SOCIAL LEARNING and CHANGE

SOCIAL LEARNING
and CHANGE:
A Cognitive Approach to Human Services

by Howard Goldstein

University of South Carolina Press

Published in Columbia, S.C., by the
University of South Carolina Press, 1981

Manufactured in the United States of America

Library of Congress Cataloging in Publication Data

Goldstein, Howard, 1922–
    Social learning and change.

    1. Social interaction.   2.   Social change.
3.   Learning, Psychology of.   4.   Cognition.
I.   Title.
HM291.G643   302   80–23446
ISBN 0–87249–402–0

To LINDA

and to

SARAH & MILDRED

Contents

vi

Figures and Tables

Preface

This book is about planned change—the intent to help people discover that their lives are in the making. This intent translates into something different than "cure," "rehabilitation," or "symptom reduction." Rather it is aimed at enriching the opportunity for people to find within themselves, their relationships, or their community the resources that will enable them to resolve their problems of living in more autonomous, self-fulfilling and socially rewarding ways. This approach is called *social learning*: "social" refers to the interpersonal context of change and includes the one-to-one, family, group, or other collective relationships; "learning" refers to the cognitive activities and processes that are the media for productive problem solving, change, and growth.

Change, in these terms, is both a process and a product of new and creative reconceptualizations of one's self, role, relationships, and goals. It involves the need to test and validate personal and shared values and aspirations and to risk taking hold of deserved power and control of the conditions that affect one's existence. Its effective outcomes are seen in a confident and principled approach to living and being.

A social learning approach does not conform to the causal or deterministic assumptions that support the traditional methods of behavior change. Human motive and action are understood as purposive and goal-directed. People act the way they do not *because* of something but *for the sake of* something, the "something" in the latter instance being their need to cope with the present as it is perceived and the future as it is envisioned.

Social learning is basically a common-sense approach insofar as it is worked out within the client's style and frame of reference. It takes account of his world view, cultural and value orientations, the nature of his environment, and his action schemes that typically shape his course of living. Learning itself can be understood as having two functions. The first involves acquisition of the knowledge tools that people require for the effective management of the contingencies of living, e.g., information, guidance, and opportunities to try out new courses of action. The second is more intensive in that it calls for the reshaping and the reconceptualization of one's essential premises and beliefs about the nature of one's personal reality. Personal reality is something more profound than the facts one accumulates over time, the ideas that conform to a conventional or shared logic, or the socially defined and rational ideas that are held about self and the world. A personal reality embodies long-standing, ingrained, and usually, unverified premises about the way things are. It is woven from an intimate and arcane logic which creates the private metaphors and symbols used by the mind to explain the world as it is perceived. We can call this personal reality our cognitions since they comprise what we *know* we know, what we *know* we believe, what we *know* we value, and what we *know* we are.

The power of these cognitions cannot be overstated: They embrace the essential proofs of our existence; they serve as unquestioned justifications for our actions; they enable us to explain past events and to redefine our respective histories to fit the present; and they shape our expectations about our futures. A corollary of these assumptions is that enduring change can be worked out in either or both of two ways: one, if the person is able to modify his accustomed premises then corresponding changes in his behavior will be observable; the other, if the person can develop new forms of adaptive behavior then changes in his conceptions of his world of experience will follow. In this regard, social learning and problem solving are not restricted to the resolution of individual troubles and conflicts but apply as well to the processes by which families, groups, and collectives concerned with broader social problems may overcome the obstacles blocking the achievement of their valued goals and needs.

It is important that something be said about the types of clientele and practitioners to whom this book is addressed. Many systems of change require a high degree of motivation on the client's part. Simply, to become a client, the individual either must be aware of the existence of a problem or, at the very least, must acknowledge that he is suffering from certain conditions. Thus, the "good" client is seen as someone who voluntarily presents himself before the practitioner in search of help or relief. This point of view is valid insofar as the particular system of change requires the client to adapt and subscribe to the practitioner's theoretical or technical orientation. Although not ignoring the plight of the voluntary client, a social learning approach is also aimed at those persons who are often described as "hard-to-reach," "resistant," "multi-problem," "involuntary," "lacking in insight," or in other terms that are subsumed under the spurious label of "unmotivated." These labels tend to echo the frustrations of the practitioner rather than accurately reflect the needs and incentives of the client in question.

I am not proclaiming that a social learning approach will offer certain success in practice with such a client. However, given that this approach begins with careful regard for and appreciation of the client's frame of reference, the possibility is improved that he will be more willing to risk his participation in the change experience. The non-voluntary client's world view is often tainted by fear, distrust, or misgivings. These perceptions might well be distortions of the way things are or perhaps the consequences of his cultural outlook or his less than rewarding experiences with previous professionals. At any rate, these cognitions need not be seen as unyielding obstacles to change; depending on the creativity and skill of the practitioner, they are as subject to modification as are any other conceptions of reality. In short, this book hopes to expand the range of possible methods of meeting the needs of people in trouble.

As far as the practitioner is concerned, I am not directing this book to a special discipline or field of practice. For this reason, I use the generic term "human services worker" throughout the text. Empirical evidence and observation show that differences among the various helping disciplines have more to do with matters of status, title, and oftentimes financial recompense than they do with function. I am not disputing the fact that each discipline possesses a special realm of competence; yet, in the main, professionals who carry the title of psychologist, social worker, psychiatric nurse, psychiatrist, guidance counselor, rehabilitation worker, community worker, mental health specialist, group or family therapist, or others occupy a common ground—a shared concern with problems of living and the well-being of the people they serve. However they go about it, these practitioners provide a human service. Thus, this book is aimed at people who help people.

The logic and format of this book are derived from Dr. Perry London's penetrating critique of the field of behavior change.* He asserts that all systems of behavior change contain three elements, either enunciated or implied. They are (1) a superordinate moral code or a social philosophy that expresses certain assumptions about man and his relations with society; (2) a theory of personality that explains the nature of the person and his behavior; and (3) a body of techniques that are deliberately used to influence behavior. For the sake of the internal consistency of the change system, each of these elements should be interdependent on the other two.

London complains that the somewhat muddled state of the field is a result of the many substantive works on behavior change that fail to credit or analyze these elements and more important, neglect to discriminate between the moral and scientific dimensions of change. Thus we find theories that exclude reference to technique or social philosophy, techniques that are indifferent to a foundational behavior theory or to a social philosophy, or a social philosophy that may seem to be persuasive but is inevitably speculative since it does not include an operational motif. As a result, the functions of practitioners become confused when they act as applied scientists while ignoring the impact of their philosophical and moral premises or as arbiters of morality who fail to acknowledge their use of technical and scientific methods.

The division of this book into three major sections is designed to render the three elements of behavior change as explicit as possible. The first section comprises an anthropological philosophy as a foundation for this theory and method of change. The second presents a general theory of human behavior, adaptation, and perception. The third attempts to translate this philosophy and theory into active and operational strategies of learning and change. Yet, it will be seen that this division is somewhat

---

*Perry London, *The Modes and Morals of Psychotherapy* (New York: Holt, Rinehart & Winston, 1964).

arbitrary since, in the final analysis, philosophy, theory, and practice unite to form the indivisible whole of this approach to change.

More specifically, Part I acquaints the reader with the philosophic premises (and the biases) that undergird this work. These ideas are, in a generic sense, of a humanistic-existential nature and attempt to encompass the quality of personal-social-societal relations. The optimal goal of learning and change (within a social context) is the development of the person's potential for autonomous choice and action. In its best sense, adaptation of this type connotes the emergence of a lifestyle that is principled, responsible, and accountable—to one's self, to one's values and commitments, to one's relationships, and to one's community. It is assumed that the proper understanding of human behavior must take account of its transactional implications (how it involves significant others), its meanings in the immediacy of the here and now, and its goal-directed purposes. To organize the substantive foundations for a cognitive and learning approach to change, considerable attention is given to the historical derivations of modern social and psychological thought. In Chapter 2, the role of theory and its relation to behavior change is discussed. The use of a case example allows for the analysis of some major systems of change and their relation to the cognitive, social learning approach.

Part II builds on these assumptions by developing a theory of the person in action and adaptation—or what is termed self theory. The value of this theory is that it places the person squarely in his world of experience and so defines him as both actively unique and interactively social. In attempting to unify psychological and social factors, self theory portrays the person as one who strives to maintain balance, stability, and integrity while coping with the innumerable and pressing demands of living. Perception, the ability to interpret and attempt to create meaning out of experience, is seen as the critical link between the inner person and his outer environment. As such, it becomes the focus and the medium of social learning and change.

Perception is defined here in phenomenological terms and therefore takes account of the significant influences in the perceiver's social field that affect his interpretations of reality, e.g., social and cultural norms and expectations, the nature of one's relationships. Perception in individual terms involves the primary functions of consciousness and attention, the process of thinking and conceptualizing, and the tendency to ascribe personal meanings to experience.

Chapter 6 recapitulates these theories in a comprehensive model of the self and goes on to show their implications for personal and social adaptation in the real world. Speculations about the origins of personal conflict and dissonance give heed to the kinds of social and institutional responses that troubled behavior might engender. In short, personal troubles are also seen as a social phenomenon that can evoke public rewards or penalties, either posing challenges to the individual's mode of adaption.

This philosophical and theoretical content converge in Part III to support specific operational strategies for social learning and change. Following a definition and analysis of social learning, the next chapters deal with the sequential and increasingly complex stages of learning and problem solving. Discrimination learning considers the interventions aimed at helping people become more conscious of themselves, their actions and interactions, and the nuances of their environment. Concept learning is the core of change. It focuses on personal, symbolic, and social constructions of reality and is directed toward changes in perception and cognition. Principle learning is concerned with the person's unique style of and approach to living and attempts to develop a measure of congruence between value and wisdom. A discussion of problem-solving processes serves to place the preceding stages of learning and change into an holistic perspective.

The issue of motivation as the energy of change is the topic of Chapter 13. This discussion could have been placed first because of the centrality of motivation to change. Here special attention is given to the dilemmas of practice with nonvoluntary clients. Chapter 14 restates the basic principles of this approach to change.

I sincerely hope that the reader will not be greatly distressed by my consistent use of the masculine gender in my references to the human services worker. It is used only to avoid the cumbersome "he/she," the neutered "they," and the distractions caused by switches from one gender to the other—in short to insure consistency in literary style.

The acknowledgment of the contributions of clients and students has become an established convention, if not a cliché, of writers in the field of social and behavioral theory and practice. Yet, the frequency with which we see this type of acknowledgment underscores the fact that ideas about something as enigmatic as human and social behavior are rarely the virginal properties of a single mind. This is certainly the case in this instance. Often unwittingly, my many clients and students forced me to confront the errors and inconsistencies in my thinking over the years of the development of these ideas. By their forthrightness and wisdom, they helped me close certain gaps, resolve certain quandaries, and defend my logic. Very special and warm thanks are extended to those former students (now creative professionals in their own right) whose enthusiasm and penetrating minds enriched and encouraged the development of this book. They include Dr. D. Kinley Sturkie III for his early interest in the concept of social learning and for the rich friendship and exchange of ideas that we have shared over the years; Patrick Mabey, the artist, for his willingness to experiment with and validate the embryonic conceptions of learning and change and for his eager curiosity and support; Karl Burger, for her incisive and laconic wit that gave me some real-life perspectives on work with people; Richard Kushner for his discerning critiques of work in progress; and Donald Spencer, for the creative ways in which he translated these ideas into effective practice.

With deep gratitude I express my thanks to all of my children for their caring interest in me as a father while I attempted the role of an author. James, Lani, and Lora in particular showed understanding and tolerance during my affair with my typewriter over these past many years. Linda, my wife, has been my partner in this project as she has been my partner in all aspects of our good life together. A fine and creative writer in her own right, she has been of inestimable help from the very inception of this endeavor—as a candid and sometimes discomfiting critic, as a patient listener to untried ideas, as an editor, as a source of inspiration and knowledge—but most of all, as a caring and loving friend. And finally, there is "Harriet" who is enduringly loyal and accepting.

PART ONE

Learning and Change:
Philosophical and Theoretical Foundations

Chapter 1
A Philosophy of Change

A book is but one of many forms of human communication; as such, it typically imparts two levels of information. The more apparent level contains the author's explicit statement—his words and ideas that fill the pages in a logical and straightforward fashion. The second level may be less evident to the reader since it often comprises the author's unstated premises, his world view that molds, tempers, and supports his expressed ideas.

The coherence and intelligibility of this form of written communication depend on the degree to which both levels are accessible to the reader's understanding. In novels, poetry, or biographies, the reader is free to reckon the author's covert thesis and in fact may enjoy the inferential experience. With regard to books that are essentially narrative or factual, the author's premises may be merely a matter of curiosity. When it comes to this type of book—one that strives to explain something as indeterminate and ambiguous as the psychological and social factors in learning and change—the author's guiding assumptions need to be made explicit. Theories and ideas that intend to represent a personal or social event cannot be based on verifiable facts alone or on any sort of universal wisdom; even the attempt to report seemingly reliable scientific or statistical evidence is colored by the reporter's selectivity and interpretation of the data. Inevitably, conceptions about the human state reflect a certain social philosophy that expresses outright or implicit beliefs and values about man.

Learning and Change

In this chapter I intend to make the underlying philosophical assumptions of this work as explicit as possible, not only to inform the reader but also to propose the rationale for the theories and principles of learning and change that will follow. These assumptions stress, first of all, the vital role of personal autonomy relative to the participants and process of the planned change event. Autonomy is more than an empty creed or desired ideal; it is the valued outcome of the change experience. It is also assumed that this outcome is more readily achieved when personal and social behavior is understood (a) within its phenomenal field or the immediacy of the person's existence, (b) in a relational or transactional context, and (c) as an expression of the person's search for and movement toward personally or socially valued ends. As these ideas about immediacy, transaction, and intention are developed, I will attempt to show how they support the principles leading to a cognitive, adaptive, and goal-oriented approach to learning and change.

SOME ASSUMPTIONS ABOUT THE PERSON

If there is anything consistent or enduring about the nature of humankind, it is the compelling need to seek answers to such questions as "Who am I?" "What am I?" and "Why am I?" These concerns may arise at odd moments of reflection or at times of despair and hopelessness. They are sometimes evident in the quest for religious certainty or in the search for an ideological, political, or social identity. Uncertainties of this sort tend to become even more pressing in a world where traditions fail, where the rules of living are both elusive and elastic, and where secure relations and locations are not easy to find.

The ideal solutions to these questions, particularly with the rise of modern technology, tend to be sought in methods of inquiry that strive to emulate the controlled and experimental approaches of the physical and natural sciences. The hope persists that somehow human behavior can be regularized, that certain laws, taxonomies, or models will be found that will order the human state in accord with defensible facts, causes, and predictions. We hope that science, which has done so much to bring the physical world under control, will do the same for the peculiarities of human experience. But as we shall see, what has been achieved is not a science of human behavior but, instead, a kind of scientism—a collection

4

of doctrines, attitudes, or findings that, at best, offer some directions for yet further inquiry.

The development of the following assumptions represents other kinds of thinking. They are based on a rhetorical form of argumentation, in its literal sense, a discursive technique designed to encourage a dialogue of sorts between author and reader. I hope to avoid the common meaning of rhetoric (the attempt to persuade by the manipulation of words) and want to promote discourse on the ideas that follow. Furthermore, these assumptions are presented within a philosophical orientation. In this regard they are largely first principles that do not propose the existence of final answers. These ideas simply serve to initiate a process of thinking that involves the pursuit of inquiry and explanation but not a solution.

To begin with, it is assumed that the proper study of man can best proceed along the lines that correspond with a holistic perspective. This is an attitude, a way of understanding, that captures at once the nature of the inner person, the acting person, persons in relation, and the relations that exist between the person and his social and physical world. Any attempt to define conditions of existence that does not in some way interrelate physical, psychological, social, and environmental influences will only succeed in reducing the understanding of man to a number of isolated "facts." The terms *organic* or *systemic* are equally useful and can be substituted for *holistic*. An organic view also admits to the irreducibility of the human state and, moreover, conceives of man as something more than the sum of these influences. At the same time, the person is understood as an integral part of such other organic structures as the family, community, labor force, and social institutions. In a similar sense, a systems perspective attempts to order and interrelate such functions as role, status, relations, and effects. Persons are defined as vital systems in their own right as well as active members of still larger systems.

Whichever framework is selected as a means of organizing what we know about man, it should include the requirement that it remain open-ended and mutable. In other words, its purpose should not be the attainment of fixed or final conclusions about the human state. The framework should be constructed in a way that retains a certain openness either to new data or to data that have not before been recognized or accepted. This criterion suggests that we do not yet have the tools of perception or logic that would enable us to arrive at some definitive conclusions. But we can speculate that the absence of these tools is not merely a consequence of the raw state of the behavioral sciences but an indication that the intricate and equivocal nature of the human state does not lend itself to any sort of universal conceptualization.

The principle of autonomy is central to this study of behavior and change. This principle refers to the person's potential and responsibility for self-governed action and his capability for spontaneous and creative expression. How does this highly individualized conception square with a holistic view of the human experience? Can one be autonomous and yet be an inseparable part of a whole? Does this idea not do violence to the notion of an organic reality? The answer is contained in the principle that applies to well-working systems or organizations: any system—whether a human body, a group, a love relationship, a family, or a bureaucracy—functions best when its constituents are able to act with freedom, spontaneity, and choice in the pursuit of its natural purposes. The physical body is healthy when its various elements and systems (cardiovascular, lymphatic, neural, etc.) can function without the impedence of disease, chemical intrusions, and the like. When one organ or system is affected so is the entire body. The mind works at its best when it is not besieged by anxieties, fears, or confusions. Families can fulfill their major purposes when each member is relatively free to pursue his own values and aspirations. Organizations and institutions that give credence to the individual needs, contributions, and aptitudes of their members operate more productively. Simply put, the autonomy of any organic whole and the potential that it has for realizing its objectives depend in large part on the autonomous actions of its members. Moreover, the extent to which any one system is autonomous bears directly on the autonomous operations of still other systems to which it is related. We see this when the illness or depression of one family member affects the usual functions of the family or when families that become dysfunctional intrude into the usual workings of the community.

The term *autonomy* is not used without some qualifications. First, the principle of autonomy will be recognized as having much in common with an existentialist philosophy, a conception of man that is directly opposed to naturalistic or causal orientations. It disaffirms the idea that the individual is molded by extraneous conditions and underscores man's potential for managing, if not modifying, his world of experience. More important, autonomy also signals the critical importance and role of self-determined action. It is not enough to say that the person *has* the ability to redefine his role, self, and behavior at any point in time. The crucial point is whether he *chooses* to use this ability when he is challenged to preserve his sense of identity, integrity, and individuality. In the ordinary course of living where obstacles and threats are not encountered, we ride along easily, feeling that our freedom to act is intact and certain. There are moments, however, when this is not the case, when the opportunity for personal choice and action appears to be thwarted, when the integrity of the self is at risk. It is at these moments when the failure to act in an autonomous fashion results in a diminishing of the experienced quality of one's self. If one chooses not to cope with the strains of his immediate world he must then acknowledge his helplessness. If one loses or abdicates his sense of personal power, he must experience the state of degradation or worthlessness, or must blame others or other circumstances for his plight. If one comes to see his world as fearful or threatening, he must acknowledge his hopelessness or his role as a victim. In other words, one not only can, he also *must* call on novel and creative responses when he finds himself in conflict with conditions that assault his integrity or the integrity of the system of which he is a part.

Before examining the broader implication of the principle of autonomy it is worthwhile noting the kinds of resistances that it evokes in current thinking. Ironically, one source of negation comes from a field that, at its core, is fully committed to these notions of integrity and individuality, although its commitment can at times take on the character of religious zeal. I am speaking of the emergence of the more exotic and romantic brands of the "human growth-and-potential" movements, as well as the humanists who lean towards extravagant notions about humanity. Their fervor in extolling human virtues and potentialities virtually denies the many-sided nature of man and overlooks his more mundane if not nefarious attributes. It is unfortunate that these movements have succeeded in cheapening terms that otherwise symbolize rare and profound states of being. Not unlike the advertising hucksters who indiscriminately attach uncommon superlatives to such inconsequential things as soap powder and sanitary pads, these psychological zealots have carelessly reduced such meaningful terms as "self-realization," "self-assertiveness," and "personal authenticity" to banal expressions that have few referents in the painful choices and actions of ordinary living. In their terms, something called "self-actualization" can be achieved in the sacred "group" where risk is minimal and idiosyncracy is applauded as a common norm. These movements have discredited the principle of autonomy by their shallow and superficial explanations of the human state. Robert Ornstein, expressing some question of the value of "growth centers," states his fears that they "are to be understood more in the sense of 'growth stocks' and childish self-indulgence than as anything seriously concerned with human development."[1]

Another source of opposition is far more substantial because it emerges from the agonized awareness that rights, equality, and opportunity are not equitably distributed. Workers in the field of human services who painfully confront the despair and futility of people who have been shunted aside and deprived of their rights by an uncaring society will argue and dispute a conception of the human state that emphasizes the importance of autonomy, responsible choice, and personal integrity. They say that these ideas are trinkets, luxuries possessed by the fortunate middle or upper classes. They argue further that choices, opportunities, and alternatives are not available to the disadvantaged and unfortunate, and that major changes must be made in the political structure, in the purposes of social institutions, and in the way that power and the commodities of living are distributed.

Because it is committed to the importance of individual choice, action, and responsibility, the principle of autonomy may appear to some to smack of old-time liberalism—a concern with the rights of the individual that excludes the significance of the group or collective actions that may effect important changes in society. Others may see this principle as supporting the more conservative ideologies that seek to perpetuate the selfsame continuity of social processes and institutions. No one of these definitions captures the essence of autonomy since it includes the need for distributive justice or substantial social change. Autonomy resists and argues against the inclination to apply simplistic solutions to complex problems, particularly those solutions that reduce enormous and pernicious social problems to elementary cause-and-effect equations. Dignifying individuality, the principle of autonomy places the individual squarely within a transactional relationship with his interpersonal, economic, and political contingencies of living. It is a person's perceptions of his plight and his convictions about his goals that determine whether and how equitable change should be effected.

It is the individual, alone or joined with others, who must have the decisive say at some point about the changes that will affect his life. Social or political action undertaken without regard for this principle often succeeds only in shifting the scenery while the human drama remains unchanged. Of greater risk, such actions may come to convince its presumed beneficiaries that they are indeed incompetent, dependent, and helpless. In speaking of individual involvement I am not referring either to token participation or a repetition of the massive but sometimes mindless programs of the 1960s that thrust ill-prepared people into ill-defined community action programs. I am referring to the creation of a system that offers people the opportunity to reexamine their place in society, to reaffirm their cherished values and ideals, and to give new thought to new alternatives and the skills and responsibilities that attend them.

As the principle of autonomous action is developed, we will not ignore the obstacles to fulfilling the individual's potential, obstacles confronting the person as well as those who appear to be a part of economic and political environments.

Yet another source of resistance to the principle of autonomy can be found in systems of thought that picture man as a product of the procession of events in his life. These events include the influences of his environment and the nature of his personal history. This deterministic view suggests a process of human development that is not unlike the mechanical extrusion of metals or plastics into predetermined shapes; therefore, the potentiality for spontaneous or original action would be considerably limited or skewed by extraneous forces. With the exception of such theorists as B. F. Skinner,[2] who picture the individual as a bundle of behaviors shaped by his environment, these systems of thought do not necessarily ignore the importance of personal choice and independent action. But the value of autonomy is certainly diminished when attention is directed to the specific causes and influences that are thought to mold a person in special ways. The individual comes to be seen as somehow incapable of choice and action, at least until the time when particular impediments are "worked through," brought to consciousness, or in some way mitigated. This thinking is exemplified by the rule in psychoanalytic therapy that prohibits the patient from making any significant decisions until his unconscious conflicts are resolved. Deterministic notions will be challenged in many sections of this book; however, we need to give some brief attention to the question of historical determinism if only to clarify the perspective of the stated principles.

Are our personal histories real and substantial facts or are they illusions we create for very cogent needs and reasons? Although some may find the word *illusion* disagreeable, it does seem apparent that the account of one's past experiences is open to many interpretations and meanings. This is partly because we tend to ascribe form and substance to our chronologies by arbitrarily arranging past events that we think we experienced as if they had occurred in an ordered fashion. We cull certain experiences from our pasts and place them in some sort of serial relationship. Of more importance is the way in which we establish a sense of continuity by creating certain mental links and relations among the selected experiences: "I did poorly in elementary school because my parents had never been interested in my work, and because I did poorly, I couldn't catch up with the other kids in the upper grades." This is a plausible explanation of the subject's educational problems, if simple explanation is all that is intended, but this sort of causal explanation usually exceeds the intention of being plausible or factual. It tries to fulfill the need to build the erratic chronicle of our lives into a neat and rational package, one that we can reach into when challenged to extract reasonable and acceptable renditions about why we are as we are and why we do what we do.[3]

Beyond such "utilitarian" purposes, this selective recall and association of happenings also serves us in broader existential terms. The autobiographies that we construct simply enable us to verify our being. They also authenticate our beliefs that we are unique, special, and right-minded in our own ways. A consciousness of the past gives credence to our existence in the present and a rationale for projecting ourselves into future living. Since we tend to select and associate events in self-fulfilling ways, the process of self-authentification proceeds rather smoothly. Certainly corrections and reinterpretations are required from time to time to maintain a degree of reasonableness in how we conceive ourselves, but by and large, a secure measure of coherence is sustained.

All that I suggest for the moment is the idea that one's history, one's accretion of life experiences, is not in itself an ineluctable force that conditions, shapes, or unconsciously determines one's destiny. If the past does pattern one's life, it is not because it must but because a person requires it to do so. At the same time, this idea does not negate the importance of the chronic and critical things that are part of human development and emergence. Deprivation, personal loss, and ill health or abundance, freedom, and opportunity are conditions that blend with the less exotic affairs of living to add to the climate in which evolvement takes place. But a climate differs from a cause. A cause can be construed as an objective and denotable force that generates fairly specific results (e.g., homosexuality is linked with mothers who are demanding and controlling, or low achievement is a behavior that is acquired as a result of specific conditioning variables). A climate or social environment or atmosphere refers to a "field" in Lewinian terms or a gestalt wherein the transactions of its members continually act to modify meanings and implications. Its significance at any given time involves how its members perceive their environment and how they are acting in relation to it.

Biographies and autobiographies offer poignant examples of the ingenuity with which people have succeeded in transcending experiences in their lives that would ordinarily be seen as crippling or retarding. These literary works stand in sharp contrast to conceptions of human adaptation coming from the fields of psychology and the behavioral sciences in general. With the exception of the existentialists and humanists, these disciplines tend to ignore the human need not only to cope with but also to surpass or rise beyond the assaults and inflictions of ordinary living. Perhaps this is because such concepts as normalcy, growth, emergence, and creativity are so elusive as to become suspect in fields engrossed in the pursuit of scientific methods. No doubt this preoccupation with disability is also part of the heritage of medical psychiatry with its sophisticated systems for the classification and treatment of pathological states. This absorption with sickness only succeeds in equating health and well-being with the *absence* of illness, thereby overlooking the human attributes that make for a more expansive expression of the self. In any case, we must turn to literature (biography, diaries, novels, and poetry) to find the more heroic and celebrated aspects of the human state.

Consider Robert Frost's life and poetry. His work is clean, simple, and profound and stands as a paradox in relation to the terrible suffering and deprivation that he experienced as a child and man. Virginia Woolf would now be diagnosed as having a severe psychiatric problem. She underwent a lifetime of wrenching bouts with depression; yet, she used her awareness of impending "madness" to ready herself for some of her most creative writing. Jean-Paul Sartre eloquently captures the way in which he escaped, even exploited, the stifling relationships imposed on him by his effusive mother and his stern, demanding grandfather.[4] We know that his childhood traumas did not cause him to wither and fade. They inspired a lifetime of thought and energy that has significantly altered modern conceptions of man and his dilemmas.

Contradiction can also be found in the lives of the great psychologists who did so much to overstate the deterministic potency of early life experiences. Freud, Jung, Adler, and Wilhelm Reich each endured disturbing and painful events in his early years. Not only did each one's respective experience fail to produce a lesser person, the systems of thought and therapy that each created are linked quite strikingly to the strife that he had outlasted. It is not coincidental that Jung's search for something resembling the "soul" is tied to his early life with a strict, religious, and ungiving father. Nor is it odd that Alfred Adler's departure from classic Freudian theory was somehow related to his own personal version of the meaning of childhood that deviated from Freud's. Freud's early years were marked by struggles with his parents, particularly with his mother. Adler was more poignantly aware of the conflict in being the second born and the feelings of inferiority that came with the inability to compete with a superior brother. Each great psychologist premised his particular system of thought on his own conception of his early life.

I am not suggesting that hardship or deprivation is a necessary precursor to a creative and generous life any more than to say that it is a cause of disability or failure. In relation to the principle of autonomous action I am attempting to place the role of history in a useful perspective. Without diminishing the significance of life experiences, I stress the centrality of the individual, the perceiver and the experiencer, as the one who gives final meaning to the character and quality of his life as it has been lived.

The principle of autonomous action is a point of departure for the search for philosophical positions that supplant naturalistic, endogenous, or causal explanations of the human state. More precisely, we are concerned with an anthropological philosophy—a reflective process that endeavors to find order in the study of the humanity of man. It does not deny the importance of scientific enterprise but finds its place before and after the more formal work of science. As a discipline it encompasses an interest in human values, human relations, self-concept, and culture; moreover, anthropological philosophy grapples with the irreducible mysteries of personal life.

TRANSACTIONAL INQUIRY

There is a most uneasy position occupied by some students of mankind who find themselves indecisively caught between a pair of incompatible conceptions of man and his universe. Each of the two conceptions may be persuasive; yet both are found lacking in important ways, and the individual cannot commit himself to either one. One of these versions falls into the conservative or Parsonian perspective and is restricted to ideas about the structure, continuity, and stability of larger systems.[5] The other stands for the classical psychological perspective that seeks either to penetrate the inner workings of the psyche or to reduce human behavior to the most elemental forms. The sociological conception captures the complex patterns and structures of social life but ignores the passions, needs, and adaptive functions of people that are sometimes out of harmony with the idea of a stable well-balanced social system. The psychological perspective produces either an exotic panorama of the inner life or a somewhat desiccated portrait of the person as a conditioned reactor to his environment.

Awareness that one perspective ignores the uniqueness of the individual in its conception of a social universe, whereas the other excludes the importance of the social field in its focus on the person has led to ambitious attempts to develop a unified picture of personal and social life.

John Spiegel's scheme of transactional inquiry is noteworthy in that it offers a useful organization of the relations between physiological, personal, social, cultural, and environmental variables.[6] His scheme builds on the assumptions of Alfred North Whitehead and John Dewey.[7] Whitehead describes the universe as a huge process, a whole in its own right. But man's need to reduce things to their manageable parts abstracts that which is substantial and fragments that which is complete. Dewey also presents a holistic conception of reality, but he speaks of the universe as a system comprised of infinite transactions. He also condemns man's need to pulverize the system, but he sees his need arising out of the human tendency to explain reality in self-actional or interactional terms. A self-actional conception assumes that entities do in fact exist, that they can be understood as independent of all other entities, springing into action in response to stimuli arising from within. The interactional perspective identifies the things that coact with other things. The self-actional view, best represented by personality theories, locates the source of behavior within the person or the institution. For example, when we talk about the force of the superego or the press of a drive we are assuming that the outcome derives solely from one or the other of these sources. The interactional view does attempt to capture what is taking place *between* certain entities, but it does so by assuming that something is known about the things that are interacting.

In contrast with self-actional or interactional approaches, the transactional perspective extends beyond the entities themselves and inquires into the space between them, where we find the informative messages about what is actually taking place. It encompasses, first of all, the needs, motivations, and intentions of the participants. It provides some clues about the way in which the members are related to and are interdependent on one another. And most important, the space contains the functional relationships of the members of the particular transactional system. If, for example, we were to observe something that was going on between an employer and his employee in interactional terms, we would begin with some ideas about their respective roles, how they should be enacted, and so forth. These ideas might include some presuppositions about how a fair-minded boss ought to act or how he should best maintain his status. We would also have some notions about the role of the employee—his responsibility, punctuality, commitment, or other role characteristics. Our impressions would be biased by these preconceptions. Our judgments about the event would inevitably be determined by

ting with at the time and what is going on within the group.[9]
ese attempts to appreciate the many factors that shape any per-
ansactional field challenge our tendency to fall back on categorical
eotypical thinking. Not only are we socialized and educated to
de our world into discrete and manageable compartments but we
nce a sense of uneasiness about the idea that knowing as it
s to the human event is infinite and final meaning will always
s.

e nature of existing behavioral science theories offers only limited
building a conditional and holistic perspective of personal and
ality. To a considerable extent, we do not have the linking ideas,
Spiegel calls the "transformational hypotheses," that would
s to achieve an integration of the parts of any phenomenon
of their simple addition. For example, psychosomatic medicine
from the assumption that critical transactions link a person's
gical and the psychological functions; yet this field cannot
ly explain how the two functions bear on each other. As I have
e specialized nature of the various sciences has succeeded in
a clutter of theories, concepts, and constructs that differ widely
evel of abstraction, referents in the real world, and the basic
ons from which they are derived. Ziller comments that even
e narrow confines of the behavioral sciences there has been a
tion of studies of such ideas as role, attitude, behavior, values,
n a manner that suggests that each concept has little bearing on
s.[10]

actional inquiry also runs into difficulty in the applied social
where theory is called upon to assist in the resolution of social
nal problems. To the practitioner engaged in counseling, plan-
munity action, and the like, the need to attend to wholes, fields,
and transactions may appear to be a diversion from the im-
sk. The numbers and the complexity of the problems requiring
he absence of resources, or the press of time tends to encour-
the symptomatic or the residual effects of persistent social
owing of vision. The cost of such a microscopic view is ap-
continue to be the focus of serious but doubtful professional
e transactional links of these problems with other flawed or

the way in which our observations did or did not fit our definitions of the respective roles. A transactional inquiry, however, would not commence with firm presuppositions about the persons we are observing. Instead, it would focus on the process, the dynamics of the interchange between the persons that would disclose not only a more incisive understanding about who they are but also what they are doing in relation to one another.

This perspective does not repudiate the other two but adds still another valuable dimension to the understanding of complex social phenomena. Although, as Dewey asserts, there is nothing in this world that is purely self-actional and independent of other contingencies, there are times when a need for knowledge makes it necessary to construct an artificial version of an event in order to gain an approximate understanding of its inner workings. For example, we shall be examining concepts about the self and the learning process as if they are isolated or self-contained entities. An interactional perspective is useful when we want to understand how things that we know something about are coacting with one another; for example, in the study of the manner in which a specific organization is serving a particular population or how a special parent-child relationship is working. Transactional inquiry, however, is especially germane to the search for the meaning of the indivisible whole of a social situation and for the appreciation of the idea that the whole is considerably greater than the sum of its parts. With the preceding observations in mind, it is now possible to examine Spiegel's paradigm (Figure 1) of what he calls the transactional field.[8]

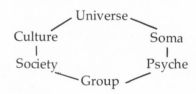

FIGURE 1. Spiegel's Paradigm

Spiegel calls on the familiar concepts that, in abstract terms, mark off the major units of the personal, social, and physical world. The definitions given for these units are essentially nominal in nature; the actual meanings are evoked only by relationships and not by their purely intrinsic characteristics. Inasmuch as there are no beginning or end points in this totality, I will begin arbitrarily with what he chooses to call the *Universe*, the natural environment involving such factors as the peculiarities of climate, the nature of the terrain, how the habitat is constituted, and the availability of natural resources. The *Soma* refers to the knowledge of all the vital processes including the anatomical, physiological, and physical adaptations to the universe. The *Psyche* represents all of the complex mental processes employed in personal adaptation, including the symbolic, cognitive, perceptual, and problem-solving activities that are part of conflict elaboration or reduction, coping mechanisms, self-development, and creativity. *Group* alludes to the transactions of small face-to-face clusters of people and takes account of the processes of problem solving, decision making, conflict stimulation and reduction, communication, division of labor, leadership development, cohesion, and task fulfillment. *Society* is a progression of groups incorporated into a number of larger social systems. It encompasses the social operations occurring within these systems; for example, the mechanisms of social class, existing power structures, and the occupational, economic, family, educational, religious, and recreational systems that form the particular social order. The notion of a society also takes into account the norms and behaviors characteristic of any and all of the subsystems. Finally, *Culture* refers to the special meanings of social behavior to members of social systems. It covers not only material elements but also symbolic, linguistic, and value factors.

As a paradigm this may be judged to be too extensive or too restrictive. For example, I could accept the inclusion of other foci such as the family and the community since they are significant units that need not be subsumed under other regions of the whole. However, I do not believe that Spiegel designed this arrangement as a representation of a particular reality but instead for heuristic purposes.

This type of transactional inquiry pertains to all other regions of existence as well. For example, the locale where this book was begun, Nova Scotia, is distinguished by its hard-bitten, rocky terrain and its raw and unpredictable weather. The visitor, tourist, or newcomer, would probably capture a vista in his mind or on film and give it some such adjective as lovely, harsh, or forbidding, depending on how he contrasts

what he sees with what he has experienced e[...]
extends beyond an interest in scenery, he [...]
inquiry to determine what this terrain mean[...]
like to live here? This draws in the cultura[...]
important meanings that the ruggedness [...]
bolizes a way of life marked by independe[...]
from mastering the elements. His inquiry [...]
whereby the terrain meets the survival n[...]
Fishing, lumbering, and mining continue t[...]
place where people can live in at least m[...]

This abridgment of Spiegel's transact[...]
of the philosophic modes of inquiry that [...]
of this book. It is a somewhat abrasive ide[...]
the grain of the ways by which human b[...]
versions of what the "real" world is. Li[...]
further confounding it with queries abo[...]

It is difficult to resist thinking about [...]
separate entities. This kind of molecula[...]
scholarship. Each of these aspects has [...]
domain of the various knowledge discip[...]
physical and natural sciences; the soma[...]
groups to psychology and psychiatry; a[...]
to the social sciences. Each part of the[...]
claimed. Each has earned its own par[...]
such a degree that only specialists can[...]
its wisdom.

If we can escape this parochial v[...]
meaningful knowledge of any one thi[...]
with things that stand in immediate re[...]
point, the personality of young Sam[...]
delinquent activity and school failu[...]
inquiry, other questions and prescri[...]
such somatic factors as malnourishm[...]
correlate with his psychological stat[...]
behavior relates to the norms of his[...]
would have to ask about his relatio[...]
expression of his "personality" will[...]

impaired systems are ignored and remain unresolved; thus, the problems endure, worsen, or reappear. The circle becomes tighter.

Transactional inquiry offers a point of view, a framework for gathering useful impressions of social phenomena. Moreover, it complements a principle of autonomy that does not subtract the individuality of the person from his social and physical field. The eminent ideas of personal integrity, self-determination, and individuality become something more than creeds or ideals when they are understood as functions interdependent with other aspects of a person's world. We reach a richer understanding of what, say, self-determination really means when it is studied in relation to the particular physiological and psychological characteristics of the person and to the social, political, cultural, and environmental context in which it is exercised.

If we carry the notion of transactional inquiry to its logical conclusions, it leads to other prescriptions about the way by which an approximate understanding of human processes and motives can be achieved. It suggests that meaning is located within the actual experience, that the most reliable knowledge comes from the observation of the functions, operations, and substance of the social event and not from reifications or presuppositions fabricated about that event. This perspective represents what is termed a *phenomenological* approach to the organization of reality. A transactional view also discloses that behavior can best be understood in terms of its purposes rather than as a response to its causes. Behavior represents intentional movement towards some goal, end, or solution rather than an action that is preordained by other forces. This concept is indicative of a *teleological* orientation to life in terms of growth and direction towards particular ends.

PHENOMENOLOGICAL INQUIRY

Phenomenology as a philosophic movement evolved from the work of Edmund Husserl (1859-1938). That it is not a fixed or final system of thought is apparent in the fact that Husserl's own conceptions changed in many ways during his later years of writing. Since then, phenomenology has taken on various interpretations and complexions. In recent decades it has also become linked to and somewhat modified by the existentialist positions of Sartre, Jaspers, and others.[11]

Our concern with this mode of inquiry and understanding touches its operational importance for the processes of planned change. We shall consider phenomenology in the way it is ordinarily understood: it urges the observer to search for understanding without initial recourse to preconceptions or a priori assumptions. It does not assume that there are initial causes nor does it rely on explanatory frameworks. The phenomenological perspective prescribes a fresh approach to each situation, an intent to grasp and comprehend an event in relation to its intrinsic structure and meaning. In this regard, it resists the tendency to force the event into correspondence with some preexisting mental construct. As it applies to the human event, phenomenology attempts to evoke the subjective meanings that are experienced by the participants rather than to impose the observer's presumptions. Some implications of this approach are readily apparent. In one respect, it encourages a measure of naïveté on the part of the observer, a willingness to understand that is tempered by humility and wonderment. At the same time, its very nature grants a certain dignity to the person as the final source of knowing. This approach does not close out the use of theories or other explanatory constructs as a means of organizing what is known, but it does set them aside as tools until the situation itself generates its own meanings.

Immediately a paradox is created: the idea that the human mind, itself a composite of beliefs, cognitions, and facts, can apprehend an occurrence without bias or presupposition. How is it possible to "unknow" what is well known? This question is peculiarly relevant when attempting to make sense out of a social situation, a distinctly human experience marked by certain behaviors, values, feelings, and needs. How does the observer divest himself of his own humanness, his own values, conceptions, ethics and other beliefs that naturally arise in social intercourse? Our basic stock in trade is the ability to maneuver through complex person-to-person networks. We are able to render these delicate turns and movements because of the social skills and standards learned over our lifetimes. These skills and standards hold something more than practical meanings; they build into and express who and what we feel we are and thus place our self-image at stake. Thus, the observation of another's actions will in some way have positive or negative implications for ourselves.

The question becomes more complicated when considering the

functions of the observing mind itself. As F. A. Hayek states, our perception of the external world is made possible by a mind that possesses an organizing capacity and an ability to generalize.[12] He characterizes the mind as a system of rules, a set of abstract categories that dispose one to a certain way of "recognizing" and explaining a particular phenomenon. But when this system of rules is imposed and the observed event abstracted, there is no assurance whatsoever that the resulting impression or interpretation will even remotely approximate what the event is all about. However the "objective" nature of the episode may be defined, each perceiver will construct his own peculiar "reality" about the event. Our deeply entrenched values, standards, and expectations (including those that escape our conscious awareness) predispose us to make at least a few preemptory judgments. The way the mind operates makes it apparent that full objectivity is not possible, that we cannot perceive a human situation either in its pristine form or in accord with its intrinsic meanings.

This is not to deny the value of phenomenological inquiry. If the human mind is innately biased, prejudiced, and bound by its cognitive structures, why pretend that one man can even begin to grasp the subjective qualities of another's experiences? The point is that phenomenological inquiry offers a means of offsetting this tendency to fall back on categorical thinking. In this sense, it not only provides entry into the experienced nature of a human event but also raises the observer's consciousness about the way in which he is perceiving and interpreting that event. Human service workers who have suffered the acute embarrassment of finding that their "expert" appraisal or diagnosis entirely missed the point of their client's problem will appreciate the importance of this kind of consciousness.

Phenomenological inquiry fills yet another role in the vagaries of work with people and their environment. It is a safeguard against the possible error inherent in the numerous taxonomies and classifications available to the worker. The behavioral sciences have succeeded in producing many categorical schemes and constructs that are useful; they are largely middle-range typologies that help to organize impressions about problems, populations, and behaviors and assist in larger-scaled efforts, such as policy and program planning and research and data collection. However, when these schemes are used to classify people within their vital existence, when people are sorted into specific compartments like biological specimens, certain injustices and assaults on dignity arise. Despite the absence of malicious intent, the act of labeling another person does something to demean his being. From my own experience, I have some pertinent recollections. My parents, from my earliest years onward, operated a small shoe store. As a small child I would overhear their discussions about the day's business; it would go something like this:

FATHER: "Do you remember the 6½B that came in today?"
MOTHER: "Oh, do you mean the patent leather pump?"
FATHER: "No, no—the low-heeled brown wedge."

For some time I carried with me weird impressions of the kind of people that came to our store—visions of large shoes walking around with nebulous bodies attached to them. In another way, I recall the confusion about who I was as a person, a boy, and a son when someone would say to me, "Oh, you're a Jew!" and let it go at that.

In any case, the act of encompassing a whole complex of disparate behaviors, attitudes, and intentions under such labels as "simple schizophrenia" or "alcoholic," or the attempt to reduce a number of cultural identifications, relations, and social and economic conditions to such terms as "hard-core family" or "minority group member," inhibits our potential for gaining an organic understanding of the persons who are so categorized. Labeling tends to abstract the vital reality of an intricate human situation and to freeze that situation into a rigid and permanent frame. Moreover, labeling also has a prescriptive quality since it informs the subject person or persons how they are to construe their future and how others ought to act towards them.

Phenomenological inquiry abhors the imposition of such presumptions about human processes. It also opposes the notion that one person can determine how another came to be as he is, what he is, and prognostically, what he will be even when the attempt to do so reflects the wish to be therapeutic or scientific. Basically, it is indicative of a mode of analysis and understanding, a commitment to the intrinsic meanings contained within the "here and now" of a person's existence. It is a start toward a continually deepening and broadening of the experience of knowing.

TELEOLOGICAL INQUIRY

The third form of philosophic questioning incorporates the transactional and phenomenological modes and endeavors to find the authentic, albeit, approximate, meanings of individual and social behavior. Here we are concerned with the study of ends, motives, intentions, and goals— the purposes that human behavior tries to fulfill for adaptation and existence in the social and physical world. The idea of human motivation as a force that presses towards certain ends has been a familiar conception since the time of the early Greeks. The teleological perspective proposes that a more profound and accurate understanding of human behavior will result from the study of its purposes, goals, and terminal values, referring, of course, to the behaviors of persons in groups as well as individuals. Putting this in another way, the actions, relations, sentiments, needs, and motivations of people will take on more dynamic meanings when they are appreciated as a process of coping with immediate and future perceptions of the world rather than as the inevitable outcomes of past experience or extraneous causes. This mode of inquiry in no way discards the importance of past experience; instead, the biographical past is accepted as the reservoir of learnings, perceptions, and experiences from which the individual selects well-practiced patterns, attitudes, and expectations as they apply to immediate purposes.

A further discussion of the difficulties that accompany an attempt to employ teleological inquiry will assist in defining the method. Not surprisingly, this mode of questioning also runs counter to our typical ways of explaining reality. The logic involved in the search for causes feels more comfortable. A cause is explicit—something one can point to and feel that it is quite real. The idea that finding the cause will give the answer is well illustrated by a story in the *Cleveland Plain Dealer*, August 13, 1977, about a captured murderer:

As the details of the enigmatic life of the 24-year old postal clerk emerged, *there appeared to have been no single incident or trauma that might explain his abrupt transformation* little more than a year ago from the quiet suburbanite that he was to the murderous night stalker that the police say that he became. [*Emphasis added.*]

The question "Why?" is a natural and spontaneous reaction to anything that puzzles us. The telelogical question, "What for?" is, on the other hand, unwieldy—ends and goals are abstract and are as unrealized as are the intentions behind them.

Anatol Rapoport offers some possible reasons why the mind strives for cause and effect explanations. [13] We habitually associate events with one another and come to see a simple, sequential relationship between them, helping us in making our worlds easier to understand and explain. In the course of ordinary living, this inclination is a useful way of coping with life's puzzles; this kind of oversimplification is risky when it comes to making sense out of intricate social problems.

Another reason for the easy application of causal explanations is tied to our attitudes and convictions about how and why the world is the way it is. Because we cling to our beliefs, we seek grounds that will verify them. If I am convinced that man is basically well intentioned, I search for one set of causal explanations when I learn someone has committed an evil act (e.g., "No wonder—he was deprived at an early age"). If I am convinced that man is evil, I seek another set of causes (e.g., "No wonder—he never learned to control his baser instincts").

Furthermore, man's possession of a memory allows him to recall one event and transfer it to a similar one, even though the two events bear only a superficial relationship; for example, an attempt to equate the unemployment and problems of the recession of the 1970s with the cause of the Great Depression of the 1930s. The final reason for this tendency stems from the ability to substitute words for experiences, providing pseudo-explanations for particular occurences. Someone asks, "Why did John and Mary get divorced?" Another answers, "Because they can't stand each other anymore." Everyone seems satisfied even though the answer is tautological and gives no enlightening information. It does, however, verify the belief that people do things as a result of certain causes.

The teleological approach directs us to ask "what" questions instead of "why" questions when confronted with a baffling situation, "what" in this instance referring to possible intentions and outcomes. Let us say that we are involved with a working group that begins to act in belligerent and recalcitrant ways. The findings of a "why" inquiry lead to the conclusion that this odd behavior is a result of the angry feeling of the group members because another new member was forced on them. If we are satisfied with this explanation of cause, we are left with few alternatives to resolve this problem: we can remove the member, encourage the group to adjust to the change, or use some other technique to "work through" the conflict.

If we are concerned, however, with the purpose and intention of the group's behavior (what members hope to express and achieve as a group), our attention and understanding is not directed only to the critical event, but more significantly, to the state of the group at that particular time. We want to understand what the group is doing in transactional terms, how its members conceive of themselves and the group as an organism in phenomenological terms, and in the course of teleological inquiry, where and toward what goals the group is heading. This does not ignore the importance of the presence of a new member, which is not seen as an extraneous cause forcing the members to act in certain ways. His presence is granted reality, but it is understood within the context— the existential flow of perceptions, transactions, and goals of those involved. Other options become available as we pursue the question "what?" "What do you wish to do?" "What does it mean to you?" "What are the possible solutions?" Since the group is not asked to justify or defend its position (the typical response to a "why" question), a climate is fostered wherein more energy can be directed toward problem resolution than toward self-justification. Ascribing credibility to the sentiments and aspirations of the group members encourages a growing feeling of self-worth, enlarging their responsibilities for assertive action and reducing passive reaction. Thus, a number of possible alternatives may arise out of the multiple perceptions of the group members. Certainly the group may decide to exclude the new member, but since it would be the members' decision, they would have to equate this action with their purposes and aims and their projections about the group's future. In this regard, such a decision becomes a critical part of the group's existence rather than a simple act of dealing with a temporary obstacle.

This points to the issue of the locus of control, the matter of autonomy in persons' choices and actions about crucial occurences in their lives. A concern with causes tends to place controls somewhere outside of ourselves. It implies that something is happening *to* us that more or less eludes our command. We find ourselves in an awkward, defensive position when someone puts a "why" question to us. When it becomes necessary to explain or defend our actions or attitudes, the balance of control is shifted towards the questioner, particularly if confirmation or approval is at stake. In contrast, queries aimed at the understanding of purposes, goals, and values tend to support and maintain personal autonomy. A causal perspective directs vision backward and outward from the self; teleological inquiry is concerned with the momentum that propels a person forward as a potential creator of his own future.

We can look at the teleological position in still another way. Quite simply, it meets a need for a common-sense approach to the study of human affairs. The desire to understand values and goals more closely approximates the way we actually treat others with whom we are involved in substantial relationships. I am suggesting that the closer we are to others, the more we are likely to try to understand their attitudes and actions in terms of personal motives, values, and goals. Conversely, the greater the distance we experience between ourselves and others, the more we tend to explain their behavior in causal, descriptive, or abstract terms. I came to use this discrimination as a principle in my counseling experience, particularly with people who were enmeshed in a relationship conflict of one kind or another. How people defined their dilemma offered helpful directions in regard to what my counseling role should be if I were to help them. If a husband described his wife's actions and attitudes in causal terms (i.e., "She treats me this way because she is (a) neurotic, or (b) listens to her mother too much, or (c) she has always hated men, or (d) all of the preceding) then he was telling me that (a) he had arrived at conclusions that served to close off any need for the pursuit of further understanding, or (b) his major concern was to protect what was left of his integrity, or (c) it was necessary for him to explain his sense of helplessness, or (d) any and all combinations of these justifications.

If, however, this man used explanatory terms such as, "something is troubling her . . .," "she is frustrated, she wants something . . .," "I don't know for sure where we are heading . . .," he is telling me that their relationship is still somewhat open, and more important, they are concerned about each other and the future of their marriage. Understanding and realization, and not mere justification, are their motivations.

A causal view attempts to capture the other person in the way I think he should be in my own world. A teleological view tries to capture the other person in the way he is in his own world, conveying a sense of dignity to him because his world as he sees it is respected. It also resists the reductionistic trap of labeling or classifying behavior; in fact, it connotes a constantly expanding process of understanding that acknowledges that a final, fixed portrait of another person can never be reached because he is seen as constantly moving into his own future.

It is apparent that this way of understanding also avoids the propensity for making final value or moral judgments about the behavior of others. When it is possible to fathom or even to conjecture about the other person's conception of himself, behavior that once outwardly appeared puzzling, perhaps even defeating and sometimes crazy, changes in meaning and purpose. Seen as a logical extension of the person's perceptions of himself and his world, his behavior makes sense. This does not propose that we ignore actions that result in pain, conflict, rejection, or alienation; such value-free objectivity is improbable. But the dreadful things people are able to do to themselves or to others are more amenable to change when their underlying intentions are brought to light instead of their being judged according to one moral criterion or another. In other words, a search for human purpose endeavors to take in the existential meanings of behavior; it attempts to find the crucial balance between the tendency to accept unequivocally all behavior, no matter how nefarious, and the proclivity for moralizing and judging. If the teleological perspective assumes anything, it is that the intentions of man are inevitably obscure and enigmatic; knowing is an ongoing process and not a final product.

If human motives are often elusive or deceptive, we must wonder why the behavioral sciences have so often expended so much time and energy in attempting to explain behavior in narrow and confining terms, as if it could be captured in equations or causal hypotheses. Certainly this approach meets some of the requirements of scientific precision and respectability. Yet, the major novelists and writers have recognized and prized man's natural struggle with his progressive and ascendant tendencies—his need to become. Unhampered by theoretical fetters, the writer attempts to capture the irony, the tragedy, and the tensions inherent in man's struggles to realize himself.

Philip Roth, in an essay about his objectives as a writer, discusses how he created the central characters in three of his novels:

Now, how Portnoy conceives of Portnoy is not much of an issue in that book [*Portnoy's Complaint*]. Portnoy knows precisely how to present himself—a good

27

part of his complaint is that his sense of himself, his past, and his ridiculous destiny is so *fixed*. In *The Breast*, Kepesh must be educated to understand what he is, and very much against the grain of his own defiant hopelessness. Only by the end of the book does he capitulate and take the doctor's word for what has seemed so utterly impossible all along, accepting finally both the preposterous description as to what now to do about it. But for Tarnopol [in *My Life as a Man*] the presentation or description of himself is what is most problematical—and what remains unresolved. To my mind, Tarnopol's attempt to realize himself with the right words—as earlier in life he attempted to realize himself through the right deeds—is what's at the heart of the book, and accounts for my joining his fictions about his life with his autobiography. I hope it will be understood as Tarnopol's struggle to achieve description. [14]

Where Roth speaks of the signal importance of meaning and being as arising out of self-definitions and self-realization, Anaïs Nin alludes to the significance of the act. Talking about the significance of symbolism, she says:

The unconscious cannot express itself directly because it is a composite of past, present, future, a timeless alchemy of many dimensions. A direct statement, as for an act, would deprive it of its effectiveness. It is an image which bypasses the censor of the mind, affects our emotions and senses. An act has to be interpreted on two levels—one as action, the other as meaning. . . . this fascinating under-world of symbolic act has always been known to the poets. It was Freud who complained that every time he made a discovery he found some poet who had been there before him. [15]

Maurice Friedman is a philosopher, not a novelist. But he has explored the realms of literature to uncover the nature and meanings of man, his images, and the ways in which he creates his reality. [16] In his latest work, Friedman also speaks of the significance of the immediate act as the source of meaning. He argues that even the philosophy of existentialism with its concern with the current human experience does not deal adequately with the lived, unique event. Authenticity, the burden of the existentialist position, is not an amorphous state of being but is located in each concrete human act. The meaning of what and who we are is not a general thing but an element of each of our acts that reveals the emergent person. [17]

What many poets, novelists, and philosophers have known all along is that meaning lies in the lived experience. Meaning, as it bears on the human state, is not the property of exotic, unconscious manipulations or instincts. Nor does it derive from the intrusion of some cosmic controls or the final influences of environmental forces. Meaning lies in relations and transactions, the inseparability of the person from all other persons and things. It is the essence of the experience as it is lived and as it bears on how we define where we are going into the future and what we expect that future holds for us.

Some Historical Perspectives

A basic human need is to create a sense of reality about the self, the world, and the relations between the two. This is done by searching for or creating explanations that demystify and reduce uncertainty by discovering or inventing relationships between things or events, and by attempting to find some measure of predictability in the occurrence of events. This unrelenting activity is one special attribute that distinguishes the human organism from all other living forms.

One highly respectable way of fulfilling this compulsion is theory building, which involves the deliberate use of inductive or deductive reasoning to achieve the sought-for explanations and a semblance of predictability. These efforts may produce useful hypotheses and propositions that then enable us to put some of our constructions of reality to a logical test. The obvious risk is the possibility that not only the theories might be wrong but the tests we put them to might also be in error. The result is a gross misconception of reality that may lead us down some perilous paths.

But even in the best of circumstances, where error is minimized, there is yet another risk—the possibility that the particular theory, especially one that tries to bind some of the complexities of human behavior or the social processes into a coherent whole, can be mistaken for reality itself. In Goethe's terms, theories and their hypotheses are only the pieces of scaffolding erected around a building during the course of construction and taken away as soon as the edifice is completed. In our intoxication with the delights of explanation that a theory offers, it is easy to lose sight of its transient and partial characteristics. We may ignore the fact that the theory only reflects the state of available knowledge at a particular point in time, and we may overlook the way the theory is colored and formed by the peculiar perspectives of the theorizer.

The greatest hazard is ignorance about the assumptions on which the theory is founded and the derivations of these assumptions. Any abstract construction of reality is inevitably a symbol of a history of thought that contains a number of ideas that have evolved over time. This risk is offset somewhat by recourse to epistemological thought or the search for the derivations of knowledge as it bears on our understanding of our worlds. We shall be describing and examining theories, constructs, and conceptions of self, behavior, relationships, learning, and change. It is essential for us to anticipate these ideas with at least a brief look at their antecedent assumptions. More precisely, I think it is important for us to look at these derivations according to the way that I, as author, arrange and interpret them as foundations for the theories that follow.

Let me first state a general impression about mankind's attempts over time to secure a meaningful (whatever that happens to mean in any period) approximation of his nature and raison d'être. No matter what form these attempts have assumed, they have been marked by conflicting ideas, not by a progressive sequence. At times these conceptions have coexisted; in other periods they have acted and reacted upon each other much in the way of the Hegelian dialectic: a thesis leads to antithesis which combine and lead to yet a new thesis. The controversial ideas have centered around a number of critical questions: whether man is essentially rational or irrational or is some blend of both; the question of separateness of mind and body, soul and mind, or mind and brain; the significance of morality, ethics and values; whether man is an actor or merely a reactor to the determinants in his world; the nature-nurture puzzle, and so forth.

The roots of these controversies lie in early Greek thought, which established broadly contrasting ideas about the human purview. The two major views were organized under two systems of thought, the Apollonian and the Dionysian.[18] The Apollonian tradition was rooted in Socrates' identification of the virtues of knowledge and became the parent of European intellectualism and Newtonian mechanism. It offered the notion of perfect intelligibility, the idea that all events of the world could be explained by deduction from first principles. The Dionysian tradition developed outside the early academies of learning and was more concerned with action, sentiment, experience, and the internal world than with reason. Its emphasis was more on passion than on logic, on excitement than on rationality. With the emergence of science and the

Age of Reason, the Dionysian heritage fell to the poets. The effects of these two systems on the social and behavioral sciences began to become apparent.

Even these ideas were products of still earlier attempts by man to explain himself. The need to know one's place within an enigmatic, uncertain world was assuaged by explanations coming from religion, mythology, and animism. The beliefs that flowed from these sources imbued nature with spirit and will; the world itself became a kind of living organism, and because of the way its vitality was understood, the fear of the powerful Unknown was reduced.[19] More important, perhaps, was the possibility that these beliefs helped the individual achieve a greater sense of connectedness with his natural world. A world that is alive and vital, that is populated by spirits and forces, seems to create the aura of mystery. But it also contains meaning and purpose; there are things out there to which one can relate, talk, and pray and most important, there are things in which one can believe. As Ernest Becker puts it, Newton's work in the seventeenth and eighteenth centuries brought this connection between man and his world to a close. The personal, moral, living world became transformed into "a completely material, mechanized world, utterly abstracted, utterly devoid of personal significance to us, emptied of spiritual qualities."[20] With this change the human task was transformed into one of controlling this now foreign, external, impersonal universe. Meaning had to be found elsewhere.

Newton's discoveries and inventions were, of course, the culmination of many centuries of exploration and wonder. Even the early Greeks found that mere explanation would not suffice. If man was to achieve greater understanding of and, hence, more control over his environment, he also had to establish some semblance of order and predictability in the things of his world. As nature came to be observed according to its regularities, it also became possible to envision a degree of order in certain aspects of the universe. Out of this order arose the potential for predicting the sequence of things and events. Tides, lunar cycles, the movement of planets, and apparent motion of stars were no longer random and spiritual occurrences but indications that nature did operate according to a set of "laws." Man could define not only the unknowns of his immediate world, he could also envision those that were part of his future as well. Out of these realizations a pre-science emerged, a type of organismic philosophy that supplanted the conceptions of the animistic, spirit-dominated world. A whole new system of thought contained the archaic beginnings of the teleological orientation. The things of the world were understood as having their own "essences" that were expressed through perpetual strivings to be realized and attained in their own peculiar ways. The meaning and cause of natural experiences could be comprehended in terms of their movement towards the goals they were supposed to attain.

The teleological perspective did persist as an acceptable principle in the biological sciences for a longer period since notions of a "vital force" and "will" continued to be ascribed to living organisms. Life was seen as having purpose and meaning in its own right and could be explained in these terms. However, this perspective came to an end with the emergence of the theory of natural selection proposed by Charles Darwin and Alfred Russel Wallace in the nineteenth century. The belief that living processes have ultimate purposes fell aside. Life no longer had intention; instead it reflected a "struggle for existence" that was based on the idea that only the fit and the strong can survive.

Although the biological sciences did continue to entertain teleological notions well into the nineteenth century, the demise of these ideas had begun with the work of Newton in the seventeenth century. Newtonian mechanics terminated ponderings about essences, meanings, or any elaborations about the *intrinsic* character of natural phenomena. What mechanics illuminated, in a narrow sense, was the production of motion by the action of *external* forces on things. Central to this new science was the concern with the external matters, the energies that could be quantified, objectified, and most important for man's relations to his world, mastered and controlled. The character of scientific questioning shifted from interests in *why* and "for what reasons" to *how* things worked. Put in other terms, the revolution that Newton generated was the idea that laws and causes could ultimately explain the nature of the world. In a more expansive sense, it nurtured the seeds of the deterministic assumption, the belief that, if everything is known about the world at a given moment then, everything can be known about it for all time. Each present state will determine the state immediately following—a scientific verification of the primary significance of cause. Moreover, the new science ennobled the Apollonian mode of rational thought, order, and control.[21]

The age of mechanics flowered and by the nineteenth century the field of physics comprised four distinct branches: mechanics, concerned with material bodies as influenced by forces; thermodynamics, concerned with temperature and its conversion into energy and work; electrodynamics, concerned with electricity and magnetic phenomena; and optics, concerned with the propagation of light. Each field continued to develop its theoretical schemes and the logical systems that could be verified under experimental conditions. The development of these theories increased the belief in the certainty and predictability of natural phenomena and offered assurance that total understanding of all things that make up our universe would somehow be achieved someday. [22] This promise has persisted in our thinking, especially in the belief that we should be able to achieve a fairly complete and predictable understanding of something as complex and elusive as human and social behavior. We still seem to be burdened and frustrated by our inability to construct the one grand theory that is the final disclosure.

The hope of a "grand theory" captured the attention of the sciences, which sought the ultimate goal of reducing all physics to theories of mechanics and unifying the four separate fields under one set of universal laws. It was this very search that came to reveal the flaws in the concept of universality. What would have been required was a concept that served as a link between the different fields, and since it did not exist, one had to be invented. This was the theory of "ether," a chemically or physically undetectable substance that permeated all matter and space and served as a medium for the transmission of electromagnetic waves. The experiments of A. A. Michelson and E. W. Morley in the late nineteenth century clearly disproved the existence of any such substance. The study of the structure of the atom and the realization that atoms are not the ultimate and indivisible foundations for all physical matter further hastened the abandonment of notions of deterministic certainty and the adoption of a mathematics of probability. With the rise of modern physics, the ambiguities and contradictions inherent in the idea of absolute causality became even more apparent. Science came to understand that all things are related and interdependent. All things that appear to present themselves as entities are inevitably integral aspects of smaller and larger systems. As such, they can be grasped only in their relations and transformations, the manner in which they stand in some sort of exchange with other seeming entities. Ervin Laszlo disputes the assumption that natural structures can in any way be considered inert, atomic, or discrete. [23]

> Suborganic nature turns out to be rather different from the mechanistic universe of Newtonian physics. It is a dynamic realm of interacting forces, resulting in the emergence of systems of increasingly organized complexity. Physical nature is not a machine, just as organic nature is not infused with a separate life force. The patterns of development parallel one another, although they take place on different levels and exhibit different, in practice irreducible characteristics.

Although a relativistic, probablistic, and systemic view came to characterize the position of science, there still remained some question about modes of inquiry. What methods of study will best reveal what we wish to know? As it pertained to the natural sciences, this was not a pressing question: the controllable and concrete nature of the objects under study in many ways influenced the manner in which explorations were undertaken. In the social and behavioral sciences, however, the usual targets for inquiry are typically abstract, not readily subject to scientific controls, and are usually devoid of definable boundaries. These anthropomorphic targets cannot in themselves reveal their fundamental structures or operations when subjected to "pure" scientific investigation.

Broadly speaking, two major solutions emerged: modern scientific empiricism and modern teleology, each having roots in antecedent forms. The empirical or positivistic approach resolves the problems inherent in the study of human conditions by limiting its investigations to what is apparent or to what "sense data" alone can describe and explain. Reality is postulated in terms of an empirical "fact," an observable event that follows some other observable event in what appears to be a direct relationship.

The rationale for a positivistic approximation of social reality was established by Auguste Comte, who set the foundations for the discipline of sociology. Comte envisaged positivism as the logical third and ultimate stage in the evolution of scientific thought. The first stage, the archaic, explained events in terms of supernatural control and intervention. The second contained a metaphysical perspective made up of abstract causes and principles. Comte's third stage, the positivistic, represented a fully scientific position, one that encompassed a set of devices for solving problems in a manner that does not extend beyond what is observable and measurable.

The modern teleological view does not limit itself to the empirical nature of things; it revives the postulate of final cause and purpose. This position is expressed by K. W. Wild in *Intuition*, published in 1938. Wild contends that modern science either assumes or asserts a teleological position up to a point.[24] Even if we limit our considerations to the material world and the exact sciences, we come to appreciate what appears to be the developing order of things. Any study of the physical or natural sciences makes it impossible to believe that this order is a consequence of specific causes or the workings of blind chance. Certainly physical laws can be understood as descriptions of how nature does behave. But they do not describe *how* nature must behave since there is no reason why nature should behave in these particular ways. There are no specific reasons for the existence of regularity, repetition, and effect following cause. Is it therefore possible to accept the reality of order without admitting to the realm of ends? The very meaning of life seems to be the seeking of ends, even in nature's most complex workings. The stem grows toward the light *in order that* the plant can get oxygen, carbon dioxide, etc.; it grows *in order to* store and manufacture food; it develops colored petals *in order to* attract insects; and so on. In human life, when consciousness develops into self-consciousness, not only do we act as though we perceived certain ends, but we also act as if we are convinced that there are such ends. In short, organisms organize, evolve, and transform themselves not because of the press of antecedent conditions but because of their tendency to move towards increasing order and wholeness out of which realization may take place.

A moment's reflection on this brief development of ideas about science and the study of man reveals a process not entirely based on pure reason or objectivity. We see the activation of the need to know and understand. We also see that the pursuit of knowledge is not without the influence of ideology and belief, that man-made assumptions shape the nature of the search as well as its outcome. We again confront the inevitable dialectic, the way in which ideas impinge upon and react to one another generating conclusions that ineluctably lead to yet other conclusions. At this point, we have two major systems of thought that represent, at least in the thinking of the Western world, the desirable ap-

35

proaches to the elaboration of reality. Because of their influence, it will be useful to outline briefly their basic characteristics (Table 1).

Table 1. Two Major Approaches to the Study of Man

Reality Sought	Positivistic	Teleological
Source of knowledge	Man as an object	Man as a subject
Nature of phenomenon	Structure/form	Process
Source of change	Extrinsic	Intrinsic
Nature of change	Cause	Intention
Effectors of change	Manipulation	Growth/vitality

The positivistic position strives for the methodological ideal and asserts that man can best be studied in objective terms. We can know about him through observational or experimental means that permit the observer to measure, appraise, explain, and otherwise arrive at conclusions about the situation in question. Findings can be ordered within particular categorical or statistical structures or according to established models. Change is understood as the consequence of denotable forces acting on the individual in some way that evokes modifications in behavior, attitude, values, etc. Change is seen as a response to something external, which implies that reordering, removing, increasing, intensifying, or in some way altering the nature and quality of the impinging force will effect the desired change. The positivistic approach relies heavily on objectifications of and reliance on empirical facts within specific parameters.

The teleological position asserts that the individual can be best understood in subjective terms. Critical data accrue from the observed person's experience with and perception about his own situation. As a result, organizing frameworks or form have less importance because it is the process of the person's interactions and not the structure that provides meaning and knowledge. Since the person is understood as an actor and not as a responder, attention is directed towards the purposeful, intentional forces within the individual that influence his interactions. Change occurs as a consequence of inner modifications of purpose, motivation, value, goals, and the like—leading to the central importance of growth as the major effector of change. As the person is consciously able to reconceptualize his own aspirations, values, and goals, as well as their derivations, change in behavior, role, or self-concept should follow.

Although modern systems of thought and method relative to human problems arrange themselves across a spectrum, each does tend to lean towards one or the other of these positions.[25]

Positivistic Systems

The systems falling within the positivistic spectrum of social and psychological theories generally strive to bring into clearer definition and control some specific variants in the human state. Certainly these systems are not totally unconcerned with the more imprecise and intangible factors such as sentiments, values, morals, and self-realization. However, the theoretical and methodological structures within the positivistic tradition are constructed with a focus on behavior or attitudes that lend themselves to isolation and manipulation. I use the term *manipulation* in its literal sense and not in accord with its negative implications. These systems tend towards a reductionistic outlook, and conditions within the human state are conceptualized in terms of particular nominal categories, causes, effects, and the like. In short, this approach strives towards a respectable scientific position that limits its scope and control to defined parameters, variables, hypotheses, and definitions. H. J. Eysenck and H. R. Beech, speaking from the behaviorist point of view, offer a cogent defense of the scientific position against the charge of gross oversimplification of the complexity of real life: "If we begin by considering all the complexities involved in real-life events, we will never arrive at a scientific theory: if we are willing to oversimplify, we are at least able to make a beginning and thus correct our errors. . . . to accuse behavior therapy of oversimplification is therefore little more than to accuse it of following the usual scientific lines of advance."[26]

Their statement, while representing the scientific point of view, also establishes the position of the behaviorists within the positivistic purlieus. The behaviorists (and we could include the Skinnerians and learning theorists) are basically committed to conclusions that derive from the laboratory methodology of experimental psychology. Their methodologies are directed towards identifying specific maladaptive behaviors, subjecting them to planned procedures that will diminish or extinguish these behaviors, and establishing desired behaviors in their place.

A number of approaches to behavior change have evolved based on psychological learning theories developed in experimental laboratories over the past fifty years. Certain behavior therapists base their practice on the work of Ivan Pavlov, J. B. Watson, and E. R. Guthrie. The emphasis is on conditioned learning based on the effects of situational stimuli. Others draw from the reinforcement theories of B. F. Skinner, E. L. Thorndyke, and C. L. Hull and are concerned with the different consequences that determine which types of behavior will be acquired.[27]

A second system rooted in the positivistic view of man is the Freudian or other classical form of the psychoanalytic schools. This system, however, does not derive from the arena of experimentalism as such, and fits more clearly in the domain of logical positivism. Freud drew his ideas and methods from many philosophic springs; but foremost among them was the belief in the supreme value of empirical science as the major means of achieving valid knowledge about man. Freud did not limit his scientific method to the rigors of the laboratory; it could also be extended to incorporate clinical evidence. Hence, the large substance of his formulations derives from the empirical experience in his direct work with his patients.

Psychoanalytic therapy is rooted in a theoretical model that concep-tualizes psychic events in terms of the following propositions:

Genetic: The complex interplay between the inborn maturational phases and the environment of the child.
Dynamic: The qualitative forces, e.g., jealousy, love, and rage.
Economic: The quantitative aspects of these forces, i.e., whether they are greater or lesser, increasing or diminishing.
Structural: The schematized area of the psychic structure and function that includes the ego, id, and superego.
Topographical: Designation of a psychic event as to whether it is con-scious, preconscious, or unconscious.
Biological and Adaptational: The view of man as a biological organism in particular periods of his life.[28]

Psychoanalytic thought and practice have unfolded in many forms and variations over the past decades; yet basic assumptions remain within the positivistic fold. The critical experimentalist would question the scientific validity of psychoanalytic propositions, since they are hardly subject to the procedures of the laboratory, but these ideas do fit the model. While postulates about the psychic processes are largely rhetorical in nature, they do serve as the framework wherein observations of the person can be ordered and, in so doing, can then be manipulated towards the attainment of preconceived ends.

Another model is neither clearly experimental or logical in its development and form. This expression of positivism is something loosely called the medical model in its approach to the diagnosis and treatment of mental disorders. The medical model represents an effort to simulate other branches of physical medicine by attempting to conceptualize mental states and behavioral forms into a set of disease categories. Patients are studied and observed through the use of psychiatric evaluations, diagnosed, and given a clinical label. Treatment may take many forms including psychotherapy, chemotherapy, and electro-convulsive therapy. In many respects, the medical model is an accident of time and circumstance. This medico-scientific orientation springs from a period when medicine assumed responsibility for diagnosis and treatment because of the absence of other relevant disciplines. Referring to its beginnings over one hundred years ago, Becker says:

> It is the history of the ascendance of mental psychiatry, of the complete annexation of mental malfunctioning as a medical prerogative. Nineteenth century diagnosticians redoubled efforts to keep man under medical wraps and dress his behavioral disorders in Greco-Latin cant. Thus the science that knew least about total symbolic man and most about the animal body fully established its sacrosanct domain. We are coming to know now that it had no business there. In 1860, those who could have shed light on the malfunction of the symbolic animal had not yet arrived and developed their anthropological, sociological, and psychological ideas. [29]

Developmentally or accidentally, these three approaches to the conflicts and strains of human living (particularly in the way they are manifested in individuals) represent the positivistic tradition. They subscribe to the preeminence of scientism and establish the superordinate position of the therapist and the theoretician. Each possesses the final answers about his patients' existence.

More expansive forms of social change also subscribe in some significant ways to the positivistic view. This is the case insofar as man is seen in objective terms, as a victim of his environment and as requiring the intervention by forces outside of himself to remedy whatever his particular form of social malaise happens to be. To some extent social action movements based on Marxist or neo-Marxist ideologies express this position. I doubt that Karl Marx, himself, would find comfort in being cast into the positivistic mold because of the importance that he assigned to the subjective nature of man. Yet movements that spring from this ideology sometimes neglect the dialectics of Marx and, instead, take the unilateral positions that fundamentally are not unlike the behavioristic or psychoanalytic constructions of the human state. It is when people are defined as conditioned products of their economic or political institutions that these social movements take on the behaviorist attitude. The types of social action and change that are proposed become a new reinforcement mechanism designed to replace the influence of noxious social institutions. These social movements resemble the psychoanalytic school when it is assumed that man is essentially a determined animal, unthinkingly governed by forces to which he is largely oblivious. The Freudians would refer to these forces as essentially internal—the unconscious or instinctual influences. The neo-Marxians would conceive of these forces as essentially external—the subtle but powerful exploitation of people by corrupt institutions. In either case, the conception of the human state is essentially reductionistic, placing the responsibilities and the incentives of individuals, whether acting alone or with others, in a somewhat secondary dimension.

This short discussion of the positivist approach to the human situation is intended to be no more than a concise summary that captures its more distinguishing characteristics. The last few decades have witnessed many departures from these positions and theories. For example, the purity of the experimental model relative to its singular concern with observable behavior has been relaxed to include the influence of sentiments, needs, and motivations. Classical psychoanalysis has also endured many modifications that have altered the valence of instinctual and unconscious determinants. Some Marxian approaches to social change have extended greater credit to the ability of people to initiate changes in their own lives and environments. Yet, I find it important to state the polar qualities of the positivistic position: first, to point to one of the major directions of psychological and social thought, and second, to delineate and contrast more clearly the quality of the teleological position.

The Teleological Position

Since I have already indicated that the teleogical point of view provides one of the philosophical and conceptual substrata of this book, I seek now to serve two purposes: (1) to show the derivations and the evolvement of a modern teleological perspective; and (2) to elaborate further the description of this position.

Let me first restate the premise of the teleological approach: human adaptive processes, whether manifested by individuals, by persons in interaction, or by groups, are indicative of strivings toward the fulfillment of particular intentions, values, or goals. This position avoids a reductionistic course of thought and reaches toward an increasingly dynamic and expansive conception of human existence. Although this idea does not deny the value of rational scientific methods, neither is it bound by the constraints of their parameters. Inasmuch as the desire to comprehend motive and purpose encompasses such elusive concepts as mind, perception, self, sentiment, relations, and value, this in itself suggests a blending of conceptions that, in some cases, reflects the metaphysical tradition and, in others, the scientific. It is a form of inquiry that would lean more towards an open-ended rather than a circumscribed approach to the study of behavior.

It is doubtful that one can point to the origins of teleological thought. Ideas about the nature of the human state seem to flow as an errant stream, crossing and recrossing itself in many places, sending out new branches that again return and take on new directions. Moreover, notions about man's intentionality appear, retreat, and reappear again over the course of time. Early in the course of philosophic thought, Aristotle asserted that "All that we do is done with an eye to something else." In this Aristotelian tradition, the Scholastic theme in the thirteenth century developed the teleological argument that portrayed man as the major creation of the universe, motivated toward the ultimate goal of union with God. Again, in the eighteenth century we find Immanuel Kant's philosophy expressing the idea of purposiveness in adaptation.

If it is necessary to point to an arbitrary place in the stream that marks the beginning of modern teleological inquiry, the work of Charles S.

41

Peirce is a reasonable place to start. Peirce is generally regarded as the founder of the philosophy of pragmatism (1839–1914) and a major influence on William James and John Dewey. He was a philosopher, a psychologist, a mathematician, and the founder of semiotics (the study of signs and symbols). Peirce's pragmatism assumes that meaning always occurs in a human context, a context of action. Words mean something only because people give meaning to them in the way they are used. Language is an abstraction of concrete acts of speech, acts that have their origin in the desire to achieve certain human ends; i.e., the meaning of anything can only be achieved by reference to its genesis in the context of purposive human behavior.[30]

Within the existing texture of ideas about the human state, Peirce introduced a notion of the self that was dynamic rather than abstract. He defined it as an energy, constantly moving forward, constantly in the process of emergence and development. Since its character is process and not structure, the human self can never attain a state of completion or finality, and since symbols are things that are exchanged among people, Peirce necessarily placed the emergence of the self within a social matrix. Anticipating the symbolic interactionism of George Herbert Mead and the communication theorists, Peirce contended that what takes place among people in social interchange depends not only on the symbols used but also on the way these symbols are interpreted.[31] Peirce's pragmatic conception of man as active and purposeful and as a crafter of symbols was a departure from the speculative philosophy of his time. By placing human emergence in a social context, he created the logic that would allow man to be studied as a vital phenomenon rather than as a mechanistic or psychic entity. If man tends to move towards a greater sense of particularization and coherence, it is possible to think of a self that is in the process of learning and development. If man is understood as an essential part of a social context, it is possible to grapple with ideas of relationship and social consciousness. If man's motives involve the exchange and manipulation of symbols, it is possible to consider the role of perception as the medium of exchange.

William James, a contemporary of Peirce, advanced the study of the self as a vital, forward-looking structure. Basic to his idea of the integrity of the self is the element of self-esteem, which is not a fixed measure or a descriptive judgment but the consequences of the person's aspirations as expressed in real behavior. Self-esteem cannot be hoarded like a material possession; it must be realized again and again in the pursuit of personal objectives and, so, is always at risk. The self is not a thing but a composite of two aspects. The empirical self or the *Me*, encompasses all the things I consider as my own. There is the *material Me*, my body, my family, my home, my goods—all those things that I consider to be parts and extensions of what I believe I am. The *social Me* takes in all my relationships of which I feel my self is a part, including my friends, my family, my allies, and the groups to which I belong. The *spiritual Me* is more nebulous, an "active-feeling state of consciousness" or an identification with particular beliefs and faiths. Standing in balance with the empirical Me is the knowing *I*. Here James is speaking of the consciousness of the self, the ability of the self to be aware of what it is, what it has been, and to what it belongs. But more important, it also refers to a consciousness in the form of a stream, an awareness of the fluidity of past into present. It is this knowing *I* that creates a self-awareness that is aggregate and coherent, that attaches credibility to the existence of one's self.[32]

The importance of James' work lies in his elaboration of the self as intentional, conscious, and cognitive. The fundamental need for self-esteem is an inner force that impels man towards material, social, and spiritual ends. This is hardly a mechanistic drive since human intentionality is monitored by a prevailing consciousness of being and acting.

John Dewey followed in the pragmatist tradition of Peirce and was a substantial contributor to the school of Pragmatism. Although he wrote primarily as a social philosopher, his ideas ultimately found their way (often controversially) into the fields of psychology and education. Whether or not one agrees with his conceptions, the power and substance of his logic merits serious attention.

Dewey was not much concerned with speculations about causes and mechanics relative to the human state. He characterized the human experience as the attempt to achieve what he called "ends-in-view." Man moves forward through his life towards the goals that he envisions. They are not ends in themselves because as soon as one approaches the achievement of a particular goal new and different ones are bound to arise. Dewey diverged from the traditional conceptions of man that celebrate his rational and thinking abilities; he portrayed the person as an acting being, one who proceeded through life and towards his goals

43

without much thought about either his path or his destination. Dewey did not assume in any way that this was an aimless journey. Because the person is convinced that there *is* a destination, little thought is required about his course of travel. However, it is when an obstacle blocks his path that thought and contemplation are evoked to find the means of overcoming the obstacle. To find a solution, the individual will call on his past experiences that seem to be relevant to his immediate ambitions and his forecasts of the future. If he is successful, a unity of thought and conduct is achieved, and he again progresses onward. If, however, the person's past experiences bear little relation to or have little utility for the resolution of the immediate problem, it becomes necessary to engage in new types of learning and problem-solving activity before he can go on toward his desired goal.

This brief discussion reveals little about the remarkable scope of Dewey's work. It does, however, establish the momentous importance of the role of learning and problem solving in human adaptation, particularly when movement towards realization is thwarted. Dewey's conceptions give some perspective to the past and its influence on present adaptations. Although history is not a determinant, it does exist in our minds as a repository of habits, patterns, solutions, and experiences in general, so that we may draw from that storehouse to find remedies for present difficulties. But as Dewey points out, these experiences may fail or delude us and thus force us to learn—finding new solutions and discovering formerly unrecognized capabilities within ourselves. His approach stresses the ability to symbolize and to think in terms of futures, and it is the future that characterizes and gives meaning to the present. It is some aim, an anticipated end, that enriches present activities that would otherwise seem to be blind, disorderly, and mechanical. "An end in view is a *means* of present action; present action is not a means to a remote end. Men do not shoot because targets exist but they set up targets in order that throwing and shooting may be more effective and significant."[33]

In the pursuit of our ends, it now becomes necessary to turn away from thought *about* the nature of human intentionality and turn our attention to the means of effecting change *in* people. We shift from the purely explanatory assumptions to the more operational.

Harry Stack Sullivan was a practicing psychiatrist and somewhat of a revisionist who left the fold of traditional medical and intrapsychic therapies. Sullivan was influenced by the ideas of the sociologists and social psychologists of his time, particularly the work of Charles Cooley, James M. Baldwin, and George Herbert Mead. He borrowed their ideas about social and interpersonal processes and translated them into new psychiatric applications for the treatment of pathological behaviors.[34] Like James and others before him, Sullivan understood the self as a system or what he called "an organization of educative experience called into being by the necessity to avoid or minimize incidents of anxiety."[35] There is considerable similarity between Sullivan's ideas about the function of the self to minimize anxiety and the Jamesian notion of self-esteem. The self is neither driven by instinct nor unconsciously shaped; it is a composite of earlier learnings that is aroused to combat anxiety and threats to safety. The self evolves and develops out of a social history. It is also influenced by the "reflected appraisals" of other persons as well as the roles one plays within a given social context. A bifocal view is required to fathom the self—a view that gives credence to developmental factors as well as the social and interpersonal conditions operating at any given time.

Anxiety is the concept central to Sullivan's thesis. It is experienced in one's interpersonal environment—a consequence of the behavior of others directed toward the self. When threat is felt a "paralyzing effect" ensues, affecting such responses as one's range of awareness and the adequacy of one's cognitive processes. In this regard, its presence serves to diminish one's sense of security and feelings of competence. At the same time, the individual has recourse to what Sullivan calls the "power motive," a need to maintain control in order to deal with and overcome the threat, thereby restoring a feeling of security. Sullivan's elaboration of these adaptive mechanisms is far more extensive than this brief discussion indicates. All I wish to emphasize at this point is his proposition about disordered behavior: The individual is not a psychiatric casualty or a passive victim; he is an active participant in an ongoing process of adaptation (whether productive or unproductive) involving his perceptions and responses to an interpersonal system.

What Sullivan had to say about the processes of cognition greatly helped to expand some rather static and constricted versions of how people come to perceive their social realities. There is still Freud's concept

45

of the "transference," which was designed to explain why people tend to distort the nature and quality of their interpersonal relationships by displacing onto them the unresolved and conflicted feelings that were aroused in very early intimate relationships. This is a valid concept insofar as it captures the human tendency to establish irrational linkages between past and present experiences; however, it falls short of explaining how and under what circumstances these kinds of cognitions develop. It is descriptive rather than explanatory and forces the therapist to make risky interpretations about the connections between the patient's past and present life. It is true that Freud did distinguish between the primary processes, the primitive and unconscious operations of the mind, and the secondary processes, the rational and logical functions of the mind. However, these differentiations are also descriptive in nature and are ineffective in qualifying what is meant by transference in its common usage.

Sullivan proposed three different modes of perception that influence the manner in which a person will come to interpret subsequent experiences. The *prototaxic* refers to the primary modes of thinking—the infantile, raw, and undifferentiated. One experiences his own world in a more or less sensory manner without reference to the temporal or physical nature of the things in his view. The result is gross impressions, largely within the range of feelings and sensations with little logical or rational control.

The *parataxic* mode represents very personal constructions and distortions of reality. It involves the use of symbols, but these are symbols of a most private nature. The impressions are quite idiosyncratic and are more related to inner needs and processes than to the actualities of the outer event. A good example is the tendency of a person to personify all authority figures as frightening or threatening as he recalls anxieties aroused in earlier experiences with similar persons.

The *syntaxic* is indicative of the person as a social creature. It refers to the logical and rational thought processes that also involve the use of symbols. These, however, are consensual symbols that are similarly defined by most of the participants in a social context. Perception in Sullivan's view is a multilevel process and not a simple transfer of gross impressions from the past into the present. Sullivan also shuns the deterministic view of man and portrays him as a complex, symbolic, and learning organism striving to ward off or to cope with threats to his mastery. The individual is capable of understanding his world on a number of levels that are not fixed but are subject to change by reeducation.

These ideas of man's intentional and interpreting nature are implicit in Sullivan's model. Another system of thought emerged that was based quite explicitly on the conception of purposiveness and goal-directedness. This is the Hormic Psychology of William McDougall; he set the foundations for his position in 1925 and elaborated in 1930 a more comprehensive version of the hormic concept. The essence of his theory can be simply stated: man or animal seeks this or that because it is his nature to do so.

In some respects, McDougall was not only creating new conceptions, he was also reacting to the prevailing mechanistic concepts of behavior. These, he believed, did not adequately explain the active, striving potentials of the human organism. He also opposed theories that asserted that human behavior was simply a response to the need to reduce pain or discomfort or that these drives were the forces that effected and shaped behavior. In contrast with the idea that human striving sprung into being only to diminish discomfort, McDougall asserted that this striving was consistently present.

McDougall's argument is clearly teleological, but apparently he could not permit his theory to rest on a purely philosophical or assumptive foundation, and he searched for "respectable" and "scientific" explanations of the sources of human behavior. While he asserted that the organism was primarily a purposive, goal-oriented being, McDougall paradoxically drew on the causal, deterministic positions to defend his point of view. His juxtaposition of these ideas is rather vague; nonetheless, he implied the presence of causal antecedents in the form of instincts and energy potential in chemical form in human tissue. Although he avoided the causal forces of mechanics, he did acknowledge the influence of a biological determinism. He asserted that human cognitive capabilities are more powerful than biological sources of energy since it is man's cognitive attributes that enable him to master the biological determinants. Although innate energies are present, as the organism approaches its goal these energies are channeled and guided by cognitive activity—the awareness, vague though it may be, of the immediate situation and the desired goal.

Despite some inconsistencies in his argument (apparent in the confusion of conflicting teleological and causal principles), McDougall's work cannot be minimized. His purposive psychology did illuminate the force of human intention and its meanings. He points to the crucial ability of the individual to use his awareness to overcome all that he is. This is expressed in McDougall's quotation of a contemporary: "A human being's inheritance would seem to include a capacity for discovering and conating tendencies beyond the inherited nature of his own organism or his own biological needs."[36] McDougall's psychology did not pretend to postulate final answers; in fact, hormic psychology recognizes the "littleness" of our present understanding and encourages an open mind to all empirical evidence and all legitimate speculations.

Hormic theory influenced succeeding personality theorists but became more of a significant reference than a school of psychology in its own right. Sullivan's interpersonal theories, however, did flower into a model of theory and practice and a school, The Washington School of Psychiatry. Nevertheless, both were overshadowed by Freudian psychoanalysis and its deterministic construction of the human psyche. Yet, Freudian psychology itself did not ignore the importance of the role of perception. It is implicitly evident in the concept of transference phenomena and in the technique of "working through," whereby the patient reconceptualizes his illusions and beliefs and their connections with significant experiences.

Despite its endeavor to maintain a pure, uniform, and classic form, the psychoanalytic school did not remain intact. Revisionists include Karl Jung, Otto Rank, and Alfred Adler, who asserted that psychologists' reliance on causal explanations was an intent to disguise their dogma in mechanistic or physical similes. "Causes, powers, instincts, impulses and the like cannot serve as explanatory principles. The final goal alone can, . . . that mysterious creative power of life which expresses itself in the desire to develop, to strive, to achieve. . . . This power is *teleological*, it expresses itself in the striving after a goal and, in this striving, every bodily and psychological movement is made to cooperate."[37]

Adler, in his antithetical position, argued that purpose and not cause is the force that mobilizes action. He offered the concept of a *lifestyle*, his term for a unifying, complex, and pervasive adaptive pattern. It is his lifestyle that represents the characteristic manner in which the individual conducts himself in his life situation, a pattern that is based mainly on his conception of himself and perception of his relationships and his place within them. Adlerian therapy as an operational form of these ideas aims at helping the person to reconstruct the concepts and precepts that accrue from his learning and interfere with his goals and contributions to the social order.

It is worthwhile reflecting on how theories about the nature of man and his behavior develop. Unlike the theories of the physical or natural sciences, which tend more to be additive or incremental, linearity is not as evident in the behavioral sciences. One tends to see the dialectic influence of one upon the other rather than a systematic progression and development, partly because of the different epistemological foundations of the various thought systems. For example, logical analysis undergirds the work of Peirce and Dewey, whereas clinical experience and observation support the ideas of Sullivan and Adler. And in instances such as in McDougall's theories, personal constructs and preexisting belief systems appear to be the influences that shape the origins as well as the eventual structures of these theories.

When we come to current systems of thought that take an intentional view of the person we find that they seem to be woven of whole parts and sometimes merely fragments of some of the preceding ideas. Arthur W. Combs and Donald Snygg select the notion of *self concept* as the focal point of their assumption of what they call the "phenomenal self."[38] The self concept of any individual comprises all of the most enduring and important perceptions that both symbolize and generalize that individual. In other words, how I understand myself, how I define myself, is a composite of what I believe I have experienced as well as what I now do experience. If this is the case, human motivation is guided by the fundamental need to maintain and enhance that self-concept according to how it is perceived. Anything inconsistent with these perceptions inevitably must be regarded as a threat since challenges to these perceptions casts the existing concept of self, the phenomenal self, in doubt. The individual copes with uncertainty by either narrowing his perceptions of his field or distorting or excluding those aspects that disturb his perceptions. Since something is ignored or twisted, some kind of inadequate or unproductive behavior must follow. Combs and Snygg believe that these dysfunctional tendencies can be remedied by enabling the person to explore a fuller breadth of his psychological field including his self-concept and his relationships. He is able to escape the circularity of patterns which, in rigidly safeguarding the self-concept, also creates an infelicitous life arrangement.

The logotherapy of Victor Frankl also reflects a phenomenological position relative to the self in interaction with its world;[39] however, Frankl translates the intentions of the self in terms of the existential search for meaning. He speaks of the "will to meaning" or the inherent tendency of man to grasp values that he can actualize and to reach out to fulfill his significant ideals. Personal meanings can derive from a number of sources including the individual himself, his pattern of living, and his social environment. Ultimately, however, each person must create the substance and design of his existence inasmuch as one cannot depend on either tradition or instinct to tell him how or what to be.

When an individual refuses to define his own life's meanings and purposes or even denies that these meanings and purposes exist, the remaining alternatives are inevitably self-diminishing. He can turn away from himself to emulate others' actions or beliefs—this leads to conformism. He may submit to others' controls and directions—this leads to totalitarianism. In both instances he is bound to experience an existential vacuum, a kind of neuroticism.

Frankl also warns against the eagerness to explain meaning through the use of scientific methods, which can only reduce or fractionalize understanding. If, for example, the person is placed in a biological frame it will only generate somatic data about him; placing him in a purely psychological frame will only produce psychic data. In either instance what is achieved is a closed system instead of a more expansive and meaningful understanding of the person.

A man is helped out of the morass of meaninglessness by the endeavor to reconsider and perhaps even renounce preconceived structures and patterns that he uses to perceive and translate his immediate experiences. He must examine his ways of understanding his world which can only disclose meaning in partial, inadequate, or devious terms.

We can see some similarity between the ideas of Frankl and those of

Combs and Snygg. Both stress the idea that change and enrichment in living can come only from the willingness of the individual to reorient his perceptual patterns. This does not merely refer to how the individual apprehends his world but also the the frame of reference he uses to interpret what is perceived. We can also add Maslow's proposition to this point of view. He advocates a parallel view except that he notes that growth and self-awareness do not necessarily arise from the reconstruction of perceptual patterns. Instead, or in addition, growth emerges from the realization of pressures within the person "toward a unity of personality, toward spontaneous expressiveness, toward full individuality and identity, toward seeing the truth . . ., toward being creative. . . ."[40]

This catalogue of ideas would not be complete without at least a brief reference to certain cognitive theorists who stress the relation of perception to human purpose. Albert Mehrabian first assumes that the person is an active and structuring agent in his environment. How the individual deals with or manages his environment partly depends on how he construes his particular situation. In other words, the cognitive construction that he applies to the event bears on how that event is understood and handled. This construction derives from the fusion of both experiential and personal factors. One factor is the individual's identification with a particular culture that informs him about the approved and common modes of thinking about certain events. The second encompasses the person's physiological processes that will influence how and what he apprehends in a given situation. A third takes into account the mental categories or the preset cognitions that the person uses to find sense and meaning in that which is perceived.

The perceptual experience is a crucial component of Mehrabian's construct of *adaptation*, defined as the typical mode used by the individual to cope with problems of his environment. Adaptation becomes problematic when it is distorted by either *assimilation*, the disposition to process incoming information so as to succeed in avoiding any change in the cognitive structure, or *accommodation*, transient changes in the cognitive structure to cope with an event. In assimilation, people act *as if* they are truly living through the experience; actually the rigidity of their cognitions precludes any significant change in understanding or awareness. In accommodation, they permit themselves to be changed by the happening but only to avoid dealing with the event in an assertive and direct fashion. The attainment of productive or adequate adaptation, or what Mehrabian calls "equilibration," requires some balance and blending of these traits.[41]

Victor Raimy translates cognitive theory into its application to psychological counseling.[42] His basic premise is that there is nothing that can be called an "objective reality." Instead, there is the notion of reality created by the person that is dependent on the circumstances of the observer. The act of creating personal versions of reality may result in some misconception, and it is these misconceptions that lead to personal maladjustments. Raimy postulates that these maladjustments are likely to be reduced if ideas or conceptions relevant to psychological problems can be changed with greater accuracy where one's reality is concerned. He does not suggest that misrepresentations can readily be modified by substituting the "right" data for the "wrong." Misconception refers to well-entrenched modes of perceiving that have been learned and practiced over time. More important, these misconceptions become systematized—clustered into groups that contribute to the personality characteristics of the person and, ultimately, provide the rationale for the way he understands himself and his world. The focus of this approach is not on the change of perceptions as such but on the change in the styles and patterns of perceiving.

RECAPITULATION

In this attempt to trace the epistemological sources of intentionality, I have incorporated diverse ideas and have cut across a number of philosophical and theoretical approaches. Briefly, what we have covered is an account of the unrelenting attempt to search for and to construct purposeful explanations of the nature of our world and our place within it. As we are able to decipher and demystify the unknowns we also attempt to place what we have discovered in some semblance of order and form to achieve the security and mastery that comes with the ability to predict what our world will yet be. Archaic man depended largely on the animistic, religious, and mythical explanations that complemented his own vitality. These explanations were displaced by teleological conceptions that continued to be concerned with the essences of things. The age of scientism followed with the emergence of the mechanistic theories that centered on forces and energies acting upon other things. Mechanism offered the promise of ultimate understanding and universal laws, but this hope died with the rise of modern science. In its place there developed less grandiose but more functional and probabilistic theories about the natural world and the social and psychological worlds. With the inevitable arbitrariness that accompanies the attempt to reconstruct pieces of historical development, I proposed that the evolving theoretical explanations tended to fall within one of two orientations: a) the positivistic model is linked to understandings provided only by sense data—what our senses and not our conjectures and speculations can tell us about specific phenomena; and b) the teleological model seeks understanding in the purposes, aims, and goals of events.

I dealt with the positivistic model only briefly, enough to clarify its various forms in relation to psychological and social conditions and to provide a contrasting statement relative to the teleological model. It was the latter model that was the major focus of attention since it serves as the assumptive foundation for the theoretical content of material to follow. Some of the major threads and theses of the teleological position can now be sorted out.

1. *The fundamental nature of the person can best be appreciated when it is understood as a search for and movement towards his own goals.* In some instances, this idea serves as a counterargument to the assumptions that man is essentially determined by his environment or other forces, that he is blindly impelled by inner drives, or that he is a victim of certain urgings, conditions, and influences about which he is largely unaware. McDougall views this directedness as a primary characteristic intrinsically present in man's being. Other theorists cite more specific ends that draw the individual towards an orientation to the future. Peirce and Dewey place this movement within a social matrix that leads towards learning and unfoldment of the self. Adler and Maslow define it in terms of self-activation and self-actualization. James, Sullivan, and Combs and Snygg point to those intentions that will protect, maintain, or enhance existing conceptions of the self. Frankl accents the human need to discover and act on personal and existential meanings.

Whether in explicit or implicit terms, these thinkers base their deductions on the conviction that the person is or strives to be something more than a machine or an animal driven by force or by instincts. In more ontological terms, they assume that a man *needs to believe* that he is more than a machine or an animal if his life is to contain any dignity or meaning. It is conceivable that this idea is no more than a myth or an idea that eludes scientific proof. Yet, as William Blake contends, "everything possible to be believed in is an image of truth."

2. *It is through his learning, previously or currently acquired, that the individual constructs his versions of reality.* The importance of learning is that it provides access to the understanding of the processes by which the person shapes his conceptions of the past as he interprets it, the present as he constructs it, and the future as he envisions it. Learning as both a personal and interpersonal phenomenon also calls attention to the social factors in man's being since it is the product of the interplay between the person and his social field. Sullivan is most explicit about this process when he describes the emergence of the self as an educative experience derived from interpersonal relations. This corresponds with Adler's view that includes the notion of "lifestyle," a characteristic manner of living learned in an extended period of social relations. Peirce speaks of the continuous construction of the self arising out of error and ignorance, two important ingredients of learning. And both Mehrabian and Frankl refer to the personal frames of reference wherein perceptions are given meaning. Mehrabian uses the term "learned cognitive constructs," whereas Frankl talks about "preconceptions"—both referring to the associations about the world that are learned through experience.

If behavior can be understood as part of an educative process, it becomes possible to find a trace of rationality and purpose in persons' attitudes, values, and motives. What is meant by rationality is not preconceived forms of "rightness" or "correctness" but the ability to discover that actions, which otherwise might be labeled insane, random, or bizarre, do reflect purposeful objectives given the manner in which the actor understands himself and his world.

3. *Adaptation is a process by which the individual manages and strives to achieve a measure of constancy in his life situation.* The term "adaptation" has been much abused, particularly when it is used interchangeably with such concepts as "accommodation" or "adjustment," the latter two connoting some form of conformity to existing standards. Here, adaptation refers to the active and purposeful involvement of the total self (including its mental, physical, spiritual, and value aspects) in dealing with problems of living. Its purpose is to sustain or to add to one's

integrity and continuity. Although Sullivan considers this intent as man's primary motive, all of our theorists speak in one way or another about one's need to manage his proximal world. McDougall and Mehrabian say that the individual is capable of altering as well as restructuring his reality; life itself, according to Dewey and Adler is an ongoing, problem-solving venture.

The adaptational perspective negates a reactive view of the person and underscores his managing, controlling, and reorganizing potentials. Because it is tied to learning experiences, this perspective also helps to avoid labels: the moralistic labels ("bad," "wrong"), the pathological labels ("sick," "psychotic"), and the deviant labels ("delinquent," "deprived"). Again, the understanding of the adaptive purposes of behavior takes into account the person's frame of reference—how and what he has learned about particular means of coping with his world and why he acts as he does.

4. *The perceiving self is the central influence in the process of adaptation.* The concept of self incorporates a number of aspects and functions. What we are now concerned with is its perceiving function, a complex of processes that not only takes in impressions but also attaches a certain organization and meaning to them. The perceptual process is the key to an understanding of the characteristic intentions, learnings, and adaptations of persons whether as individuals or as groups of individuals. Both Peirce and Sullivan depict the symbolic nature of man—his ability to transform impressions into distinctly personal meanings. William James refers to what may be called the reflective self—the ability of the person to turn his perceptions inward. McDougall describes what he calls "cognitive awareness"—the frame of reference that mediates and channels instinctual energies. The other writers stress the importance of perception as the crucial mechanism that mediates the person's transactions with his environment and becomes the core of adaptive competency. Perception is the means by which we "make sense" of our experiences and find the rationale for our life patterns.

These four basic assumptions of the teleological position portray the individual as an animate and vital actor in his social and physical environment, engaged a good deal of the time in preparing for, or actually contending with, his phenomenal world. How he accomplishes this end partly depends on the cognitive equipment that has matured over time—his sentiments, past experiences, wisdom, his values and aspirations, and his habits of thought. He needs to find a semblance of order and meaning in his environment in order to find his way through the obstacles and problems of ordinary living. Fundamentally, however, the need to make sense, to create a substantial reality, serves to quell the threat of chaos that comes from uncertainty. Man needs to have a constant grasp of his sanity.

I am not necessarily speaking of the legal forms of sanity or the rules and standards for "sane" activity that society creates. Instead, I refer to personal definitions, the inner notions of balance and soundness that are inevitably tied to feelings of integrity and wholeness. Seymour Krim has given his account of what it was like to be diagnosed as a "psychotic."

When I was considered out of my mind during the original upward thrust into the sheer ecstasy of 100 percent uninhibitedness, I was aware of the "daringness" of my every move; it represented at heart an existential *choice* rather than mindless discharge . . . when I flipped I was nevertheless instinctively rebelling against a fact which I think is objectively true in our society and time; and that is the lack of alignment between the immense inner world and the outer one which one has not yet legalized, or officially recognized, the forms that can tolerate the flood of communication from the mind to the stage of action.[43]

Krim's eloquence reveals that somewhere within the personal concept of sanity there is something called the self, or more precisely, a belief about what that self should be. It is here that fundamental reality inheres: the conviction that there is, indeed, something that can be called a *Me* that has substance, continuity, and some purpose and value. Even if that self is to maintain an illusion of purpose it must continue to create certain aims and ends, whether or not they conform to the social rules, to project a future holding some meaning and hope.

I am not attempting to draw a romantic or exalted portrait of the person. Certainly there is a measure of inspiration and idealism in the notion of the human search for truth, meaning, and design; but we also know that sought-for goals are as likely to be quixotic, possibly even damaging or malicious. If there is any merit in the idea of the felt fragility or vulnerability of the self-concept, self-defeating or pernicious aspirations would not be an oddity in a world of portentous threat and danger. Jean-Paul Sartre drew his philosophy of existentialism from his preoccupation with the human tendency to search almost compulsively for inauthentic ends. For we sometimes search for the safety that comes with conformity or control to avoid the obligation to create a free, open, and fluid future. It is this persistent denial of the self that brings about a "nothingness" of the self, the experience of self-deception or what Sartre calls "bad faith."

Because these assumptions point to the centrality of the self, along with its perceiving, adaptive, and aspiring tendencies, one may erroneously conclude that I have intentionally separated the person from the community of other lives, relationships, and groups. Or, in thinking about these assumptions as they apply to the intentional processes of change, they may appear to be restricted only to the counseling or psychotherapeutic methods aimed primarily at the inner world of people. This is not the case. These assumptions presume an actional and transactional view of the individual that places him squarely within a social context, because it is in the quality and character of social interactions that the self and its functions are so richly revealed. It is there that each individual discloses by his actions what he has at stake, what his values are, and what he seeks. As these motivations become increasingly apparent, it is possible to glimpse the compelling nature of the self, its cognitions, and its intentions.

The move in the past two decades to the use of the family, the group, or the immediate milieu of persons as the context of planned change gives at least tacit recognition of the value of these social stages on which persons can openly enact and disclose their conceptions of self and their perceptions of their reality. [44] In addition, whatever other purposes these newer approaches serve, they also provide the opportunity for the self to verify its perceptions and cognitions, to experiment, to learn new adaptions, and to unlearn whatever is no longer functional.

These assumptions are equally relevant to other forms of change where the intention is not directly related to the resolution of specific personal or interpersonal problems. For example, there is an increased interest in what has come to be called "consciousness-raising" groups. These groups, whether they are composed of women, minorities, or others seeking liberation, are concerned with the ultimate correctives of oppression that is self or otherwise inflicted. But they also see as preconditions for this goal the attainment of a greater self-awareness, a consciousness of personal conceptions of self-esteem and personal objectives. These groups are designed to offer members the possibility of heightened cognitive awareness of their plight as well as their position within it and their contributions to it. Perceptions and preconceptions that serve to rigidify prevailing status and to insure continued conformity to presumed roles are subjected to rethinking and reevaluation. In sum, the basic premise of these groups stresses that free and liberated movement forward can take place more or less spontaneously when people are no longer able to deny the essential character of their respective selves, the validity of their own dissent, and the meaning and worth of their values and goals—in all, their autonomy.

And, finally, we come to the implications of these assumptions for the broadest forms of social change that involve change in institutions, laws, or economic structures. I have already indicated the critical importance of the active involvement of the people who are affected by proposed social change. The significance and weight of personal ideologies and perceptions cannot be overestimated as influences on how even the most beneficent plan or policy will turn out. After more than fifty years, a period in which social reform has become identified with Western culture, Dewey's cautions about social change still offer a fresh and instructive perspective:

Actual social change is never so great as is apparent change. Ways of belief, of expectation, of judgment, and attendant emotional dispositions of like and dislike, are not easily modified after they have once taken shape. Political and legal institutions may be altered, even abolished: but the bulk of popular thought which has been shaped to their pattern persists. This is why glowing predictions of the immediate coming of a social millenium terminate so uniformly in disappointment. . . . Habits of thought outlive modifications in habits of overt action. The former are vital, the latter, without the sustaining life of the former, are muscular tricks.[45]

Chapter 2

Theory and Change

Having explored the derivations of the ideas that undergird the theoretical content, it is appropriate to give at least brief attention to the functions and limitations of theory, particularly since I will be relying on this type of mental construct to explain and define the nature of the reality that is the focus of this work. Theories are means and not ends in and of themselves. They are the mental tools that we use at the moment to create a suggestion of order and sense out of an otherwise confounding reality.

FUNCTIONS OF THEORY

Walter Wallace in *The Logic of Science in Sociology* states that theories serve the purpose of providing the rules of the game.[1] In more specific terms, a theory may be defined as a set of two or more constructions (abstractions, concepts, items, images, etc.) that are framed as hypotheses, and assumed if not demonstrated to bear a certain relationship, one to the other.[2] We have seen that a theory, especially one that attempts to account for the nature of personal and social phenomena, can offer only tentative guidelines to knowledge. It is essentially an intellectual device that allows us to discover a measure of logic and rationality in events that would otherwise defy comprehension. Yet it must be said that theory in its scientific garb is but one means of uncovering and explaining the nature of reality. Religious beliefs, mysticism, or other more arcane perspectives offer sufficient, if not more enlightening, explanations about the nature of the world to some of us. We need only to pay heed to the current debate between theologians and scientists about the origins of our solar system and the Big Bang Theory to find that each can present a persuasive and justifiable version of that imponderable event. We would also find that the two versions, derived from the most disparate assumptions, tend to correspond in some interesting ways.[3]

A theory might well serve two purposes. The first includes its conventional function, to demystify and bring a phenomenon into some degree of order and comprehension. The second is somewhat less specific and less deliberate. The purpose of the theory may extend beyond its specific intent and may become a necessary step or link in the ongoing development of knowledge. Both purposes deserve further amplification.

Demystification

Demystification can be demonstrated by indicating briefly the criteria against which the effectiveness or the validity of a theory might be measured. These criteria are borrowed from the natural and physical sciences which, in contrast to the social and behavioral sciences, deal with phenomena that, to some extent, can be manipulated, objectified, controlled, quantified, and otherwise subjected to the experimental methods of science. The human sciences are concerned with the more elusive and inchoate quality of human affairs that do not lend themselves very readily to these methods. For this reason, the following criteria might best be considered as guidelines or perhaps ideals for theory construction rather than absolute benchmarks. We can also expect that any one behavioral or social theory will tend to conform to certain criteria more so than others.

1. A given theory should be internally consistent in the way that it organizes, unifies, and defines the concepts and constructs that it embodies. A theory can be seen as an explanatory system within which its constituent elements stand in a coherent and intelligent relationship with one another. Recalling my brief reference to psychoanalytic theory, this explanation of the human mind is entirely consistent when concepts such as dynamism, economy, and structure generally contribute to and support the theory of a psyche and, in addition, combine to shape a coherent whole.

2. Another criterion concerns the question of the theory's level of

abstraction. Given a human event, how closely do the relevant concepts represent the actual nature of the condition to which they allude? Group dynamics theory, for example, employs the concept of group cohesion. Since it refers to the observable patterns of interaction, the glue of interdependence and affinity that acts to bind an aggregation of people into a definable unit of action, we can say that this concept conforms to this criterion. In contrast, psychoanalytic theory submits the concepts of ego, id, and superego. Since these concepts do not point to demonstrable references, they must then be considered to be highly abstract inferences or reifications about the dynamics of the impenetrable mind.

3. A theory should have some predictive value. As part of its explanatory functions it should also be able to tell us something about a phenomenon in prognostic terms. Under given conditions what might be expected to occur? Learning theory, derived from the field of experimental psychology and the basis for behavior modification techniques, stands as an exemplar of this criterion. Social systems theory, on the other hand, offers a most useful, albeit abstract, description of the relationships among the elements of any form of social organization. However, there is little that it can tell us about the system in question in any sort of predictive sense.

4. A theory should have some correspondence with method. Simply stated, it should be subject to verification by empirical or cognitive means or have some direct application to the event that it represents. If we wish to restrict this criterion to the scientific ideal, an empirical approach using an experimental design would be the method of choice. But as Rychlak argues, the cognitive method is also valid as a means of verification; theoretical propositions are verified in the mind by the use of philosophical and mathematical rationalism. Procedurally, thinking moves forward by steps of plausibility and common sense and our ideas are tested against the consistency of other ideas. Although this method does not result in definitive proof or conviction, it can generate confidence about our assumptions.[4] This common sense approach also pertains to the testing of theory by its application to actual events. Particularly in the case of the applied social sciences, we may also validate a theory by determining whether it appears to propose a relevant means of action or intervention in work with people.

Developmental Purpose

In addition to its explanatory functions, the second purpose of a theory might be contained in the role that it plays in the ongoing development of knowledge about our social universe. We have seen that the formal development of knowledge about our world, the social as well as the physical, proceeds in an irregular, sometimes spasmodic, but generally in an incremental fashion. At times, knowledge is the product of a circumstance, when by chance or accident, one stumbles upon a discovery or realization. In other instances, a special theory may be the well-earned product of painstaking deduction or experimentation. On occasion, brilliant insights flow from revelations or what appear to be the peculiar workings of the mind. And not infrequently, the test of whether or not a particular piece of wisdom or a theory becomes accepted into the existing body of knowledge depends on timing and the readiness of people to see its value.

In any case, any one theory, regardless of its apparent novelty or brilliance, is neither self-contained nor independent of preexisting knowledge. Albert Einstein's enormous contribution of the theory of relativity, for example, cannot be fully appreciated without reference to A. A. Michelson's and E. W. Morley's earlier studies of Earth motion in relation to surrounding space. They had depended on other scientists' knowledge and equipment for their work—and so on. In the review of the development of social theory, a similar developmental pattern can be observed. The evolvement of a particular theory needs to be seen within a developmental perspective in terms of its dialectical or expansive relations with antecedent knowledge and, if it is at all meaningful, as a stimulus for the advance of yet other knowledge.

Although this condensed discussion of the explanatory and developmental functions of theory is presented for clarification, it is also intended to add to the body of premises that support the theoretical content to follow. The content on self, perception, learning, and change derives from a variety of conceptual sources in the social and behavioral sciences and the field of educational theory. In many instances, I will attempt to synthesize various concepts and constructs with the ultimate purpose of demonstrating their applicability to practice within the human services. My intent is to capture and articulate what can only be a fraction of human reality, with the understanding that a theoretical approach can bring us a bit closer to an appreciation of that reality but, in the final analysis, cannot fully replicate it. As Henri Bergson asserts, the attempt to construct and understand a theory involves the use of our intellectual processes which, as extensions of our senses, perceive things as divisible and discontinuous. Perception, in this way, loses sight of the actual nature of things as being continuous, mobile, and constantly in the process of change. Bergson also warns: "We see that the intellect, so skillful in dealing with the inert, is awkward the moment it touches the living. Whether it wants to treat the life of the body or the life of the mind, it proceeds with the rigor, the stiffness and the brutality of an instrument not designed for such use."[5]

Bergson's questions about the competency of the intellect arise each time we attempt to ascribe meaning to or explain a human event. This problem is seriously compounded when we attempt to devise a plan of action to do something about or to that human situation. Hence, we need to employ our theoretical instruments with an appreciation of their limitations and with a sense of humility.

Keeping these caveats in mind, I now want to move away from these generalizations about the nature and application of theory toward more specific considerations. This is best accomplished by stepping back into a real-life situation and using it as a means of testing the relevance of some major constructs and concepts for understanding the meaning of what occurred.

MARY ADAMS: A CASE IN POINT

There is a Mary Adams, although this is not her real name. I have observed her, but I have never met her; perhaps what is more significant is the fact that she does not know me or the fact that I have observed her since this says something about her status, her dignity, and her vulnerability. Thus, it is her circumstances more so than her problem that lead me to select Mary Adams as a case study. The way I came to know about her reveals not only her plight but where she stands and where she is moving within a broader social context.

I learned about Mary's life quite by chance. Not long ago I visited a modern, somewhat reputable mental hospital to discuss a program that involved a few of my students. I was invited to sit in on a weekly "staffing" of a patient, and I accepted because I had not had an opportunity to observe this aspect of the hospital's procedures. Entering a huge amphitheatre, I saw two hundred or more "professionals," all attired in long white coats. The chief psychiatrist sat at the head of a table facing tiers of professionals and a row of young residents. Flanking him were a psychologist and a social worker. Each had a pile of charts and folders.

In the account of Mary's puzzling condition, each person at the table contributed to a three-dimensional view of this patient: social history, psyche, and pathology. The social worker described the sordid and depreciating conditions of Mary's life to this moment. The psychologist discussed what was going on in Mary's head—findings that were the products of an array of projective and intelligence tests. The psychiatrist gave his own conjectures about the nature and causes of Mary's disorder. It was left to the listener to weave these disparate conceptions of a human life and mind into a coherent whole. Obviously, the psychiatric residents had little difficulty with the inconsistency of her portrait. The idea of the divisible person seemed quite acceptable, and the diverse points of view enabled each one to take a different tack in his attempt to outshine the others by the brilliance of his diagnostic and prognostic skills.

Up to this point, I could observe this exhibition with tolerable bemusement. My acquaintance with the theater of the absurd and my knowledge of the practices of many mental facilities allowed me to view the proceedings in a farcical but innocent context. Most of all, I was aware that this exercise would do little to change the essentially custodial care that Mary was receiving. Then the farce was transformed into a horror. To my astonishment, the psychiatrist announced that it was now time to see the patient in action. Apparently, this day offered an "extra added attraction": not only was Mary to be brought into the arena, but we were to see her husband as well.

Perhaps this fiasco was more shattering to me than it was to Mary and her husband; perhaps this violation of whatever dignity and privacy they had left was no longer of consequence to them; perhaps dignity was no longer an issue, having been drugged, shocked, or institutionalized out of existence. At any rate, Mr. and Mrs. Adams showed no overt signs of animosity and passively subjected themselves to self-display. Both sat hunched in their chairs, only once or twice turning their stares from the floor to the hundreds of curious eyes. The psychiatrist benignly directed a few probing questions at each of them. Mary and her husband grunted back some appropriate responses, and when their act was completed they were led out of the arena by a nurse.

Our concern here is not with Mary's psychiatric problem as a basis for considering the role of theory in the explanation of human and social predicaments. If we could reduce her condition to the level of a psychiatric, disease-oriented model, it would be possible to append an appropriate clinical label and leave it at that. But that would merely dispose and not expose, would classify and not clarify, the intricate nature of her predicament. Her symptoms do not involve merely the strange things occurring in her mind and behavior, but she also now finds herself occupying a bizarre role, acting in a peculiar scenario that was devised by the very people who claim a willingness to help or cure her. What requires understanding is why she is now a psychiatric curiosity sitting before two hundred strangers. To further this understanding let us consider what information we have about Mary's life and circumstances. The following are the facts; however, since she did not report them directly to me they must be treated speculatively and with circumspection.

At this time, Mary was in her mid-twenties, a housewife in the sixth month of her first pregnancy. She appeared rather drab looking and not particularly intelligent, characteristics that could be partly attributed to her institutionalization and tranquilization. She was and had always been poor. I believe that if she were asked to identify herself she would have said that she was a mental patient. Her clinical diagnosis was ''borderline schizophrenic with depressive tendencies,'' a label that gave her easy access to the hospital on a number of previous occasions at her and others' requests.

Mary was born in a remote fishing village on the North Atlantic coast. Her birth was the first indication of bad timing on her part. She arrived just at the time when the village was undergoing financial disaster; the fishing industry was suffering from a depletion of fish stock. Even under the best conditions, life had been marginal and unpredictable, and during her first years her family gradually slipped into a state of poverty. Despite the historically close kinship patterns of the region, her immediate family began to unravel. The details are not clear, but we do know that her father, who worked and drank with equal intensity, disappeared, and her mother soon became ill and helpless and, after a brief period, died. Mary was sent to live with her aging grandparents nearby.

Her grandparents got by on meager welfare payments while Mary attended the local school. Her education was spotty because even untrained teachers were not always available. The school was frequently closed because either the school bus or the furnace would break down. She does not feel that she was particularly lonely, yet in many ways, she was quite isolated. Her grandparents had already raised their family, and although they had little interest in her, they did provide what material needs they could. Mary tended to stay apart from others and demanded little attention from anyone.

At sixteen, Mary gave up her schooling and moved to the city. We do not know whether she aspired to anything more, but she worked at low-paying, menial waitress and store clerk jobs or was dependent on unemployment insurance. No one suggested further training and education, nor did this idea occur to her as an alternative.

Her relationships with men had been sporadic and inevitably followed the same dismal pattern: a brief acquaintance and a casual sexual relationship, followed by the man's departure. Her sense of detachment and isolation grew.

Then she met Stan, a quiet, homely man some twenty years her senior who had never married. Stan was a taxi driver, working many hours to earn enough to get by. Mary was vaguely puzzled by his persistent attention to her. He also seemed strange, particularly when expressing affection in an unfamiliar European idiom. She was even more perplexed when she found that she could ridicule him and mock his peculiar manner without fear of penalty or rejection. Since this was the first time she could allow herself to play with her otherwise restrained hostility, she would suffer sieges of what appeared to be feelings of guilt or depression. But Stan offered his simple solace and assurance that he cared.

She finally married Stan because there was no reason not to. With the same lack of preparation that marked her shift in roles from adolescent to adult, she now assumed the role of housewife. Little would be added to this account by detailing the predictable circumstances of their marriage: the growing boredom of a tiny apartment; increasing indebtedness; and brief periods on welfare or unemployment insurance. In these demeaning conditions, Mary's "irrational behavior" began to blossom. Her mimicry, petulance, and sarcasm matured into outright violence toward Stan, often followed by vaguely suicidal attempts when she would nick her wrists enough to draw blood and create consternation. As Stan's commiseration about her unhappiness continued, so did her periods of wretched depression.

In the midst of one of their frequent, violent, and usually one-sided battles, the neighbors called the police. A well-meaning officer advised Stan to take his wife to a mental hospital. Stan, whose respect for authority was absolute, immediately complied, and Mary offered no resistance. She was promptly admitted, tranquilized, and initiated into the role of mental patient. Stan was a conscientious visitor, and offered all the details he could when asked to provide information to complete Mary's social history. The doctor tried to explain the nature of Mary's illness and the treatment that she required, and Stan agreed to do all that he could, although he was confused because he had never before heard of such an illness. He understood neither why she acted so strangely nor what that had to do with her being sick. But his awe of the doctor stopped him from asking any but simple questions.

Mary's aggressive behavior quickly subsided. She acted remorseful, and asked if she could go home. The hospital staff thought she had improved and released her, mentioning in passing that she could visit the outpatient clinic when she felt troubled. Soon the previous patterns recurred: drabness turned into violence and self-torment. Her return to the hospital became the usual alternative. The treatment she received during her various stays differed from time to time, sometimes depending on the ward and psychiatrist to whom she was assigned. She almost always received chemotherapy. On occasion electro-convulsive therapy was administered. Sometimes she would have talks with a psychiatrist and a social worker. But since none of these methods appeared to have any positive lasting effects, it was decided to bring Mary before the professional staff to see if altogether they might suggest a better course of action. This is where we first found Mary. One other detail needs to be reported about Mary's pregnancy. The role of mother-to-be was one of the few in her existence that she had assumed voluntarily. She told a psychiatrist that she wanted to "have someone to love who will make me happy and mean something to."

The story of Mary Adams' life and career to this point captures only the more apparent outlines. Incomplete and inaccurate as it is, this profile provides sufficient information against which we can balance some types of conceptual explanations and consider their utility as expository devices.

If we do not limit our perception of Mary to the parameters of her clinical diagnosis, if we see her as something more than a diseased entity, we are immediately confronted with dilemmas that are at once common to many and peculiar to Mary as an individual. In one respect, Mary represents countless others who become society's deviant minority. They are those who have been cast into cramped roles because of their nonconforming or subconforming behavior and who have been labeled, classified, and subjected to various forms of treatment that may or may not be effective. In many cases, they are the "beneficiaries" of institutionalized programs that are more concerned with the perpetuation of the institution than with solving the problems of the clients whom they are supposed to treat.

In some other respects, Mary is not unlike any other mortal. As an individual, she personifies the needs, the strivings, and the yearnings that are common to the pursuits of all human beings. It is not some exotic malaise that causes Mary to be in her present state. It is not just her mind or body that is diseased; her entire existence is sick.

Discarding the limitations of the clinical diagnosis, how can we begin to make some sense of her personal, social, and societal predicament? Can we move beyond static description toward a more dynamic understanding that might yield some ideas about remedy or change? Is it possible to explain why an individual, already caught in a deplorable situation, persists in resorting to beliefs and actions that only succeed in worsening her debacle? Why do some people seem either to seek or to accept defeat? How do such sorry relationships get formed and why do they persist? And what should be the role of society, and what should be its concerns about the welfare of its members trapped by such problems?

Social Systems and Role Theory

One approach to these questions takes a broader view, an approach that attempts to encompass the variety of impinging factors and arrange them in some sort of interdependent structure. This comprehensive perspective is found in general systems theory, or in its more specific application to social phenomena, social systems theory. For our purposes I will limit the discussion of this approach (and the related role theory) to its general outlines and functions because a number of useful sources are available to those who want to pursue the subject.[6]

Simply speaking, social systems theory attempts to define the *ecology* of a social situation. It is largely an analytic device, a conceptual matrix that enables the observer to locate the elements of a particular situation and determine how they are transactionally interrelated. This approach helps us to understand how the system that is formed means something more than the sum of its parts. In its application it enables us to study the constituents of a living system (for example, a family, community, or organization) and understand how its parts oppose and complement one another and produce a particular effect. It also allows us to appreciate the roles of the members of the system and how they interact and maintain or disturb the stability of the system. In sum, a systems view discloses critical transactional patterns, the conditions that sustain the steady state of the unit, those that are open to change, and the relationships between one system and another (for example, the transactions between a family and its community).

In Mary Adams' situation, a number of critical conditions become apparent. Examining the various systems she has occupied, there are a number of significant shifts in her status and role. Her early roles as orphan, child, and student were rather depleted and passive. As she moved into the larger society she was ascribed and assumed the role of a nonentity. Marriage did little to enhance her identity, and as she came into contact with the aspects of the system concerned with social control and treatment, she occupied the general role of a deviant and the specific role of a mental patient. This status subjected her to special types of attention, prescriptions, and expectations. A systems view takes in the transactions between subordinates and control elements and shows how the former are vulnerable to the rules and definitions that maintain the system.

At the same time, this perspective directs attention to the operations and transactions of the power aspects of a given system. For example, in Mary's case we could study the nature of the economic institutions that are not concerned with equity or with remedies for those who are the casualties of the way the system functions. The frailty of the community becomes apparent when we can observe how the social fabric comes apart when traditional patterns and the resources that supported the community system are no longer viable. The educational system also deserves scrutiny in terms of the way it operates to deprive its members of their rights to an education that might prepare them for the rigors of living. The social welfare and mental health systems could be regarded as sieves through which the individual is filtered and ineluctably separated from a sense of self and value.

This is not to say that a social system approach ignores the strengths and potentialities of the whole. As we observe these various systems in transaction, we are able to grasp the dominant ideologies and values that energize their activities.

In sum, systems theory offers the conceptual tools for appreciating the meaning of individual problems within a social and ecological context. It forestalls the easy tendency to circumscribe the plight of an individual within the limits of his immediate life situation. Although it may show how his predicament is intertwined with the conditions of his larger environment, a systems perspective may also reveal where effective intervention might be indicated.

Although a systems approach is very useful in offering a holistic view of the person in a larger social situation, it also poses certain limitations to understanding. Because of the scope and level of abstraction, it is inevitable that critical factors will be overlooked. The fact that we call certain arrangements of things systems means that the resultant approximation of the event in question will be somewhat removed from reality. Specifically, this theory cannot tell us any of the meanings of what is taking place and how events appear to and are interpreted by the members of the system. Moreover, it does not capture the dynamics of behavior and cannot disclose the motives, needs, and purposes linked to human action. Our tendency toward probabilistic thinking could lead to certain assumptions about the consequences of a given system's operations. For example, if the system is marked by discrimination, inequities, and the lack of opportunities, certain of its members are likely to respond in a self-defeating, asocial, or otherwise ineffective manner. But we would have to see Mary as a victim or as one of the failures of a flawed environment. This simplistic appraisal would omit the way that Mary understands her reality and the alternatives that she can or cannot see as a way out of her dilemma. Thus, although a systems orientation can depict the behavioral transactions occurring within the organic whole, it cannot disclose the social and exclusive meanings these behaviors hold for those who enact them.[7] Moreover, the theory cannot explain how, even within the most punitive and oppressive system, certain members emerge not only unscathed but perhaps greatly matured by their trials.

Behavioral Theory

Because of the macroscopic breadth of systems theory, one might consider the alternative of more microscopic theories, such as the approach to behavior change based on methods of conditioning and reinforcement. This framework would explain Mary's irrational behavior as learned and involuntary responses to cues that she perceives as a threat. We would need to examine her environment in greater detail and to learn what within it acts as a stimulus to evoke inappropriate responses. For example, we might find that a violent reaction follows even the slightest indication of disapproval by Stan. If we were able to discern a linkage between the stimulus and the response, we would need further to determine what acts as a means of continued reinforcement, the rewards or gains that perpetuate this learned pattern. This theory proposes that if either the stimulus or the reinforcing mechanism were changed then her response would gradually cease.

This might be a useful approach if Mary's behavior was out of line with an otherwise well-balanced existence—if all else was in order, all that would be required would be to study the causal factors and establish the protocols that would serve to extinguish the noxious response. Obviously, Mary's life is something less than stable or secure. Thus, her behavioral reactions are something more complex than a specific response to a specific stimulus. They would appear to be well-entrenched patterns of coping—not conditioned responses but the means she uses in attempting to manage her reality. In addition, we might ask whether she would have recourse to other more productive behaviors were it possible to extinguish her problematic reactions.

A behavioral orientation would probably be useful if our intentions were limited to manipulating and changing some small portion of Mary's complex of responses. It is also quite possible, but not necessarily predictable, that a ripple effect might modify other behaviors if the more troublesome actions were changed. Insofar as this theory limits its objectives to the definition and remediation of isolated response patterns, the explanatory potential of the theory is not at all extensive. The theory has little interest in the quality of a person's environment other than the extent to which certain elements within it are effective enough to serve as stimuli. The theory in its classic form specifically avoids the ideas of psychological states, needs, and motives; it provides no information about the individual as a person moving forward in a world of his own understanding. The theory does not concern itself with inferences about personal values, aspirations, feelings, or the other more nebulous fragments of humanity that are disclosed in one's overt expressions of self. It would tell us little about Mary Adams as a unique individual.

Psychodynamic Theory

Psychodynamic theory delves into the interior provinces of the human personality. This orientation to the human state is essentially concerned with underlying causes—the drives, instincts, or unconscious mechanisms that compel the individual to respond to his world in determined ways. The individual is no more than a casualty of his life experiences, a condition that can be changed by achieving awareness of past events that influence his present life. Awareness loosens their control or modifies it to the extent that it is possible for one's ego-adaptive functions to take over. In Mary's case, this approach would give special emphasis to the traumas of her earlier life. However, if we took this route we would have to make certain inferences about both the nature of these events and their meaning and impact. Hence, we would generate a number of personally created constructs or fictions about Mary's beginnings. Moreover, we would have to fit our findings into the compartments of this explanatory framework (e.g., oral, anal, and genital levels of development) and reduce extremely variegated and complex aspects of living to semiscientific equations. This process tends to exclude Mary's participation in the definition of what all of these events mean.

The "truth" that is produced is dependent largely on the acceptance of questionable assumptions (e.g., the existence of an "unconscious" or an "id"). For example, the concept of the "Oedipus Complex" could easily lead to the assumption that the desertion of Mary's father and her marriage to a man much older than herself were somehow connected, if not inevitable. This concept, after all, does argue that a child retains an unconscious attraction to the parent of the opposite sex as a love object. This is a most tempting explanation and seems to make sense in Mary's case. Her unseemly marriage to Stan appears to be more comprehensible: the marriage served to terminate her search for the longed-for father figure.

But transposition of circumstance into inference is not as simple and convenient as it might seem. A number of mental and conceptual leaps are required. To accomplish this transposition, (a) we would have to accept an assumption, convert it into a fact, and grant reality to something that, in this instance, we agree to call "Oedipal"; (b) we would have to assume that this is a universal concept not affected by the cultural and social conditions of a person's life; (c) we would then have to accept Mary's behavior as an unwitting pursuit and herself as blind to her own motivations and choices; (d) to some extent, we would have to excuse her for her lack of discrimination and responsibility and overlook the possible influences of her values, expectations, and perceptions on her choice; and (e) we would have to ignore the family, group, or other environmental factors that may have had some bearing on her behavior. In so doing, we would find her somewhat diminished as an autonomous individual.

In developing his ideas about the classic problems of "human nature" contained in the issue of personal freedom versus psychological compulsion Maurice Friedman says:

> The problem . . . cannot be solved by the attempt to reduce man to a bundle of instinctual drives, unconscious complexes, the need for security, or any other single factor. . . . Motivation is inextricably bound up within the wholeness of the person, with his struggles to authenticate himself. . . . No general theory of psychogenesis and no general knowledge of the person will tell us in advance what will be his actual mixture of spontaneity and compulsion in any particular situation. [8]

SUMMARY AND IMPLICATIONS

The three theoretical models—the macro-systemic, the behavioral-mechanistic, and the psychodynamic—do not, of course, exhaust the available explanatory theories. Under the rubric of "humanistic psychology" there are also intimations or fragments of theory; however, it is an approach that defies definition. Wertheimer, after a serious attempt to define this field, admits to despair as he states: " 'Humanistic psychology' is a phrase that has been used with so many different, and such vague, meanings that it is highly unlikely that an explicit definition of it could be written that would satisfy even a small fraction of the people who call themselves 'humanistic psychologists.' "[9]

The three models do serve our purpose of showing the functions and limitations of theoretical constructs. Each explanatory theory defines its conception of reality in accordance with its own assumptions about the nature of the social world and the place of the person within it. Simply, each offers its version of "truth"; but, inevitably, it is a fabricated "truth" that is lacking in some serious respects.

When a human event is so defined as to fit into the confines of a theoretical model, something critical is lost from understanding. A systems perspective quite effectively magnifies and draws attention to the weight of social forces, but gives little or no attention to the mind and body aspects of the transactional whole. Thus, this theory has little predictive value and does little to explain the meaningful effect of systemic forces on the members of the system. Behavioral theories shrink the field of understanding and narrow human reality to include only observable behavior and its causal and reinforcing contingencies. It does not provide an understanding of the impact of social and environmental forces or give any credence to the motive needs of the individual and the interpersonal influences that bear on behavior. Psychodynamic theory probes into the deeper recesses of personality and creates a somewhat chimerical reality based on unverifiable assumptions.

Admittedly, I have done some disservice to this sample of theories if only by radically compressing them. I have arbitrarily selected and simplified certain aspects of each theory so as to make my point. Nonetheless, that point has some merit: a behavioral theory inevitably recreates reality in a way that results in some degree of distortion or omission relative to the event it intends to explain. [10] Considering my established criteria, let us consider some additional shortcomings of social and behavioral theory. Having already commented on the risk of high level abstractions that tend to separate the concept from the real event, it is also important to note the inherent risks in attempting to limit conceptions to only those events that can be empirically determined. Reliance on only our senses rejects the less perceptible characteristics of the person and results in a measure of dehumanization. A theory may disclose the structural attributes of a human event, but it may ignore the transactional and energetic processes by which the vitality of the event is manifested. A concern with structure without reference to process results in an austere and static construct. Likewise, a concern with process without reference to structure results in randomness or behavior that is misunderstood because it is out of context. A preoccupation with underlying and psychodynamic causal forces detracts from the appreciation of motivational, situational, or purposive needs that bear on the individual's behavior in his immediate and real world. Reliance on inferential constructs can fragment the essentially holistic nature of the human state.

I am by no means suggesting that we should reject the value of theory any more than I would discount the use of intellect. Theories do serve as one means by which we are able to make some sense of an ambiguous reality. What I am suggesting is that we must be careful to appreciate that this "sense" is tentative—it is limited by the language and semantics that we use to explain reality, and it is biased by the presuppositions we impose on our observations.

It seems that the use of the intellect would be somewhat more precise if we could achieve a clearer view of the person's reality as he experiences it, as well as the premises that govern his view. Such understanding should lead to a greater degree of accuracy and circumspection in our responses to people and to a more helpful approach toward enabling people to find rewarding solutions to their problems of living. *Empathy* can realize this ideal to some extent, and I am convinced that at special moments it does. But there are certain drawbacks associated with the notion of empathic understanding: (a) we are not exactly sure what empathy is or how it works; (b) it cannot be counted on or willed; and (c) empathic capabilities vary from person to person and situation to situation.

Certain aspects of the human state that are omitted in the theories do offer some pathways toward an ideal of awareness. Although the theories tell us something about the systemic forces that impinge on behavior, the learned or conditioned drives that reiterate behavior, and the psychodynamics that compel behavior, they do not inform us about the personal or shared "truths"—the versions of reality that the individual constructs as foundations for his actions in a given situation.

I use the verb "construct" advisedly to reaffirm the thesis that a person's (acting individually or in concert) elaboration of the nature of his experience is part of an active, deliberate, and purposeful process. It is not a simple and reactive process in which the image mirrors the object; it is what Rapaport calls "a tortuous chain of reasoning, inference, and evaluation of what one observes and concludes."[11] If we can catch a fraction of understanding of this chain of reality, we stand a better chance of grasping a trace of the meaning and the logic that lies behind an individual's actions. Conversely, if behavior is seen as an expression of inner intent, this point of view directs our attention to questions about the inner logic and design of reality that supports his actions. Hence, in attempting to comprehend a man's perceptions, our thinking would be guided by such questions as the following:

How did the person come to perceive his world in the way that he does? What is the nature of his past experience and learning?

What does it do for him or his relationships to perceive in this way? Does it serve a particular purpose, protect him, provide security, justify his actions?

Are there inconsistencies, gaps of information, or misconceptions that sustain his perceptions?

Is his style of perceiving rigid, concrete, or accommodative?

Are these perceptions bounded by a particular frame of reference? Is the individual oriented to reality in a way that predisposes him to interpret his experiences in a particular manner?

How do one's perceptions correspond with or how are they influenced by the system and situation he is occupying? Are they supported by or in conflict with others' norms and views? Are cultural influences operative? Is his position within the system a significant factor?

Do one's perceptions indicate his expectations of himself and others? How will the future unfold? What is his ability to cope with the contingencies of living?

Are there indications of error stemming from his lack of attention to important details, a lack of discrimination, or a difficulty in organizing his impressions into meaningful language and concepts?

As guides to understanding and intervention, such questions could inform us about an individual's (or groups of individuals') place in his social and physical environment *as he defines and envisions* his role and status. We learn how people have come to build their image of self, what they value, and who they are as social beings. A clearer and certainly more accurate judgment regarding persons' sense of mastery and power, their beliefs about their control of their destiny, and the aims and meanings of their motives would come from such understanding. Perhaps most important, this awareness would tell us something about the individual's lacks, strengths, potentials, and intentions relative to the way he copes with the problems of living. This knowledge would support a responsive, sensitive, and intelligent entry into the person's life circumstances so as to induce more effective learning and adaptation.

This approach is in accord with the teleological and phenomenological forms of inquiry. It attempts to cast some light not only on the person in the situation but also on his conceptions of the event and his role and purposes within it. The transactional theme is also evident as it is concerned with the dialectical nature of persons' relations with their world of experience, including primary groups, normative standards, and cultural influences and values. Not the least of these factors is the quality of life that one enjoys or endures.

PART TWO

Self, Perception, and Learning

Chapter 3
Self in Transaction

From a cognitive standpoint, the processes of perception, learning and adaptation are meaningless unless they are linked in some way to the person in action. Perception as the major intermediating function that connects the person with his world can be studied from three perspectives, each having its own design and purpose although interrelated with the other two. The *neurophysiological* perspective inquires into the structure and function of the nervous system. The *psychological* is frequently concerned with external stimuli and the corresponding perceptual experience. The two are largely reductionistic approaches following the lines of the scientific method. The approach here is, of course, *phenomenological* and nonreductionistic, a perspective that attempts to take account of the I-world nature of perception.[1] Without minimizing the other two perspectives, it is the last that is most pertinent to this study of learning, adaptation, and ultimately, change.

Thus, it is essential that we have some appreciation of the "I" that is the perceiver. To achieve this intent, this chapter will develop the construct of the *self* in adaptational and transactional terms. As a point of departure we will consider the place of self theory in current thinking. What may be called an anatomy of the self will show that the self is really a composite of a number of interacting selves which, together, shape the human system. It will then be possible to go on to study the adaptive functions of the self. These functions include, first, its variant and constant nature as the individual interacts with the social and physical environment. Second, the self may also be seen as a system that strives to maintain a modicum of balance and integrity within the tensions of living. And finally, we will consider the intentional and forward-moving tendencies of the self.

CURRENT PERSPECTIVES ON SELF THEORY

The notion of a self is not uncommon insofar as it has found its way into everyday parlance in such frequently used terms as self-esteem, self-concept, self-awareness, self-confidence, and self-doubt. It is also an ancient concept: over the centuries, philosophers and theologians have speculated and deliberated about the person's relations with the good, with God, with beauty, with morality, and so on. However, only in the past century have there emerged definitive studies of the *nature* of the self as an active and reflective dynamic.

These studies continue to serve as the foundations for human services practice with individuals, either singly or within families, groups, and community affiliations. Knowledge afforded by the various conceptions of self and personality theories offers the practitioner a map of sorts that enables him to employ certain assumptions about the psychic and social terrain he and his client are traversing, what their destinations might be, and how they will get there.

The concept of self as an emergent and sentient energy is also exploited by the burgeoning "third force" of humanistic psychology that has broken away from the behavioristic and analytic psychologies. It is central to the work of Carl Rogers, as well as the encounter, self-help group movements, and other self-realization denominations. The ultimate if not paramount importance of the inner-being shapes the wave of popular psychology that has swept across the western countries in the past decades. Self theory is used in the multitude of workshops, seminars, and "weekends" that train people for better self-assertiveness, parent effectiveness, and sexual competency. In fact, self theory has swollen into what is now known as the New Narcissism and the encouragement to "deify the isolated self."[2]

If the notion of self has been elevated to an excessive degree in some cases, in others it has been either actively discredited or benignly ignored. This attitude is often expressed in the broad field of social change concerned with collective political and social action and, to some extent, social policy development. Once incidental to the human services professions, these pursuits are now accepted as additional means to enhance the well-being of certain populations. We find suggestions of these intentions in community psychology and psychiatry and in the community organization and development, social action, and planning functions of social work. To some extent, these movements are spurred by the emergence of social theories and the resurgence of critical and radical perspectives on the existence of inequity and discrimination in society.

Either for ideological or theoretical reasons, the more radical collective approaches to social change have tended to deprecate the role of the individual and the concept of self. Individualization in the ideological view has come to be equated with the kind of liberalism that promotes a laissez-faire attitude or the self-aggrandizing characteristics of capitalism. The notion of a self conflicts with the central importance of collective action wherein individual initiative must be restrained. It is the group's values and needs that take precedence over the individual's aspirations.

Some radical theories about social change replace the intricate map of self or personality with a grander blueprint for change—made up of ideas drawn from political and economic concepts of power, conflict, and intergroup relations. Built into these ideas are assumptions about desirable large-scale goals and the means by which they are to be achieved. Certainly these social movements are not oblivious to the plight of people as individuals; however, they assume that it is through change, improvement, or elimination of certain deficient social institutions that the individual's ordeal will be remedied.

I have no argument with and in fact would commend many of the ideological or theoretical approaches to social change. However, I want to suggest that personal autonomy and dignity are placed at risk when social movements overlook the needs and participation of the individual. Neil Gilbert and Harry Specht believe that human rights and self-determination are violated when "champions of advocacy" deny individuals' prerogatives. They note that "perhaps it is easier to endorse professional arrogance when support is called for in the name of 'social victims' and the disadvantaged.' "[3]

It is not surprising that ideas about the nature of man and his behavior are entangled in prevailing social, philosophical, and ideological strains of thought. It is not accidental that in one world-view individuality is venerated and selfhood is elevated to a supreme value while in another the person is devalued or ignored and selfhood is viewed with scorn. We are in an era when social problems seem to be out of control, when ordinary living itself is fraught with insecurity and grim doubts about the future. The absence of easy and ready solutions and the failure of former promises create a pressure for polar conclusions about and unequivocal answers to perplexing social conditions. We find one set of proponents urging a retreat into narcissistic fantasy and preoccupation with the unfoldment of self and another zealously decrying the merits of individuality and exalting the worth of the collective. Each promises the best possible escape from the present miasma.

A POINT OF VIEW

Given the many uses of and attitudes toward the concept, can we say that there is something consistent and meaningful about the phenomenon called the self? As the concept will be used here, it is not understood as a given or as a thing. It does not have actual form and substance that can be located within the person nor can it be quantified. The self is a state and a process that eludes exactitude and circumscription; thus, we will treat self as an explanatory concept, or more specifically, as a construct that is composed of hypothetical properties.[4] As an introduction to a more explicit definition of the construct to follow, a few of these hypothetical properties can be noted briefly.

Self as a phenomenon has certain *temporal qualities* in that it can be expressed in a number of tenses. We can view the self in historical terms when we reflect on "what I was" or "what I might have been." Its present tense is expressed by statements that refer to "what or who I am." And a future tense is evident in projections such as "what I might yet be" or "what I would like to be."

In some respects, the self is objectified when we are able to stand back and view ourselves in past, present, and future terms. At the same time, the self also has *subjective characteristics* as it turns back on itself to observe and evaluate its attitudes and process. We are able to reproach or admire ourselves, measure who and what we are against personal standards, judge ourselves, and in other ways engage in some reflective commentary about our being.

The self may also be known in *experiential* terms in the way it

84

undergoes certain aspects of living. We can experience an awareness of self through our senses: the aesthetic self may arise out of the vision of the beauty or the color and composition of a particular scene; we could be conscious of the erotic self that is aroused by the touch, sight, or smell of another's body; or the savor of a delicious meal could bestir the epicurian self. Our emotions allow us to encounter ourselves in countless ways: reactions to death or trauma may reveal a morbid self, a release of social inhibitions may permit the childish self to appear, and great stress may illuminate the presence of a dependent self.

A peculiar human quality is the ability to experience one's self in symbolic ways that transcend conventional reason and logic. Within the loving and intimate relationship the boundaries of the self appear to dissolve as, in some ineffable fashion, one self flows into another. In other ways we are able to escape the confines of ordinary reality and, through imagery and fantasy, transport ourselves into a personally created world. To the extent that we can trust our empathic tendencies, we may be able to experience the communion of another's self with our own. But the opposite realization is also possible; as we are able to sense the nature of another's inner world we may discover the many ways in which we are essentially different and separate from others.

Self, as an explanatory construct, is neither static nor bounded by certain limits. I am compelled to say this because the following definitions necessitate the use of concepts and frameworks that, by their very nature, tend to freeze the thing they refer to into inert and concrete forms. What is intended, of course, is a more animate and vital picture of what we call the self.

An Anatomy of the Self

Scholarly disciplines concerned with questions about the human state have given ample attention to the notion of selfhood. Within the vast amount of literature, Gordon Allport's work stands out in its cogency. His study of the self lends itself to the transactional perspective of this book.

Allport's premise about the essential unity of the self is outlined in *Becoming*, published in 1955.[5] His ideas are an expansion of William James' taxonomic scheme. Allport defines the concept of the *proprium* as all of the aspects of personality that are intimately and essentially our own that collectively create a sense of inner unity. An important proviso is that unity does not necessarily connote harmony since the aspects of self may stand in conflict with one another. The concept of the proprium is his answer to the persistent problem of how to understand something as complex as the personality without doing violence to its essential wholeness. This idea contributes to an appreciation of the dynamic processes of living and growing, and it forestalls the temptation to consign these processes to simplistic or discrete categories. As an example, Allport cites the misuse of the concept of the "ego," which he believes "looks suspiciously like a homunculus." The following are the eight aspects of the proprium:

1. *Bodily sense* refers to our sense of physical reality or the awareness of a "bodily *me*." Our bodies are an enduring anchor to which a consciousness of a palpable self is tied. This consciousness comprises our streams of sensations that create cognizance of our vitality, our appearance, and our distinguishing physical characteristics. This sense of self tells us that we are alive and *how* we are alive. The somatic and aesthetic adjectives that we use to describe ourselves (e.g., "thin," "handsome," "strong") arise from this sense. Although we are usually somewhat aware of our physical state, the sense of self is very important during periods of bodily change such as pregnancy, adolescence, and senescence, and its impact is unavoidable when we are faced with radical surgery.

2. *Self identity* encompasses conditions that extend beyond the body and involves a subjective awareness of characteristics peculiar to the individual. It changes and grows as a result of the individual's interactions with his world. It is evident in consciousness of our existence over time and the ability to construct a sense of self based on personal evidence of our past history. When we recall our thoughts of yesterday, they tell us that we did actually exist; moreover, the knowledge that we shall recall today's thoughts tomorrow assures us that we shall continue to exist.

Self identity includes the special characteristics that differentiate one person from another. Nominal characteristics (one's name, religion, occupation, and roles) give each person a special definition. Affiliations and identifications also add to one's identity, particularly as the individual sees himself as an integral part of a family or group, or allies himself with special ideologies, beliefs, and values.

This aspect of self stands out most clearly because it is the one we rely on when we are in a position of needing to say who or what we are. Responses such as "I am a single, thirty-eight-year-old school teacher," or "I am an unemployed father of seven children," are direct expressions of the identity aspect of self.

3. *Self (ego) enhancement* is one of the conative aspects of the self that helps to portray the self in its relation to and dependence on the outer world. It expresses the need to search for self-seeking and self-satisfying conditions such as love, physical gratification, admiration, or approval. It is largely a process of taking in someone or something and appeasing the needs that we feel necessary for physical and emotional survival. It also reminds us of our basic dependence on others or the conditions about us.

4. *Self (ego) extension* refers to the tendency to reach out and become part of something rather than to incorporate and take it in. It enables the self to go beyond its own boundaries and become part of something larger. The child becomes identified with the material things that are "mine;" as he matures, the self enters into loyalties and commitments (love relationships, causes, and group affiliations) that disclose motives of wishing to care for and protect others or preserving cherished values and ideals. Allport asserts, "Indeed, a mark of maturity seems to be the range and extent of one's feelings of self involvement in abstract ideals."

5. *Rational process* is the central function of the proprium, the cognitive aspect of the self that enables the person to accomplish considered adaptations to the world as it is experienced. Rational faculties provide for effective problem solving as a means of dealing with life; accumulated knowledge is called upon, or new solutions are invented, when problems of living are encountered.

6. *Self-image* can be called the *phenomenal self* because it is most closely associated with the core of the total self. It involves the impression of our essential state of being and integrates all other aspects of self. The image we create about ourselves depends on the ideals and standards against which we measure what we are. Judgments about adequacy, worth, morality, or competency derive from our accomplishments and from our expectations of accomplishment. Self-image is also an interac-

tional aspect insofar as it encompasses the impressions of what others think about us. In some respects, it refers to the tension within the individual as he struggles to balance his actions and accomplishments against his own ideals, aspirations, and definition of self, and against his own interpretations of the expectations of significant others.

7. *Propriate striving* endows the individual with the ability to reach beyond his more mundane needs. Allport disagrees with the preoccupation of psychology with the peripheral forms of motivation. Allport underscores human ingenuity—the inclination to set long-range goals and to persist against all obstacles toward their realization. Such motivational pursuits are akin to Victor Frankl's idea of the "search for meaning." Propriate striving is consonant with the willingness to live with tension and to endure the strains that accompany the pursuit of valued ideals. ("The possession of long-range goals, regarded as central to one's personal existence, distinguishes the human being from the animal, the adult from the child, the healthy person from the sick.")[6] It is the purposive aspect of self in the process of defining and projecting a future.

8. *The knower* is the cognizing self or the *reflective self*, the "I" that is able to pull back and recognize all other aspects of what I am. "It is I who have bodily sensations, I who recognize my self-identity from day to day; I who note and reflect on my self-assertion, self-extension, my own rationalizations, as well as my own interests and strivings."[7] Moreover, it is my ability to reflect upon the essential unity of my self and the extent to which harmony or dissonance characterizes my state of being in various situations and at various times.

The concept of a proprium takes us some distance beyond the relatively static, cramped, or deterministic notions of the self that dominate psychological thinking. It does not ignore the elegant and intricate inner processes unique to the individual; but it emphasizes the social and transactional nature of the self. It captures the essential unity of the self without losing sight of the dynamic tension that characterizes life as we live it.

Further amplification of the proprium should heed Allport's warning that it is all too easy to revert to a view of the self as a homogeneous force in the attempt to explain personality and behavior. The self is really organized in a number of dimensions: (a) it is *adaptive* insofar as it represents the attempt to maintain a sense of continuity in time and space while coping with the world of experience; (b) it typifies the striving for a sense of *congruence* and *wholeness* while undergoing change; (c) the conative aspects of self depict the *intentional* and *purposive* motives of the individual; and (d) the self has a *perceiving* function that is evident in its rational and reflective tendencies.

The Self as a Variant and Constant

A moment's pause to reflect on how we are dealing with the business of daily living is likely to reveal that a number of inner pulls and strains are occurring. We may be modifying our attitudes and responses to retain a measure of control and effectiveness relative to an event itself. We may also be striving to maintain a sense of continuity and integrity, an impression of ourselves that is relatively constant; at certain times, the self may thus be pulled between the need for stability and demands for accommodation.

Literature and the arts seem to have much more to tell us about this normally variegated nature of the human state than do the theoretical or applied social sciences that strive almost compulsively to sort human ingredients into sets of neat and static abstractions.

The behavioral scientist is concerned with some sort of taxonomical precision about the human state, but the writer is often in search of its boundless meanings, and he is quite comfortable with ambiguity and variability—portraying good and evil as coexisting and in conflict, but essentially as an irresolvable dilemma. Kazantzakis gives us a Dionysian character in *Zorba the Greek* whose excesses of behavior reveal power, passion, and sensitivity, a maleness and femaleness that blend but never lose their separateness. Edgar Allan Poe and Franz Kafka turn back into their inner experiences and create uncanny and bizarre accounts of reality. Harold Pinter's plays are essentially reflections of the non sequiturs of living. Voltaire, Dostoevsky, Strindberg, Camus, Woolf, and Eliot all travel within the enigmatic realm of the ambiguous and versatile self. It is no wonder that able practitioners in the field of human relations sometimes find their way into their career not by the conventional route of the behavioral or social sciences but through an exposure in depth to literature.

Allport's conception of the proprium defines the self as a composite of many aspects or the self as a composite of a number of selves. However, these aspects do not have equal valence at all times: at a given *time* and in a given *situation* one or more aspects of the self may assume greater hierarchical importance than the others.

The concepts of time and situation are not necessarily used here in concrete or categorical terms. Both may, indeed, be "real" in certain circumstances, "real" meaning that there is an intersubjective agreement about the specifics of time and space by a community of persons. But the experience of time and situation can be imagined, dreamed, fantasized, or hallucinated and still succeed in evoking the expression of certain aspects of self. The awareness and the interpretation of time and space is often an *intra*personal experience, construed by the individual and his perception of reality.

TIME   Time can be experienced in periodic terms involving the consciousness of beginnings and endings, of phases, or of the measurable spans of minutes, days, weeks, and years. It can also be experienced subjectively when the passage of time is judged by a distinctly personal chronometer. Although not mutually exclusive, the determination of which aspect of self will be evoked depends on which experience is dominant.

We tend to understand the stages of maturation and development in periodic terms. Certain years and junctures make up to each phase. Within an expected range, we know when childhood ends and adolescence begins, when adolescence ends and early adulthood begins, and so on. At each stage of development, certain aspects of self take precedence while others retreat. Allport notes that preoccupation with the bodily self, self-identity, and self-enhancement are relatively early manifestations of personality development. With learning and growth, the self extends to include its valued possessions, loved objects, and loyalties and causes, and we see the emergence of self-enhancing and self-extending aspects of the individual.[8]

The range of many ordinary activities and needs involves certain aspects of self in relation to a particular time frame. Planning and problem solving are affected by the consciousness of temporal limits. This cognitive aspect of self becomes especially dominant when we become uncomfortably aware that time is running out and a project or plan remains uncompleted.

How we appraise our abilities and achievements often depends on our personal timetable or the temporal expectations of others. It is not uncommon to append a chronological qualifier when we estimate how far we have come in life or how far we have yet to go; e.g., "I haven't done too badly for a guy with only two years experience," or "I don't expect to hit my stride until I am about thirty-five."

Our acquisitive needs are sometimes linked to temporal variables if only because of the credit-oriented, time-payment nature of the economic system. Because of the aging process, body sense has a powerful chronological component. We judge changes in our appearance as signs of the passing of time. If there is something that we must do about our health, it too, is placed in a time frame. Diets are tolerable when we believe they will terminate after a specified period.

We can extend time relationships even further by linking certain attributes of the self with the particular seasons of the year or even with our own biological rhythms. Spring evokes one part of ourselves and winter another. Robert Ornstein sees these seasonal cycles replicated in the human state in the form of a particular periodicity appearing in our personal and biological cycles. The assumption that personality is stable, he argues, no longer withstands rigorous empirical analysis. There are cycles in our daily lives just as there are cycles in the Earth; moreover, they can be recorded, studied, and exploited for better personal adaptation.[9]

This conscious awareness of the chronological periods is only one dimension of the time experience. The other is the subjective, personal tempo felt without reference to the clock or calendar. Time, as it is experienced, can expand or contract.

The effects of poverty and deprivation on one's self image depend to some extent on how time is personally construed. If these conditions are short lived and if the person affected can foresee their eventual termination, it is quite possible that their effects will be negligible and perhaps even self enhancing. The young student, artist, or apprentice may rise out of a period of severe indigence with feelings of strength and an identity and image enlarged by the realization that he has met the challenge of privation. But dispossessed persons who are cast into an interminable state of destitution come to understand the nature of time in ways that erode conceptions of self, esteem, and identity. The loss of control of time corresponds with a loss of control of one's destiny; self-esteem may dissolve into feelings of powerlessness, helplessness, and futile anger.

Pointless work tends to dull the use of rational processes and depletes strivings and motivations. If one feels inescapably trapped into the endless routine of work of no intrinsic value, to survive the self must be trimmed and constricted. Higher goals and aspirations have to be denied or rejected in one way or another, and thinking must be shaped to fit the monotony of day-by-day living interrupted only by payday, vacations, retirement, and death.

Another example of the effects of the perception of time involves the anxiety that accompanies the anticipation of an impending event. The situation may be as ordinary as a planned appearance before an audience or as exceptional as scheduled surgery. Since the person cannot control or cope with something that lies in the future, time may be an ally. But it can also be overwhelming when it is experienced as a void, an interminable period that gives rise to an acute sense of helplessness.

The manner in which time is experienced has some important implications for one's social roles. Since a subjective response to time evokes only special aspects of self, there is a good possibility that the person may be judged or characterized by others in relation to the behavior that follows. This may explain why those who are trapped in the timelessness of poverty are often criticized for their lack of a "future orientation." The long view would appear pointless under these circumstances given the immediate need to preserve their self-image, security, and identity.

SITUATION People ordinarily spend the major part of their lives in predictable and dependable environments. The need for identity and a sense of belonging and continuity urges us to remain as members of stable and secure relationships, families, jobs, and communities. The rules, routines, and expectations that characterize these social structures allow us to pursue the business of living without much thought. Only when habitual patterns break down is there a need to engage in self-questioning about our actions, purposes, or goals.

Once removed from the protective boundaries of routine existence, the ease of a nonintrospective lifestyle begins to diminish. Confronted with the unfamiliar, our assumptions about our roles and status in the world become subject to challenge and doubt. There are, of course, exceptional people who move from one social environment to another without any marked change in their habitual ways of presenting themselves. The rigid and unyielding nature of their self-conceptions assures that any new demand will only elicit a methodical response. There are also those who welcome a change in environment as a break from a dull routine, actively seeking new experiences or contacts with new groups for purposes of self-renewal and discovery. In any case, it is not only the nature of the environment that bears on the emergence of certain aspects of self, but how it is perceived and understood.

Consciousness of the total self is raised and sharpened when one recognizes that his new situation contrasts strongly with predictable and comfortable patterns. This acute consciousness has certain regulating functions: an increased sense of alertness readies special aspects of self for their emergence as coping operations. When the person is exposed to physical danger, *body senses* are aroused, signaling fear in the form of tension, accelerated heart rate, and so on. Entry into new settings—the first day on the job or in the classroom or movement into an unfamiliar culture—challenges one's sense of competency and worth. But the same event can also intensify one's *propriate strivings* as he perceives the experience as an impetus for achievement. *Self-identity* is awakened.

Since the situational variable also has the effect of revealing only special aspects of self to public view the risk is again present that the person will come to be characterized by the narrow set of behaviors that express only the emergent aspects of self. What is lost from sight is the mixture of personal attributes that make up the total self. In some instances, an individual might welcome the idea of wearing a single mask; by assuming a narrow persona he achieves a sense of control over others' responses and over what he wishes to disclose to himself to others. This abridgment of the larger self becomes problematic, however, in situations where the individual has lost control over how he will present and define himself. This is often the case when a person is subjected to the controls of certain societal institutions and agents. In *Asylums,* Goffman depicts the mortification of self that results when inmates or mental patients are pecularized by the application of pathological labels to certain observed behaviors.[10] Even in the case of physical illness, hospitalized patients may be ridiculed or treated as dependent and childlike because of their temporary preoccupation with the body senses.

The diverse ways in which we respond to perceived time and place, depict only one side of the adaptive equation. The other involves the invariable and enduring nature of the self. A self bereft of an integrative force, without a sense of inner unity, experiences a jumble of unpredictable tendencies responding erratically or reflexively to passing stimuli. A so-called psychotic, preoccupied with his physical self, studying his heartbeats or listening to the "voices" of his stomach or brain, or struggling to fashion a figment of identity by assuming the guise of Christ, the devil, or Winston Churchill, acts as if he were "crazy" or "mentally ill" or "schizophrenic." But this person is neither demented nor ill; if one takes the time to understand, his behaviors might be seen as meaningful statements. They stand for the futile attempt to create a small semblance of a self, to affirm that he is, indeed, real. His attempt necessarily fails since he lacks a central core of being—the ability to recognize and experience an inner sense of unity. Unable to locate this core, the "madman" flounders in his search for a suitable alternative by trying to salvage small scraps of self or by appropriating other roles and images. His "success" is that he only creates a bizarre caricature of humanity.

This central core is contained within one's self-image—the conceptions of one's worth and esteem balanced against his ideals and standards at a particular point in time. Self-image is derived from judgments about past life experiences and expectations about the present and future. It is not so much what one has done or is doing but rather how one's actions and accomplishments measure up to a deep-rooted set of personal expectations. Hence, the person moves through life dealing with the dialectic between a personal model of self (derived in part from the process of socialization) and lived experience. For this reason, self-image and esteem cannot be finally formed or totally secure. Although it serves as the substantial center of our being, self-image is constantly vulnerable—exposed to the contingencies of living and the awareness that one cannot fully control all that lies ahead.

Confronted with this dilemma, the individual must make a choice. He can declare himself a victim—one who defines his past, present, and future as conditions that are beyond his control and determination. This allows him to escape responsibility for his actions and puts him in touch with many others who will willingly complement and support the victim's role. Or he may be far more assertive and thus incur greater personal risks and dangers. Here the person affirms that within the limitations of his existence he has the right, obligation, and capacity to participate in the decisions and choices that will bear on his dignity, worth, and well-being. These decisions and choices may involve the few critical episodes that arise rather infrequently: marriage, career planning, education, and retirement. Of greater consequence are the seemingly insignificant choices and decisions that must be made within the ordinary flow of daily living. These determinations may appear to be insignificant, yet the cumulative quality of this succession of choices affects our image of ourselves. As Tom Wicker says:

. . . a man seldom has to make one decisive all-or-nothing choice, either to go down in flames or to bed with the devil. Instead a man has to constantly make lesser choices, the meaning of which was not clear at the time he chose. And then suddenly all of those incessant, troubling choices became together the one big one, and a man has gone round the bend before he knew it, with the damage all done—not in the same romantic instant of clear-eyed knowledge that had at least the dignity of comprehension, but inch by inch, step by step, day by day.[11]

The self-image or the phenomenal self is the major and familiar target of most forms of traditional psychotherapy. Enhancement of what is called the "self-concept," "self-esteem," "ego state," or "self-ideal," is considered a means to achieving such aims as individuation, self-actualization, self-realization, improved social functioning, better reality testing, and even deeper orgasmic experiences. The role of the self-image is equally relevant to other types of social change involving families, groups, or other collectives. Although the major focus in these instances is on interactional patterns and processes, the outcomes of these ventures would be doubtful if serious attention was not extended to the participants' basic valuations of self.

The Self as a System

The self's need to enjoy congruence and integration can also be understood in systemic terms. Sharing the characteristics of all living systems, the self strives for a sense of balance and stability (or self-maintenance) when confronted with the inevitable stresses of living. System, as the term is used here, is an explanatory construct, one that does not have a denotable referent in reality.[12] Thus we are speaking of "the self as a system" in analogous terms, the self acting *as if* it were a system, with a more or less persistent movement toward the goal of balance, integration, and the maintenance of a steady state. This idea corresponds with Walter Buckley's conception of the morphogenetic tendency of systems, which proposes that systems are in the process of maintaining stability and continuity while undergoing change.[13]

The concept of the self as a system is best explained by looking at some of the more common occasions of living and the threats that they pose to the unity and the harmony of the self. They include the confusion that may be aroused by intense self-reflection; the disturbing doubts about our beliefs that follow a reconsideration of past events; and the vulnerability that is felt upon entry into a group or into the commitments of a loving and caring relationship.

SELF-REFLECTION   Self-reflection is something more profound than the familiar musings and ruminations that we all engage in from time to time. These musings are usually eliptical: we begin with certain firm assumptions about ourselves and our actions and allow these assumptions to verify what we believed in the first place. If I entertain some queasy feelings about my behavior at a certain social gathering, my initial premises about my role or my relationships with those present permits me to justify my actions and resolve my doubts, and I can dismiss these thoughts leaving the integrity of self only slightly tarnished.

Self-reflection is the kind of thinking that dares to question our fundamental premises about ourselves and others. It is thinking that steps beyond our conventional rationalizations leaving us open to the possible realization that we have been deceiving ourselves.

I suspect that this sort of profound self-examination is not deliberately willed, and more often than not, either arises spontaneously in an unguarded moment or seems forced upon us by unforeseen circumstances. Unpremeditated thoughts and revelations about the self may spring into being during a sleepless night or in the early hours of the morning when the mind has not yet erected its proper barriers. But we are forced to examine our essential premises (although being forced does not necessarily mean that we follow through) when we encounter circumstances that seem to peel off the thin covering of self-assurance or contentment. The contingencies we face remind us that our control over our fate is not as secure as we believed. We may work out our tomorrows with a measure of confidence, but something unforeseen intrudes and forces us back into questioning where we stand in relation to our proximal world. We may disclaim the notion of control, nonetheless, we are likely to feel a sense of dreadful loss when others who are depended on for confirmation fail us. An even more pervasive threat is the impression that the world increasingly appears to be spinning out of control. The bizarre political and economic systems are beyond the reach of the human mind; it is more than their sheer size and complexity that generate our feelings of insignificance. It becomes difficult to give any credence to beliefs about the essential goodness of man when our beliefs are constantly shattered by news and pictures of violence, terrorism, starvation, and persecution. The Holocaust seems ever with us in one form or another; and even personal security seems to be directly threatened.

It is a natural tendency to react to these threats reflexively, to cling to our beliefs and so short circuit the need to turn inward and to reevaluate the whole of our being. If this is so, it begins to tell us something about the contingencies of intentional change through counseling, group work, or other approaches. Any one in a relationship for the purpose of bringing about some kind of change relative to problems of living will experience this sort of threat to the self. At some point the counselor or group leader will in some way ask his client to pause for a moment and reconsider his beliefs, his aspirations, his motivations, or the meaning of his actions. The worker is appealing to the reflective self to account for the individual's needs, thoughts, and actions. Depending on the state of the individual, even an innocuous query may have the effect of disturbing his vulnerable beliefs. An interviewer asks an applicant for financial assistance why he has been unemployed for so long a time. The response is sharpened by anger: "You mean you don't know that they don't hire people like me—ex cons?" A new employee asks his supervisor why he must adhere to a policy that appears to harm his clients. The answer is hard and to the point: "You will understand when you have enough experience!"

Whether or not these responses are distortions of the truth is not the issue. What they do reveal is the role of our essential premises in averting the need to reflect on our motives, identities, or any part of the self that might pose a threat to inner integrity.

RECONSIDERING THE PAST   We can appreciate the hazards of reflective thinking by considering how each of us creates his own biography. Since the self as a whole, and the self-image specifically, is shaped out of the meanings that we attach to past experiences, our perceived histories become the ballasts of our sense of reality and self. [14] Since this historical sense is crucial to our stability, it is exceptionally vulnerable.

The vulnerability of our versions of the past is striking when we consider how the historical sense is put together. Since we cannot objectify or reproduce past events, we are forced to fabricate an autobiography by selectively assembling certain pieces and parts and translating them into special meanings that have special purposes at particular times. We also use cause and effect thinking to bolster our self-justifying premises. One needs only to examine the social history that is routinely gathered during the initial phase of counseling or psychotherapy to see how the respondent will explain his present predicament by pointing to certain causes and events in his past.

Inwardly, we sense that these constructions and past referents are not particularly dependable even though they are fundamental to our immediate reality. We need only to return to the place of early childhood to be shaken by the realization that things were really not as they are remembered. Our dwellings seem much smaller and familiar objects have disappeared. If these simple physical anchors have been distorted by our minds, is there more about the past that is in doubt? In *The Crack Up*, F. Scott Fitzgerald admonishes: "It is sadder to find the past again and find it inadequate to the present than it is to have it elude you and remain forever a harmonious conception of memory." [15]

THE RISK OF INTERPERSONAL AND INTIMATE RELATIONSHIPS   In some respects, the solitary thinker faced with the need to reconceptualize his notions about his present self or past experience retains some control in maintaining the stability of the self. He has a number of options open: he may rechannel his thoughts into more comfortable streams; he may rationalize and dismiss any apparent dissonance; or he may stop his cogitations. If these tactics do not work, delusions may provide an escape from self-reflection. Any such control, however, diminishes considerably once the individual enters into an interpersonal or group relationship.

Now I do not mean to suggest that human relationships should be avoided in order to assure the self's remaining intact. I do want to show how intimate involvement with others is a double-edged experience. It is through close association with others that an authentic self evolves; yet the emergence of an authentic self is usually a consequence of the tensions and disruptions of human relationships.

From infancy onward, the nature and quality of an individual's relationships continue to fill and shape the self and the ways in which it finds expression. He evolves from the childish, constricted "I" into a more expansive sense of selfhood by means of his bonds with his family and his relations with significant groups and his cultural community. Dependence on and regard for others enable one to discover and develop the personal characteristics that mark him off as a unique individual and social being. Body sense grows out of standards of beauty, prowess, and health that we accept as our own, and how we judge ourselves is greatly affected by the prevailing standards, values, and ideals of the surrounding culture. How we reflect on and monitor our thoughts and actions partly depends on the perceived expectations of family, community, and culture. This combination of forces is what Lewin calls the "life space" of the individual: the interplay of influences that provide the context in which learning and development takes place. The way the individual interacts with these forces affects the development of a particular cognitive style and structure that comes to characterize his way of knowing, explaining, and coping with his world of experience.[16]

Personal development does not take place in a simple, additive, or predictable fashion. Although dependent to a considerable extent on the orderly maturation of the biological system, the emergence of the psychological and social self follows a spasmodic course. From birth onward, the human organism strives toward integration; however, since he must live in an anomalous world, he is bound to encounter experiences that tend to undermine his sense of unity. These conditions call for further learning and the development of fresh adaptive patterns to enable the person to move to the next level of integration. If he were able to counter these threats to the integrity of self by avoiding relationships, the consequences would be worse. Inevitably, the self would become vitiated; individuality and spontaneity require challenge and stimulation in order to develop. Their absence leads to depression or retreat.

This double-edged quality of human relationships illustrates the dialectics of balance and tension. Let us first consider some of the general characteristics of the intimate, loving relationship. Erich Fromm in defining love speaks of mature love as a "union under the condition of preserving one's integrity, one's individuality."[17] Loving does *not* connote a fusion of two souls in which the uniqueness of the individual is dissolved in a mystic symbiosis. Fromm's definition also presents a paradox: the notion of two seemingly contradictory states, union and individuality, coexisting and nurturing each other. How do we maintain individuality while blending sentiments, needs, and values with another? How is union sustained in a way that preserves individuality?

In the matter of individuality, a person undergoes some remarkable changes in loving and in being loved. Intimacy does not necessarily change the person but it may evoke qualities of self that were formerly unrecognized. In the rich intensity of the experience the lover "finds" himself, sees himself as a "new person" or "reborn." Being a man or a woman takes on new meanings, and he or she discovers desires and needs that never before seemed to exist. But this elation is not without its costs, because although the lover becomes more keenly aware of the new self as it is revealed in relation to another, the old rules of living no longer pertain. If true individuality rises out of the mature love relationship, how far ought he take it? At what point does his individuality violate hers? Other questions arise: Are these feelings and visions real? Will they endure? Can they be disclosed without risk? Can this relationship continue without imposing controls? Loving another provides an escape from estrangement, but it also brings previously unrecognized anxieties and doubts about the self.

If the act of loving sharpens sensibilities about what is distinctively *my*self, it also heightens awareness of much that is definitively *you*rself. And out of this resonance between lovers another state of being emerges: the peculiar bond of "*we*-ness." Perhaps this is what Fromm refers to as "union" which, like other overexploited terms such as "togetherness," is merely a vague abstraction of a quality that is sensed and experienced by lovers.

Loving places the qualities of self in a new light, stirs a more

100

penetrating awareness of the partner, and creates a sense of "how *we* are." It is perhaps in "*we*-ness" that the paradox finds resolution: Stability is achieved, the exposed and vulnerable selves of the lovers find a measure of refuge, and individuality is nurtured.

Is this a real state of being, or just a delightful illusion concocted by lovers to fashion a needed version of reality that is peculiarly theirs? The behavioral sciences are not particularly revealing about this quality of relationship in other than clinical terms, but the literary world is replete with descriptions of the world of lovers.

Apparently musing about the meaning of the love between herself and her husband, Katherine Mansfield became aware of how her room had "gained life" and how the order in which she lived was enriched ("in some strange way it is enlarged").

This is *en effet* just the effect of his mind upon mine. Mysterious fitness of our relationship! And all those things which he does impose on my mind please me so deeply that they seem to be *natural* to me. It is all part of this feeling that he and I, different beyond the dream of difference, are yet an *organic whole*. We are, as I said yesterday, the two sides of the medal, separate, distinct and yet making one. I do not feel that I need another to fulfil my being, and yet having him, I possess something that without him I would lack. In fact we are—apart from everything else—each other's *critic* in that he 'sees' me, I see myself reflected as more than I appear and yet not more than I AM, and so I believe it is with him. So, to be together is apart from all else *an act of faith in ourselves.* [18]

Although Mansfield describes a uniquely personal relationship, her reflections hold universal meanings. The experience of loving, when free of control and coercion, sets the climate within which the uneasy expression of the more authentic self is exacted; at the same time, the self is protected by "what we believe we are."

This dialectic is an attribute of any serious human relationship. We can see its potential when a person enters and begins to become part of some group experience, whether his entry is made because of choice, necessity, or interest. In this regard, I am emphasizing experience with secondary groups rather than such primary groups as the family or natural friendships. Secondary groups are usually devised to achieve certain purposes and to meet particular needs. Some may have an educational orientation to teach the participants about special roles, skills, or fields of knowledge. Another may have as its aim achievement of social change. There are also groups that are designed to provide a medium for enhancing human relations skills or to resolve various personal or interpersonal conflicts.

In any of these situations, many personal gains may accrue to the members whether or not the stated purpose of the group is or is not achieved. The closeness of human contact and the opportunity for the exchange and confirmation of sentiments and ideas are likely to be gratifying in their own right. It is not uncommon for people to return again and again to their therapy or encounter group in order to continue to experience the fulfillment generated by the relative safety of controlled intimacy. The group can come to be the alternative for the emptiness of daily living. Similarly, groups that coalesce out of a set of commonly shared ideologies and beliefs offer a feeling of identification and a sense of camaraderie that can hardly be experienced elsewhere. They engender a quality of passion and excitement that is rarely experienced by the solitary individual. In any of these cases, personal involvement in a human network can provide novel opportunities for the expression and the elaboration of many aspects of the self. A greater feeling of worth and purpose can emerge as the group encourages the altruistic self to find that it can extend help to others as well as get something helpful back. Personal strivings and aspirations that are usually hidden by diffidence or uncertainty can find expression through the encouragement and interest of a peer group.

The idea behind and the entry into a group is not without some threat to the coherence of the self however. Even if the newcomer can imagine certain rewards, the initial period is typically one characterized by a sense of dislocation. Even a sincerely motivated newcomer finds that he must modulate or temporarily suspend certain of his values and standards in favor of the norms of the group.

The secondary group is congregated for some special purpose and develops its own character and ethos in a way different from the family group. The norms and principles that distinguish the particular group represent a compromise of a variety of idiosyncratic ideas from people who have gone through very different life experiences. Whereas synthesis of beliefs occurs in a family group, the secondary group must work out a set of shared beliefs in a relatively short period of time if it is to prosper. The individual member must sacrifice at least a segment of his belief system in order to remain an active and accepted part of the whole. For example, in the therapy group the individual may need to readjust his convictions about privacy and self-disclosure in favor of the group's demand for self-revelation. Certain social action groups require that individual aspirations must be set aside in favor of the general good. In addition to the ethical climate that characterizes the particular group, a set of norms and rules emerges. Whether tacitly understood or specifically expressed, these standards govern the operations of the group. They may determine the ways in which the members relate and interact, what can and cannot be opened for discussion, how intimacy is defined, the way in which conflict will be managed, and other matters of human interaction. The person coming into an established group or who participates in the formation of a new group finds his usual patterns of relating and his essential convictions somewhat out of harmony with the emerging group norms. The balance that formerly seemed to shape the wholeness of the self now comes into question, the values that shored up the self-image are at least slightly in doubt, and rational processes require some realignment. The group member may need to give more than he gets back in relation to the needs of the self. Depending on the stability of the self as it confronts the power of the group, some dissonance is inevitable.

An animate and vigorous group does provide some significant countervailing benefits. The tension-creating experience becomes the impetus for learning and change and the eventual restabilization of self. The group offers the potential for intense and substantial relationships that provide confirmation and support in the midst of personal crisis. Group members also create a sense of "we-ness" that adds up to the emergence of a new identity.

The systemic characteristics of self have several implications for the activity of planned change since they disclose the adaptive patterns that people rely on to achieve and experience a sense of self integration. Healthy patterns are fairly straightforward and are reflected in the self-assertive tendencies of the person. Less successful patterns can take a variety of forms, the most obvious being the deliberate or habitual avoidance of situations or relationships that could possibly arouse the need to reflect upon one's beliefs, identity, or conceptions of self. In a more roundabout way, people may immerse themselves in the compulsive pursuit of routine activity or take on an unyielding lifestyle that seems to assure them relatively predictable outcomes. If the need for a relationship cannot be denied, a person may attempt to construct a controlled affiliation with others governed by his own boundaries and rules. Moreover, relationships may be sought with seeming inferiors who can or wish to be dominated. At any rate, the self, in systems language, "reduces the number of possible inputs," thereby assuring a minimum of personal disturbance.

Accommodation or deference to a higher authority is another adaptive technique that reduces the potential for internal strain by taking on or capitulating to the beliefs and commands of a superior. In a like manner, people may willingly admit to their weakness and obviate the need for assertive action. A cruder but no less effective means is the tendency to deny the experience of tension.

In contrast to passive patterns of adaptation, challenges to the stability of self might be met with self-righteous resistance ("It is beneath my dignity to respond to that statement"), over-intellectualization ("Let us consider for a moment what you really mean"), or veiled hostility ("If that's the way you feel about it, I'm leaving," or "I hope God punishes you for what you say about me!").

Such patterns ultimately defeat their desired purposes. As the individual denies himself the opportunity to learn and experience or to undergo the tension and agony accompanying reflection and relationship, he becomes habitually dependent on a cramped set of behavioral responses. His relationships suffer either because his actions soon become transparent to others or they evoke negative responses. The most damaging consequences result from a failure to recognize that efforts toward total control over self, others, or the environment will inevitably fail. As the person encounters unexpected affronts to his version and control of reality, he finds himself lacking the flexibility needed to cope. As a result, the self either crumbles a bit more or hardens; in either case, it becomes even more unreliable than before.

It is apparent that the attempt to effect change in adaptive patterns is not restricted to problems of personal adjustment or interpersonal stress. The work of Paulo Freire, the South American educator, shows how arousing the potential for self-reflection can activate large numbers of people to change the oppressive and demanding conditions in their social system. He calls this method "conscientization," a radical politicizing approach that urges people to reconceptualize their illusions about their inferior status and to think about alternatives never before considered. This approach begins to challenge the self system by disturbing the balance produced by resignation and passive beliefs. As people reassess their rights, obligations, and status through collective self-reflection, it becomes possible to press for humanistic changes in the larger social system.[19]

The Intentional Self—In Search of Purpose and Meaning

Complementing the process and systems conception of the self in adaptation, the idea of intentionality refers to the human need to press forward toward valued ends. The person not only strives for adaptability and integration but also for the realization of personally or socially defined goals. In this regard, intentionality represents the motivational nature of self, the aspects of the proprium that stand for the self-seeking, self-extending, and the self-expanding pursuits of living.

A purposive or future-oriented conception of motive and behavior does not dismiss the significance of the past life of the individual. As the person moves forward into his future, his ideas about the goals that are desirable depend in part on what he has already learned and experienced. In other words, his selective perceptions of his past will influence his choices about his future. As a person encounters unanticipated problems, he will summon up former experiences to see if they will offer helpful clues or solutions. The individual must then judge whether this old solution is really germane to the nature of his immediate problem and his ongoing intentions.

I have argued that one's history neither causes no determines behavior in the present; rather, it is a self-created mental construct. Yet, many people behave *as if* their histories were irresistible influences, particularly when they are used as authoritative scripts or guides rather than as helpful resources for learning and adaptation. In these cases, the person appears to be oblivious to the evidence that shows that these old precepts are irrelevant to his immediate problem. Quite possibly, this evidence may induce the person to apply these precepts with even greater insistence. Closer examination of such compulsive and repetitive behavior and its motives will disclose that it is *not* the product of one or more causes; it is the *choice* of the person to be a victim of or to submit to the past as he sees it that leads to these archaic patterns. The individual is not acting in some way *because of* past condition but instead, *for the sake of* something, e.g., to avoid change, to escape guilt, or to deny responsibility. The "something" that one is acting for the sake of is located not in one's history but in the present or anticipated future as it is perceived. The past is merely the store of selected experiences from which the person draws what is needed to cope with immediate problems of living.

How we cope with the problems of living is more reasonably (and more commonsensically) explained in adaptive rather than causal terms. This is representative of the phenomenological perspective that attempts to find meaning and purpose in what we are actually doing rather than inferring the reasons *why* we are doing it. Moreover, perception plays a central role in this process. What past, present, and future are all about depends on our definitions and interpretations of our experiences. If this is the case, we see ourselves as capable of changing by means of new learning or relearning, which involves the reconceptualization or reconstruction of aspects of our life experiences that interfere with a more gratifying way of life. What makes for a more gratifying way of life is the search for meaning in what we are, and in what we might yet be.

The Pursuit of Meaning

From the beginning of life there is a growing preoccupation with the need to locate, define, and assimilate the matter that comes to shape our identities. Early years involve concerns about the elemental nature of self. It is a time when the fundamental values and expectations of family, community, and culture are assimilated. These years mark the beginning of the lifelong tendency to look outward and ahead into our environments and relationships as the process of self-differentiation unfolds.

This process is actually a dialectic or what Gordon refers to as the interplay between *social identity* and *personal characteristics.* [20] Social identity is expressed in categorical, descriptive, or nounlike terms: "I am a Methodist, married with two children, and I am employed as a computer programmer." The effect of one's personal characteristics tends to be more adjectival in nature, thereby indicating the special qualities of the individual. For example, "I am a devoted father, responsible in whatever I do, and I am committed to liberal ideals."

Identity is only partially based on affiliation with particular groups and classes and on the various roles that we come to assume. As important are the personal assumptions we make about our affiliative and role identities and the values we ascribe to them. If I had grown up in an agricultural community and had taken over the family farm when I came of age, my role as a farmer would possibly be seen as "good" and "proper," particularly if it corresponded with family tradition.

The objectives of the search for identity involve not only substance but meaning as well. The substantial aspects of identity give the individual a sense of social reality. There are referents that he can point to (e.g., occupation, family, religion,) that evoke individual recognition and approval. These referents verify his "me-ness" and differentiate him from others. At the same time, the social substance of his identity discloses all that he calls "ours," the characteristics that are shared with other humans and that assure his sense of belonging and fraternity. The *meaning* of his identity is an elusive quality but a crucial one that is not securely rooted in his roles, affiliations, or accomplishments. Meaning, has to do with his ontology—his distinctly personal awareness that his existence is worth something more than the sum total of his roles or affiliations. Meaning is somehow tied with the images he creates of himself, what he ought to be, and what the world ought to provide. is the incentive for an individual's intensional and goal-seeking tendencies.

Much of great literature, is built on the theme of the loss of meaning in one's identity and the resulting state of alienation and existential emptiness. Marx wrote most powerfully about the meaninglessness of labor when it is exploited for the profit of others, and the individual becomes an alienated object.[21] Horney speaks of the "alienation from the actual self" that blots out all of what a person is or was when he ceases to be an active and determining force in how he lives.[22] R. D. Laing underscores the nature of ontological insecurity that comes from the inability to find meaning within one's self.[23] From a deeply personal perspective, Pirsig chronicles his suffering arising out of the search for the meaning of "quality."

Man is the measure of all things. Yes, that is what he is saying about Quality. Man is not the *source* of all things, as the subjective idealists would say. Nor is he the passive observer of all things, as the objective realists and materialists would say. The Quality which creates the world emerges as a *relationship* between man and his experience. He is a *participant* in the creation of all things. The *measure* of all things—it fits. [24]

Even a meager knowledge of history tells us that the pursuit of meaning is not a trait that is peculiar to contemporary man. From Plato to Eric Hoffer, the philosophers and the common man have debated and questioned the meaning of existence. Today's society is more than accommodating in providing its members with standards and prescriptions that define how one ought to be and act as a parent, moral individual, sexual partner, or employee. But the roles that society defines are contradictory and their longevity is often measured in terms of a single decade. Whether or not basic roles have really changed, the average person is regularly assaulted by new sets of expectations concerning his fundamental commitments. One may read or hear that the family is no longer a viable concept, or it is an enduring institution, or it is rapidly being transformed by alternative lifestyles. Even a search for some substantive ideas about one's identity flounders in ambiguity. What options remain? Is a person to plant his feet firmly in the foundation of his more credible beliefs? Is he to resign himself to inconsistency and accept each new trend as it appears? Is he to go on with the search?

The individual is also dependent on his social system for guiding ideas that are more abstract. Prevailing standards and expectations permeate human relations. Friedman calls them the "images of man" and describes them in this way:

> Man comes to awareness of himself as a self not just through his individuality and not just through his difference from others but in dialogue with other selves—in their response to him and in the way they call him into being. Because man lives as a separate self, yet in relation to other persons and to society, past, present, and to come, he needs an image of man to aid him in finding a meaningful way of life, in choosing between conflicting sets of values, in realizing his own unique potentialities. Our human existence itself is at once tradition and unexplored future, acceptance and rebellion. The image of man is an embodiment of an attitude and a response. Whether it is an image shared by only one man or by a society as a whole, the individual stands in a unique personal relation to it. [25]

The images that one must contend with are many and, often contradictory. Let us consider one that happens to be dominant in most cultures: the paragon of the promethean man who can endure and surmount the hardships that accompany his striving toward a prodigious goal. Myths, fables, and folklore celebrate this valor, tenacity, and courage. This image is certainly important to the child who needs a hero of some sort from whom he can borrow a vicarious identity for a time. Such a hero opens possibilities for being that the child's more ordinary world cannot provide. Although we are supposed to divest ourselves of the hero fantasy in adulthood, this image remains in our minds as a symbol that gets to be translated into more pragmatic terms. Standards of wealth, success, power, and sexual prowess intrude into our self-definitions and draw us forward. These standards become the extrinsic values to be pursued to excite our more mundane lifestyles. But even if this image is realized in some way, we are bound to find that it is but a one-dimensional state that cannot satisfy the search for a meaningful identity.

Social and cultural images are not only inconsistent but they also present different implications for the various stages of living. Even the expectations for basic gender roles undergo substantial change in each phase of life.

The significance of these changes has become more evident now that new fields of study have opened up concerning the long neglected period of adulthood.[26] The times of childhood, adolescence, and aging are well documented in the literature on human development. But only lately has attention been given to the four decades of adulthood as a span of time encompassing its own developmental phases, each demanding certain personal changes and adaptations as far as images, roles, and expectations are concerned.

The age bracket of the twenties are understood as the period in which the individual begins to consolidate the experience of emancipation by experimentation, self-redefinition, and other actions that come to differentiate a self. In the thirties, this new-found identity becomes subject to question and perhaps doubt. The intention to this point has been to develop a sense of individuality; the question now becomes: "What will I do with it?" As a person looks ahead, he puzzles over whether to settle into the lifestyle that he has built for one set of reasons or whether to revise it or reject it altogether for another set. The aim now is less concerned with "what I am" and more with the reevaluation of "what I want to be" in the life ahead.

Depending on how these questions are settled, the forties and fifties can be a period of realization and self-confirmation or possibly one of emptiness and estrangement. By this time, the merit of prior commitments are inescapably evident. In a manner of speaking, the results are in. The choices made about marriage, lifestyle, and career now take on a palpable reality. A person's appraisal about the meaningfulness of life is influenced not only by his reflections about how far he has come but also by the acute realization of his finitude. The consciousness of a future that has an end cannot be dismissed as easily as it had been in the formative years. The concept of "fifteen or twenty years" between now and retirement is no longer the vague abstraction it once was. Having already lived through this length of time and more, a person is painfully aware of the speed with which time passes as well as what can be missed or remain unaccomplished in this relatively brief span. The period of "mid-life transition" is a time of intense reevaluation of identity past and the possibilities of identity that might be.

The idea of pursuit of meaning is consonant with the reality of identity being in a constant state of flux. There are plateaus in the course of living where the individual can rest his search for a time. However, if he resists the blandishments of predictability and routine or does not consign his future to the control of fate or greater powers, his estimations of meaning will compel him to move forward again into the future.

These estimations and the decisions that follow are not necessarily the products of heroic moments and crucial times. It is within the seemingly prosaic ventures of daily living that what Wicker calls "the lesser choices" are made. They are the moments when we are able to make slight yet critical variations in our course, variations that depend on our willingness to act, to choose, and to accept responsibility for our values.

Questions of identity and intentionality are the dominant concerns of the existentialist approaches to behavior change. The existentialists argue that anxiety is an inescapable quality of living; however, they differentiate between "existential anxiety" and "neurotic anxiety." Bugental makes this point succinctly:

The existential givens of our being, (I am finite, able to act, able to choose, and separate) once recognized, occasion deep feelings of existential anxiety. That anxiety is natural to our being, but it may seem too overwhelming at times. Genuine confrontation of existential anxiety means taking into our awareness of ourselves certain attributes of being in the world that may seem more than we can sustain. In such instances we may try to avoid being overwhelmed by distorting the nature of the givens of our existence. When we do so, we experience dread and the feelings of neurotic anxiety. If, on the other hand, we confront existential anxiety authentically and take into our experience of ourselves the aspects of being that seem so threatening, we are making the courageous response and are freed for authentic being. Only when we are authentic in our being can we truly satisfy our basic existential needs.[27]

Summary

The development of an active and transactional conception of self is a foundation for the study of perception and learning. The *self* is used as an explanatory construct and not as a denotable part of the individual or an "homunculus" that, in itself, impels behavior. Allport's formulation of a *proprium* discloses the many dimensions of the construct. From this, eight aspects of self were outlined to reveal the self as a state and as a process rather than as static entity.

This framework led to the examination of three vital operations of the self, reflecting the individual's relations with his world of experience. The first involves adaptation and takes account of the self as both constant and variant in its commerce with reality. The self (or aspects of it) can be understood only in a situational and temporal context. How the individual makes himself known depends not only on place and time, but more importantly on how the individual perceives and interprets that experience. Connected with this view is the possible risk that any one person may come to be defined by others in terms of the way he presents himself in the given time and place. The variance of self that is accommodative or adaptive to the situation is balanced by one's self-image, which, in optimal circumstances, is the energy that unifies the self and infuses the other aspects with meaning.

The second function considered the self as a system that strives for stability although undergoing change, maintaining balance while experiencing tension. Certain threats to the integrity of self include the risks that come with reflective thinking. The contemplation of serious change in lifestyle, or the need to reconceptualize one's understanding of past or present reality can be sources of inner dissonance. The individual's entry into and commitments to serious intimate and interpersonal relationships are also potential threats to security and balance.

111

Finally, the self is intentional, future oriented, and in pursuit of meaning. In this regard individual behavior is not programmed (except if one wills it). Rather one has the potential and obligation to create the design and meaning of his life to some extent and is able to transcend his history and his immediacy. One source of the movement of the self into the future is one's need for identity that is subject to the transactions between personal and social images of the self.

Hence, the self is understood to be adaptive, reflective, and intentional and in a constant process of change. A dialectic exists between past, present, and future as well as between inner image and outer reality. What needs to be understood is the process involved in this dialectic—the experience of perception.

Chapter 4

The Perceiving Self

The terms *transaction* and *dialectic* have been used interchangeably to capture the state of tension existing between the inner self and its outer reality. Individuality, both a private experience and a social process, is a product of this tension. The social process is the interchange between the person and his phenomenal world; the private experience involves the personal and unique meanings attached to this interchange. Carolyn Sherif and Muzafer Sherif declare: "Regardless of the nature of the environment, the individual is the center of his social space. It is the individual's apprehension of the environment that is incorporated and translated into beliefs, values, and actions."[1]

Their view assumes that the person is not responding blindly either to special inner drives and instincts or to some outer controls; rather, his understanding of and response to his world of experience are functions of certain inferential and cognitive operations. These operations occur in the process of perception, the activities of mind and emotion that enable the individual to apprehend, order, symbolize, and interpret his experiences. An understanding of the perceptual processes is essential to the understanding of human behavior: "The perceiving self is the central influence in the process of adaptation."

PERCEPTION: A PHENOMENOLOGICAL PERSPECTIVE

The mechanics and processes of perception have been the subjects of study by the various disciplines concerned with the enigmatic nature of

113

human behavior. Partialization and differentiation of the phenomenon have resulted, and, as Floyd H. Allport concluded in his critical analysis of perceptual theories, different theories provide different explanations of the same phenomenon and place conflicting emphases on different operations of perception.[2] The findings of the field of neurophysiology dealing with the physical correlates of perception include the operations of the optic and neural systems and their responses to types of sensory stimuli.[3] Certain psychological studies are directed toward the role of perception in learning and social relations; others are concerned with its functions in relation to the discrimination of space, depth, and form.[4] Anthropology has examined how perception influences the formation and sharing of cultural concepts by groups and societies.[5] Some philosophers relate perception to an explanation of the derivation of knowledge and meaning.[6]

Allport proposed that a functional theory of perception should include a phenomenological account of the individual's perceptual experience.[7] Such an approach does not ignore the physiological, psychological, social, and cultural factors; they are, however, considered within the context of the perceived experience itself and in relation to the inferred meanings of that experience. From a phenomenological standpoint, perception is seen as a selective process because only certain aspects of any event are apprehended by the perceiver whereas other aspects are disregarded, rejected, or unrecognized. This means that the initial impressions that are formed, the interpretations that are made about them, and the behaviors that follow are frequently based on insufficient data. Selectivity may be unintentional or in some ways deliberate: in either case, adaptation is affected in small or large ways.

A phenomenological perspective grants a pivotal role to the perceptual functions since they bear on how the individual shapes his basic premises about himself and his world and on how he elects to behave toward it. Obviously these functions involve something more complex than simple sensory responses to a stimulus. In actuality, it is possible to define perception as an interactional sequence of functions that include:

Awareness or *consciousness*—the openness of the individual to his world

Attention—the more selective functions including readiness, vigilance and focus

114

Strategic or *organizational* operations—the cognitive style in which the person orders incoming impressions

Schema or *interpretive* functions—the preexisting frame of reference that gives meaning to the perceived event

These four functions are meaningful only when they are considered in relation to direct experience; thus, it is necessary to add two other variables that complete the picture of the person in a situation. One is the nature of the *stimulus,* the object or event to which the perceiver is (or is not) responding since the quality, strength, and nature of the cue will in some ways impinge on the perceptual experience. The second variable is the individual's *perceptual field* or the *social context* of perception. This takes account of the person's location within that field and its influential and social and cultural conditions. Figure 2 shows the relations between these factors and serves to introduce the nature of perception.

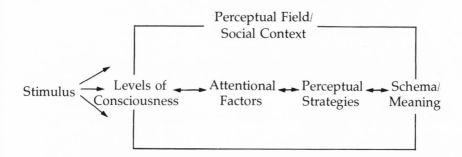

FIGURE 2. Perceptual Field/Social Context

Experience tells us that perception does not occur in the neat and sequential fashion of Figure 2. Moreover, various functions are not discrete but do stand in a reciprocal relationship, one with the others, and together they form the gestalt of the perceptual experience.

ROLE OF THE STIMULUS IN PERCEPTION

If we give any thought at all to how we come to "know" the events and the conditions that make up our proximal worlds, the tendency is to split the experience of understanding into objective and subjective terms. We grant a certain reality to the things "out there" and apart from ourselves by objectifying and disassociating them from ourselves. At the same time, we tend to internalize these events and conditions and make them our own by giving them our own special meanings. In this regard, it may seem as if certain objective stimuli present themselves to us. If these stimuli are potent enough our awareness will be aroused. This being the case, we then respond by apprehending the stimulus and ascribing some type of meaning to it. But is this really the case? Does this duality exist in the form of an objective stimulus that is divorced from the subjective self?

Gustav Ichheiser questions the artificiality of this duality when he distinguishes between "collectively and individually perceivable data."[8] Collectively refers to data that can be perceived in more or less the same way by everyone, such as the fact that a particular object is a house or a surface is rough or smooth. Individually perceived data is unshared and unique to the individual. Although two people might react to the same event with emotions or impressions that are similar, each of their reactions would belong to two separate universes of experience. The collectively perceivable world is definitely and unambiguously the same for everyone; the world of individual experiences is unique.

We objectify reality if only for the sake of being able to share the same world in a reasonable fashion; however, what we arrive at is not an objective reality but an *intersubjective* one that depends on a common language and a socially derived consensus about the nature of the shared world. When we consider how an individual ascribes personal meanings to the perceived experience, the idea of duality is no longer tenable. The synthetic separation between the perceiver and the stimulus seems to fade. The stimulus ceases to be a detached and objective fact; it becomes what the perceiver thinks it is or wants it to be in the process of translating it into personal symbols and meanings.

As an example, we can consider a study that appeared a few years back. Some researchers investigated statistics indicating that more deaths resulted from tornadoes in the southern United States than in the North, despite indications that tornadoes were suffered by both regions in similar numbers and intensities. The significant variable was the "average" southerner's identification with a fundamentalist religion. Unrelenting faith that God would intercede and protect them from harm appeared to relieve anxiety about the danger and made them disinclined to prepare for it. Northerners held a more pragmatic view and built tornado shelters. Obviously, the objective reality of the event was significantly altered by the meanings that each group ascribed to it.

The dubious assumption that the stimulus is an incontrovertible fact or that subjective perceptions are irrelevant also accounts for the erratic practices that creep into the delivery of human services. The "collective fact" is the assumption that "mental illness" or "psychosis" exists and can be diagnosed with accuracy. These "illnesses" have been objectified and classified in many psychiatric texts and in the official manual of mental disorders of the American Psychiatric Association.

A case in point is D. L. Rosenhan's study of the diagnostic and admissions procedures used by reputable mental hospitals. It shows how subjective impressions are easily accorded the status and reputation of objective or collective facts and, despite conflicting evidence, are employed as rationalizations for irrational practices. The question that prompted this investigation was: "If sanity and insanity exist, how shall we know them?"[9] Rosenhan's premise was stated in these terms: ". . . the view has grown that psychological categorization of mental illness is useless at best and downright harmful, misleading, and pejorative at worst. Psychiatric diagnoses . . . *are in the minds of the observers* and are not valid summaries of characteristics displayed by the observed." (Emphasis added.)

Rosenhan collected a group of ordinary people who were instructed to apply at the admissions services of selected mental hospitals, some of which were university training centers. The mock patients were told to report their own life histories and to add the information that they were "hearing voices." All were admitted without question. The "patients" then resumed their normal patterns of behavior: they told staff that the voices had ceased, they responded to the regimen, and generally presented no outward problems. All were discharged after varying periods of time and all except one were given the diagnosis of "schizophrenia in remission."

The results of a follow-up study indicate that even if the stimulus is clearly identified and the perceiver is deliberately prepared for its appearance, it continues to remain subject to idiosyncratic impressions. Representatives of the first hospitals challenged the reliability of the findings and asked that the study be replicated. Rosenhan agreed to send other "pseudo-patients" for admission during a specified time period. The staff then tried to weed out these persons from the overall number of applicants for admission. At the end, each hospital reported the number of people refused admission on the grounds of feigning mental illness. But, Rosenhan had not sent any pseudo-patients to these hospitals during this period!

The outcome of this study points to the fallacy of the notion that we can objectify reality merely by calling it something. But as Spiegel points out, even this attempt at precision and detachment inevitably involves the subjective versions of the namer.

Knowing, as naming, has no properties of exactness, reality, or truth beyond the observational procedures and their limitations involved in the naming process. . . . The naming process, the name (word), and what is named are to be regarded as one process of observation to which [John] Dewey and [Arthur F.] Bentley applied the title "transaction." Naming cannot take place without the simultaneous operations of the observer, the event observed, and the name attached to the event-as-observed. The transaction, in other words, is so mutually organized as a process that to impute a separate "reality" to either the name, the event, or the observer-in-process-of-naming would be to fragment beyond justification the unitary character of the process. The name is thus "double-faced," participating simultaneously in the behavior of the named object or event and in the namer and his behavior. [10]

Stimulus and perceiver form an inseparable union; yet for purposes of analysis, it becomes necessary to consider the stimulus in its own right and artificially separate it from the perceiver who gives it meaning. This matter is complicated by the fact that Webster's International Dictionary defines a stimulus as unidirectional, "something that rouses or incites to activity." This is the precise notion that I have been challenging. I shall take the liberty to redefine "stimulus" as something that may have the *potential* for arousing or inciting a perceptual response, given that certain conditions are present within the perceiver.

The Locus of the Stimulus

Most commonly, we tend to think of a stimulus as something coming from our palpable environment that succeeds in arousing any of our senses. There are, in addition, two other possible sources of arousal: our physical and emotional state of being and our deeper, more subjective levels of imagination and fantasy.

The cues arising from our inner state of being can take a number of forms. We are subject to certain physical sensations that are consciously accepted as hunger, pain, or fatigue. The neural, muscular, or glandular systems that are activated by deprivation or tension emit signals to the brain that provide information about the state of the organism. Emotion as a potential stimulus may also be understood as a physical response involving visceral or hypothalmic activity, or emotion might be seen as a flooding of the system occurring when rational processes are no longer capable of coping with a threat. Either way, the feelings that we identify as fear, anxiety, guilt, joy, or anger are capable of inciting the perceptual process. Such feelings may be the consequence of antecedent perceptions or they may appear to arise spontaneously for no apparent reason.

Both the external and the physical and emotional sources of arousal are usually directly or indirectly linked to some referent in reality. In other words, we are either aware of the cause and source of the thing arousing our perceptions, or we tend to create a cause of our thinking.

The sensations arising from the deeper self have a much more tenuous relationship with the world of reality. Their origins are elusive, a circumstance that in itself may be discomfiting. They are the illusions, visions, fantasies, and dreams that flow from the inexplicable chambers of the inner being. Despite their illusive nature, they are no less powerful than the more "real" stimuli as potentials for evoking sensation and response; however, because they seem to be extraneous to the material nature of existence, we are prone to dismiss these cues.

The human ability to alternate between palpable and ephemeral realities opens to question the actual differences between sanity and insanity or normality and abnormality. I suspect that the "psychotic" spends some of his time responding to the cues coming from this peculiar inner realm of stimulation. Whether or not his visions are designated as hallucinatory or delusionary, they are neither subhuman productions nor products of a sick mind. They are distinctly human creations that happen to differ radically from others' conceptions of reality: they are symbols contrived in the interior of an exclusive world.

It may be argued that the difference between the "psychotic" and the "normal" is that the former acts as if he is unable to make a proper distinction between his inner world of fantasy and the outer world of reality. But a more critical variable is whether a "qualified" observer makes this judgment and determines whether the label of psychosis is to be appended and solemnized. "Normals" do have peculiar visions and fantasies—"unreal" experiences that are usually passed off as weird but transient events. If a person is able to keep these occurrences to himself, he is allowed to retain the status of a "normal." If these flights become public information, he risks becoming the recipient of a medical classification. What might have been a transient paranormal experience becomes the critical variable that is used to characterize the entire, complex personality: "He suffers from delusions; therefore he is psychotic."

Qualities of the Stimulus

Obviously, the cues that are capable of arousing the perceptual experience are neither uniform nor equivalent. Whether they are externally or internally based, their form, structure, and intensity will have some bearing on perceptual response. Ralph Garry and Howard Kingsley emphasize the importance of the structural qualities of the stimulus. How the stimulus is apprehended depends on the following characteristics: its *figure-ground* relationships, the *proximity* and *similarity* of its components, its *continuity* and *consistency*, and the extent to which it is whole and complete allowing for *closure*.[11]

The relationship of figure to ground has much to do with whether we can discern a particular cue in our environment or in ourselves. The figure is the central and unified aspect of the stimulus. Although it may be either sharply defined or complex and patterned, its prominence depends on qualities of the ground against which it appears; for the figure to be discerned, it must stand in some contrast to its ground. For example, we may hear the sound of a bird but be unable to locate its source until the bird is distinguished from the foliage around it.

The peculiar resonance between figure and ground creates many optical and other sensory illusions, and this quality of the stimulus is equally pertinent to the problems of perception and comprehension of complex social situations. For example, there is the plight of the child in a family that is constantly in the midst of pandemonium and uproar. Communications are marked by high decibel levels, and all issues, regardless of their importance, are dealt with in the same clamorous terms. How does the child begin to sort out and find meaning in the noises that are supposed to convey instruction, discipline, or affection (the figure) when these messages are indistinguishable from the other noises that the family is constantly creating (the ground)? In other instances, the relations between figure and ground may be so radical as to create a bizarre situation, for example, a burst of uncontrollable laughter at a funeral.

Proximity and similarity refer to the relations between the elements of the stimulus. Proximity points to the extent to which the parts are grouped together so as to permit them to be perceived as a whole. An example is the constellation of the Big Dipper whose configuration of stars in apparent proximity suggests a particular form. In ordinary living, we are able to apprehend the whole of an event when we are able to recognize how its parts shape a gestalt; otherwise, it would appear to be random. A mother perceives "the need for attention" when she discovers that her child's disparate actions, such as kicking, crying, and throwing toys, combine into one meaningful expression of behavior when the child is left alone. Similarity refers to the extent to which the parts of the stimulus share a common set of features, permitting observation as a cluster or unit. The perception of "the need for attention" might result from the mother's awareness that kicking, crying, and throwing toys all mean the same thing.

Stimulus qualities also involve the matter of their *continuity* and *consistency*. The possibility that the event will be perceived depends on whether it persists over time and retains its intensity and strength. Anxiety arising from time to time in an erratic fashion and in varying degrees of intensity is likely to be ignored or tolerated. Should anxiety feelings persist in an acute way, they would tend to become intolerable forms of agitation.

A final variable, *closure*, alludes to the completeness of the stimulus, the extent to which the sufficiency and quality of the elements allow for the perception of the integrity of the event. In many respects, the matter of closure has as much to do with the tendencies of the perceiver as it does with the object or event itself. It is quite natural to experience a sense of confusion or discomfort when observing something incomplete or lacking a meaningful ingredient. There are many examples: an overheard scrap of conversation in which the context is missing; an electric sign with burnt out letters; or the abrupt awakening from the midst of a dream. I would surmise that an urgency for closure often accounts for the inventive explanations of people undergoing a painfully confusing problem. Although risking charges of distortion, irresponsibility, and craziness, their motive may be to bring about closure and reduce ambiguity, even when they are giving patently absurd explanations or excuses.

These attributes of the stimulus are not mutually exclusive; they coexist in varying degrees of strength. However, the nature of the stimulus may depend on which of these characteristics is dominant. Anxiety may be perceived because of its continuity and consistency; the perception of a subtle social situation requires an opportunity to observe closure and proximity.

When we speak of a human services worker as being especially perceptive we are referring to his keen responses to qualities of the stimulus. The community worker may have an acute sense of the nature of the community because of his ability to identify and relate a number of seemingly disparate variables that shape something more than a geographical entity—variables that include social customs, power structures, institutions, attitudes, and belief systems. Only when he can perceive these features as significant figures standing against less important grounds, or when he can see their continuity and relations does the impression of "community" emerge. Similarly, a social problem does not present itself in sharp relief but must be deduced from an awareness of the coexistence of a number of obscure conditions. The problem of alcoholism would seem much less important if such collateral factors as rates of hospitalization, absenteeism, and family conflict could be ignored.

THE PERCEPTUAL EXPERIENCE

The logic of perception is the process involving the reception of impressions, the focalizing influence of attention, and the transformation of these impressions into concepts and meanings. The crucial first phase of this process is the moment of conscious awareness when what Julian Jaynes calls *assimilation*[12] takes place. It deserves considerable attention since the subsequent stages of perception are obviously dependent on it.

Levels of Conscious Awareness

How do we begin to "know"? At one moment certain phenomena do not exist as far as we are concerned; in the next, these phenomena seem to join us and become implanted into our consciousness, a term all too often abused and misconstrued. What is the nature of this moment when outer and inner reality unite? The field of sensory psychology limits the explanation of this event to the operations of the optical, aural, or other sense mechanisms. It also proposes the concept of the *threshold,* the point on the scale of intensity below which stimuli are not detected and above which they are. [13] Awareness of reality is restricted to the "facts" provided by our sensory functions; moreover, the notion of a threshold or gate-keeper splits awareness into "go" and "no go" compartments ignoring the possibility of equivocal in-between states of consciousness. This point of view is enticing if only because it reduces a puzzling and complex experience to some definite and plausible boundaries. Yet, this sort of reductionism also dwarfs our appreciation of the myriad ways in which each of us is able to apprehend his universe. As humans, we are neither passive receptors of incoming stimuli nor well-designed computers programmed to process the input of data in a predetermined fashion.

From varying perspectives, other theorists argue that the arousal of consciousness about the world of experience may take many forms in addition to sensory impression and may appear on any of a number of levels. Jerome Bruner uses the concept "models of the world" to describe the ways that experience can be assimilated. [14] He differentiates between three forms of representation. *Enactive representation,* the awareness of something by its expression in action does not require the use of words or schemes. We are able to learn about something purely by behavioral means or by observing another's model of behavior. *Iconic representation* is a form of awareness that arises from the creation of visual images that organize perception by filling in, completing, or extrapolating what is otherwise unavailable to understanding. *Symbolic representation* is the familiar use of language and symbols to account for the things in our world.

Carl Jung's earlier work makes the point of differentiating between rational and irrational sensibilities although both are pathways to consciousness of experience. In his pursuit of a grand theory of intuition he elaborated four possible ways of understanding reality: thinking, feeling, sensation, and intuition. [15] The first two stand for the rational modes of achieving awareness. Thinking involves the exercise of judgment, inference, and other cognitive acts. Feeling covers the appreciation of things in positive or negative, or pleasant or unpleasant terms. Both rational modes involve something more than simple awareness of the stimulus since these impressions become meaningful as they are related to the effects of preexisting frameworks of understanding.

Sensation and intuition exclude preconceptions because they are the primal modes by which people become conscious of experience. Sensation is the unadulterated reception of sense data as truth. The experience is the basic and total event expressed in the form of joy, pain, or passion. Intuition is equally rudimentary but it encompasses a realization of the possibilities and implications of an experience without recourse to details or facts. "Knowing," in this instance, is pure awareness that is uncontaminated by cognitive schemes or judgments.

Modern thought and investigation provides increasing data about the more esoteric levels of consciousness. For example, E. L. Rossi states that the act of dreaming is a critical mode by which the individual can develop deeper consciousness of himself and his world. [16] The symbolic messages contained within the dream state allow creation of new frames of references for understanding experience and development of a new identity. Brain research offers some valid but fragmentary knowledge about mental capabilities that were formerly unrecognized or not understood. The emerging transpersonal psychologies and psychic research provide persuasive assumptions about the unusual ways in which reality may be apprehended.

In the final analysis, however, we are left bearing a host of speculative material about the phenomenon of consciousness. There is little clear-cut evidence that tells us how we come to assimilate and "know" the nature of our reality. Yet it is not necessary to retreat to the safe ground of empirical knowledge that reveals only the mechanics of data reception. We turn instead to the conjectural but pregnant realm of the experience of consciousness, what Jaynes calls the "mind-space inside of you." [17]

SENSORY AWARENESS   Sensory awareness is the level where sense organs collect information about the stimulus and transmit the data to the brain for processing. Analogically, this fundamental aspect of the complex perceptual process represents the computerlike functions of human physiology. Within this narrow conception of awareness the idea of the threshold may have merit because it determines what will and what will not be recognized as input. However, this analogy has only limited applicability because even within the confines of sensory awareness there is considerable room for differential forms of awareness.

In his review of recent research on the brain, G. R. Taylor reports some revealing findings about the operations of the senses. Noting that it is possible to have an indefinite number of possible types of subjective sensory experiences, he adds that the belief that we have only five senses is entirely misleading. The word "touch" for example covers such sensations as heat and cold, deformation, pressure, roughness, weight, softness, and so on. Moreover, it is not possible for the mind to represent the world as it really is since analysis of the stimulus occurs even before the sensed impression reaches the brain. With regard to sight, the stimulus is transformed by nerve nets in the retina before the information is sent to the brain. [18]

In its function of providing access to the real world, sensory awareness is infinitely more sophisticated and complex than the most modern information processing devices. The sensory system does not reduce incoming data to discrete or binary categories, and it does not function in strict compliance with preprogrammed instructions. Reflexive responses (say, to unexpected heat or sound) may approximate the computer model but beyond these automatic reactions, the awareness response is mediated by a number of selective mechanisms that affect the reception of data. Typical environments include any number of visible, audible, textural, and olfactory features, but only a select few of these stimuli are permitted to filter through into awareness. Anyone who tapes a sound recording of a counseling session or group meeting will be surprised at the number and variety of sounds recorded—sounds not heard at the time despite a heightened state of consciousness. Among other factors, attention and the "set" or "tuning" of the perceiver influence what is sensed and what is filtered out.

The sensory system is not totally accessible to the stimuli in its environment, even to those events that would seem to be manifestly apparent. For protection and stability, the inhibiting functions of the mind act to shield the person from what would feel like a barrage of sounds, sights, and smells. The selective process also insures the possibility that the individual will achieve only a partial awareness of his personal or environmental reality. Despite the intricacy of his sensory mechanisms, he finds himself muddling through his world with less information, oblivious to some actualities of his surroundings.

At the same time it is evident that we hardly exploit the potentialities for a more penetrating consciousness than our senses can afford. Engrossed in the demands of daily living as we are, we use our senses only for expedient purposes: we touch, smell, or see something merely to identify what it is or what it does, and then move on to other interests. We need only to open our senses to really *see* what we normally just look at, to *listen* to what we ordinarily hear. Commonplace things take on new meanings and sensualities: the grain of wood, the veins and hues of a leaf, the fragrance of herbs. Such openness can also subject us to the ugliness of the world, the contamination and violence of what we call civilization. In either instance, a more profound consciousness thrusts us into the center of the existential space that we occupy; the things that fill this space can no longer remain as transient and meaningless objects. Items that we figuratively bump into in a random fashion as they are allowed entry into consciousness must be dealt with in some way. Our familiar and workaday senses are something more than merely pragmatic connectors linking the inner self with the gross features of the outer world. Within the sensory experience itself, we are capable of making delicate discriminations that can lead to a more arresting appreciation and construction of reality, one that allows us to enter the core of experience.

SENTIENT AWARENESS   Although our senses can serve as informants about the nuances of our immediate world, our emotions begin to tell us something about the quality of the experience itself. On this level of sentiency, consciousness is the result of the arousal of feelings in response to the stimulus. An emotional response may well complement sensations stirred by sensory functions.

Sentient awareness is not necessarily linked to sensory data when it becomes the primary means of assimilating experience. Our emotional response to a particular stimulus may oppose or even nullify what our senses tell us. Our sentiments may raise our consciousness of the essence of an event, whereas our sensory system may tell us only about its more manifest characteristics. We speak of having "gut feelings" about something or that we "feel it in our bones" to explain that we know that there is more to a situation than its apparent form reveals. These are not inaccurate metaphors since our physiological state acts as a sounding board that not only alerts us to the essential nature of incoming stimuli but may also warn us of possible risk or danger. Consciousness arising from emotion is not correct at all times; feelings can distort the nature of the event and lead to erroneous cognitions. Even in this case, such emotional reactions are no less relevant. Although they may be inaccurate as responses to the particular event, they may tell us something about ourselves; for example, the immediate response of fear or anxiety to what is clearly a benign stimulus informs us of our apprehensions.

This form of consciousness serves as a dialectic link between the uniqueness of the inner self and the actuality of outer experience. The singular resonance that is created between real and felt experience also comes to explain the idiosyncratic nature of perception since the felt impression is likely to lead to a highly personal construct about the nature of the occasion. Perhaps it is for this reason that we tend to discount this type of consciousness or at least assign it a secondary role in the business of living. The rapid succession of encounters with new and unfamiliar events that characterizes modern living impels us to rely primarily on our sensory and rational faculties. It seems that these happenings need to be grasped and understood as expeditiously as possible: what really counts are the "facts" and "realities." Feelings, on the other hand, get in the way, particularly when they disclose the discrepancies and the contingencies that tend to clutter our thoughts and actions.

Social conventions and a lifetime of socialization tend to discourage the credibility of sentiency. The rules and norms of the social order invite the rational and objective response or what is considered to be the "masculine" style of perceiving. Awareness arising from the emotions is assigned the "feminine" mode. It is the woman who can feel and intuit, but it is the man who is able to meet reality head on in a sensible and no-nonsense fashion.

Self, Perception, and Learning

The emergence and endorsement of the concept of androgyny challenges the notion that rationality is the exclusive property of males and that emotional sensibilities belong to women. That any person, woman or man, is possessed of both types of consciousness was keenly appreciated by Virginia Woolf:

. . . I went on amateurishly to sketch a plan of the soul so that in each of us two powers preside, one male, one female. . . . The normal and comfortable state of being is that when the two live in harmony together, spiritually cooperating. If one is a man, still the woman part of the brain must have effect; and a woman must also have intercourse with the man in her. Coleridge perhaps meant this when he said that a great mind is androgynous. It is when this fusion takes place that the mind is fully fertilized and uses all its faculties. . . . He meant, perhaps, that the androgynous mind is resonant and porous; that it transmits emotion without impediment; that it is naturally creative, incandescent, and undivided. [19]

The rational and irrational planes of consciousness are essentially complementary in relation to the question of sentiency. The matter of complementarity is very important when contrasted with the notion of hierarchy. The mind that is open to the varied meanings of experience is not marked by the supremacy of only one type of awareness, but by its freedom to discover realities on many levels of consciousness. It is the reverberations between these levels that enhances a richer appreciation of the self and its universe.

BEHAVIORAL AWARENESS   There is a form of consciousness in which rational and cognitive process are extraneous or a hindrance. Here awareness is reached by way of conduct and the exercise of physical faculties. many activities that require balance, coordination, and the use of fine motor skills can be learned only by witnessing and participating in the behavior itself. Verbal instruction or the use of other cognitive symbols may serve to introduce the person to the type of performance that is desired; but it can also confound the person who is intending to carry out the act. For example, in teaching a child how to play table tennis, he can be instructed in how to hold the paddle and hit the ball. While he is heeding these instructions, his play will be self-conscious and tense, but once he shifts awareness from mind to body his movements become spontaneous and effective. He does not need to think about what to do next; as in swimming and bicycling, bodily motion becomes the medium of learning.

Children's play also shows how conceptions of the world are realized by means of behavioral awareness. Children come to assimilate and understand some of the major roles they will one day enact by actively experimenting in play with being a mother, father, or teacher. Vicariously, they become the hero or the heroine by devising all sorts of scenarios for their dolls and toys. Words may be superfluous to this kind of consciousness as awareness of different forms of being seeps into and becomes an inchoate yet integral part of self.

Perhaps the fervid and unconstrained nature of the sexual experience is the best example of consciousness in action. When the experience is open and free the partners transcend the boundaries of the mind and senses and the roles that are conventionally assumed. Alan Watts has said:

Anyone who has become conscious of role-playing will swiftly discover that just about *all* his attitudes are roles, that he cannot find out what he is genuinely and is therefore at loss as to what to do to express himself sincerely. Thereupon he is self conscious and blocked in his relationships . . . where every road is closed This leaves him in a state of complete paralysis if he persists in thinking that there is some "right" course of action and some particular set of feelings which constitutes his real self.

Referring to the discovery that arises from the unrestrained relations of lovers, he adds:

If we say that from such contacts the movement toward sexual intercourse grows of itself, it may be supposed that this is no more than what ordinarily happens. Intimacy just leads to passion; it certainly does not have to be willed. . . . It is not merely that appetite needs restraint; it needs awareness—awareness of the total process of the organism—environment moving into action of itself. As the lead and response of good dancers appear to be almost simultaneous, as if they were a single entity, there comes a moment when more intimate sexual contact occurs with extraordinary mutuality.[20]

The behavioral level of awareness is central to some approaches to education as well as to systems of planned change. One is Bruner's concept of enactive representation, which he sees as a mode by which serious learning takes place. Bandura has actually developed a scheme of social learning that depends on the use of modeling, vicarious observation, and direct behavior.[21] Both Bruner's and Bandura's learning models emphasize that novel forms of behavior and awareness can result from the enactment of behavior without reference to cognitive knowledge. Behavioral modification as a therapeutic system aimed solely at actional experience gives little attention to emotional or cognitive perspectives. Although the behaviorist would discount the possibility that behavior change would lead to a deeper consciousness, it is doubtful that one could undergo such change without some effect on how reality is understood, given the inseparability of thought and action. Many behavioral forms— dance, group activity, and even jogging—offer a means of entry into an adventure that releases and enlarges a richer consciousness of the total self.

IMAGERY The ability to apprehend sensation in imaginal and personally symbolic terms is something apart from the confines of rational or conventional thought. It is a form of consciousness that is largely nonintellectual, although the experience may later be reported in intellectual terms that another can understand. The use of imagery may involve the translation of experience into strange forms of awareness where meanings are obscured or paradoxical. This level also embodies day or night dreams, reveries, flights of fancy, or any other retreat from the rational ideations that are tied to an apparent reality. As another form of nonrational consciousness, imagery allows one to encounter his inner or outer world without the benefit of logic, reason, or words.

Dreaming is a form of imagery that is both common and necessary to existence. It is neither an extraneous nor an exotic happening but an experience that Rossi calls a "living encounter" with one's self and one's existence. [22] Through the dream the self can create a new dimension of awareness, a new phenomenological structure of reality. In daily living a person constantly confronts events that upset his balance: something shakes his image of himself, his comfortable belief systems become vulnerable, or a serious problem eludes a proper solution. Quite naturally he attempts to resolve these dilemmas by rational and practical means, which are often satisfactory. But there are other times when cognitive abilities fail, when insight is out of reach, or certain parts of the solution are missing. The dream becomes a potential alternative for understanding to the extent that it pierces the boundaries of familiar logic and leaps beyond the limits of intellectuality. The dream is an expression of a mind that is freed, one that is no longer obligated to remain within the perimeters of fact, truth, or reason. In the dream, man is able to render reality into its many forms or turn that reality inside out to unleash whatever meanings are hidden within it.

We tend to limit the idea of imagery to the purview of the fields of psychotherapy and counseling. To do so overlooks its role in other realms of change or in other human events. This form of consciousness is often the force that binds together the members of a group as they come to share unspoken symbols; this is typically the energy that creates the mob. In an assemblage of humanity that is being exhorted by a demagogue, the literal content of his words may have little effect until the moment when the listeners are moved by the suasive quality of the orator and allow the rational constraints to fall aside. Imagery takes over. The demagogue is now transformed into a crusader or saviour. What was a group of reasonable citizens, is now transformed into a mob sharing a common delusion.

Imagery enters into more normal pursuits as well. In many ways, our deeper beliefs and convictions and the human causes to which we subscribe contain an element of this level of consciousness. The persuasiveness of certain ideologies lies in their appeal to our imaginal and visionary approaches to reality. Such appeal seems to stir the energy that drives social movements and keeps them alive in the face of imminent failure. Perhaps the power of this type of consciousness is the explanation of the durable resistance of these beliefs against the blandishments of reason and logic.

Humanity has an extraordinary ability to be conscious of the experiences of living in peculiarly metaphorical terms. This ingenuity is the currency of the artist, the poet, and the writer who are able to transform a prosaic reality into a masterpiece. This attribute may be part of the brief span of childhood when ordinariness becomes magic, and the world at certain moments is changed into whatever the child wants it to be. Adulthood is too often the time of austere rationality when personal visions are rendered sterile by the need to hold to the proper syntax.

IDENTIFICATION   In many respects, identification and imagery are quite similar as they appear to spring from the same level of consciousness. Both represent images of reality that are distinctly unique to the individual. Identification, however, refers to the sense of oneness that we feel in relation to another or to an experience of some sort. Identification is something more profound than a cognitive awareness of the more apparent characteristics that we hold in common with someone or something apart from ourselves.

Empathy might be considered as an expression of identification having depth and meaning. When I am able to experience a sense of empathy about your state of being it is as if the objective distance that separates us has dissolved. Your inner world is experienced by me with enough congruence to permit me to "know" subjectively what you are undergoing at the moment; thus, I can now say with a sense of confidence that "I can identify with you." This awareness seems to emanate almost spontaneously and without effort. Yet such empathic knowing is not a magical act; it depends on a willing consciousness of nuances of mood, posture, and disposition that the observer can relate to his own inner state. Charles Truax and Kevin Mitchell have said: ". . . many of the cues used for deciding what is true, or is false, and what is meaningful in things we hear from another person come from the root ground of our own experience and existence. We can often recognize from our own awareness of ourselves the outward signs that relate to inner feelings and experiences."[23]

In addition to its role in enriching and intensifying interpersonal relationships, this form of consciousness can shape and sustain those aspects of the self that were previously referred to as self-identity, self-extension, and the striving of self toward transcendent goals. We talk easily about "identifying with" some cause or movement or that we are part of or belong to a worthwhile institution or belief system. If it has any depth, such identification is something more than the mere borrowing of ideals for our temporary use. Rather it connotes a kind of sharing or a blurring of boundaries that previously existed between the individual and the ideal or group. Each becomes part of the other; each is meaningless without the other. The sense of community that immediately emerges intensifies one's appreciation of his individuality and affiliation. In feeling as one and in communion at the same time, it seems natural to give and extend one's self even if it might mean placing well-being or one's life at risk.

This kind of consciousness is expressed in Irving Howe's account of the immigration of Eastern European Jews to America in *The World of Our*

Fathers. Speaking about the vital significance of the identification of these Jews with the socialist movement during the late nineteenth and early twentieth centuries, he argues that Jewish socialism was not merely a "colorful trauma in the process of adjustment . . . a mere sublimated version of unfulfilled historical yearnings or a mere social agency holding in check oppressed masses." Something of greater depth was at stake, as Howe adds:

> But just as international socialism helped to transform the consciousness of humanity, so did Jewish socialism transform the consciousness of the Jews. International socialism placed upon the historical agenda the idea of human liberation; it brought to unprecedented intensity the vision of a secular utopia; it enabled masses of previously mute workers to enter the arena of history. Jewish socialism (and Zionism also) transformed the posture of Jewish life, creating a new type of person: combative, worldly, spirited, and intent upon sharing the future of industrial society with the rest of the world.[24]

Socialism and its ideals are not seen as a rational or pragmatic solution to the despair of alienation in a foreign land. As a movement and cause it was capable of arousing inner images of power and participation—a vision of status in what was otherwise seen as an indifferent if not an oppressive society. Socialism offered an ideal, perhaps somewhat utopian, that one could take as his own and yet give to. In one respect it allowed the remnants of another land and culture to join together and reaffirm former beliefs; in another, socialism evoked new images of reality and new aspirations that redeemed the emptiness of labor.

Identification also plays a part in more ordinary experiences of living. The caring mother can realize the hurt, joy, or yearnings of her child as if these feelings were her own, and such realization occurs with surprising veridicality. Identification is the powerful ingredient that strengthens the bond of intimacy between partners who "know" each other and know that each "knows" without recourse to words and explanations. It is present in the camaraderie and the fellowship of people who share the same cultural, religious, or ethnic ties. It is the cement that transforms the conglomeration of separate and isolated individuals into a cohesive group or family in the full meaning of these terms. Identification means more than the sharing of a reality with another; the sense of reality is deepened by the sharing.

ARCHETYPAL AWARENESS   Jung's work enters into another realm of thinking about consciousness and the manner in which persons make contact with their world of experience. These ideas deserve mention for two reasons: Jung's system of analytic psychology offers a bridge between the familiar Western ideas of awareness and the conceptions of an Eastern philosophy that is somewhat more elusive to Westerners; he urges us to put aside our more comfortable pragmatic or empirical modes of thinking about human consciousness.

Although Jung used the customary logic and rhetoric of the Western thinker, his ideas portray I-world relations in somewhat arcane ways.[25] Central to Jung's system is the concept of *individuation*, which refers to the ongoing process of personal emergence and growth. It is not restricted to special periods or phases of living but persists over a person's total existence. This emergence does not just happen; it depends on the way in which the individual comes to realize the essential nature of the self. Jung identifies three aspects of the human psyche that need to be found in their obscure inner state and brought to conscious awareness: (a) the *archetype*, our immediate concern; (b) the *persona*, the mask of conventional attitudes and behaviors adopted to adjust to our social milieu; and (c) the *shadow*, private and personal characteristics that we hide from our own awareness and from the observation of others.

Persona and shadow are the social and learned parts of the self that stand in a state of tension. The persona is the personality that we expose in our social relations; the shadow is the personality-containing characteristics that we reject and cannot accept within ourselves. Archetypes, however, are intrinsic to the individual and not a learned product of experience. Jung surmised that archetypes are somewhat instinctual, either a part of the structure of the brain or representations of neo-Platonic ideals; they are the inborn and indwelling aspects of the human mind.

As an overarching matrix, archetypes have an immense influence on how we become aware of the things that compose our universe. Archetypes are essentially the array of universal images of critical characters that we hold in our mind—the fixed conceptions of what it is to be a man, woman, parent, child, hero, or sage. They correspond with the images that appear and reappear in dreams and in mythological forms; these images shape the manner in which consciousness of reality evolves.

Jung asserts that we cannot apprehend ourselves or others in a way that is free from distortion and prejudgment. This idea stands as a contradiction to the human wish to see ourselves as open-minded and unprejudiced. Jung cautions that we are subject to an inheritance of myths and ideals that are products of previous generations. As a means of countervailing these distorting tendencies, Jung proposes that we turn to our conscious selves to translate these archetypal images into perceptible and symbolic forms. This act serves to achieve a greater measure of self-awareness; it also leads to the exploitation of these energies in more creative forms. If these images are not brought to consciousness, the individual persists in his blind gropings and remains oblivious to the true meaning of human experience.

Jung's ideas about the human predisposition toward, or preconception of, reality is but one argument in a long-standing debate about the nature of human mentality. Two antithetical models have dominated the last two centuries of thought about the nature of meaning and, more recently, the psychology of the mind. One is the tradition of John Locke and the concept of the *tabula rasa* intellect. At birth the mind of the infant is like a blank tablet upon which is imprinted the subsequent sensory inputs coming from outside the person. The real world exists outside of the person, and it is known purely by the information that is sent in and received. The mind is limited to the ideas produced by these inputs and can do no more than recall, add, or manipulate these ideas as far as thought and meaning are concerned.

Immanuel Kant argued for a conceptual model of the mind. The individual mind is not a blank tablet but possesses certain inborn abilities to endow experience with meaning. External reality cannot be known directly because the mind acts as a barrier that transforms the qualities of that reality. Although he agreed that there is a palpable world (the *noumena*) apart from the person, this world can only be known as the mind forms sensations into a meaningful understanding (the *phenomena*). Thus the mind has no limits as Locke proposed. The mind is capable of creative and fanciful impressions and can think in opposites and opposites of opposites. [26]

CONSCIOUSNESS IN EASTERN THOUGHT   A appreciation of the Jungian-Kantian idea of meaning will reduce the radical or mystical qualities of

Eastern thought. However, the Western writer can hardly do justice to Eastern philosophy which, by its very nature, calls for understanding through experience rather than through intellect. This qualification is particularly relevant to discussion of Zen, an exemplar of Eastern thought.

Kaplan states that Zen cannot be considered a philosophy in the Western sense of the term.[27] It does not offer a new logic or special ethics nor does it resemble any familiar form of transcendentalism. Zen eludes words, symbols, or instruction; as a way of life, it must be experienced and grasped in its own form. Yet, an outcome of the state of Zen appears to be enlightenment or *satori*. Paradoxically, in its pure meaning *satori* cannot be an outcome because Zen thought militates against strivings towards final states of being.

A rough approximation of the meaning of *satori* is an ever-deepening awareness that comes from intuitive insights.[28] These insights involve a primary ability to see into one's "true-nature" through the nature of all existences. The self is an inseparable part of all things, which form an inseparable whole. Its purpose is not to add anything of substance to the person but to open all possibilities for disclosing and discovering the formerly unrecognized qualities of nature which would disclose the self. Enlightenment does not emerge from the act of observation but from the experience of becoming part of that which was formerly not a part of the self. It is a state of being that grows out of meditation (*zazen*) wherein the conscious mind is becalmed and the intuitive mind is freed to contemplate everything and nothing.

As a level of consciousness, Zen enlightenment soars above and dips below that which our senses, thoughts, and imagery can tell us about our existence. Zen implies a detachment from the senses and rationality, and it is from this detachment that harmony arises. Foreign as Zen is to Western modes of thought, does it hold any meaning for us? Is it possible to contemplate the act of contemplating nothing?

If nothing else, a serious consideration of the Zen mode would give pause for some rethinking about prevalent ideas that we tend to accept without much question, such as the notions of dualism, empiricism, and rationality. In Zen thinking things do not exist in separate spheres as in the concept of dualism. There is no separation in reality nor is there the idea of divisibility that is evident in notions such as mind and body, light and darkness, and sanity and insanity. The world also cannot be known through experimentation and the use of the empirical method, techniques that can only reveal what is known or what is accessible to the senses alone; they cannot cast any light on things that exist beyond concrete boundaries. The rational mind is similarly restricted in what it can know and understand because it is governed by rules that the mind believes indispensable. The rule of Zen is the rejection of rules. Alan Watts refers to the contrast between Western thought and Zen when he speaks of *kuan*, the ability to feel without seeing. *Kuan* implies an openness to the world as it is, a receptiveness to reality that is not distorted by the intellect. Watts sees this state to be as essential to rigorous scientific thinking as it is to the mind of the poet. Lin Ching-hsi, the nineteenth-century poet and revolutionary, wrote:

Scholars of the old time said that the mind is originally empty, and only because of this it can respond (resonate) to natural things without prejudices. Only the empty mind can respond to the things of Nature. Though everything resonates with the mind, the mind should be as if it never resonated, and things should not remain in it. But once the mind has received (impression of) natural things, they tend to remain and not to disappear, thus leaving traces in the mind. It should be like a river gorge with swans flying overhead; the river has no desire to retain the swan, yet the swan's passage is traced out by its shadow without any omission. Take another example. All things, whether beautiful or ugly, are reflected perfectly in a mirror; it never refuses to show anything, nor retains anything afterwards. [29]

SCIENTIFIC PERSPECTIVE   To Western ways of thinking, these Eastern ideas are not only confounding but are also open to dispute. It beggars the mind to think of "experiencing" reality without recourse at some point to intellectual processes. Can we *not* think about our experience? Can the mind reject what is already in it and attain a state of unbiased openness? Can our perceptions transcend our sensory states, particularly when we seem to depend on our senses for a measure of certainty about our perceptions? There are, indeed, some responsible Western affirmations of these possibilities. Interestingly, they do not come from the arts or the humanities but rather are products of reputable physiological and psychological research.

Recent developments in the experimentation with and application of biofeedback mechanisms depend hardly at all on rational processes.

Ornstein reports that through the use of electroencephalography, the alpha waves of the brain are filtered out and converted to either an audible tone or a visible light. The subject is able to hear or see these signals that indicate the presence or absence of alpha waves, placing the person in a novel and intimate relationship with his self and his body. He is able to discriminate among certain internal states and discover how they are related to the production of alpha waves; moreover, he may be able to find the internal manipulations that produce desired changes in the brain's emissions. If such control is achieved, he no longer needs the electronic gear. He is fully in tune with his inner state of being in a way that was formerly inconceivable.

Even though still in its early stages, this discovery shows that the individual can become conscious of physical signals and use this awareness of self to regulate brain, heart, and muscular activity. Ornstein sees this research offering great promise for medicine and education insofar as it enlarges the possibility for allowing people to develop an external index of inner states of being and consciousness. The applications of biofeedback research may begin to return the responsibility for healing to the patient, particularly in cases of hypertension, gastrointestinal disorders, and tension headaches. It is quite possible that biofeedback also might increase the efficiency of ordinary education by expanding and refining the processes of awareness by teaching students how to contact their own internal states. In sum, biofeedback poses the interesting possibility of scientific and objective self-observation and subjective self-discovery.[30]

Other scientific research has disclosed that the brain is not a single instrument of thought; it is an organ comprising two distinct hemispheres, each with its own function. Michael Gazzaniga reports on the results of surgery that severed the structures connecting the two halves of the cerebral cortex. The presence of *two* brains was conclusively demonstrated: each is independently capable of a form of mental functioning of a high order indicating the presence of two separate spheres of consciousness within a single cranium.[31] Arthur Deikman distinguishes between the two modes of consciousness, defining one as the "action" mode, the other as the "receptive" mode.[32]

The action mode of consciousness is reality-based and organized to manipulate the environment. It is manifested in focalized attention and depends on an object-based logic; it is related to a heightened perception of boundaries emphasizing shapes and meanings rather than colors or textures. The action mode relies on the specific qualities of perception that set outer objects and the inner self in distinctly separate fields. Language and rationality are at its core and are the instruments by which the world can be analyzed, divided, and reduced to literal concepts that facilitate the individual's ability to define and control his own world of reality.

The receptive mode is of particular concern to understanding consciousness, because it is organized around the *intake* of the environment rather than its manipulation. It is characterized by diffuse attention and use of paralogical thought processes. Considerably less regard is given to perception of boundaries than is given to perception of wholes and the relationships of things. Sensory and feeling responses obviate the need for cognitive perceptions. The world is taken in more or less as it is without reference to a rational or cognitive frame.

The action mode assumes priority since it acts to insure biological survival. It is the means by which we are able to reduce or subdivide our reality and thereby bring it into more manageable proportions. In response to the dictates of our Western culture, it is also the proper mode for adult behavior—at least in terms of the definition of maleness since the receptive mode is seen as regressive or feminine. Deikman suggests that the receptive mode is operative in the various forms of mystical consciousness. He notes that this mode may provide a way of "knowing" about certain aspects of reality that the action mode cannot perceive because it is grossly selective, gives priority only to certain features of the world, and excludes other possibilities. "That the view of the world thus obtained is relative rather than absolute, and incorrect in certain applications is held by many theoretical physicists. . . . The correspondence between the cosmology of mystics and that of contemporary physicists is striking."[33]

Three conclusions appear to be valid in attempting to understand the concepts of action and receptive modes:

1. Evidence of the presence of a receptive mode supports the assumption that assimilation of the world is not restricted to sensory and rational functions. Since the activity of this mode is nonverbal and nonconceptual, credibility can be given to the idea of a consciousness based on imagery and identification. Because the receptive mode does

not deal with boundaries and divisions, the notion of identification as fusion or communion becomes clearly plausible.

2. The coexistence of the active and receptive modes casts some light on the reality of androgynous thinking. Rational and intuitive constructions of the world can no longer be considered peculiarly male or female, but they are basic attributes of both. Definitions of separate maleness and femaleness must be seen as social constructs and expectations. Woolf's assumption is valid: "The normal state of being is that when the two live in harmony together. . . ."

3. The findings about bimodal consciousness seem to explain the Lockean and Kantian polarity, not in "either-or" terms but in "both-and" terms. The active mode seems to be somewhat in accord with Lockean principles since it is restricted to the lexical symbols that more or less correspond with the outer reality. Because we respond to certain stimuli by naming and classifying them, it appears *as if* we are registering in our minds the idea form of input received by us. The receptive mode conforms to Kantian philosophy. Our brains are unhampered by ideographic constraints and are free to modulate or even recast reality into any of the possible forms. Moreover, it appears *as if* a preexisting framework may be in operation influencing the manner in which reality is transformed.

Chapter 5
Perception and Adaptation

In a heated discussion, a father argues that his son's interest in poetry is peculiar, even unmanly; the mother insists that it is creative and a sign of the boy's brilliance.

A community agency convenes a meeting to encourage local residents to share their concerns about the rapid deterioration of their neighborhood. Hardly anyone shows up.

After his team loses a crucial game, Bill leaves his classroom without noticing the announcement of tomorrow's exam displayed prominently on the blackboard.

At a home for the aging, a visitor is puzzled by the fact that the television sets are turned on but no one is watching them.

A family counselor observes that every time the father shouts at the mother their daughter breaks into tears and their son grins broadly.

A teacher assigns a project requiring the students to study climactic conditions. George writes a report based on what he has found in the encyclopedia. Helen keeps a precise record and chart of weather conditions for one month. Alice creates a collage of pictures of various kinds of weather.

A group leader is frustrated because he cannot get the members to agree on the problem they want to tackle.

Even within such commonplace occurrences involving people who are trying to relate to one another, define ordinary problems, or cope with

141

life's tasks, we find that they are as likely to disagree about the nature of reality as they are to agree. In these illustrations we find a number of possible reasons why people arrive at different perceptions of the same event: (a) some of the participants take heed of the event while others remain inattentive; (b) different people are attentive to different aspects of the same happening; (c) some people may be observant of the event but will reject or modify their perceptions because of their sensitivity to the demands of the particular social setting; (d) people generally differ in the way they organize and think about their impressions of the experience; and (e) although people may be equally aware of a given event they are likely to ascribe different interpretations and meanings to it.

These variations are further expressions of the premise that human perception is a selective process that assures that the images formed in the mind of the perceiver are not likely to mirror or capture the totality of his experience. The misrepresentations that result from perceptual selectivity are not usually random or capricious. And despite the protests of the observer, neither are they necessarily the consequences of deliberate distortion or craziness. Persons' idiosyncratic renderings of reality can be understood as an adaptive pursuit, the need to preserve authenticity and integrity while attempting to make sense of and manage the confounding problems of living.

We have already considered how consciousness allows us to be open to our respective worlds in different ways, and for different reasons at different times. The variables of attention, the felt influence of the social context, the contrasts in styles of thinking and interpretation will further add to our understanding of the complex and unique nature of perception.

ATTENTIONAL PROCESSES

The distinction between consciousness and attention is perhaps more definitional than real since both concepts represent the manner in which we initially respond to the things that are the "non-self." Consciousness can be likened to a radar beam that, with some measure of constancy, sweeps the surrounding environment. As it signals and registers the presence of things "out there" in a number of forms, consciousness records certain general impressions. In contrast, attention is analogous to an optical instrument that focuses on, particularizes, and refines the elements of the stimulus. Where consciousness is directed to form and essence, attention is concerned with discrimination and analysis.

An explanation of the attentional processes needs to include consideration of the qualities of the stimulus since a transactional relationship exists between the two. The extent to which one is mindful of a particular event depends on such characteristics as the intensity, figure-ground relations, similarity, continuity, and consistency of that event. This does not mean that the ambiguity of the stimulus will necessarily repel attention. Its vagueness or confusing qualities may be the very factor that stirs the curiosity and interest of the perceiver. But it is just as likely that complex or inchoate stimuli will generate feelings of frustration or indifference. Modern abstract paintings or atonal music, for example, that lack conventional figure-ground or consistency characteristics will fascinate some observers but will repulse others who find them incomprehensible.

At the same time, the qualities of the stimulus are not, in themselves, sufficient to attract attention. Whether and how an event is observed depends on two major dispositions within the attentional process—*vigilance* and *filtering*.[1] Vigilance or watchfulness covers the various factors that prepare the individual to attend to a particular occurrence. Filtering or discrimination refers to the activities of the mind that enable the person to sort the important features of the stimulus from the extraneous elements. Neither of these dispositions arise automatically since a number of attention-controlling conditions (some that reflect personal characteristics, others more motivational in nature) will influence the person's readiness to attend and his ability to differentiate.

Physical and Emotional Conditions

How an individual feels, both physically and emotionally, will have a great deal to do with how he responds to particular aspects of his world. If he is experiencing some sort of physical ailment it is quite likely that he will be more preoccupied with his inner discomfort, thus reducing the amount of attention that he might otherwise direct to his outer environment. When he does attend to events that seem to be irrelevant to his well-being they are often blurred by the lack of perceptual acuity or perhaps even confused or distorted in some way. Similarly, forms of personal deprivation of such needs as food, shelter, and rest would also narrow the person's scope of attention and exclude to a considerable extent the parts of his environment that are not directly related to the satisfaction of his needs. Although he might be acutely vigilant, his attentiveness would be restricted to the things that he deems necessary for survival.

Emotional stress can also bias attention in various ways, partly depending on whether the individual is turned inward or outward in his inner torment. The depressed individual undergoing some kind of personal loss or self-devaluation typically rejects what is occurring in the world about him, possessed as he is by his sense of inner melancholy and alienation. In contrast, the anxious person beset by feelings of insecurity and apprehension is likely to be keenly alert to the possible dangers lurking in his environment.

Personal Characteristics

Whether as a consequence of learning, habit, or physiology, certain people appear to be predisposed to responding to particular events in characteristic and often predictable ways. For example, an individual may be regarded as "sharp" or "quick-witted" insofar as he appears able to discern and grasp with remarkable alacrity even the more obscure features of a situation. Often, he seems to relish the more ambiguous circumstances, and he quickly seizes the whole of the occurrence even before its parts are clarified. He appears to absorb reality on many levels of consciousness and thus does not need to wait until the particular event is fully crystallized. Another individual may be more deliberate and contemplative in his approach to certain conditions. He needs to pay heed to the special parts of the occurrence and then determine how they relate to the whole. The responsive teacher is quite aware of the strengths and weaknesses in both of these attentional styles. The impetuous, keen-witted student may generate a lot of enthusiasm but may also overlook critical elements of a problem. The slower and more calculating student may be less attractive and may be penalized for his lack of spontaneity. But through careful analysis, he may arrive at a more thorough understanding of the problem.

A second example of an attentional characteristic concerns the individual's span of attention or the amount of time and energy that he typically extends toward an object or event. Certainly the nature of the occurrence itself and the person's interests at the moment will have important bearing on the intensity and breadth of his attention. Yet, over the course of time people appear to respond to the things that attract them in distinctive ways. Some become intensely absorbed with the incident and seem to fixate on it for inordinate periods of time. At the other extreme, others seem to bounce from one stimulus to another, momentarily snatching what they can from each situation.

These and other personal traits are no doubt behavioral expressions of the reverberation of the individual's neurophysiological make-up and his acquired values and orientation to his world. As to the former, J. P. Guilford states that vigilance and filtering are functions of the brain's reticular formation located in the center of the brainstem. It acts to arouse and alert the cortex to incoming excitations and can be regarded as the "traffic-control" center of the mind. It also regulates and coordinates the output of the motor organs that under normal conditions may be modulated by socialization.[2] For example, even the person who is usually overresponsive to sudden, sharp sounds might try to restrain his reactions in social situations where he might suffer certain penalties. If these filtering operations are disturbed by a neurological disorder it is probable that socialization and learning will not be sufficient to control these reactions. The perceptually handicapped child is an example of filtering functions gone awry; they are no longer efficient in screening irrelevant stimuli in the child's environment, and he becomes "flooded" or overloaded by the wholesale flow of sensory exciters. The child's attention span and focus are debilitated, and he responds to his chaotic environment in a fractious and hyperactive manner.

The value base of these attentional traits can reflect the individual's commitments to broad or exclusive elements of his world. The power of these tendencies comes forth when one person's outlook contradicts another's—especially when something important is at stake. At the very least, these differences may obstruct harmonious communication. Should they persist over time, an otherwise caring relationship may break down. A case in point is a young couple who clearly shared warm and enduring feelings about their marriage. The wife, a schoolteacher, had a curious mind and was easily enthralled by the many things that captured her attention. The husband, an engineer, had a more parochial and linear outlook on his world and would concentrate only on those things that had practical importance. Despite his good intentions, he would quickly become bored and restless when his wife wanted to talk about the many things that piqued her interest. On the other hand, all he wanted was his wife's quiet presence while he spent hours tinkering with his hi-fi rig. Feeling stifled by these restrictions, she would soon find an excuse to leave. It was not long before each became despondent, interpreting the other's actions as signs of rejection and disconfirmation.

Such distinctly individual differences not only characterize the individual's basic perceptual style but also will affect how he comes to define the reality of his circumstances and how he begins to involve himself in the kinds of learning and problem solving critical to his life situation.

Mental Set

The concept of mental set is a variation of the idea of vigilance or the readiness to apprehend a particular internal or exogenous occurrence. Attentional readiness may be situational (depending on whether the individual happens to be open to the stimulus at the moment) or it may hinge on the person's expectations or preconceptions. If the event occurs unexpectedly or if it is unrecognizably novel, it is possible that it will pass unnoticed.

How the individual anticipates and thus attends to the happenings in his field can also reflect his characteristic approach to reality. Some people, for example, may be other-oriented while others are I-oriented. The former tends to be receptive to more of the things taking place about him; the latter is more self-centered, restricting his attention to those things that bear on his personal needs. The seasoned and secure human services worker exemplifies the other-oriented mode of attention. As a result of much experience and success in dealing with human problems, he is alert to the many nuances of tone, posture, and demeanor which enable him to "read" his clients with considerable accuracy. In contrast, the novice or learner who is self-consciously preoccupied with questions about his own role or what he ought to be doing next will likely have some difficulty in discriminating even among the more apparent needs of his client. The idea of a mental set is not far removed from the concept of levels of consciousness. The readiness to be receptive to and appreciative of a heterogeneous reality appears to depend on the individual's ability to have recourse to various levels of consciousness. The reliance on sensory awareness alone tends to restrict attention; the person's intuitive or imaginal resources nurtures and enlarges his responsiveness to his world.

The discriminatory and analytical properties of attention are shown in the influences of physical and emotional conditions, personal traits, and the authority of mental set. I have also implied that certain situational variables (the immediate interests, pursuits, and circumstances of the person) also bear on the scope and acuity of attention. The perceiver's need to sort and fragment a reality that is essentially irreducible (and that he does so in an unreflective and spontaneous manner) assures that his initial conclusions about that reality will be necessarily incomplete. This consequence will inevitably prejudice the ensuing perceptual processes as well as the act of learning and adaptation.

THE SOCIAL CONTEXT OF PERCEPTION

Perception is as much a social phenomenon as it is an individual act. The process of perception springs from the inner self; what is actually perceived and how it is understood can be affected by prior socialization, how the person regards his immediate environment, and where he stands within it. This person-environment relationship brings to mind the lesson in the "Emperor's New Clothes": what we allow ourselves to see depends on what we believe is socially desirable. Where we happen to be located will also bias our version of what is occurring within our field. Perhaps the low angle of view explains why the child was the only observer who could not ignore the emperor's nakedness.

An understanding of how people arrive at their impressions of reality requires consideration of the dimensions of the social context. First, there is the topography of the physical environment and the position within it that the perceiver occupies. Even though two people are observing the same event at the same time in the same setting, their perceptions will vary to the degree that there is a difference in their angles of vision. Second, a social context can be characterized by its prevailing expectations, norms, and rules for conduct, which will resonate with the thoughts and conceptions of the individual perceiver.

This topographic and sociocultural perspective on the social field corresponds with Kurt Lewin's "field theory."[3] Lewin refers to the "life space" of the individual or his construction of his situation that more or less conforms with the environment that he is occupying at the time. Each person has a number of life spaces that are related to his various roles (work, familial, recreational). Each may be characterized by the opportunities they provide or the frustrations they incur relative to the individual's goals. "Adjustment" therefore depends on the satisfaction found in each life space and the congruence between the various life spaces.

Topography of the Field

Topography refers to the qualities of the environment and the location of the perceiver within it. The importance of these features is recognized by educators and group workers who attempt to make it possible for class or group members to have relatively equal access to what is going on in the field by the use of circular seating arrangements. The matter of quality is dealt with by creating a pleasing atmosphere with proper lighting, good acoustics, and conditions generally conducive to effective learning. Accordingly, human services workers strive to provide their clients with a climate in which distractions and intrusions are kept to a minimum and clients are free to concentrate on their own concerns.

The impact of topographical factors can be easily overlooked in the attempt to comprehend certain social problems. For example, explanations of the common as well as the exceptional problems of family living often ignore the environmental variable. Among its other attributes, the typical family comprises a group of people in relation sharing the same physical space. They also share certain values, expectations, relationships, and themes of living—all colored by powerful emotions. The family's affective-relational state is enclosed within a particular structural arrangement that strongly influences how that state is perceived and experienced.

This structural factor is significant because the typical modern home is a product of economic expedience or necessity; its design is based on the cost of labor and materials that go into each square foot of space rather than on the essential requirements for adequate family living. Even people living in housing that is fairly decent are enclosed in a cramped space—visually and audibly exposed to whatever is taking place. Privacy needed for a few moments of regeneration of self, for contemplation, or merely to be alone is not only denied the individual but also no longer seems to be a priority of living. Family members must now cope with all sorts of matters: from questions about what will be cooked for dinner to serious conflicts over money and from petty spats between children to major battles that seem to threaten the stability of the marriage. The family's function as a refuge from the other cares of living is greatly diminished; family life itself becomes a source of tension as a consequence of environmental constraints.

Cultural and Normative Features

The social and cultural forces that permeate the field of human relations are somewhat more difficult to discern. Particularly, there are the shared beliefs of the social experience that are far less palpable than factors of space, distance, or angle. "Culture" can be conceptualized in various ways: as an all-enveloping constellation of controls determining the nature of a particular society, as a spiritual community based on common beliefs and attitudes, or as a series of historically created patterns serving as guides for human conduct.[4] In any case, culture contains the beliefs, rules, and norms recommended as the standards for active membership in and acceptance by a particular social group. These prescriptions and constraints become most powerful at times when they are violated or ignored.

Cultural influences have a significant effect on the individual's way of perceiving and interpreting his living experiences, and they become assimilated within the person without much objective scrutiny or judgment. Since we are born into and mature within a unitary culture, we naturally come to accept its norms and standards for conduct without question. Acceptance is then rewarded and reinforced by the other bearers of cultural beliefs. This type of social learning becomes the framework on which each of us forms his notions of what reality is all about. This is not an interpretive mechanism that simply translates our impressions of the world into special meanings; cultural forces also influence the perceptual experience itself. Depending on the circumstances, our belief systems may lead us to narrow or broaden our perceptions of a particular event, focus or diffuse our senses, or entirely negate the information produced by consciousness or attention.

These observations are supported by a number of subcultural and cross-cultural studies. Minuchin and his associates investigated the characteristics of slum families living in large metropolitan areas and found that the children living in the community or in institutions behaved in distinctive ways. They participated in activities without experiencing their participation and reacted immediately and without restraint to incoming stimuli, but they could not recapture and explore the event when asked to do so. [5] Because of narrow social learning experiences in a closed cultural system, these children tended to restrict their perceptions to exclude what Minuchin calls "the rich, subtle complexities of their surrounding life-field." A form of adaptation was developed that limited perceptual skills only to immediate needs for survival and gratification. Moreover, their behavior was supported by existing social norms that did not require the children to delay need fulfillment or to reflect on or be responsible for the implications of their actions. Perception was narrowed to exclude all things extraneous to adaptive needs.

Basil Bernstein's studies center on language factor differentials in certain subcultural groups, finding that linguistic differences are most marked between high and low socioeconomic groups. Two distinct forms of language use are apparent when the middle class and the lower working class are compared because of the different emphases placed on language potential. Since language is the medium by which people organize their perceptions of reality, members of each group can be characterized by their special orientation to relationships, objects, and persons—an orientation that has little reference to levels of measured intelligence. [6]

In recent years, the sociology of deviance has emerged with the basic premise that within any social order different groups tend to perceive the same behaviors in different ways and for different purposes. People who are seen by the dominant group as immoral, sick, or driven by the devil are victims of a kind of cultural relativism that defines and explains behavior in relation to the extent to which it violates or deviates from preferred majority standards. The formal studies of deviancy take account of the cultural, sociological, and situational factors that play an important role in the evolvement of particular social and personal problems. Of special interest are the groups who have come to be stigmatized by such labels as "the mentally ill," "delinquent," or "the poor," or still others who have been cast out of the mainstream of society not because of an innate disability or illness but because of divergent conceptions of reality.[7]

In its generic sense, the notion of deviancy can also be extended to the behaviors of other groups who pose less of a threat to the larger society. These are people who have elected "an alternative lifestyle" or who, though a minority, are reluctant to abdicate their essential beliefs. For example, the "liberated" woman is considered a deviant in a culture of complacent homemakers or women who willingly accept a secondary role. The Catholic or Jew experiences a sense of displacement if he tries to take his place in a distinctly Protestant community. The couple practicing an open marriage is considered aberrant if they live in a neighborhood dominated by conventional standards.

Whether deviancy is considered major or minor, what is important is the impact of prevailing cultural criteria on the individual's perception of self, his relationships, and his status within his community. A person's outlook on his world must contend with criteria and the penalties or rewards they mete out.

The weight of cultural demands also falls on the professional whose motives are of the highest order. The person who chooses a career in the human services must endure a socializing process and the particular rites of passage that insure his membership in the culture of his profession. Geoffrey Pearson writes about how this affiliation can affect professional outlooks:

> The shared understandings and beliefs of an occupation—its "collective repre-sentation" of reality—are rarely, if at all, made articulate even though they sometimes approach the status of a world-view. Recruits to a profession are socialised into this shared view of the world—which can differ sharply from lay conceptions of the world and from other professional world-views—by a number of subtle (and not so subtle) means. Everett Hughes (*The Sociological Eye*, Vol. II, Aldine Atherton, 1971, p. 399) has suggested that professional socialisation puts the subject into a kind of professional daze: in the extreme case, he writes, entry into a profession is like "a passing through the mirror so that one looks out at the world from behind it . . . [creating] a sense of seeing the world in reverse." . . . The professionally socialised subject goes about his (or her) business in a more-or-less routine fashion which embodies certain assumptions about himself, his

occupational group, and the world at large and these assumptions are not open to reflection.[8]

Pearson's statement underscores the point that the individual's cultural and social field (whether benign, contentious, or neutral) is a persistent force bearing on perception. It impinges on whether or not he attends to internal or external events and, if an event is assimilated, how it will be understood. This social influence poses certain implications. It supports the premise that a perceptual experience is not a random happening. Since the stability of the self and the comfort of the self-image are at stake in any serious conception of reality, the person's identification with a particular group or culture is equally at stake in the world view that is assumed. A man perceives things in a certain way because his image of who and what he is rests in a special version of reality. Concomitantly, he clings to a particular perspective, not necessarily because it is rational or true, but because it signifies his belonging to a league of people who will verify his existence because he holds that perspective.

In operational terms, this bond between cultural demands and perceptual processes is evident to anyone who attempts to question or challenge the perceptions of any one member of a cohesive family, ethnic group, religious group, bureaucracy, or other unified structure. The resourceful social actionist, for example, is aware that within certain community or neighborhood affiliations some group perspectives must change before single members will modify their own views. The able family counselor deliberately avoids pitting the beliefs of one member of the family against the others' (unless it is his express intention to stir conflict) and directs his interventions toward the perspectives of the family as a whole. Even the worker in the one-to-one relationship keeps in mind the fact that he is not dealing with his client in a vacuum but is contending with the perceptions of the client's reference group that play into their interchange.

It is more important for the practitioner to be cognizant of the extent to which his own personal and professional culture dictates and colors his perceptions of his work. It is all too easy to fall into a set of parochial views that affect every level of his activities from his basic techniques to the overarching ideologies that direct and support the system in which he is working.

Concepts of stimulus, consciousness, attention, and social context represent the receptive phase of the perceptual experience. They explain the conditions that affect the manner in which the self is able to grasp limited segments of reality and show how certain biases come into being. These perceptual functions anticipate the ensuing phases within which gained images and impressions come to be transformed into the personal symbols that explain reality and serve as motives and justifications for behavior.

It is apparent that the person is something far more complex than a reactive organism controlled by the order of incoming stimuli and the structure of his neural machinery.[9] The fact that humans do share a similar neurophysiology means that it is possible (providing there is no impairment) for everyone to respond to and participate in a common universe in a more or less concordant fashion. But these basic neurological and sensory operations provide only the raw data of experience; these data are subject to certain mental processes which succeed in recasting the basic imprint into what can be a uniquely personal construct. The ability to create novel and unprecedented interpretations is indeed astonishing. It can also lead to charges of "craziness" and "weirdness," particularly when these idiosyncratic interpretations violate a consensual and valued "truth." Our reluctance to debate political, religious, or aesthetic issues often signifies our awareness of the potential distance that can separate our and others' secure versions of reality.

The processes of organization and inference that transform raw impressions into personal forms of ideation involve thought and reasoning or what is termed cognitive patterns.[10] The term "patterns" refers to the individual's accustomed manner of thinking and it conforms with the stated premise that human behavior (including thinking) is a composite of characteristic tendencies and styles that shape the person's adaptations to his world and problems of living. It is within these cognitive patterns that we begin to discover the purposive reasons for the manner in which the individual comes to construct his unique or shared conceptions of reality. More important, this understanding draws us closer to an appreciation of the phenomenal self. If, even in tentative ways, we can fathom the person's elaboration of reality, we are then able to discard our own unverified assumptions about the meaning of his behavior in a particular situation.

For purposes of explanation, the concept of cognitive patterns needs to be seen as two complementary functions. The first takes account of the perceiver's typical method of concept or construct formation or the transformation of image into symbol. This function can be called *cognitive mode* since it calls on certain types of reasoning. The mode employed at one time may be relatively simple and direct as when I am conscious of the arrangement of features on my friend Henry's face and conclude that he is frowning. "Frown" is my explanatory concept for my mind's description of his appearance. At another time and for other reasons, this mode may represent a number of complex mental operations. A farmer, for example, is sensitive to a variety of nature's signs and concludes that a severe winter lies ahead. Here the perceiver conceptualizes a number of diverse impressions, sets them into a special class (predictive guides), and places these classes into a prognostic relationship. Quite often, the perceptual process will terminate at this level of cognition. Whether evolving from simple or complex reasoning, the derived concepts provide the person with the information required to carry on with his business of living. By naming the event he is better able to explain or predict its implications and therefore feels better able to deal with it.

In other instances, the derived conceptions are insufficient insofar as they fail to provide the understanding that will allow for effective behavior. These are the points when a cognition, if it is to be useful, needs to be qualified by some sort of judgment, valuation, or meaning. My conclusion that "Henry is frowning" is adequate only as a passing explanation for some differences in his appearance. If I believe that I ought to respond to Henry, I must ascribe some meaning to his frown. I might interpret his frown in sentient terms ("He must be unhappy"), in judgmental terms ("He always picks the wrong time to get upset"), or in aesthetic terms ("He sure looks ugly when he frowns"). How I will or will not respond to him depends on my personal rendition of the concept. In these circumstances, the other set of cognitive functions comes into play, those that make the derived conceptions meaningful by placing them into a personal frame of reference or *schema*. It is the uniquely private schema that ultimately ascribes meaning to the human experience and, in conjunction with distinctive cognitive patterns, shapes the individual's knowledge of and approach to his world.

Cognitive Modes

We have little conclusive evidence about complex human thought. It seems apparent, however, that the mind attempts to create patterns of incoming data and constructs more elaborate patterns from the original patterns until a single explanatory pattern is achieved. When this occurs, the individual experiences a sense of knowing and comprehension.

What is of interest to us here is the special cognitive styles by which these patterns are shaped—i.e., the typical modes of thinking and reasoning that result in a particular kind of knowing. It is possible to differentiate these styles in various ways. For example, the *analytic* thinker tends to break down information into its manageable parts; the *synthetic* thinker characteristically tries to integrate perceived information and transform it into a related whole. Some persons rely on *deductive* thought, using their preexisting knowledge to explain the particular impression; in effect, they move from the general to the specific. Conversely, others use an *inductive* approach, generating new knowledge from their explanation of the specific event. Certain people appear to be *verbalizers* insofar as their thinking largely depends on the use of words. Others are *visualizers* and tend to think in terms of images and symbols. The *concrete* thinker is concerned with the attempt to achieve a specific and accurate representation of reality in his mind. The *abstract* thinker, on the other hand, is comfortable dealing with metaphorical and analogical representations of his world. We can observe that some people appear to be *field dependent*, meaning that their thinking is influenced by perceived directions in their environment, while others are more self-reliant and therefore *field independent*. In simpler terms, the thinking of some people reflects an amount of *faith* while others are more *skeptical*. [11]

Obviously, these sets of characteristics are not always as distinct or polar as this outline suggests. In addition, many of these pairs are not mutually exclusive; they may coexist in different combinations and reflect a number of other influences including past learning and experience, the nature of the immediate task, expectations, situational factors, and so on. Yet, it is possible to characterize and understand people to some extent by observing the customary styles of reasoning and thinking that they depend on when contending with certain demands of living. Some tend to focus solely on the units or parts of a particular happening; others seem able to grasp the complex relations that represent the same event. For example, in their study of family problems some students insist on defining individual roles and behaviors, whereas others see the family as a general network or system of interactions. Some people think in terms of answers in response to an event ("That must be a ———") and others are more concerned with questions ("I wonder why it seems to be a ———"). Some are mostly concerned with distinct probabilities; others are able to grapple with any number of possibilities. Some seem to require precise solutions; others can go on dealing with enigmas and ambiguities. Some attempt to find solutions to their problems in systematic and dependable ways; others pursue what appears to be a rather curious and unpredictable course. Some are judged to be thoroughly practical and down-to-earth; others display an odd flair for ingenious or quixotic behaviors.

Evidence of these distinct personal and cognitive traits can be found in the way people behave in interpersonal relationships. As we come to know someone we find ourselves responding to him in a manner that more or less corresponds with or complements his typical style of thinking; the quality of our relationship, the topics that can or cannot be discussed, our respective approaches to special issues—these and other matters reflect the similarities or differences in our modes of thinking.

On the other hand, people do not employ the same reasoning modes in all circumstances; certain situations and problems will evoke different kinds of response. In daily living we encounter a vast number of tasks of an ordinary variety where the modes of thinking and organization are of no great consequence. Whether we approach preparing a meal or gardening in a practical and systematic fashion or in an inventive and exploratory way will generally have few lingering effects. There is, however, another level of problems that call for the use of either one or the other of these modes. For example, if we are attempting to figure out why our car won't start, we will be best equipped to solve this difficulty if we follow a systematic, linear, and practical approach, searching for a specific probability. If, however, as parents we are attempting to fathom the reasons for a child's poor performance in school, we need to take a more holistic tack, considering a wide range of possibilities and relations that may yield some tentative conclusions.

Some problems of living confront us with a serious difficulty for which there is no apparent practical solution. Neither past experience nor present circumstances seem to provide the answer. And, of greater consequence, something personal is at stake in how the problem is resolved. It is in this realm of living that the individual tends to fall back on the mode of reasoning that is characteristically his own, despite the seemingly undeniable evidence that the mode may be entirely inappropriate to the problem. For instance, a couple's sexual relationship may have for no clear reason deteriorated to a point where each feels rejected, deprived, or threatened. One partner has retreated to a concrete and practical explanation ("I've just been working too hard"); the other is grappling with the enigmatic and relational possibilities ("I wonder whether it has something to do with our worries about the kids").

The pattern of organization of thinking that centers on the perception of units, answers, probabilities, solutions, and order is called *convergent*. The pattern that attempts to grasp relations, questions, possibilities, and ambiguities is called *divergent*. [12] In convergent thinking the perceiver converts the impression gained through consciousness and attention into a single symbolic or conceptual form. He classifies, orders, or names the impression so as to make it comprehensible. In the example, the first partner became conscious of a number of sensations, feelings, and actions and may call these "a sex problem." The definition of the concept or symbol, however, derives from a body of knowledge. The perceiver draws from what he knows and has learned and applies or "converges" this knowledge onto the symbol. Thus the implications of the symbol or concept are limited by what the individual comprehends and believes, and his understanding of the event cannot exceed these boundaries.

Divergent thinking may be initiated in much the same way by means of consciousness and attentional processes. However, the definition of the symbol or concept used to organize the incoming set of impressions does not obtain from the perceiver's knowledge alone; he allows his images to generate all sorts of possible definitions and meanings. Although the second partner might agree with the nomimal concept of a "sex problem," this idea might expand (diverge) into any number of possible implications.

Much of relational strife is possibly a product of the conflict between these two patterns of thinking. Another example might involve a son's inclination to drop out of high school a few months before graduation. His father is adamant in his insistence that his son complete schooling. The father knows that a diploma is a *sine qua non* for contemporary life and should be obtained at all costs. There is no place in his thinking for any deviation from this concept. His son cannot accept education and diplomas as absolutes. He does not grant them an intrinsic validity and feels that knowledge can come from a number of possible experiences. He doubts that graduation is a worthwhile achievement in itself and proposes a number of possible alternatives, such as travel, work, or merely the opportunity to think about his future. Again, the example shows convergent and divergent modes in operation. It also reveals the kind of insoluble conflict that arises when two or more people conceive of the same phenomenon differently.

Implications of Convergent and Divergent Patterns

It is apparent that convergent thinking is the means by which we most commonly attempt to make sense out of our perceptions of experience. Convergent patterns are essential to ordinary forms of adaptation because the cognitions that are learned and acquired over time serve as useful guides to problem solving and action. Life would be overwhelming if it were necessary to pause at each new encounter and, through analysis, attempt to figure out what it is and what it means. Thus the accumulation of knowledge that we carry usually allows an intelligent pursuit of many of life's tasks.

There is also a certain circular and self-verifying quality in convergent thought that is linked to the image that we hold of ourselves. Our beliefs and certainties about various aspects of our world are critical elements that add to our self-esteem and identity. The self is a composite of premises which, for the sake of personal stability, need to be guarded and authenticated. The convergent mode functions when what we know is used to explain what we perceive. If the explanation works, we are once more assured that self and reality are what we believed they were in the first place. It is this need to buttress the unity of the self that often accounts for the hostility that surfaces when one's perceptions are contradicted.

Society also offers some persuasive supports for the convergent mode of thought. Conventional educational methods stressing rote learning and the accumulation of facts and information can foster a ready dependency on this style of reasoning. Scheffler calls this the "impression model" of teaching, and he sees it as the simplest and most widespread method. [13] Its desired result is an accumulation in the learner of basic elements fed in from without and organized and processed in standard ways, but the process is not generated by the learner himself. Although the learner emerges with a body of knowledge shaped by the teacher's design and selection, he is not prepared for the kinds of problems that require radical innovation and experimentation.

The ongoing process of socialization to which all are exposed also encourages this pattern. If one wishes to become an accepted and participating member of any social group, he must largely assimilate the commonly shared approximations of what the world is all about. The group's consensual view of reality becomes an important part of the individual's cognitive orientation guiding his organization of experience.

In a world that is becoming more complex and undecipherable, we become increasingly subject to the convenient wisdom of the many authorities, experts, and specialists who eagerly offer the fund of knowledge that obviates any need for us to grapple with the inexplicable. In saying this, I am not suggesting that the average person is incapable of more innovative perceptions; yet these educational, social, and authoritative influences do tend to increase a feeling of uncertainty about our private estimations of reality and encourage the inclination to rely on conventional precepts. If we take a divergent approach to special aspects of our real world, we stand out as being unconventional or deviant. This does not mean that we necessarily abdicate a convergent view or the value of accumulated knowledge, but we may also be able to leap the established cognitive fences and contemplate any and all contingencies of a given event.

Guilford offers an example of a person whose curious mind transforms a conventional problem into a divergent adventure.

A resourceful student, however else he might be described, in college physics was given the problem: "Show how it is possible to determine the height of a tall building with the aid of a barometer." The student's answer was to take the barometer to the top of the building, attach a long rope to it, lower the barometer to the street, bring it back and measure the length of rope needed to reach the ground.

The answer was not what the instructor was evidently expecting and he asked the student to try again. His second plan was to take the barometer to the top of the building and drop it to the ground, timing its fall with a stopwatch. By using the formula $S = \frac{1}{2}gt^2$, one could then calculate the height of the building. Other answers he gave were also ingenious. One was to take the barometer out on a sunny day, measure its height and the length of the shadow and the length of the shadow of the building and use the simple ratios. His fourth method was the simplest of all: take the barometer to the superintendent of the building, promising him that he will receive a gift of a nice barometer if he will tell the height of the building. [14]

There is a note of humor in this kind of experience as long as we are detached observers and do not need to deal with exceptional behaviors and ideas. But the person inclined toward expanding his perceptions into diverse or even extravagant premises often runs into trouble, particularly in relationships that require a measure of conformity. The child who is called "the problem" or the "difficult one" by his family is sometimes a child that insists on upsetting, without malicious intent, the usual family rules and arrangements by creating his own schedules and procedures or by pursuing a range of interests that are confounding as far as the others are concerned. E. P. Torrance has written:

Society in general is downright savage towards creative thinkers, especially when they are young. To some extent, the educational system must be coercive and emphasize the establishment of behavior norms. Teachers and administrators can rarely escape this coercive role. Counselors and other guidance workers are in a much better position to free themselves of it. . . . From the studies of Getzels and Jackson (J. W. Getzels and P. W. Jackson, "The Meaning of 'Giftedness'—an Examination of an Exploratory Concept," Phi Delta Kappan, 40, 1958, pp. 75–77), we know that highly creative adolescents are estranged from their teachers and peers. Our Minnesota studies indicate that the same holds true for children in the elementary school. The reasons are easy to understand. Who can blame teachers for being irritated when a pupil presents an original answer which differs from what is expected. It doesn't fit in with the rest of the grading scheme. They don't know how the unusual answer should be treated. They have to stop and think themselves. Peers have the same difficulty and label the creative child's unusual questions and answers as "crazy" or "silly." [15]

Paradoxically, a disquieting, divergent thinker can sometimes be found within the orthodox confines of the large organizations·or bureaucracies—probably because he insists on interpreting and imple-

menting policies and protocols in ways that their designers never anticipated. Occasionally such a person turns up in human services systems
where he is tagged either as a "culprit" or a "creative person" depending
on how his ability to manipulate absurd policies to meet his clients' or
superiors' needs is viewed. A professional in a community clinic had a
client receiving public assistance based on a disability diagnosed as
"schizophrenia." This female client was searching for a measure of
independence and had applied to the vocational rehabilitation department for additional support to pursue an educational program to prepare
herself for a suitable career. The client's aspirations were frustrated by a
set of contradictory policies: the public assistance agency required that
she remain classified as a disabled schizophrenic to continue to receive
financial aid; vocational rehabilitation required a diagnosis of "normal" or
"considerably improved" if they were to provide assistance. She could
not pursue her educational ambitions if she lost her welfare payments,
and if she gave up these ambitions she knew that she would remain
helplessly trapped in a state of dependence.

How could her worker reconcile these incongruous requirements?
Could the client be evaluated simultaneously as "sick" and "normal"?
The worker gave these questions considerable thought. Drawing from
her knowledge about how bureaucracies work and her awareness of how
professional jargon can be used to say something without communicating
anything meaningful, she wrote a letter to each agency. The letter to the
welfare department included the following: "Although the diagnosis of
'Simple Schizophrenia, Undifferentiated' remains unchanged, it is apparent that Ms. X is manifesting excellent indications of remission. Her
prognosis is quite good and will clearly benefit from the continuing
financial support of your organization."

She wrote to vocational rehabilitation: "I am pleased to report that
Ms. X is well stabilized. Personality and behavior are integrated indicating that her ongoing state of remission predicts a substantial competency
to pursue and succeed in a rehabilitative educational program."

Being aware that each agency would consider these statements valid
and using professional double-talk, this worker was able to secure the
needed services for her client without having to resort to prevarication.

The ability to perceive experience in divergent terms is, in some
ways, linked to the creative potential. Quite literally, divergent thinking

connotes a departure from established arrangements of reality into a search for novel conceptions and possibilities. It is the kind of thinking that is willing to question ideas that others accept as demonstrably true or to reorder them into a new set of relationships and meanings that were previously unrecognized. It is this last ability that represents the genius of Albert Einstein in the way he transposed the accepted theories of the universal and absolute nature of time and space into his theory of relativity.

However, divergent thought that contributes to the creative process does not always result in creative outcomes. If Nietzsche was correct in saying that "one must still have chaos in one's self to be able to give birth to a dancing star," then it is also possible that the chaos will remain and the birth will be aborted. In this regard, Anthony Davis speculates that there is a complicated interrelationship between divergent thinking and madness since both the creative and the psychotic individual reveal a preference for complexity and a tolerance for ambiguity. What distinguishes the two is that the former is far better able to manage his inner strivings and his interactions with his world than is the latter. [16]

I doubt that Davis' differentiation even begins to approach the ineffable factors that bear on the reason why one person comes to be celebrated as creative while another is rejected as being mad. What divides the two are relative conditions that have as much to do with the individual's social circumstances as they do with the peculiar way his mind operates. The judgment of insanity is by no means objective: how an individual thinks may be of less importance than what others think about how he thinks. Conceptions of "madness" and "badness" arise from cultural and social definitions reflecting the norms of time and circumstance. Galileo and Copernicus stand as classic examples of the persecution and ostracism that are suffered should one have the temerity to contradict socially accepted views of reality.

From another perspective, consider the case of nine-year-old Joey, the "mechanical boy," described by Bruno Bettelheim. [17] Joey, who was institutionalized, appeared to reject the human world and in his isolation believed that he was a machine. "He functioned as if by remote control, run by machines of his own powerfully created fantasy." But more important, everyone about him including the sophisticated professionals responded as if they too were convinced that Joey was mechanical. He would carry imaginary wires about and from time to time elaborately plug himself into some unseen circuitry. Only when the "current" was on did Joey show any signs of life. The people around him were cautious about not stepping on his wires. Yet, the professionals diagnosed Joey as being schizophrenic—a convergent impression striving to encapsulate divergent behavior. By any standards, Joey's behavior was certainly peculiar. But is his imaginative view of his world really "madness"? Should he be "treated" and urged to become like all other nine year olds? Or, should his imagery be celebrated and his fertile mind nurtured? Is the difference between Joey and the barometer-bearing physics student merely qualitative and not a question that is solved by the categorical decision of the observer? Although some qualifications are called for, Silvano Arieti shed some light on this enigma when he stated:

> In contrast to what could be said about the creative product, the creative process is shorn of newness and sublimity; to a considerable extent it consists of ancient, obsolete, and primitive mental mechanisms generally relegated to those recesses of the psyche that are under the domain of what Freud called the primary processes.
> The *primary process*, for Freud, is a way in which the psyche functions, especially the unconscious part of the psyche. It prevails in dreams and some mental illness, especially psychosis. The primary process operates quite differently from the secondary process, which is the way of functioning of the mind when it is awake and uses common logic. Primary process mechanisms reappear in the creative process also, in strange, intricate combinations with secondary process mechanisms and in synthesis that, although unpredictable, are nevertheless susceptible of psychological interpretation. It is from the appropriate matching with the secondary process mechanisms that these primitive forms of cognition, generally confined to abnormal conditions or to unconscious processes, become innovating powers.[18]

If we strip away the presuppositions in this statement about the esoteric structure of the psyche as well as the hierarchy of primary and secondary processes, Arieti is telling us that the human mind in its natural form is a composite of irrational and rational dispositions. In many respects, this idea fits the recent discoveries made by the investigators of the bicameral mind and the process of bimodal consciousness. The latter give the two forms of consciousness parity rather than seeing one as normal and the other as primitive. In this sense, the symbolic and impressionistic modes of thought are no more devious than are the lexical

163

and rational functions of the mind. We may assume that the divergent thinker is one who has access to both regions of his mind: he is as free to wander in imagery as he is to rely on the functions of logic, and the creative thinker may be one who is able to achieve a measure of synthesis between the two.

The Schema and Its Interpretive Forms

The term *schema* may be strange or unfamiliar, but such other terms as *frame of reference* or *mental association* may also be employed. The term can be traced back to Kant, who used *schema* to refer to what he called the procedures of imagination by which preexisting categories of understanding are applied to incoming perceptions. *Schema* is used here because of its venerable origins and because it clearly represents the range of premises that we carry with us and bestow on the things that we encounter and perceive in the course of living.

Kant differentiated between the empirical concepts that identify the details of experience and the "categories" of the mind, or the schema, which gives the experience its general form and meaning these details will take. Kant's notion of empirical concepts roughly approximates the concepts or symbols that are the products of convergent or divergent thinking. This thinking converts raw impressions into names, classes, or other comprehensible forms: thus we know what something is. The schema, in contrast, is a set of *a priori* principles, conceptions that are already in the mind: they inform us about what something *means*. Kant's assumption was that, in knowing, *it is not the mind that conforms to things, but things conform to the mind*. This means that a fixed and immutable reality does not exist somewhere "out there" and, thus, cannot determine the nature of the individual's perception. Rather, the nature of that external reality is inevitably shaped by the explanatory categories of the individual's mind. Simply put, the human mind is not an empty screen on which the features of reality can be projected with faithful exactitude. Out of life lived and the experiences that build into one's learning, the person creates his own premises and categories of meaning that are employed to make sense of his encounters.

In effect, the interpretive product of the schema, the idea, is the end-point of a phase of thinking. The base impressions gained through consciousness of and attention to a particular stimulus are converted by thought into personally comprehensible and certain concepts. The schema, comprising the person's essential premises, converts this knowledge into ideas containing distinctly personal meanings. As Rychlak states, the schema is inherently conservative; insofar as a frame of preexisting premises is placed onto an experience, the limits of what can be known about that experience is fixed and predictable.[19]

Examples of the conservative role of the schema abound in all aspects of daily living. The extent to which we are constrained by our underlying premises is evident each time people confront an occurrence and find that they are either gratified by a shared understanding or perplexed or frustrated by their conflicting versions. Let me cite a special case that is marked by the expectation that the actors in this instance would, on the basis of their knowledge and commitments, share a kindred outlook relative to their common cause—progressive changes in education.

Benjamin DeMott has written an account of four citizens' meetings on federal educational policy. The meetings were held "to engage a broad range of citizens . . . in shaping recommendations for the development of educational policy for all societal agencies involved in the teaching and learning process."[20] There were about 120 participants representing a standard American cross-section. Ostensibly, they were people of good-will, involved in and committed to the creation of a better world. DeMott describes what happens when personal doctrines collide.

He first refers to an afternoon devoid of progress and full of repetition of old slogans "where worlds of discourse already overexplored would be scratched as virgin soil."

. . . the incident confirmed at last that the professional part of us is not necessarily inferior in what it produces or contributes in this sort of setting to the 'My Credo' part of us. . . . Fantasists that we were, we had assumed that the presence of difference near at hand wouldn't fail to entice men and women to come forward from themselves, forward toward their unwritten chapters. Error one.

DeMott's second error was his assumption that the "doers of the world, the improvers . . . cannot but introduce into a mixed assemblage qualities of flexibility that teach and refine by example."

For every expert . . . silencing his best self for a chance at the My Credo organ, there was another expert clinging to what he knew with a holy fury and dealing damnation round the land to those who knew something else. . . . Men and women on hobbyhorses are not much interested in interdependency, contradiction, complication. You say minority problems don't exist in Denmark? You say vitamins won't heal the disease of self-contempt? You say conquering self-contempt requires a (dangerous) mobilization of the resources of hatred? Ah, replies Dr. Hobbyhorse witheringly, but you don't *understand,* you are an outsider. As the ego-undertone becomes insistent, a blade of contempt begins swishing from side to side: I *am* Headstart, you see, it was my *idea.* I am a philosopher king. I have been to Denmark, my man, I am a fellow of Cambridge College. I am the people, I am *street wise,* do not question this knowledge so remote from your own.

And so DeMott sums up:

I wake up a little now. I see that molecular deeds are nothing unless the doer feels, registers, publicly insists upon the difference between the frail impulses from which the deeds spring and the infinitely more powerful habitual under-standings within himself—the unexamined feelings, the numberless unregis-tered acceptance of things as they are—that are forever obliterating true imagin-ings of change, forever insinuating that the true arena of change lies Out There, not within, Out There in the arrangements.

Indirectly, DeMott refers to the schema in operation but he calls it "My Credo." It is at the pit of any substantial disagreement—marital, ideological, political, procedural, or even in debate about how objective statistical numbers ought to be interpreted. For within the schema lies our latent categories, our premises about what I, you, and the world are all about. It persists over time, not only as a fixed map of reality but also as an indelible justification and verification of the realness of self.

As a hypothetical version of this function of the mind, the schema is a further expression of the self in transaction with its world of things, events, sensations, and relations. It involves one's self-identity since it contains one's acquired beliefs as well as the assimilated convictions of one's social group and culture. In that it embodies the individual's critical values and ideologies the schema also reveals the self as it is extended into the world of causes and ideals. It is obviously an assertion of the rational self since it expresses a cognitive appreciation of reality. Above all, it is an echo of the phenomenal self or self-image since one's standards, ideas of competency, rightness, and worth are contained in how the person ultimately explains the things that make up his existence.

The concept of the schema should not be confused with attitudes. Attitudes are the more general inclinations we feel toward or about something, tendencies that are not securely rooted in the essential self. A person may hold several varying attitudes about any one thing and may also change any one or all without any changes in the self. Attitude change is a relatively comfortable accommodative mechanism since it enables the individual to maneuver through his world without having to modify his self-image, roles, or values to any great extent.

In contrast, the schema represents a complex of emotion, value, and reason—a commitment to singular constructions of reality. This form of mentation is related to the process of principle learning or the means by which we integrate knowledge and value as guides to action. Because of its potency, this combination of mental categories comes to characterize the individual and thus provides the clues that others use to relate to him. Without any pronouncements we "know" and can even predict how someone with whom we are familiar will react in a given situation. We respond to this person according to how he does to us, and in this way we create the peculiar patterns of our relationship that differ from the patterns of our other relationships. The chances are good that a relationship will work when two people value or at least respect each other's frames of reference.

An example showing the growth of alienation and difference involves a meeting that I had with a group of teachers to discuss ways of dealing with a youngster whose incorrigible behavior had brought him to the brink of expulsion. This was by no means a casual consultation; believing that they had already overextended themselves, the teachers were searching for a forceful solution to their dilemma. We reviewed the more apparent facts including the parents' apathy, the long history of academic failure, and the boy's disturbing behaviors. Then the teachers eagerly volunteered their impressions of what they saw as the problem.

The first described the youngster in absolute and unequivocal terms. Designations such as "evil," "bad," and "malicious," crept into what was otherwise a controlled appraisal of the boy as the teacher narrated many instances to show how he seemed to insist on violating one rule after another.

The second teacher apologetically broke into this account wanting to say that he, too, was frustrated, but his frustration occurred because the youngster seemed unable to relate properly to the other children and continually disrupted the friendly climate of the classroom. He went on to explain that it was essential that each student recognize that he or she is, in the final analysis, just a single citizen within an educational community and should relate to others in an appropriate way.

The third teacher speculated about what must be going on in the mind of this unhappy boy: how must he feel trying to come to terms with his repeated failures? She spoke of the teen years and the difficulty any youngster has in attempting to find his own identity—a special problem for this boy because he had always been a loser. She wondered whether some additional psychological help might point him in a more productive direction.

The last teacher had been listening with a kind of tolerant patience. She courteously ignored the others' ideas and suggestions and observed that we really ought to get back to the reality of this boy's problems. She recited the facts of the case. His IQ score was quite low, and it was reflected in his achievement tests. The boy was warned a number of times, had been sent to the principal's office on five known occasions, and had been placed on detention at least once a week over the past few months. Then, after reviewing the data, she observed that sufficient facts were at hand to make an intelligent judgment about the best course of action.

Here, then, were four experienced and serious professionals, each addressing an issue of common concern in a thoughtful fashion. But beyond the shared acknowledgment that a problem did exist each offered a somewhat different meaning of the same phenomenon. Although they all spoke the same language, their respective portraits of the boy were diverse enough to suggest that perhaps the problem was shared by them only in terms of its severity and not by its quality.

Were these natural differences—merely the varied opinions of a number of experts called together to brainstorm a particular issue? I think not, for more than a casual opinion was at stake. The social context prescribed that their feelings would need to be couched in the lexicon of their educational roles; evidence of deep personal concern appeared, in their careful approximations of the problem, indicating that their respective conceptions of self were somehow entangled in their professional roles and this boy had succeeded in undermining feelings of competency. In terms of the operations of the schema the overtones of their respective statements contained the message: "This is how *I* see the problem, what it means to *me*, and what *I* know needs to be done!"

The first teacher used what could be called an *ethical* or *moral* category that judges behavior in polar terms. This outlook involves a set of personal criteria about what is "right" and what is "wrong," what is "good," "bad," "evil," or "virtuous." As in all personal schemata, this is not merely an intellectual judgment based on thoughtful logic; it shows a powerful sentiment that expresses the ideals and standards of the self-image. It proclaims a quality of self that is committed to precise beliefs and values about how people ought to act—and the penalties that violations should incur.

The second teacher interpreted the same problem with a *social* or *interpersonal* cast. Here behavior is interpreted in relational terms, its meaning dependent on the effect it has on others or on the social context. This interpretation can have humanistic implications or it may reflect the perceiver's reliance on others' thoughts and feelings for an adequate self-concept. This frame of reference may represent self-extension, a deep concern for the welfare of others, or self-enhancement in the need for others' approval.

The third teacher's version of the problem was a product of a schema that arranged reality according to *psychological* or *intrapersonal* premises. This view finds meanings in the needs and motives that may be indicative of any of a number of the strivings of the self; for example, a tendency toward self-reflection and introspection, a willingness to feel with and identify with others' inner needs, or a desire to excuse behavior because of its compelling interior determinants.

The fourth teacher revealed a rather intellectual frame of reference that stripped the problem of its affective elements and reduced it to a neat and precise skeleton. The rational self is in control, again for a number of possible purposes: to verify a position of competence and authority, to overrule the emergence of latent frustration or anger, or to ward off the emotional insinuations of the other teachers.

These illustrations show only one aspect of an otherwise complex human event. They serve the purpose of explaining how, in a situation where something personally important is at stake, the individual will resort to an established belief system that at once acts to verify the substance of the self and the appraisal of the episode. These examples do not exhaust the kinds of categories that people use. One may fall back on an aesthetic schema that captures reality in terms of perceived form, relations, and composition as well as its elegance, style, and beauty. A *politically oriented* schema would interpret certain events in regard to matters of power, ascendency, influence, or conflict. An *economic* or *utilitarian* schema would tend to evaluate things in relation to their worth, possible gain, or practical functions. This brings to mind an ongoing conflict between a father and son. The son is proud of his coin collection as specimens of the art of minting. His father, on the other hand, can only see their value as an investment. Each feels grossly misunderstood and rebuffed by the other. There are also associative frames that resist classification. These are the ways of interpreting the real world in highly autistic or symbolic forms that are idiosyncratic to the person and probably undecipherable to others. We can also surmise that the open and responsive perceiver differs from the more rigid and narrowly focused person by the ease with which he is able to shift from one associative frame to another depending on the nature of the experience.

The power of the schema is at the core of all meaningful human relations. The family in its vital form can be seen as an interdependent group of people striving to secure a degree of validation of their individual categorical definitions of the nature of their common reality. For that matter, even the outwardly stolid bureaucratic organization can be riven by intense disagreements that are only superficially related to factual issues. Whether we label this interpretive function of the mind as a schema, as "My Credo," as a weltanschauung, or as a personal frame of reference, it is important to be aware of the special human need to re-form aspects of our universe into meanings that are ultimately tied to conceptions of self. In Nietzsche's terms, "If we have our own *why* of life, we shall get along with almost any *how*."

The Shaping of Cognitive Patterns

The organizing and interpreting functions in perception are obviously interdependent. At the moment we order our impressions into a particular conceptual form certain meanings become evident. If we rely on convergent thinking to organize an image of something, that something will be appreciated in a way different from the conclusions of divergent thought. As I grant my own special meaning to a perception, I am also organizing that perception in some way. If, for example, I regard a winter's storm within an aesthetic frame and see nature's splendor, I will think in terms of its poetry and beauty—concepts that place the elements into a special configuration. If, however, the meaning of the event is more utilitarian, I will be attentive to rather different concepts. It is from this peculiar blending of reasoning and interpreting that the unique cognitive patterns of the individual come to be shaped. And when we consider the role of the variables that affect the initial impression (the level of consciousness, the nature of attention, and the individual's response to the social environment), it becomes clear why the perceptual episode can be a singularly idiosyncratic experience.

If we carry this premise to its logical extreme, we would have to conclude that each individual exists, to one degree or another, alone and in the midst of his own version of reality. In significant ways he is isolated from all others. Because each person perceives his world in his own unique manner, what he takes out of that world will in some ways be alien to others. In this regard, a certain "strangeness" exists between people even when there is the shared desire to know, love, and understand. No matter how intensely driven I am to know you, I will in some way be frustrated. Even the slight variations in our respective perceptual lenses mean that we will experience one another in somewhat disparate ways. The extent to which I come to know you better will change your outlook in some ways that then require new understandings on my part.

The curious architecture of the mind comprising private and hidden places as well as common and shared quarters reflects the dialectical nature of the self. The separateness of an individual's versions of reality is at once essential and intolerable. It is essential insofar as the person needs to come to terms with and value what is unique to him. Yet, without meaningful human association his uniqueness risks becoming transformed into alienation. Although the individual must preserve his personal divinations of reality, he needs to seek the authentication of self found only in the responses of other significant persons. But how is authentication possible if individual perceptual schemes are at such variance? Sartre wrote on "intersubjectivity":

. . . through the *I think* we reach our own self in the presence of others, and the others are just as real to us as our own self. Thus, the man who becomes aware of himself through the *cogito* also perceives all others, and he perceives them as the condition of his own existence.
He realizes that he cannot be anything (in the sense that we say that someone is

171

witty or nasty or jealous) unless others recognize it as such. In order to get any truth about myself, I must have contact with another person. . . . In discovering my inner being I discover the other person at the same time, like a freedom placed in front of me which thinks and wills only for or against me. Hence, let us at once announce the discovery of a world which we shall call intersubjectivity; this is the world in which man decides what he is and what others are.[21]

Sartre does not nullify the importance of the person's private and unique conceptions of reality. Intersubjectivity implies that a linking of consciousness is willed wherein each "decides what he is and others are." This linking and deciding is neither absolute nor final but is Katherine Mansfield's "act of faith."

Adaptive Implications

Since we are dependent on others' perceptions for the confirmation and authentication of self, we also face the risk that our intersubjectivity (our shared beliefs) may fail. The intersubjective relationship may be willed but it cannot be controlled; once I demand that you must define me and my reality in my terms then our shared consciousness vanishes. By this act I deprive you of the freedom to express your own reality. Thus, the individual who ventures to voice his personal conceptions, particularly those that are assertive or unconventional, risks the possibility of inviting challenge or outright disconfirmation.

How do we come to cope with the vicissitudes that are characteristic of serious human relationships? Perceptual processes take on an adaptive function, and they become purposeful and patterned means by which the individual manages the tenuous nature of his reality. Cognitive styles are the manifestation of a configuration of receptive, organizational, and interpretive mechanisms, and they are also shaped by the purpose they serve in enabling the individual to maintain a degree of self-esteem and equilibrium.

If an individual finds that he is unable to respond in a straightforward way to what he perceives as disagreement or disconfirmation, what sort of perceptual tactics might he employ? The simplest response pattern is a reflexive attempt to deny that his conceptions of the reality in question are in any way erroneous. The most flagrant act would be to totally ignore and close off the incoming threat. Here the incoming message is short-circuited at the attentional level and not allowed into awareness; or the individual may recognize the message but refuse to register it in his mind either by not ascribing any meaning to it or mislabeling it (e.g., "No, he wasn't angry because I was late again—his wife probably gave him a bad time").

Denial can also take a behavioral form when the individual actively removes himself from the threatening situation. Although withdrawal is likely to generate other conflicts, the person is able to maintain a measure of stability by not having to attend to and deal with the imminent challenges to his beliefs. Or he may resort to such ploys as "I refuse to argue with you. If you persist, I will leave this house!"

Shrewder and more devious styles of denial involve the use of external supports or purposeful attempts at the manipulation of the relationship itself. It is possible to turn to certain ultimate authorities (Freud, Spock, or the Bible) to substantiate one's beliefs, using a form of intellectual overkill to negate the threat. Or, one can employ various gambits that serve to exploit whatever is vulnerable about the relationship, (e.g., the oblique or tangentializing tactic that diverts the basic thrust of the perceived opponent: "You really are out to get me!" "I knew all along that you really didn't love me." "Why do you always have to be right?"). Such tactics place the other person in a defensive position and succeed in evading the central issue. Similarly, one could also draw attention to an irrelevant matter ("All this stuff is giving me a headache!") and throw the challenger off balance.

An individual's patterns may be of a more accommodative quality. In its more passive and primitive form, this pattern is analogous to the tropistic response of an amoeba. When confronted with a challenge to one's cognitions, the individual quickly acknowledges the possibility that his version of reality is wrong thereby voiding what must feel like an assault on the self. However, this change is made without conviction or learning; in point of fact, one's preoccupation with fear and survival needs diminishes the possibility of gaining any useful awareness of self or the surrounding world. The individual seems fixed in a convergent way of thinking and his frame of reference remains focused on control.

The *labile* personality described by Mehrabian is similar in that the thought patterns of such people are marked by inconsistency, vacillation, and instability. [22] Outwardly the person's reactions to stress appear to be random and unpredictable; actually his responses, even though groping and incongruous, are painful attempts to rescue a semblance of self-rectitude.

A more selective version of this pattern is accommodation to external threat by changing only a narrow aspect of one's view of reality so as to leave the gestalt intact. In this instance personality is marked by its rigidity rather than by its lability; by making slight accommodative shifts the individual can continue to maintain the same well-worn perceptual organization of reality. Moreover, this tactic serves to frustrate and control other members of the relationship. Since the person is acting as if he were agreeable, he can no longer be charged with being deviant. This "as if" is common in many marital or parent-child relationship problems that thwart resolution. A mother, for example, pleads with her husband to take more responsibility for the discipline and guidance of their children. The father perceives this as a threat to his self-image and does what is requested of him, not out of awareness of his children's needs, but to repair the break in the relationship. His wife is deluded into believing that a change has occurred, her criticism diminishes, and her husband returns to his rigid pattern—the frustrating cycle continues.

It is important to note the kinds of patterns that allow for learning and growth. Mehrabian refers to the *flexible* personality. The individual is able to reflect on and reorder his cognitions without loss to the wholeness of self and is also open to learning and an increase in self-esteem. This quality of responsiveness is not without some disturbance, particularly when the individual realizes that his primary vision or frame of reference is either neglecting or distorting some critical facts. Thus, he finds that he must shift from one style of thinking to another, say, from convergent to divergent, or from one category of thought to another to alter his formerly secure version of reality.

This sort of flexibility (and its accompanying strains) is best illustrated by the bright, sensitive, and potentially creative learner within any of the human services fields. He enters the educational experience with a world view that is often fixed within an ethical or moral framework. His notions about the social reality are governed by a number of "oughts" and "shoulds" in relation to personal and social matters. Quite possibly these highly idealistic values and beliefs about the nature of social living influenced his career choice in the first place.

As a student-practitioner, his first contacts with his clients are likely to be colored by his moralistic schema. He may have some difficulty in managing his righteous judgments or in overreacting may withhold opinion altogether. But with experience and new knowledge the beginnings of more relevant frames of reference come into being. If he is clinically oriented, a psychological structure begins to complement but not supplant his philosophical frame. If his field is social change, a sociological orientation may come into being. With experience, growth, and security his schematic understanding of human realities begins to expand. The psychological schema is enlarged by an appreciation of the importance of interpersonal, social, and systemic factors; the sociological schema comes to include the significance of individual needs and motivations.

It should be apparent that the experience does not unfold in this neat and additive manner. Intellect plays a large but not necessarily dominant part in this kind of personal learning. The process is marked by periods of upheaval and doubt when secure and persuasive convictions are shattered either by convincing new data or by what is learned from encounters with the exceptional qualities of his clients' existence. Most important, the flexible student learns something about learning: the immense value in being aware of the limits and constraints of one's own perceptual scheme. He discovers the advantages and limitations of convergent thinking, risks divergent explorations of the human experience, and appreciates that the complexity of social reality cannot be encapsulated in single frames and concepts. He may then go on to apprehend the politics as well as the aesthetics of interpersonal and social processes. It is this new capability for perceiving the human situation through new prisms of meaning that makes for the integration of the personal and professional selves than can lead to a more creative and humanistic quality of practice.

These patterns of adaptation suggest something more than the abstract idea of "defense mechanisms." People perceive reality in peculiar ways in defense of the self; however, these patterns are neither reflexive responses nor unconscious mechanisms that are reactive to a given threat. They are learned choices reflecting the manner in which the person has come to understand and perceive his I-world relations.

SUMMARY

In order to study the intricacies of the perceiving self, it was necessary to partialize an essentially holistic and integrated process. As it is experienced, perception is irreducible. It is a phenomenon that can neither be subtracted from or divided since it is constantly in flux—influenced by what has come before and the expectations of what might follow.

As perception is aroused, the object of interest is not apprehended in a one-to-one fashion. The rich and varied nature of human consciousness makes it possible to incorporate the stimulus on a number of levels of awareness—sensory, imaginal, behavioral, and so on. The attentional process involves other modulating influences (the social field, the state of the perceiver, mind set, vigilance, and filtering) which assure that the perceiver will grasp only selected segments of the total event and, therefore, will have only a biased appreciation of it.

As the perceptual process continues, cognitive patterns convert the original rudimentary impressions into conceptual forms that explain something to the perceiver. If convergent thought patterns are used, the derived concept will be relatively narrow and specific and suggest fairly precise implications. If divergent thought patterns are used, the original impressions may be elaborated into a complex of conceptual forms and implications. These transformations take place within certain categories of thought (the schema), the means by which the individual ascribes his own meanings and interpretations to the derived concept. This complex process does not unfold in a linear fashion like the operations of a preprogrammed computer. Given the nature of the particular perceptual event and what the person has at stake in it, the perceptual process may be modulated to suit the individual's adaptive needs.

In this phenomenological perspective, perception is understood as a creative act by which each individual constructs his own rendition of reality. These personal versions often conform to a consensual view of reality. Because our species is endowed with homogeneous neurophysiology, we are able to register in our brains and minds relatively similar impressions of the same reality. Because learning and language are acquired in similar ways, we are able to communicate with one another by the use of common symbols that are mutually understood—at least in literal terms. Because we undergo analogous socializing experiences, we tend to interpret our perceptions in accord with a compatible value system.

Despite these homologous conditions that allow for social participation and interaction, certain aspects of the self remain private and secluded from public view. No matter how closely we are thrown together, no matter how desperately we seek intimacy, there is a certain inevitability that important parts of an otherwise shared reality cannot be expressed or be understood by others. Paradoxically, this estrangement may be the source of a meaningful and intimate relationship, particularly when people care enough to try to appreciate another's exceptional versions of self and his world. This estrangement should not be confused with alienation. The former is an inescapable condition of our existence. It means that we need to come to terms with the inevitability of our separateness out of which we come to value the special nature of our distinct identities. Alienation, on the other hand, may represent the denial of one's essential individuality and may intensify when the individual chooses to remold his valued conceptions so that they will conform with a uniform, collective, or socially prescribed version or reality.

As it is defined here, perception is central to the process of human adaptation. It is a concept that helps link psychological and sociological explanations of behavior insofar as it connects inner processes of inference and meaning with the nature of the social situation and begins to make sense of the coping behavior that ensues. It is important to add that this view is in the tradition of the gestaltist and subjectivist position on human behavior that has emerged in previous decades.[23]

Chapter 6
The Social Consequences of Personal Adaptation

The idea of personal adaptation as an expression of the subjective perceptual experience goes only so far in explaining the multi-sided nature of human behavior. Personal adaptation needs to be considered as a social and transactional phenomenon as well as an individual act. Typically, adaptive behaviors are played out in some kind of interpersonal or societal setting. In these circumstances, the person's behavior may be understood as an objective social act that is observable and subject to the reaction of others. When people conduct their business of living in comfortable and amicable family, work, or friendship groups, it is quite likely that their behaviors will be casually accepted or encouraged. If this is the case, the individual needs only to make some simple adjustments from time to time in order to assure the stability of his role and relations with his group.

This benign view of personal and social adaptation fails, however, when the individual's manner of dealing with his world somehow falls out of accord with the expectations and requirements of his group. At these times he risks disapproval in any of its many forms and the possibility that he might be judged a deviant. The kind of censure he receives from others or what he tells himself when discord arises is bound to have certain serious implications for his attempt to cling to a degree of integrity and to find other productive solutions to his immediate or long-range problems of living. These are the critical points where social learning and change may be the means by which effective solutions may be achieved.

The purpose of this chapter is to give careful study to the transactional (social-personal) problems of adaptation and their implications for planned change. Attention will be given to the three major components of any social act, including the characteristics of the person (self), significant others and their expectations and needs, and the normative features of the surrounding social field.

THE SELF AND ITS ADAPTIVE FUNCTIONS

As an explanatory concept, self offers a useful way of understanding the individual in his pursuit of his valued objectives and self-fulfillment. Accordingly, the concept of adaptation stands for the self-styled manner in which the individual contends with the endogenous or external conditions that he perceives as aids or obstacles in his progress toward his valued goals. What is meant by self-fulfillment is subject to a number of interpretations. Salvatore Maddi distinguishes between two major versions of this human motive. There is the "biological blueprint" notion espoused by Carl Rogers and Abraham Maslow, which defines fulfillment as the actualization of innate potentials. In this view, the individual is able to realize his latent capabilities only as his deficiency needs (well-being, safety, and affiliation) are met. Although Gordon Allport does not minimize the implications of deficiency needs for survival, he argues that the striving for fulfillment also expresses the person's ideals about excellence and his beliefs about what will make his life meaningful and worthwhile. The meaning of life is not determined by biology alone, but by the images, ideals, and esteem that define the self. [1]

A cognitive perspective on human behavior incorporates both the biological and idealistic conceptions of self-fulfillment. However, it also takes account of the risks that often accompany the attempt to amplify the meaning of one's existence. Active realization of self is rarely a simple and straightforward enterprise; such serious changes may well jeopardize the security of the self.

Recall that the self is somewhat *ambivalent* insofar as it attempts to reconcile its protean and conservative tendencies. In one respect, the self is exceptionally versatile in its ability to accommodate to the number and

179

variety of different demands that are typical of ordinary living. At the same time, the self expresses its conservative qualities as it attempts to forestall the possibility of fragmentation. The extent to which the individual is able to tolerate the tension aroused by the two forces depends on his self image—the experienced sense of worth, unity, and authenticity. A relatively secure self-image supports movement towards one's prized goals in a freer and more vigorous manner. A self-image that is flawed by doubt and depreciation predicts a cautious, temperate, or possibly regressive response to the potentiality of these goals.

Analogously, the self can be viewed as an *open system* relative to the manner in which it copes with the range of incoming challenges to its integrity. The person's success in maintaining an adequate degree of wholeness and constancy depends on his ability to organize and reorganize his inner state in response to the strains of daily living. His freedom to pursue self-fulfilling objectives will vary with the extent to which he is open to new alternatives and experiences. Inner flexibility and responsiveness allows for the reception of new inputs of information about the world and what it has to offer. Inner rigidity or a preoccupation with the maintenance of status quo obviously reduces this possibility.

A third perspective illuminates the strains that are engendered by the *intentional* attributes of the self. Should the individual contemplate relinquishing an indifferent but predictable way of life in favor of some valued but indefinite aspirations, he must then contend with a number of troubling and elusive uncertainties. Questions of personal competency and worth may raise doubts about his ability to fulfill his ambitions and whether he really deserves to achieve them. Should he decide to give in to these doubts, what are the personal costs of renouncing his commitments? If he is convinced that he can achieve the desired goal, he will need to consider the possible consequences of his strivings, particularly if they appear to be in opposition to the values of his close associates. Given the contingencies that are bound to come into being, the individual must, above all, consider whether he possesses the courage and hope to see him through his venture.

These ambivalent, systemic, and intentional qualities represent a self that is simultaneously a *state of being* and a *process*. State of being refers to the more or less enduring attributes of the person that allow him to claim a certain identity. A more familiar term is *personality*, or the configuration of traits, characteristics, and attitudes that tend to distinguish a particular individual. The idea of the self in process may be more difficult to entertain. It stands for the mutable nature of the self, the ability to adapt, grow, and reorganize as one moves forward into an unpredictable future. Adaptation that is something more than a matter of resignation or conformity implies that one's state of being stands in a complementary relationship with the self in process. Self-fulfillment becomes an alternative to habit or stagnation when a sense of personal unity and identity frees the self to redefine and re-form its substance as assertive living requires; conversely, the freedom to risk change serves to enrich one's quality of being. However, since adaptation is a dialectical social experience and not a unilateral set of actions, further clarification is required.

THE ADAPTIVE EXPERIENCE

We can begin to examine the complexity of social adaptation by the use of a graphic view of the elements of the self and their relation to any situational event in Figure 3.

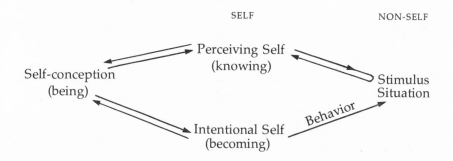

FIGURE 3. A Paradigm of the Self

The self as a whole is separated from whatever may be called the non-self by an irregular broken line indicating that this division is ambiguous. The non-self can be anything that is experienced as being apart from what is consciously perceived as self. In Jamesian terms, this would be the differentiation of what is "not Me" from what "I know is me."[2]

This division is quite rational and defensible in one respect. Through the use of our senses we are able to distinguish those things that are outside of ourselves: we can see and hear others who are separate from us; we can smell, touch, and taste things and thus objectify them. We are also able to differentiate ourselves from other objects and events by the use of categories and concepts that create a quality of distance. Thus, in saying or thinking "That is a chair," or "He is Bob," we are able to create a dichotomy between ourselves and the thing that is named. Even our emotions may be experienced as phenomena that are alien to our being. The forbidden or disturbing feelings, such as malice, lethal intent, or erotic fantasy, that arise into consciousness may be disclaimed. We might dismiss them as "something that is happening to me," a temporary possession of sorts that is humorously but not insignificantly expressed in the quip: "The devil made me do it!"

The broken line in the paradigm also indicates that the self and non-self are not always clearly divided, particularly in the case of human relationships. In a good part of the business of living, we are quite conscious of our separateness from others. When we contemplate our special identity, physical image, the roles that we enact, and the history we have lived, we are aware of the many ways in which we are uniquely different. Moreover, others define us as being different for their own reasons. We are sometimes brought up short by the realization that our beliefs and values are indeed peculiar enough to estrange us from most others. We may find ourselves looking out into a social world that seems somewhat foreign.

If fortunate, we may enter into experiences that seem to dissolve the boundaries between ourselves and others. The idea that consciousness of the world is not limited by the senses or by rational mechanisms means that we can experience a sense of intimacy with another and create a fusion of selves that eradicates detachment. This is Martin Buber's concept of the I—Thou, the ultimate blending of separate selves resulting in a deeper realization of each individual self. The person who has undergone an intense and profound revelatory or religious experience will also claim that he has found a sense of communion with others or with a spiritual essence.

In the final analysis, the divisibility of self and non-self becomes a moot question, particularly within the subjectivist and cognitive orientation. Arthur Koestler's *Janus: A Summing Up* offers some insight into this matter. As a critic of behavioral psychology and the physical science, Koestler committed himself to destroying the myth of reductionism, the idea that "all human activities can be 'reduced' to the behavioral responses of lower animals. . . ."[3] He wrote:

The single individual constitutes the apex of the organismic hierarchy, and at the same time the lowest unit of the social hierarchy. Looking inward, he sees himself as a self-contained, unique whole, looking outward as a dependent part. No man is an island, he is a holon. His *self-assertive* tendency is the dynamic manifestation of his unique wholeness as an individual; his *integrative* tendency expresses his dependence on the larger whole to which he belongs, his partness. Under normal conditions, the two opposite tendencies are more or less evenly balanced. Under conditions of stress, the equilibrium is upset, as manifested in emotional behavior.[4]

Self-assertiveness and integration can be seen as human tendencies that are both polar and interdependent. We can say that a duality does exist; each individual is autonomous and separate from all others. Yet, there is also the unity that arises out of the need to be part of a social whole. This need at times obscures the sense of duality and confuses the boundaries separating self from important others.

Figure 3 also depicts the *stimulus situation,* which is included to comply with the premise that the self is revealed and becomes subject to understanding in its relation to some situation. Again, what we speak of as the self is not a remote abstraction but the individual in active expression in relation to a life experience.

Perceiving, self-concept, and intention are shown (Figure 3) in a reciprocal and interdependent relationship. This is represented by the two-directional arrows indicating that the state of any one aspect is affected by the states of the other two. The perceptual processes link the inner self with the outer situation; however, a feedback loop shows that perception is not unidirectional. Although we may respond to certain stimuli in a reflexive manner, the ability to process incoming information means that the person is capable of checking and altering his initial impressions of the event. Thus, upon entering a room full of people engaged in conversation, my first perception may leave me with the impression that I am an intruder or that I am being ignored. Reference to self-esteem, past experiences or other data would impel me to survey the situation again and attend to details or conditions that my frame of reference excluded.

Feedback also occurs in a perception → action → perception sequence. The transactional circuit between self and situation is effected by the person's response to the event (the arrow moving from the intentional self outward in Figure 3). As one's motives find expression in some behavior or even non-response to the stimulus, the situation is altered in some ways that may change the initial impression and set another process in motion.

The Components of Self

The three aspects of self derive from and are extrapolations of the eight aspects of Allport's proprium (Table 2). Some of them have more in common with one another than they do with the rest, particularly when the self is thought of in functional and active terms. One cluster embodies the phenomenal nature of the self; another cluster includes certain motivational and conative inclinations; a third encompasses cognitive and rational faculties.

The reflective self appears twice since it is germane to both aspects. The reflective self is integral to one's self-concept inasmuch as it is through the ability to reflect that we arrive at judgments about personal worth, morality, competence, and value; and the tendency to stand back and reflect on our impressions enables us to consider and assess their meanings and implications.

SELF CONCEPT Self concept can be thought of in its literal sense since it refers to the mental picture that the individual holds about himself. It is not a permanently fixed portrait, despite the tendency some have to cling

TABLE 2. Three Aspects of Self

SELF-CONCEPT	INTENTIONAL SELF	PERCEIVING SELF
Bodily image	Self-enhancement	Rational processes
Identity	Self-extension	Reflective self
Self-image	Propriate strivings	
Reflective self		

obstinately to a personal version. It is more of a "collage," because the self concept can also be understood as a composite of a number of referents that stand in odd and changing relationships.

Basically, a conception of self is influenced by the physical basis on which a consciousness of being depends. It is not the physical actuality of our being in itself that influences a conception of self but the images that we hold in our mind about our bodies. Fundamentally, we know little about our anatomies except in rather abstract or intellectual terms. Our bodies enclose vital organs, muscles, and a skeletal structure, but these elements are not directly apparent to us. If we think about them at all, we must imagine how this thing we call our body is operating.

Even the impressions we form about our outward appearance are not clearly objective. Each time we look into a mirror what we see is a reverse image, and we can be disconcerted when a photograph reveals what we really look like. The most revealing parts of the body (face, eyes, and mouth) are least apparent to us in our daily encounters with the world. Others who have much greater access to our countenance and demeanor are sometimes better able to inform us about our feelings and attitudes than we are ourselves. Even if we were able to achieve a representative picture of our physical makeup, it would still be biased by the norms and standards of our culture and the prevailing ideas about attractiveness and desirability as well as statistical standards of weight, size, and bodily proportions. The process of aging also markedly affects how we feel about our appearance, because of the significant role of impressions of one's physical state. At any rate, bodily image is the substance of the self concept even though it is not entirely durable or dependable.

Personal identity embodies the many characteristics that are uniquely our own, the elements of the self that distinguish each of us from all that might be considered the non-self. Identity is also a part of our integrative tendencies—the need to become part of some larger group. Identity joins with the images of our physical state to shape the more evident indicators of the person's self concept. We tend to define ourselves and are defined by others through images of appearance and identity.

Lying at the core of the self concept are self-image and self-reflection. These are the most private and securely guarded facets of the self and are the last to be revealed even in the most intimate and reliable relationships.

They involve an individual's ultimate judgments that bear on his sense of worth and deservingness—his pride along with his guilt and shame.

Self concept assumes a central role in the more serious choices and pursuits of living. One's self-esteem, sense of power, attractiveness and affiliations critically influence how the person defines, deals with, and judges his problems of living. Self-concept can be said to be equivalent to the *executive* functions of the self.

INTENTIONAL SELF   The intentional self involves the motive and forward moving tendencies concerned with the goals and purposes of existence. The most elemental and self-serving of these tendencies is the need for self-enhancement, because it is the search for fulfillment that the self alone cannot provide. It cries out for gratification of survival needs and the need for approval, love, and respect. It seeks the objects and conditions that add pleasure and meaning to existence.

Self-extensive tendencies are those that impel a person to become part of something deemed valuable and significant. It is apparent in the way we are able to invest our selves into the things that have only limited value. We become "part" of a powerful car, our house and its furnishings, and the accumulation of money. We are personally affronted or feel ourselves attacked when others criticize our choices, tastes, or acquisitions. In its affiliative form, the ability of the self to extend outward involves our relationships and the need to become a meaningful part of another's or some others' existence. This need may be possessive ("*my* wife" or "*my* friend"), or it may be integrative, as when one gives to and shares with another. Self-extension may take something approaching an altruistic form in cases where the individual invests himself in and commits himself to particular causes, belief systems, or ideologies. Propriate striving is a considerably more radical motive because it stands for the search for uncommon goals representing more than the usual requirements of living. They may involve a pursuit of meaning or purpose peculiar to the individual, which may transcend the common objectives of life. Such goals may symbolize the desire to exercise and realize talents or abilities not yet put to the test. Such striving is relatively rare, and it is often regarded as heroic in that it reflects a willingness to risk the uncertainties of the search and to contend with unknown outcomes.

Any or all of the three motivational tendencies can be understood as the *self-determining* function of the self having to do with final ends and values. Behavior becomes meaningful when it is "for the sake of" something. It may be argued that people often do not choose their own goals and that the pressures and constraints of the social order are the determinants of the individual's aspirations. Although this is a common state of affairs, choice and intention are no less a part of these circumstances: The person is still acting "for the sake of" something. The goal may be the rewards of conformity, avoidance of ridicule, or relief from responsibility, but it is a valued end to which the individual is moving, even though passively. Determining not to determine obviously creates certain goals.

PERCEIVING SELF   In addition to its receptive, organizing, and interpreting faculties, the perceiving self has the role of reflection, which is the turning inward of the perceptual process to monitor the self and its purposes. Together, these faculties comprise the *rational* and *cognitive* functions of the self that connect the inner being with the field of existence and create meaning out of experience. "Rational" refers to the mental processes by which the person comes to reason, judge, recall, compare, analyze, and synthesize. In a broad cognitive sense, it also involves intuitive tendencies, imagery, and the ability to project one's self into alien types of thought. Cognitive functions of the mind are not restricted to intellect, logic, and analysis; they also embody the extensive dimensions of human awareness.

Implications

Figure 3 is an attempt to map the personal-social experience in an effort to understand the person in his social situation. It tries to show Bergson's "indivisible continuity"—not a series of parts. The intrapersonal and interpersonal experience needs to be understood in unitary terms. Yet in order to describe the whole, we are forced to cut into it and reveal its "partial views." But Bergson also said that "with these partial views put end to end, you will not make even a beginning of the reconstruction of the whole."[5]

Inevitably, we are forced to grapple with partial views as a consequence of the limitations of language, thinking, and theory. It is much more convenient to speak of units rather than a process when we attempt to deal with what transpires between people. For example, if I wanted to inform someone fully about a particular parent-child dispute it would seem more natural and it would take less effort to report what the parent (unit) or child (unit) was doing or feeling rather than to attempt to portray the nature and quality of the exchange (process) taking place. And if I attempted to describe this process in transactional terms, where would I cut into it since there are no specific beginnings or endings in persons' transactions? Even if I offered a factual account of their argument it would be an arbitrary segment of their experience that omits antecedent and subsequent events.

In addition to this need to partialize reality so as to communicate intelligibly, we also feel compelled to reinforce our belief that we really understand what we have observed. Such verification often depends on explanations that follow linear or cause-effect thinking because our conclusions are dependent on causes and partializations of reality that are tacitly accepted as truths. One observer of the parent-child incident might report that the mother was angry at the child *because* he refused to obey her wishes. Another might conclude with equal assurance that the child disobeyed his mother *because* she would not listen to him. Each observer could defend his understanding of the episode with righteous conviction because the selectivity of perception permits different but plausible conclusions. However, neither observer is really able to present the "truth" because a causal perspective can capture only the narrow sequence of events.

With these conceptual restraints in mind, I want to attempt to portray some sense of the transactional qualities of adaptation with special emphasis on what occurs when people experience a breakdown in their problem-solving capabilities. As an introduction to a more detailed analysis, a series of propositions will trace the flow, impairment, and social consequences of what can be termed maladaptive behavior.

1. The experience of personal well-being and effectiveness depends on the harmony or symmetry that exists among the three functions of self as the individual interacts with his social and physical world. Although this experience varies relative to changing circumstances, a state of inner congruence means that for the most part, there is sufficient compatibility

in how the person defines himself, his world, and his aspirations. Should a persistent conflict arise among these inner functions, it is likely that the individual will undergo some form of disturbance or dissonance.

2. When such dissonance is felt to be intolerable, the individual will feel impelled to find a solution that will ease his suffering. If he cannot locate the appropriate personal, social, informational, or material resources required to solve the problem and reduce tension and distress, the individual will resort to distorted patterns of thinking and acting as an alternative, resulting in altered premises about reality.

3. These latter patterns may become entrenched and come to characterize the person's orientation to his world, to the extent to which they continue to provide relief. More important, they also serve to invite or evoke certain reactions from significant others in the person's social field and in so doing, tend to reshape his role (often in second-rate terms) and the quality of his relationships.

4. The persistence and intensity of these patterns increase the possibility that the individual will, in some way, come to the attention of relevant community or societal institutions—particularly if they spread beyond the boundaries of his family, group, or proximate community. Should this occur, he will need to adapt to the procedures and expectations of the institution.

5. Depending on how the individual grants authority or is vulnerable to the procedures of the institution, his adaptation may involve certain redefinitions of self, role, relationships, and behavior. A consequence may be the resolution of the original state of dissonance and its social implications (e.g., its effects on marriage, family, or other relationships). But the consequence may also have less salutory implications for the person's autonomy, self-concept, and incentives. In this case, his adaptive potentials are reduced and the foregoing process continues.

It is important to note that the statement "appropriate personal, social, informational, or material resources required to solve the problem" is a pivotal issue in this outline. This may refer to actual lacks within the person, his immediate relationships, or his community; but it can also mean that effective help is indeed available, but for some reason it is not perceived by the person in distress.

Self, Perception, and Learning

Adaptation in the Case of Dissonance

Under normal conditions, the self maintains a relatively steady state as it strives to cope with the predictable and unexpected affairs of living. Stress is held within tolerable limits when the person is able to reorder his perceptions, reflect on his motives and competencies, draw from past experience, modify behavior, and otherwise manage his problems of living.

In more exceptional circumstances, the adversities of living may be experienced as an attack on one's basic security. If the person cannot find the resources, supports, or alternatives required to restore a sense of inner unity, then the threat to integrity is compounded by feelings of failure, anxiety, somatic disturbances, or other signs of distress. In these instances, radical means are required to preserve at least a fragment of a personal reality. I want to show that this preservation is selective, depending on the aspect of self that is offended. It is accomplished by distorting the particular function of the self or by attempting to force it into a shaky accord with the other functions. Although the consequence is a mode of thinking and acting that is something less than adequate—and a world view that is faulty—its purpose is to achieve a temporary respite from anguish and, above all, a semblance of integrity.

DISSONANCE BETWEEN PERCEIVING SELF AND SELF-CONCEPT   Intense stress and conflict occur when the person perceives data that inform him that his conception of reality is severely out of accord with his conception of self. What the individual discovers in his world of experience undercuts his beliefs about himself, and he is left struggling with two irreconcilable facts. Leon Festinger refers to a similar state as *cognitive dissonance* or the state of psychological tension that exists when the person holds opposing knowledge or beliefs about self and world.[6]

Tension can be generated by changes occurring in a person's environment that are beyond his control. There is the common plight of certain aging populations residing in crumbling inner city areas. These people have lived the major portion of their lives with dignity and self-esteem; however, they have watched their neighborhoods become blighted by deterioration, vandalism, and threats to personal safety. Since they cannot move, how can they escape the violation of their values and beliefs?

190

Changes affecting one's status and capabilities also generate dissonance. An individual performing well on his job is promoted to a higher position that imposes responsibilities for which he is ill prepared. Over time his performance begins to slip. His high personal standards will not let him admit his incompetence, but he is constantly confronted with tasks and obligations that overtax his skill.

Changes in culture without adequate preparation induce tension. A fourteen-year-old boy could be affected when his family moves to another part of the country because of his father's transfer. To this point he has lived in the same community and has developed a comfortable identity out of his long association with the same friends. The new school and community have strangely different standards for dress, attitudes toward school, and relationship patterns, and he cannot find the proper way to get accepted into any of the local groups. He cannot make sense about what is going on around him, and he begins to doubt his own worth.

Changes in one's central role resulting from the actions of others cause tension. Changes in relationship patterns over the various stages of marital life offer many examples of this type of discord. A woman may be quite comfortable in her role as a dutiful wife and mother over many years of marriage. Her husband had accepted her caring and attentive ways with apparent pleasure. As the children approach maturity, they not only ignore her but even disparage her attempts to show interest in their activities. Her husband, facing the doubts of his own middle years, increasingly shows signs of disappointment in his wife. She becomes bewildered by this inexplicable change.

When opposing perceptions of reality and conceptions of self collide and possibilities for resolution of conflict are not apparent, the individual feels compelled to modify one or the other of these views to restore a semblance of security and balance. Irrespective of which of these impressions is altered, some type of distortion ensues.

When the self-concept is the most vulnerable aspect and because of its instability lends itself to being twisted to conform with incoming perceptions, the distortion could take several forms. If the individual's patterns had been generally passive and seclusive, he might withdraw from any assertive involvement and retreat into some kind of depression. Feeling dejected about himself, he would be relieved of the need to do anything about the problem. His passive and depressed state also offers certain manipulative possibilities. Wallowing in hopelessness could have the effect of inveigling others into caring for his needs and even restoring a semblance of the previous balance.

If a person has a rather rigid and unyielding self-concept, he is likely to take a more assertive approach. He could compensate for diminished self-esteem by some form of defensive vanity or by magnifying his merits or ideals. The employee who is promoted into a more demanding position might reasonably assume that he is too good for or is bored by the new job. He might invent all sorts of rationalizations as to why these difficulties could not be his own shortcomings and could hold his inferiors responsible for the problems that arise.

The inevitable consequence of these or other similar tactics is a false conception of self. Nonetheless, it would continue to justify the person's attitude and preserve at least a trace of his former integrity. Since any of these adaptations are founded on misrepresentations of the self, the individual has to go on defending his outlook to sustain their effectiveness.

Dissonance may also be reduced by a distortion of the incoming perception. If impressions of reality can be managed or altered, the self-concept is immune to threat. The simplest tactic is selective inattention or down-right denial of what is going on. A person might minimize the perceived attack by ignoring it, shutting off feeling, or by insistently pursuing the desired goal. However, by narrowing his perception to such a marked degree, he would also be closing himself off from other aspects of his experience creating yet other problems.

Perception can also be distorted by the intentional misrepresentation of the facts. By altering the frame of reference or by attending only to special parts of the event, an individual can arrive at conclusions that are less painful. Again, distortions of any one aspect of the person's perceptual field are likely to spill over into other regions and further complicate his adaptive style.

DISSONANCE BETWEEN INTENTIONAL SELF AND PERCEIVING SELF   Conflict arises when there is a serious gap between conceptions of the world and goal-seeking motives. Depending on the nature of a person's intentions, one of two forms of dissonance may arise. In one case, a person may feel impelled towards certain clear-cut goals by the power of his sincere motives and aspirations. However, when he looks to his environment for possible outlets and opportunities for the fulfillment of his intentions, he finds nothing. This hiatus is sometimes a penalty of socialization. From childhood, we are imbued with the myth that virtually any goal is attainable if we are only willing to work for it. We learn that it is shameful or perhaps abnormal not to compete or aspire for the valued heights of achievement. This ethic guarantees the production of a good number of "failures" and "incompetents" since there are some goal-seekers who, despite strong incentives, are too ill-equipped to succeed in the contest. There are others who eventually discover that the society that encourages strivings for success fails to provide equal opportunities for achievement. There are highly motivated people who successfully complete educational and retraining programs only to find that their gained skills are obsolete or that proper employment is lacking.

In its obverse form, dissonance arises when the individual is offered favorable opportunities for the realization of his potentials but must find some way to deny or elude their promise because his intentions are obscure or his motivation is at an ebb. This type of dissonance is represented by some clients of ambitious remedial and vocational programs that stress the myth of success but pay little heed to the need to work on motivational problems. Since these clients cannot fit the intrinsic "goodness" of these opportunities into their own value scheme they are well on their way to becoming the "under-achievers" and "washouts" of society.

In instances of incompatibility between perception and intention, the person experiencing frustration or defeat again needs to modify one or the other function. He might disparage his intentions and abdicate his goals, or he might deny his perceptions and proceed relentlessly toward his goals with increasing frustration.

When a person is faced with the absence of outlets for his ambitions, the renouncement of his goals is the simplest way to save face. He might merely admit that these goals had no meaning in the first place and are really unimportant to him. Or he might choose to acknowledge publicly that he is incompetent, and with a plea ("Don't expect anything more of me!") adopt a predictable and risk-free lifestyle, one that no longer requires much in the way of planning or projections about his future. The individual could also devise self-justifying arguments such as "I tried, but nothing ever works for me." These arguments could be amplified into embittered judgments about the unfair or "dog-eat-dog" nature of the world further justifying his retreat from competition and aspiration.

The individual might not abdicate his ambitions and goals in a total sense but deny his responsibility for them. Seeing that his path is beset with obstacles he becomes dependent on others' judgments. He searches for guarantees that things will turn out properly, or he insistently asks, "Am I doing the right thing?" If he succeeds he cannot truly feel ownership of his achievement, but he has hedged his bets in a way that avoids the sting of failure inasmuch as he can always blame others for the dismal outcome.

When one clings to his ambitions in spite of what his perceptions tell him, the result will be frustration and meaninglessness. On closing off his perception the individual also insulates himself from the impact of his pursuits on others as well as on himself. His striving becomes compulsive and mindless regardless of personal costs or the effects on his relationships. The end becomes all that counts: the means loses importance. When ends dominate means, maliciousness and exploitation may follow and others may suffer. Pindar wrote: There is a mortal breed most full of futility. In contempt of what is at hand, they strain onto the future, hunting impossibilities on the wings of ineffectual hopes.

DISSONANCE BETWEEN SELF-CONCEPT AND INTENTIONAL SELF Dissonance can rise from disparities between a person's conception of self and his intentions when he is concerned with personal fulfillment or the realization of what the self can be. This conflict emerges each time the person confronts a critical choice of living in which he needs to determine whether "what I believe I am" will support "what I believe I want to be." Thus, how this determination is resolved will have long-termed existential implications for the person's self-esteem and the quality of life that he believes he deserves.

Where previous forms of dissonance tend to be related to certain actualities of living, strife of this type can emerge anytime the individual permits himself to engage in serious reflection about his state of being. We allow our hopes, ideals, and aspirations to come forth and, in fantasy, play with the images of our becoming. These visions take on a certain

194

poignancy, particularly when they adumbrate residual feelings of discontent, boredom, or futility about our way of living. But these feelings can be endured if the emergent visions and hopes remain generalized and ephemeral or if one agrees to settle for something less. However, if the person acknowledges his idealism and commits himself to the fulfillment of his valued expectations, he must now contemplate the active choices he will need to make to achieve these ends. In so doing, he places his security and the predictability of his lifestyle in doubt.

Examples of dissonance that are products of a diminished self-concept or rejected hopes and aspirations are not hard to locate in our society. There are the partners in floundering marriages who, having compromised their original ideals, ask for little more than the right to share the same pointless space. Others resign themselves to hollow, unrewarding occupations, settling for anything that resembles security rather than risk challenge or change. On a different stratum there are the poor and the dispossessed who have long given up the possibility that there might be other alternatives to their harsh existence. In any of these instances people define their circumstances in a way that places the control of their destinies outside themselves. They act as if they are devoid of incentive when in reality it is the consequences of an unrealized incentive that is the source of their sense of futility and hopelessness. Unable to envision how their incentives might be actualized, they come to depend on fate, surrender to the inducements of the cult or the demagogue, or become nonentities.

If goallessness is one source of inner dissonance, the blind pursuit of meaningless goals is another. It is difficult to resist the glittering inducements of a materialistic and competitive society that urge the individual to betray his intrinsic values in favor of popular but illusory extrinsic values. If the person does succeed in accumulating the conventional tokens of success he risks disillusionment. If he fails or drops out of the race, society invites him to accept other options to assuage his discontent. They include another set of extrinsic values proclaiming the virtues of conformity and acquiescence and defending the righteousness of accepting one's lot and station in a baffling system.[7]

If the dissonance resulting from any of these circumstances cannot be resolved by effective choice, the individual needs to devise other adaptive patterns to reduce the anguish of futility or meaninglessness. The most direct and least painful one obviates the need for further initiative and is expressed in such terms as "turned-off" and "burned-out." Walter Kaufmann observes that the fear of making fateful decisions has become too common in contemporary life. Modern man has succumbed to this fear and has stifled his ability to shape his future. Kaufmann calls attention to a paradox: the retreat from the need to choose and decide is often accomplished by the person making a "once-and-for-all-time" choice that rules out the need ever to make future choices again.[8] (The marriage of resignation is one such choice.) Blind belief in some religious dogma provides another way out, particularly as it offers the believer the universal rules that will determine all of his future actions. There is also the unequivocal and unreflective commitment to a political ideology, a philosophy, or even a brand of psychology which, to the true believer, offers the unyielding security of a final truth. For that matter, one may choose not to choose and drift through life unconcerned about what one will do next.

These are relatively entropic means of adaptation geared to a constantly diminishing reservoir of energy and initiative. The individual's approach to reducing inner turmoil may take more active forms. In one respect, he may turn his disappointment inward and display his self-denunciation to attract caring and attention or to convince himself and others that it is futile to attempt to change anything. In another way, the person may direct his frustration outward to justify his perception of the world as a mean and brutish place, or he may find a willing scapegoat who accepts the blame for his unfortunate existence. The dissonance under these conditions is no doubt the most intense inasmuch as a person's personal worth is so much at risk. Since the long-termed potentialities of the self are on the line it might be surmised that the individual's attempt to cope with his anguish would evolve into a life pattern, a style of thought and behavior that would serve to ward off the risk of attempting change or acknowledging failure.

Personal Adaptation and Public Meanings

Adaptive behavior has a relational as well as a self-serving function. Although it serves the need for personal coping it is also enacted to induce others in the person's social field to behave or respond in desired ways.

Communication theorists assert that all behavior has a message character.[9] Whether it is expressed in words, posture, affect, or silence, it intends to convey something of importance to those in relation. These messages may be expressed specifically or ambiguously. The person may be informing others about how he sees himself, what he needs, how he feels, what has happened, or other "facts" about his circumstances. His behavioral messages may also attempt to persuade others what ought to happen or what others should do. These messages tend to define the nature of the relationship from the actor's viewpoint; that is, how he and others stand in relation to one another and the nature of their respective roles and obligations. A husband who is withdrawn or passive may be granting his wife the control that she relishes. The employee who refrains from making independent judgments may be complementing the need of his supervisor to be directive or even exploitive. Relationships of this type continue to work and remain stable as long as the partners continue to perform their respective roles in an interlocking way. Such relationships also need to take on the characteristics of a closed system if they are to endure; that is, a relationship's internal peculiarities should not be open to an outsider, especially one who may question or cast doubts on the nature of the arrangement.

This type of mutuality and interdependence is nowhere more in evidence than in the operations of some family systems. Carter and Orfanidis explain:

Family relationships tend to be highly reciprocal, patterned, and repetitive, and to have circular rather than linear motion. In other words, cause and effect thinking, which asks why, and looks for someone to blame for a problem, is not useful in identifying patterns and tracing their flow, since all family patterns, once established, are perpetuated by everyone involved in them, including their so-called "victims." If any one of the participants change, his predictable emotional input and reaction also changes, interrupting the natural flow. Other family members will be jarred out of their own unthinking responses, and in the automatic move toward homeostasis that is inherent in all systems, will react by trying to get the disrupter back in place again. In two-person sub-systems, such as married couples or a parent-child relationship, the element of reciprocity of emotional functioning can be striking, as in the enduring marriages of the villain and the saint, the master and the slave, the dreamer and the doer, the optimist and the pessimist, or in the involvement between the nagging mother and dawdling child. From a systems point of view, there is no blame or causality on either side of these patterns; instead there is active participation of both in order to perpetuate them, with ramifications for the rest of the family and antecedents in previous generations. [10]

From a transactional perspective it is apparent that an attempt to assess the degree of pathology in any one person's behavior would prove to be meaningless without reference to others in the person's social field. We would need to know how this behavior is perceived and interpreted by others in this field, if and how it is being reinforced, how it may conform to the needs of the system, and its role in the service of systems maintenance.

The question of when any kind of behavior becomes problematic or disturbing depends on any or all of a number of social contingencies:

1. For whatever reason (crisis, overload, arousal of other needs) the individual's social system no longer can tolerate or cope with his behavior in accustomed ways;

2. His behavior becomes too extreme (too frequent, intense, or visible) and can no longer be accepted;

3. His behavior is no longer congruent with the needs of the system because of structural, role, or value changes; or,

4. His behavior spills over into the larger community and evokes censure or the threat or actuality of official control.

In any of these cases the person comes to be defined as troublesome, disturbing, or deranged, particularly as he is seen as a danger to the balance and consistency of the system. Others within the field who are affected directly by his actions would feel impelled to respond in a punitive or controlling fashion to lessen the threat and restore a measure of equilibrium.

The severity of the response will depend on how others have ordinarily regarded the problematic individual. If a substantial social distance exists between people, disturbing behavior arising within the relationship tends to be defined in causal terms rather than in terms that attempt to explain the person's needs. If the person had been considered as inferior or had been thought of in unfavorable terms in the past, it is likely that he will be declared immoral, malicious, deficient, or crazy. These labels eventually may take on more persuasive meanings when the more authoritative members of the community come to play a role in the definition of the offender.

The term "deviance" describes behavior that departs from established and valued social norms. Actions censured or labeled in negative terms reflect the attitudes of the more conventional and conforming members of the system. This sort of ostracism or reproachment has its obvious implications for the offender, not the least of which is being confronted with yet another image of himself, an image that is a product of the perceptions of disapproving others. He must now contend with this incoming image with adaptive techniques that were ineffective in the first place and that set this process in motion. Some selected examples show how this process unfolds.

AIMLESSNESS   To others about him, the aimless person acts as if nothing but emptiness lies before him and that it is pointless even to give thought to the next moment. By word and action he denies that he has any control over his destiny. He may appear willing to grant these controls to others, however, if he is given direction or advice he will either ignore it or somehow fail as he attempts to implement these instructions—incurring further wrath or rejection. All in all, he passively yet irritatingly submits to the events he encounters or stumbles into.

As he looks out into his world, his perception is shrouded by a narrowed attention that attempts to exclude any stimuli that might spark motivation or reflect his deeper sense of inadequacy. Consciousness is attenuated and imaginative or creative thoughts are forestalled. His thinking is markedly convergent to reduce the inputs of experience to their basic and most manageable form. It would appear that his schema would be rather barren or limited to mundane conceptions of the world. Yet, he could also hold a hedonistic and impulsive outlook on life, especially if gratification of momentary and immediate urges is felt to be all that one can expect out of living. He may expect very little from relationships, and assume any of several roles—passive and submissive; alienated; or because his sense of control and future is so doubtful, a more clinging, demanding, and manipulative role.

This type of futility and alienation is personified in the character Meursault in *The Stranger* by Albert Camus.

He frequently says, and even more frequently implies, that he believes life to be meaningless and his activities to be arbitrary. He is virtually always bored and apathetic. He never imagines or daydreams. He has no goals. He makes only the most minimal decisions, doing little more than is necessary to keep a simple job as a clerk. He walks in his mother's funeral cortege and makes love to a woman with the same apathy and indifference. He frequently says, "It's all the same to me." His perceptions are banal and colorless. The most difference anything makes is to be mildly irritating. . . . When Meursault finally murders a man without any premeditation or reason, without any greater decision than is involved in resolving to take a walk, the reader is not even surprised. Anything is possible for Meursault, specifically because nothing is anything of importance. His is a vegetative existence that amounts to psychological death.[11]

This excerpt draws attention to the excesses of this form of adaptation to living. Many an aimless individual may meander through most of his existence without affecting others, particularly if he is successful in falling into a relationship with another who is willing to act on his behalf and make important decisions. But what happens if this person's behavior comes to be defined as problematic? How he would be regarded and the labels he would be subject to would depend on the particular setting. In a mental health or therapeutic locale, he would be called "unmotivated" or an "inadequate personality." If he is successful in stirring the ire of the interviewer, he might be diagnosed as "passive-aggressive." In educational settings, he is known as the "underachiever" or "drop-out" or "just plain lazy." He may sometimes become a candidate for remedial or retraining programs designed to stimulate interest and motivation. His dogged passivity, however, will lead to his being treated with disdain or ignored depending on the extent to which he frustrates his helpers.

AMBIVALENCE AND INDECISIVENESS   Because of his inconsistent and equivocal approach to living, the ambivalent and indecisive person often evokes different impressions in different people at different times. His uncertainty and misgivings about his conceptions of self, his goals, and his relationships result in his being torn between his doubtful incentives and the demands of his social environment. His moods and incentives fluctuate. At times he may be aroused enough to set off on quixotic pursuits of goals which seem to offer elegant solutions to his predicaments, but these searches are likely to become ridden with doubt and pessimism. People in relation with him may at first be attracted by his florid style but soon become frustrated by his instability.

This person's perceptual style is best characterized by its kaleidoscopic temperament and its attendant feelings of anxiety and insecurity. His outlook is sometimes all embracing, other times skewed, and always variable to some extent. He functions on many levels of consciousness, sometimes experiencing remarkable flights of imagery and flashes of intuition; but these are transient events, contributing little to his understanding of himself or his world. His attention is also shifting and unfocused, often confusing figure and ground and losing sight of the salient issues in his relationships or environment. His thought organization appears to be divergent as he seems able to find many meanings in his experiences. In reality he is merely bouncing from one impression to another without much coherence. Basically, this variability reflects a schema about which the person feels no consistent sense of ownership. He has a number of essential beliefs about his existence, but cannot commit himself to any one of them. In seeing all sides of all questions he frustrates his need to choose a direction, to make a commitment, or to obligate himself to a particular life value.

Examples of this type of adaptation abound, particularly in a world where the precepts of tradition and convention have weakened. Where culture and society once guided a man's major choices and decisions and heritage gave him dependable values, it is now the individual's task to create many of his own determinations. Such strains of living are the stuff of which modern drama, novels, diaries, and the notes of psychotherapists are made. A case in point, is the complaint of a young man in his middle twenties:

> I've lived away from home for four years and yet I feel a dozen times a day as if my parents were standing behind me, watching. I'm constantly trying to decide whether what I'm doing is right or wrong according to what my parents would say. I date girls and never have any wrong thoughts about them but I always feel guilty because my parents warned me and threatened me so much about getting into trouble. Just putting my arms around a girl makes me feel like I'm doing something dangerous, or sinful.
>
> If I stay up late at night I feel it's wicked, no matter what I'm doing, because my father always laid down the law about getting home at a certain hour. I worry a lot about everything I do at my job, wondering if I'm doing it right. . . .
>
> When I go to a show I can't relax because I feel I shouldn't be having this fun. As

if my parents should know about it, and they don't know, of course. I feel like I'm doing something sly, or like I'm cheating. . . . The funny part of all this is that I know how foolish it is. I know I'm old enough not to feel this way. I get very exasperated but I can't help it. My friends laugh at me, and lose respect too. I agree with them but I can't stop it. I'm still a baby, I guess. Why can't I grow up? What's wrong with me? If you know a thing is foolish or stupid, why can't you stop doing it?[12]

People who manifest such ambivalent perceptions of themselves and their reality are readily subject to the label of "neurotic" in any and all of its diverse meanings. The specific response this person will evoke will depend on the expectations of his particular milieu. He might be viewed as charming, childlike, quaint, weird, or repulsive. Because of his sometimes flamboyant thinking and quasi-insightfulness, he may be welcomed eagerly as a candidate for psychotherapy because he appears to be "challenging" or "interesting." Since the dependent role is not exactly foreign to him, he is likely to incorporate his therapist's frame of reference and thus increase his desirability as a patient, at least during the "honeymoon" of the experience. But, his self doubt and vulnerability can also result in his acceptance of the roles of the scapegoat, the clown, or the pitiful object. In even less receptive settings his behavior might be viewed as a "nag," or "bitch," or as a "pain in the ass." If none of these roles serve as a basis for even a spurious form of identity, he may then find it necessary to turn to even more self-defeating means such as the abuse of alcohol, drugs, or food—making it certain that he will be subject to yet other designations.

DISTORTION OR MISREPRESENTATION   In contrast with other patterns where perverse perceptions are the expression of overwhelming doubt or confusion, distortion represents the unyielding need to cling to a version of reality for purposes of control. This behavior would be seen as egregious and most disturbing to others to the extent that it violates existing beliefs about what is true, proper, and dependable in the person's social field. This type of individual tends to abrade comfortable conceptions of what reality is all about, threatening others' conceptions.

A number of adaptive forms may be subsumed under this need since the tendency to distort perception may evolve into various types of behavior. Although certain people may share the same need to misrepresent, their respective personal symbols and interpretations will lead to diverse responses.

Essentially, such a person's I-world view is contaminated by the stubborn need to ward off impressions that might in any way menace his already shaky controls. He uses his consciousness to twist and manipulate incoming impressions. Reliance on imagery or sentiency excludes the use of sensory or cognitive levels of awareness as verifications of the plausibility of his impressions. Attention is selective, shutting out any data that do not conform to his conceptions. These narrow impressions are, in turn, compressed into static forms by circumscribed convergent thought. However, in cases of extreme distortion, the individual may turn to unrestrained divergent thinking that fragments and scatters ideas into bizarre meanings. Complementing these thought processes, his frame of reference might be either single-celled (reducing all things to uniform interpretations and meanings), or it might be outrageously capricious, warding off the possibility of finding any meaning whatsoever in his experience.

Depending on the specific nature of his outward behavior in combination with the social setting, this person may attract any of a number of possible labels. For example, there is the person who becomes morbidly preoccupied with special fears or aversions to avoid the acute discomfort that would be felt if he confronted his feelings about himself or his problems of living. His entire ontology is given over to warding off the overwhelming fear that he might be trapped in a terrifying situation. Others may define him in various ways depending on what it is that terrorizes him and the degree to which this condition impairs his relationships and mode of living. In psychological or psychiatric terms, he would be called "phobic."

When a person's consciousness is preoccupied with self-loathing relative to beliefs about his personal failings, undesirability, or immorality he undergoes a bleak hopelessness and succeeds in divesting himself of the need to become more aggressive in response to his problem of living. Typically, he comes to be known as "depressed," a term that may be descriptive in layman's language or used to express pathological conditions by a mental health specialist. The actual connotations of the term depend on the sympathy, tolerance, or animosity that others feel toward him. If he is able to elicit a benevolent and caring response, he is likely to be treated in a protective and dependent fashion, but his emotional state may also succeed in alienating others particularly when the kindness and support of the helper are rejected. Then the depressed state may be equated with "sickness," and the person is known as a "patient."

There are other patterns of adaptation that are turned outward toward special people, aspects of the environment, or the world in general. These projections place the blame for the individual's misery on external conditions and shield him from consciousness of his defects. The crudeness or refinement of these projections will tend to affect how the individual is regarded by others. If he merely assumes a passive orientation to the world, mottled by unfounded complaints of unfairness or maltreatment, he may escape with such epithets as "carper," "whiner," or "blamer." If his accusations and suspicions are indicative of a system of thinking that serves to verify his beliefs of persecution, he will be deemed "paranoid." In either case, the result is estrangement since others will be repelled by these implied or explicit recriminations. Moreover, this rejection comes to fit into the person's scheme of things because it succeeds in authenticating his initial belief that the world is against him.

Distorted thought can also involve a tortured and fragile perceptual system that produces what appear to be rather incoherent ideations or isolates the individual from relationships with others and the actualities of his world. In many ways, the person creates a new, bizarre version of reality that is stained with symbols and images that are meaningful to only himself. Even though ephemeral, it offers the person a fragment of security—at least his new world is "safer" than the incomprehensible, alien one out there.

If he is able to remain in the confines of a protective family or culture that can tolerate his behavior, he may be seen as somewhat "strange," "eccentric," or "weird." He may be accorded special treatment (perhaps be stigmatized within the idiom of the culture), and as he plays out his assigned role he will find his niche within the system. If his behavior becomes too extreme for or too apparent to his community, he may be classified as "mentally ill" and given the label "psychotic." He will be excluded from his familiar social field and perhaps institutionalized in a hospital with other "ill" people. Even if institutionalization does not occur, the label will isolate him psychologically from his normal role and relationships. Since the nature of the "illness" is imprecise, there is little possibility that he will ever be "cured" of something that cannot be defined. The label becomes permanently imprinted or modified to the anomalous form of "ex-mental patient."

The words of Lara Jefferson, once a patient in a mental hospital, capture the anguished inner world of such people. Originally written on scraps of paper that were discovered by the hospital superintendent, she wrote:

Because I am I, an odd piece of Egotism who could not make the riffle of living according to the precepts and standards society demands of itself, I find myself locked up with others of my kind in a "hospital" for the insane. There is nothing wrong with me—except I was born at least two thousand years too late. Ladies of Amazonian proportions and Berseker propensities have passed quite out of vogue and have no place in this too damn civilized world.

Had I been born in the age and time when the world dealt in a straightforward manner with misfits as could not meet the requirements of living, I would not have been much of a problem to my contemporaries. They would have said that I was "Possessed of the Devil" and promptly stoned me to death—or else disposed of me in some other equally effective manner.

But because the poor deluded tax-payers of America insist on the delusion that they are civilized, they strain themselves to the breaking point to keep institutions for our care in operation. Then when they break down under the strain of trying to live up to the standards they set for themselves, the officials, whom they have appointed for the office, pronounce them insane—and they are committed to institutions.

I know I cannot think straight—but the conclusions I arrive at are very convincing to me and I still think the whole system is a regular Hades itself. . . . Here I sit—mad as the hatter—with nothing to do but either become madder—or else recover enough of my sanity to be allowed to go back into the life which drove me mad.

. . .

How—how—HOW? In the name of God—How does a person learn to think differently? I am crazy wild this minute—how can I learn to think straight? Is it after all, of so much importance whether there is one more—or one less—mad woman in this world?

They have a list of long Greek and Latin words and when they observe such and such symptoms in one of us, they paste the label for our phobia on us—and that is the end of the matter. I cannot see what they have accomplished so much in merely being able to remember all those long-handled names for our madness. We, who have learned what madness is by going through it,—(and you cannot have a closer knowing than that)—are separated from all others by a gulf so wide that it cannot be bridged. And there the matter lays—divided, split, and sundered.[13]

RIGIDITY AND PERSISTENCE Even though they may be disjointed and confused, thinking and reflection do play some part in the previous adaptive patterns. In this instance, the pattern is distinguished by the virtual absence of the ability to look inward. Reflective thought and the misgivings and insecurities it might engender are averted by the person's reliance on repetitive and obdurate behavior that is enacted to manage his life and control his environment. Ritualistic and instinctive actions ward off unsettling perceptions and provide an illusion of command. If the individual chooses to reflect, he does so in order to justify his sense of righteousness.

It is not only the mindless tenacity of such behavior that makes it so offensive to the observer, but also the fact that it patently violates reason. It is true that this behavior may be attractive to some others, such as those who suffer from indecisiveness or passivity, who may then regard the person with some envy despite the fact that his behavior is meaningless in its own right. His ability to act without the tremors of anxiety and doubt is the appealing feature.

An individual bound by his compulsive drives may well be in pursuit of something—perhaps an overdetermined goal which, if it could be achieved, would offer little in the way of meaning or respite. This blind impulse, the quest for ends no matter how personally destructive the means, is portrayed by Malamud in *The Tenants*. Although this account represents the more purposive side of this adaptive pattern, it captures its nonreflective, compelling qualities.

The novel's protagonist, Lesser, is a writer gripped by the drive to finish his third book to prove that he is "a going concern, not a freak who had published a good first novel and shot his wad." He is the last tenant in a crumbling tenement that is to be razed to make way for a new building. Levenspiel, his landlord, pleads with him to move so that he can proceed, and he keeps increasing the reward that Lesser will receive if only he will leave. But Lesser is resolute and he will not vary his compulsive routine even though the walls about him are literally falling:*

The skinny ten-floor house next door is being gutted, torn down floor by floor. The wreckage chutes into the green truck-size container in the street. The huge iron ball the crane heaves at the collapsing walls, and the noise of the streams of falling bricks and broken wooden beams deafen the writer. Though he keeps his windows tightly shut his flat is foul with plaster dust; he sneezes in clusters all day. Sometimes his floor trembles, seems to move; he envisions the building cracking apart, collapsing in a dusty roar. Lesser and his unfinished book go shrieking into the exploding debris. He wouldn't put it past Levenspiel to blow up the joint with a long stick of dynamite and blame it on the times.

Lesser writes extra hours at night. He sleeps poorly, one eye on tomorrow morning when it's time to write. His heavy heartbeat shakes the bed. He dreams of drowning. When he can't sleep he gets up, snaps on his desk lamp and writes.

Autumn is dark, rainy, chilly. It scuds towards an early winter. His electric heater has pooped out and is being repaired. He writes in his overcoat, woolen scarf, cap. He warms his fingers inside the coat, under his arms, then goes on writing. Levenspiel provides a mockery of heat. Lesser complains to the housing authorities but the landlord resists cleverly: "The furnace is age fifty-one. What kind of performance does one expect of this old wreck? I had it repaired two hundred times. Should I maybe install a brand new one for one lousy uncooperative tenant?"

"Let him move out and collect $9,000 cash."

The bribe has increased but this is where Lesser's book was conceived more than a decade ago, died a premature (temporary) death, and seeks rebirth. Lesser is a man of habit, order, steady disciplined work. Habit and order fill the pages one by one. Inspiration is habit, order; ideas growing, formulated, formed. He is determined to finish his book where it was begun, created its history, still lives.

. . .

Sometimes the writing goes really badly. . . . Lesser sometimes feels despair's shovel digging. He writes against cliffs of resistance. Fear, they say, of completing the book? Once it's done what's there to finish? Fear of the ultimate confession? Why? if I can start another book after this. Confess once more. What's the distant dark mountain in my mind when I write? It won't fade from inscape, sink, evanesce; or volatilize into light. It won't become diaphanous, radiance, fire, Moses himself climbing down the burning rock, Ten lit Commandments tucked under his arm. The writer wants his pen to turn stone into sunlight, language into fire. It's an extraordinary thing to want by a man his size and shape, given all he hasn't got. Lesser lives on his nerve.[14]

Lesser's drive magnifies with each new hardship and the reader is sucked into his obsession, not by sympathy or the hope that Lesser will succeed, but by the morbid and compelling curiosity about the kind of catastrophe that will have to destroy the writer.

Such reaction is not uncommon to most of us who watch helplessly someone who is pressed to act in a heedless fashion. Caution, reason, or the gift of more rewarding alternatives cannot halt the drive, either because the compulsion must be fulfilled for the sake of fulfillment alone or because so much of the self is hooked into the momentum. Since the behavior itself denies consciousness, each failure or obstacle serves to intensity action, further separating the actor from himself.

The futility felt by the observer who cannot stem this impetuosity can be expected to be followed by the harsher feelings of hostility or rejection, but this is not always the case. The person who violates the conventional methods without apparent guilt or culpability meets the vicarious wishes of those of us who are hemmed in by the felt constraints of society. Thus we have the phenomenon of the "anti-hero," the apotheosis of the person who nonchalantly violates the codes of morality, and who may exploit, beguile, and manipulate the system for his own selfish advantage.

Because of the wide-ranging implications of this pattern of living, it succeeds in generating a number of rather diverse labels, expressing particular aspects or interpretations. Most often, even the more benign categories tend to set the person apart in negative terms. Ordinarily he may be considered "obstinate," "narrow-minded," or "incorrigible." If he appears to be driven by an uncompromising idea or belief, he is "obsessed"; if his behavior is ritualized and habituated, he is "compulsive." In psychological circles he may be known informally as "impulse-ridden" or as an "actor-outer." If a more formal designation is used, the titles "character disorder," "personality disorder," or "character neurosis" are ascribed. If it is determined that the person is acting as if he were bereft of conscience and remorse, he is diagnosed as a "psychopath" or "sociopath," depending of the observer's frame of reference. There are more innocuous labels that may also apply: "unpredictable," "hothead," "autocrat," or "free spirit."

Obviously many of these labels refer to quite different manifestations as well as those that are enacted for different purposes in different social contexts. Different personal social and psychological dynamics are in play in the various forms of this pattern.

RESIGNATION   Resignation represents the effort to diminish the conflict that arises when self-concept and intention are out of accord. This is accomplisheld by the abdication of creative impulse, individuality, or diversity and the submission to proper and conventional standards. Since the primary motive is to strive for either anonymity or to be like everybody else, it is probable that this pattern will draw the least public response or censure. Resignation is all too commonplace, and clichés are readily used to describe large sectors of society: "corporate man," "silent majority," the "faceless crowd," and the "bureaucratized society." These terms have pejorative overtones suggesting that accommodation to social standards is largely misguided, a sign of social decay, or a symptom of mass pathology. This type of social criticism is much too facile; it ignores the fact that the survival of any society depends on the degree to which the majority of its members agree about what is good, right, proper, and desirable. David Riesman, in reevaluating *The Lonely Crowd*,[15] acknowledges that people can become fully integrated into their social order without strain or maladjustment. He refers to this type as the "adjusted":

They are the typical tradition-directed, inner-directed, or other-directed people—those who respond in their character structure to the demands of their society or social class at its particular stage on the curve of the population. Such people fit the culture as though they were made for it, as in fact they are. There is, characterologically speaking, an effortless quality about their adjustment. . . . That is, the adjusted are those who reflect their society, or their class within the society, with the least distortion.[16]

We are not concerned with the "adjusted" but with the "resigned," people who gravitate towards conformity as a means of subduing the press for autonomy. If it is possible to strive for mediocrity or meaninglessness, such is their intention. Distortion in the form of a pointless existence whittled down to the mean tasks of daily survival is the outcome. George Konrad's *The Case Worker* depicts a nameless case worker, who is himself as entrapped and as caught in the empty routine of living as are his clients. He symbolizes his own existence:*

> If I sit at my desk with my head in my hands, it is because the moment I entered the office a thousand pygmy typewriters began to clatter right and left, hurling incongruous phrases into the ever shrinking field of my attention. . . .
>
> if a few drops of brandy makes my nerves pulsate as an electric current awakens a dusty old television set to life, my benumbed brain starts crackling and, liberated from the insufferable hammering, engenders images that, at first diffuse, then organized, parade across my hesitant retina . . .
>
> if nobody says anything; if the telephone keeps quiet, the radiator doesn't hiss, the loudspeaker doesn't bark, the door of the elevator doesn't clatter every minute, and diarrheal pigeons are not scratching at my windowsill; if the worn-down shoes of uncertain, nosy people are not shuffling past my window . . .
>
> if from my memory that is becoming more and more like a junk pile I expel table-pounding ministers of war, official spokesmen who communicate nothing, mass murderers dozing in bulletproof docks, double agents exchanged on the q.t., newly spawned popular dictators who string up their friends, cannibalistic monarchs by divine right, the season's celebrities whose electronic smile invades every room, who unveil statues, taste the new wine, inaugurate highways, inspect guards of honor, kiss babies, send telegrams of congratulation, and present medals and gold watches . . .
>
> if my wife and I have gone for our usual quiet walk on the hillside the night before; if rent, electric, and telephone bills have been paid and there's still enough money for milk, meat, fruit, coffee, tobacco, and wine . . .
>
> if after a good night's sleep, propelled to the washbasin by the exploding alarm, I have successfully completed the befuddled ritual of getting up; if with the aroma of fresh coffee in my head I have managed, on taking the bus, to find a seat by the window and collect my thoughts amid overcoats smelling of tobacco, rain, dishwater, and dry toast . . .
>
> then, even then, this day will still be pretty much the same as every other day. [17]

The case worker interweaves the fruitlessness of his existence with that of his clients. The difference? The fact that he is a bit less vulnerable.

Every institution makes for a specific state of mind. At the circus my client laughs, at the public baths he daydreams, on the streetcar he stares into space, at a

---

*Excerpted from *The Case Worker* by George Konrad. Copyright © 1969 by Konrad Gyorgy; English translation copyright © 1974 by Gyorgy Konrad. Reprinted by permission of Harcourt Brace Jovanovich, Inc.

boxing match he is aggressive, in the cemetery subdued, and so on. To this room he brings a few samples of his sufferings and of frustrations that he has handed on to his sons and daughters. Quite possibly the image I get—the barest tip of the fragile molehill of his life—is deceptive. Yesterday he was kicked, today he gets apologies and tomorrow he may even come in for a caress or two, but all I see is his past. Nevertheless, I trust the momentary image, though with some caution. I may not know the man himself, but I know his circumstances. A diagram of his blunders, superimposed on those of other people, brings out what is specific to him, showing that what is unpredictable in him is infinitesimal compared to what is predictable. His circumstances are, let us say, straitened. In my official capacity I am informed of his job, habits, and previous blunders; this allows me to estimate how much freedom of action he has. Of course, what I see isn't the man himself, but only the envelope in which he moves about. Yet, reluctantly, I identify my client with all these odds and ends, and feel sorry for him because so many obstacles have impeded his development. It would be commendable if his relations with his environment were somewhat more complex, if the rules he chose to live by were a little less conventional. But his system is depressingly lacking in complexity, his income wretched, his physical surroundings dreary, his vision blurred, his burden heavy. His freedom of action is below average, his drives, which are without direction, conflict and sometimes collide head on. When this happens, the traffic jams up and official intervention is needed to start it moving again. Since my job is to protect children and safeguard the interests of the state, the most I can do is reconcile him with his circumstances and oppose his propensity for suffering. I do what the law and my fumbling judgment permit; then I look on, mesmerized, as the system crushes him. [18]

We see that resignation and the rejection of the risks that come with full-blooded, autonomous living is not without its own perils. The sense of harmony created is synthetic; because so many controls are given over to the unknown powers outside ourselves, we never know when or from where the next assault will come. Thus the individual's resistance to public censure and classification is uncertain. If his failures are too frequent or spill over into the lives of others, he becomes the subject of scorn and disdain. Yiddish makes the slight but very important distinctions between the "schlemiel" and the "schlimazel" both referring to somewhat inept and unfortunate people. The "schlemiel" is the fellow who is forever spilling hot soup on others. The "schlimazel" is the guy the soup is spilled on. Less imaginative counterparts of these epithets, including "passive-aggressive" and "inadequate personality," can be found in the professional lexicon.

The "born loser" earns his share of penalties since his brand of conformity generates little respect or attention. He is often exploited and victimized by the more malicious members of his system and by the institutions and bureaucracies on which he may depend. In a society characterized by its competitive spirit, this fellow will ultimately lose out and remain forever at the end of the line.

Public Response and Personal Meanings

It has been suggested that a correlate of ineffective adaptive patterns is the relinquishment of some amount of control over one's fortunes. Thus, there is a likelihood that a person can become liable to the regulations of his larger community by reasons of chance, by his own indiscretions, or by the actions of others. Should this occur, he will find himself drawn into what Rhodes calls "the psychological protector apparatus of society."[19] The behavioral services that help form and regulate the individual and group to socially preferred patterns of behavior include the human services systems of social welfare, education, mental health, and the legal and correctional services. Since each system is endowed with a different sanction (to aid and support, to teach, to treat, and to control, punish, and rehabilitate), how the client will be handled will vary greatly depending on the "service" he is receiving.

Even within any one broad system of services, practices may vary in quality and character. Taking the mental health or social service agencies as an example, one can observe some striking contrasts in methods of service delivery even within the same community. These contrasts often represent differences in ideologies, in the way problems are defined, in specialized technologies, in the training and experience of personnel, and in other indigenous factors.

Political and pragmatic issues also bear on the administration of human services and the types and qualities of the care that is rendered. Such organizations are dependent on a superordinate body, public or private, for sanction and funding. They must be responsive to the dictates of their principals and make the necessary accommodations to changes in policy or funding. Of greater import is the actual structure of the greater social welfare and mental health system. That this structure tends to overlook the fact that human problems are of a whole is evident in the way the human services (particularly in North America) are arbitrarily divided into such categories as mental health, family and children, aging, and so on. These services must overlap to some extent. To avoid encroachment and to justify its continuity, each organization must construct its program and define its functions in an arbitrary fashion; the extent to which these rationalizations are self-serving effects the relevance of the organization's services to the needs of its constituents. Although many services do offer their consumers aid that is consistent and helpful, these conditions pose the risk that the client may be short-changed in some cases. The point is that the mere presence of human service systems designed to serve certain human needs does not necessarily insure that these needs will be met.

It is also important to clarify that the intent of these systems to regulate and control the individual or group need not be considered detrimental in all cases. Such intent does not necessarily connote the violation of personal rights or self-determination. There is often a need for authoritative social intervention and control in those instances where people are harming others or require the security of imposed boundaries within which they can begin to tackle their undisciplined problems of living.

Returning to the person who finds himself drawn into a human service system, one possible consequence of his involvement is the evolution of the deviant career process. [20] This process unfolds when the individual falls into an assigned third-rate role; like any other career role, it becomes central to his lifestyle, but without the benefits of more auspicious and socially acceptable career roles. As this role becomes internalized it distorts his perceptions of self as well as the quality of his affiliations with others. A case in point is the bright young woman who was committed to a mental health facility when her relatives became disturbed by what they saw as rather odd behavior. When she began to wonder what was really wrong with her, she was able to locate her medical chart without too much difficulty. To her surprise, she found that she was a "schizophrenic, undifferentiated." Since she was not sure what a schizophrenic was and was also troubled because "undifferentiated" seemed to imply that she was rather unexceptional, she felt further research was warranted. She gained admission to the hospital library, found some texts on abnormal psychology, and learned not only what these terms meant but also how she was supposed to act in order to fulfill this role. The definitions she secured already seemed familiar to her since, with the help of the hospital staff, she had begun to enact the prescribed role. Her release was followed by a number of readmissions facilitated by the agreement about the nature of her sick role shared by herself, her family, and the hospital personnel.

(I later had the opportunity to counsel with her and over time got her to reexamine her version of reality and the adaptive purposes it served. Doubtful about the persistence of her incongruous conduct, I urged her to be studied by a medical research group specializing in endocrinological and neurological problems. She reluctantly agreed and after a rigorous examination it was discovered that the source of her erratic behavior was an uncommon form of epilepsy—a purely organic condition. Yes, she guessed that she wasn't schizophrenic after all, but what was she going to do about her sick role? Her almost reflexive response was "My god! Now I have to start all over again and learn how to be an epileptic!")

The deviant role is not a unilateral process involving straightforward role assignment and role assumption. Even within its constraints, there is room for interaction and negotiation depending on the unique characteristics of the individual. His self-esteem, his way of defining reality, his needs and purposes will shape the nature of the career process. It is another aspect of the eliptical mode, involving a sequence of interactions between the person and the system, that arrives at a definition, validation, and a set of expectations for the role in question. This process can evolve into any of a number of types of deviant person-society relationships and roles depending on the nature of the service system, and the characteristics of its constituents.

SYMBIOTIC/COMPLEMENTARY RELATIONSHIP   On its surface, the symbiotic/complementary relationship is one of the more benevolent modes for creating the deviant role and career. A new cultural definition is imposed upon individuals or groups of people whose lifestyles are judged by the majority population to be subnormal or in some ways disturbing. This cultural definition may be a product of sociological wisdom and research, political opinion or expedience, or the judgment of an expert. In any case, it represents the attempt of parties outside of the group to recast and reinterpret the motives, patterns, and needs of the members of that group. Whether or not these definitions are valid is not the issue; the point is that they are not the inventions of the people who are being defined.

These definitions are expressed in such terms as "the culture of the poor," "welfare recipient," "hard-core families," "child abusers," and the "disadvantaged." Objectively, these terms are neutral and descriptive designations, arising out of the need to conceptualize and in some way identify troubling social phenomena. However, these terms easily become stereotypes and a way of classifying entire populations and prescribing how they are to be treated. As these classifications become popularized, they are insensitive to what is unique and special about the people to whom they refer, and they can become offensive and debasing.[21]

Certain rewards may accrue to those who accept the designation and tacitly acknowledge membership in this contrived culture. Deemed inadequate or inferior, they may be granted certain privileges (say, easy access to educational opportunities and lower expectations for performance). They may also be placed in remedial or corrective programs or retrained for certain trades even though these trades may be of little interest to the trainee. They may also be placed in sheltered workshops or in programs designed to make them better and more productive citizens. Under certain conditions, they might even be invited to participate in selected aspects of planning for their community. However, these privileges are provisional inasmuch as they are accompanied by the supposition that all such persons are occupying second-class roles, limiting the individual's say in the decisions made about him.

Benign though this approach may be, it is patronizing. The majority group, with admittedly good intentions, seeks to create a state of symbiosis with the deviant group; but it is skewed since the majority group dictates the terms. It is as if to say, "We will provide for your needs as long as you behave and respond as we expect you to." Thus the gains of this relationship are short lived because those on the receiving end come to discover that psychological segregation is demeaning. The consequence: An uneasy and lingering hostility develops on the part of both groups, each believing that it is being thwarted by the other.

THE AUTHORITARIAN RELATIONSHIP The most expedient and straightforward approach to both creating and controlling deviant behavior is the authoritarian relationship. It informs the deviant in clear and unequivocal terms who he is and what is expected of him. An official body empowered with legitimate authority defines the individual and his problems within special classifications of behavior, some of which are legally based. Reciprocally, the labeled individual is required to accept this definition and to conform to the expectations and controls imposed. Such classifications include "juvenile delinquent," "parolee" or "ex-con," "alcoholic," "child abuser," and "underachiever" or "drop out." These labels do in fact point to severely problematic and destructive behaviors, but they tend to enclose the person in narrow behavioral brackets and may exclude other personal, social, and motivational factors that distinguish the individual as a unique entity.

Compensations may be gained by both the authority and the subject. For the authority group, and the majority population group as a whole, the use of these classifications allows a convenient and simplified approach to the explanation and management of what are confounding social problems. This pseudo-theoretical orientation permits the expeditious selection of any of a number of methods and protocols designed to curb undesirable behavior. These methods can be imposed at the discretion of the authoritative system and can be alternated or combined in any way deemed feasible. Considering alcoholic behavior, Sahakian lists the following approaches aimed solely at controlling the abuse of alcohol: (1) drugs that interfere with alcohol metabolism, making the drinker sick; (2) hypnosis to alter his attitude toward alcohol; (3) conditioned reflex therapy to create an aversion to drinking; (4) Alcoholics Anonymous, a social-spiritual approach to self-control; and (5) "halfway houses" to provide the atmosphere and opportunity to stop drinking.[22] This sort of functional eclecticism applies as well to other classifications and offers the advantage of justifying the role of the behavior specialist who is called on to employ these techniques. Furthermore, it confirms the value of the specific service created to manage these problems.

Members of these deviant categories may also gain something from participation in such ventures. The mere acceptance of such a behavioral level tends to simplify life—the label providing an uncomplicated frame of reference by which one's relations with his world can be interpreted. Personal responsibility for one's role and actions is minimized to a considerable extent. If the person can say with some belief, "I am an alcoholic," or "I am a delinquent," he can claim that any of his actions are both natural and justifiable. After all, he is only doing what he is ("since I have the name, I'll play the game"). His nefarious behavior becomes someone else's problem. The willingness to accept the label also offers the opportunity to identify one's self with others who are similarly classified. This association allows the person to feel less alone or peculiar, and an affiliation with others suffering from the same problem somehow reduces the felt stigma. A newly appointed police chief facing criticism about his lack of credentials for the position was reported in a newspaper:

> Fox was also frank about another problem he has faced.
>
> "It was an illness which is contracted by millions of Americans and its called alcoholism," he said. "At one time in my life I had to face the reality that I was addicted, and I did.
>
> "Since that time, I have found a way of life which I have been able to function free from alcohol and other drugs. . . ."[23]

The individual may enjoy deliberate associations with others undergoing the same problem, such as those offered by Alcoholics Anonymous and Parents Anonymous. These organizations do offer members a measure of control and occasions to share experiences and common solutions. However, how deep and meaningful are the relationships that are formed, based as they are on the maladaptive patterns that people hold in common rather than on their respective personalities? To what extent do these bonds isolate the individual from the mainstream of society and his own social field?

Although authoritarian schemes may contain and check some socially undesirable behaviors, they often fail to touch certain elemental dilemmas of living and may not encourage new and more creative ways of dealing with problems. Their goal is not the solution of the problem of "what am I?" but an investment in the label itself and a reduction in the noxious behavior it represents. Personal autonomy cannot be gained by the surrender of one's self-definition. In Sartre's words, "We only become what we are by the radical and deep-seated refusal of that which others have made of us."

THE CLINICAL-DIAGNOSTIC RELATIONSHIP   Many of the authoritative protocols apply equally to the person diagnosed as a "mental patient" or as having a "mental illness." This deviant's predicament deserves special attention, because his life patterns are subject to a highly specialized field, a system of mental health services organized to manage and treat his problems. The clinical-diagnostic relationship concerns those programs that adhere to the medical model or disease-oriented approach to so-called problems of the mind.

People who fall into the classification of "mentally ill" and are not suffering from an organic defect are often those who are ineffectually struggling to recreate a version of reality that will in some way help them preserve a vestige of integrity. This struggle is common to all "deviants"; however, in the case of the mentally ill, it is the strange and incomprehensible nature of the person's thoughts and actions that cause him to be set apart from the "normal" members of society. The peculiar manner in which he looks into himself or out into his world stirs discomfort and fear in others. He painfully reminds them of their own sense of estrangement and startles the vestiges of their own irrationalities.

Whether or not this person is officially designated a patient or is placed in a mental institution depends only in part on the perceived severity of his condition. Socioeconomic and class status appear to have as much bearing on the disposition of his problem as his mental state. This inconsistency was noted in a study of 500 deinstitutionalized California mental patients. Steven Segal and Uri Aviram found that only about 80 (16 percent) could be considered seriously disturbed. In point of fact, 28 percent were entirely without symptoms, and more than 50 percent were seen as mildly disturbed. Although these patients shared few common characteristics as far as their mental condition was concerned, they were markedly similar with regard to demographic factors. Almost two-thirds were from the lower socioeconomic class with unskilled occupations. One-half had completed only elementary school. Most were unmarried and had no close family ties.[24] Clearly, whatever the "mental illness" in this sample, it appears to have had more to do with circumstances of living than with the classification of mental disorder.

If a person does become institutionalized, he often enters the domain of medicine with its disease-oriented taxonomy of symptoms and disorders. The labels generated by the diagnostic process may or may not have any relevance to how he is subsequently handled and treated. But, these labels also provide the patient with a definition of his role. He learns that he is sick or incompetent—designations that impede decision making, reduce wholesome motivations, and simplify his existence. This condition can have a ripple effect insofar as it is reinforced by his family and community.

Some serious difficulties arise from this diagnostic enterprise. In the Rosenhan study, well-adjusted people applying for admission to mental hospitals as pseudo-patients were easily given the diagnosis of schizophrenia. Korchin has stated that these categories are loosely empirical and descriptive, are not oriented to a particular theoretical position, and they do not refer to causes or to the treatment consequences of the disorder. The "diagnosis better fits a hypothetical 'textbook case' rather than real individuals, and there is a danger of stereotyping."[25]

If the diagnosis of the patient does not accurately represent his state of being, how will he ever know when and if he is cured? He finds himself in a double-bind: although he is "sick," there is no chance of his ever getting "better" since whatever his "sickness" is, it cannot be defined in terms of treatment or cure. The best he can hope for is that a capricious change in policy will cast him back out into his community, someone will observe that his symptoms have diminished, or the determination that he has gone into a "state of remission." In any case, he cannot return to society unstigmatized by his hospitalization as do those who are successfully treated for a physical disorder. His role is adjusted to that of "ex-mental patient," a role that continues to linger somewhere outside of the edges of the normal society.

PSYCHIATROID RELATIONSHIPS   A person can assume a deviant role by his own volition. The "psychiatroid" relationship can have a firm but peculiar hold on the lifestyles of many people. Ornstein uses this term to describe the cult system that has developed since Freud's time, a system that has overgeneralized and extended psychoanalytic and psychological theory into all aspects of everyday living.[26] It assumes that all phenomena can be explained in psychological terms of one kind or another; it is evident in the facile way such terms as "oedipus," "libido," and "id" are used *as if* they actually represented what the speaker is talking about. As the term "psychiatroid" applies here, it refers to the thinking of people who define themselves as neurotic in one way or another and are overly preoccupied with treatment as a major part of their existence.

219

Some people are fully devoted to their perennial career as patient or client. Whether or not they are seen as deviants, they claim this role as their own and eagerly set off in search of the perfect therapy. Since effective therapy requires the client to attain a measure of autonomy and independence at some point, "perfection," however it may be conceived, is always beyond reach. Consequently, these persons are in constant pursuit of the psychotherapeutic adventure—in human relations movements, growth and encounter groups, sexual seminars, meditational cults, and countless other esoteric inventions.

Unfortunately, many people influenced by psychiatroid thought confuse the search for an extended perspective on one's life with a new form of self-indulgence. It is often observed that people involved in psychotherapy become changed. What they really become is fascinated with their own personal problems. They may often discuss *ad nauseum* their emotional, sexual, and intellectual difficulties until there is little else about which they are concerned. . . . Not by coincidence, these tendencies are all too common among the "personal growth" adherents as well. The same self-preoccupation is here confused with "growth," now merely redirected from the observation of depression to the quest for ecstasy or emotion.[27]

Watzlawick and his colleagues are also concerned with this popular tendency and see it as an example of what they called the "utopia syndrome," an extreme form of human problem solving that expresses the belief that one will one day find the ultimate solution.[28] With a utopian goal, the believer can blame its unattainability on his own ineptitude instead of on the outrageous nature of the goal.

. . . if a "neurotic" symptom is merely seen as that tip of the iceberg, and if in spite of many months of uncovering therapy it has not improved, this "proves" the correctness of the assumption that emotional problems may have their roots in the deepest layers of the unconscious, which in turn explains why the patient needs further and deeper analysis. Open-ended, self-sealing doctrines win either way, as in the bitter joke about the patient who after years of treatment still wets his bed, "but now understands why I do it."[29]

The eager acceptance of the chronic-client role does offer certain pay-offs even though the role proclaims that at worst the person is incompetent and at best has not yet reached his potential. Acceptance serves for the most part as an alternative to or an avoidance of serious change; that is, the challenge to reevaluate one's purpose and goals in life, to open one's conception of self in a candid fashion, to reconsider one's premises and the thought processes that support them, and to examine how these conditions affect the way one deals with his relationships and environment. In these cases, it is not the ends that are important but the means since the client believes that "it is better to travel hopefully than to arrive."[30]

This lifestyle provides other moment-to-moment gratification. For those reluctant to show their assertive side to their social world, interminable treatment postpones the issue. They are also free to invest their assertiveness in the ethos of their particular treatment group and stand together against the world that can't or won't understand "us." For those lacking the ability or the confidence to risk themselves in closeness with others, the therapeutic or encounter group allows for many forms of pseudo-intimacy—programmed communions free of the hazards that arise in more spontaneous human relationships. There is also the joy of omniscience that grows out of one's affiliation with a cult. In that these therapeutic and growth movements have burgeoned and flourished over the past years and have extended their influence to many aspects of living, they have achieved a measure of authority and in some areas, a quality of veneration. Membership connotes an affiliation with the "true believers" or the "possessors of the real truth." The psychiatroid relationship reverses the stigma of psychological disability and displaces it onto the majority made up of "non-believers" and the "great unwashed."

THE ADVERSARY/CONFLICT RELATIONSHIP   Although the adversary/conflict relationship can be considered another form of voluntary deviance, it bears little resemblance to the psychiatroid role. An adversary or conflict relationship is created when people who consciously occupy an inferior status in their society join together to form a union to replace the deviant role assigned to them with one of their own choosing. The best examples are the various civil rights movements aimed at securing equal rights in education, employment, and housing. Welfare rights organizations have sometimes united welfare recipients to protect their interest, to combat the massive welfare bureaucracy, and to participate in decisions made about the nature and quality of services received. Other examples include neighborhood action groups, liberation groups, and even groups of institutionalized mental patients or convicts demanding a say about policies and programs affecting their lives.

These movements represent an important shift from acquiescence to political action. The individuals involved willingly and deliberately assume the role of the activist, the militant, or the ideologue knowing that it will further polarize their relations with society. An adversary relationship forces both sides to reevaluate and reconceptualize their positions. Members of the deviant group, no longer bound by external definitions, must grapple with questions of personal rights, equality, and distributive justice and their role in achieving these ends. The superior group, confronted by an intractable opposition, is also forced to reevaluate its function and policies. At the very least, the institution or service in question would need to become more accountable and to justify its operations, a process that is not likely to occur spontaneously.

Other benefits accrue to members of assertive movements. Identification with others sharing the same values and the accompanying authentication of self are obvious rewards. The opportunity for expression of pent-up aggression is another—particularly to people who have suffered an oppressed or depressed lifestyle. Such associations offer a more promising and hopeful version of reality.

Although human services workers are a minority, a growing number of them are supporting political approaches to problem solving and are reconsidering their own roles as emissaries of the major social institutions. Within the field of social work, there is a growing body of "radical" literature that critically examines the posture of the profession as an agent of social control.[31] Speaking as a psychiatrist (although it is doubtful that he represents the majority of his colleagues) Seymour Halleck asserts:

As a political force organized psychiatry could be powerful. An individual psychiatrist who writes a book or article describing the oppressive impact of institutionalized racism or technology makes a small but important contribution to social change. If psychiatric organizations presented position papers and testified before legislative bodies on similar issues, however, their opinions would directly reach those who could initiate change. An individual psychiatrist can effect small changes in structure of social systems by exposing inequalities and inconsistencies, but organized psychiatry could use its influence to change such institutions. An individual psychiatrist can make a statement exposing the medical profession's failure to provide adequate health services to the poor, but organized psychiatry could "clean its own house" and serve as a model for the other medical specialties by urging its members to de-emphasize personal profit and by searching for new means of providing adequate care for all people.[32]

The Client's Predicament

When the individual's adaptive behavior casts him into the role of the deviant, his entry into the "protector apparatus" of society may lead to the resolution of some of his problems, but it is also probable that he will be presented with some new ones. Aside from the adversary/conflict arrangement, these types of public response are variations on the theme of social control. In one way or another, once the person becomes a client of these services he is compelled to relinquish or waive some of his rights to decide about the nature and course of his existence.

Within the symbiotic relationship, there may be a margin of benevolence in the way social control is imposed. What is offered is ostensibly for the good and the welfare of the client. Even disregarding the stigma that comes with being a "client," a "case," or a "recipient," there is still the question of what is "good" for people and who makes this determination. Given the labyrinthian nature of the bureaucracies created to deal with residual problems of human distress, it is inevitable that decisions about the welfare of people are made on echelons far removed from the clients' real life circumstances. In accord with the pragmatic philosophy of Western society, the decision about what is "good" is more likely to be based on what is best for the most rather than what is needed by the person. Thus the client is beset by contradictions. How does he manage his own existence on terms that are not his own?

In its most straightforward form, the authoritarian relationship does have the virtue of honesty. It does inform the client about the purpose of the relationship and who, within it, has the final word. The client should know where he stands and what options are open to him, but this is not always the case. Power is not always a comfortable property; the helping person may need to discredit his authoritarian role. The behavioral engineer, the environmental manipulator, or the drug dispenser may be convinced that his controls are being used in the client's best interests. The correctional officer may hide or minimize the immense power he wields in order to "prove" to his client that he really cares and wants to help. The worker responsible for determining who should get what commodities may find his authority distasteful and uneasily deny its part in the process. The client again finds himself confronting a contradiction.

Clinical-diagnostic and psychiatroid relationships are also not devoid of contradictions, especially in the way they are presented as the means by which mental health can be restored or rehabilitated. A liberal-minded observer might agree that medical technologies that include conditioning, psychosurgery, and the use of mind numbing drugs are questionable forms of behavior control. But he would also argue that the many forms of psychotherapy in the medical-psychiatric context are not methods of control but means of inducing freedom. The rhetoric of these therapies is persuasive although we question whether freedom can be induced. In any case, it is worth questioning whether the psychotherapeutic technique is bereft of control. Perry London has written:

> Psychotherapy is a technologically primitive means of behavior control compared to what will come after it, but it is significant in its own right because of the breadth of its applications, if not their power, and because it embodies virtually all the ethical problems which conscientious students of behavior control must encounter. There are literally millions of people undergoing psychotherapy at any time in the United States alone, and millions more probably would be if it were up to many psychotherapists, educators, clergymen, parents, or their enemies to decide. . . .
>
> Without counting sub-professional mental health workers . . . it is plain that an entire industry is engaged in psychotherapeutic practice. Its techniques, therefore, are not merely abstract discourses on influencing human beings but practical plans for doing so, promoted and supported by several fullblown professions, by associations for promoting its use, by manuals of practice, by journals of the trade and by codes of fair exchange between practitioners and their customers. What is more, its operation is often protected by legislation and by custom and nurtured by enormous public and private funds. . . . Considering the huge amounts of public concern, energy, and funds expended on the search for means to cope with behavior problems in one form or another, and thus with behavior control, by one name or another, psychotherapy is a force to be reckoned with. . . .
>
> All forms of psychotherapy aim to control behavior which, by one standard or another, is considered mentally deranged, diseased, disturbed, or otherwise disordered. For this reason, psychotherapists commonly refer to their methods as techniques of treatment rather than control. Such terminology makes no difference to their operations.[33]

Whatever psychotherapy is, it is not a single entity. For this reason, it would be important to heed London's conjectures about its controlling functions, leaving open the possibility that under optimal conditions psychotherapy could offer the consumer the option for personal choice and freedom. Because of its variability and the number of contingencies that are part of its application, whether this option is offered or accepted still depends somewhat on chance.

The predictable result of the client's involvement with societal organizations is his exposure to a number of possible contradictions. Whatever his problems were at the outset of this process, they are bound to become more entangled and confused. Michael Weinstein sums up this plight without much equivocation:

When I become related to an organization I am immediately thrown into the position of a beggar. If I have come with a problem, I realize that the major purpose of the administrators is to insure a smooth flow of work, to avoid excessive complaints and pressures, and to get the most money possible from me while delivering the least services. . . . As for the specialists and workers, I realize that their first aim is to get through the day without excessive discomfort and, perhaps, to distinguish themselves before their superiors. It is also possible that some of them will take pleasure in dominating me. And do I exclude the possibility that some of them will want to help me? No. But in that case I will feel lucky, and I can never give them the benefit of the doubt.

My situation is even worse when I am placed under an organization's control. The managers, specialists, and workers already have the legal right to dispose of much of my existence, and they are under no obligation to show any consideration for me. Some organizations will treat me as an object to be warehoused for a certain period of time, while others will treat me as a deviant to be reformed. I will have little or no choice about the kind of treatment that I will receive. And I will probably also have to confront an inmate hierarchy with powers of its own and links with the official hierarchy. . . . And what if it is my bad luck to deal with a spiteful pariah? I may not get the information I need easily. People may mumble to me unintelligibly, ignore me, keep me waiting for hours, address me in administrative or technical jargon that I cannot understand, give me systematically incomplete information, send me to the wrong office, and so on. They may order me to sign statements or fill out forms, claiming that nothing can be done for me until I do so. And, after all, I have either come with a problem or I have been forced to come. I am likely to be uncertain and worried and thinking about myself more than about my surroundings. I am at a radical disadvantage.

Weinstein considers the possible roles the "client as a beggar" may assume in response to his dilemma.

The closest approximation to dignity for a client is persistent badgering and nagging. Submissiveness breeds contempt; aggressiveness breeds resentment and revenge; badgering and nagging and subtle threats breed exasperation and, sometimes, concession.[34]

SUMMARY AND IMPLICATIONS

This chapter concludes the section on theory and translates the assumptions about self and its cognitive functions into implications for personal and social adaptation. It also defines the personal-social-societal context in which learning and change can be explained. This definition cannot be fully accomplished; the shift from a monadic or closed-system analysis of human behavior (e.g., personality theory, clinical taxonomies, or sociological and statistical) toward an inclusive and transactional perspective on the state of human affairs limits the number of variables that can be incorporated.

The individual becomes comprehensible when his relations with his social situation are understood. The nature of I-world transactions discloses the unique characteristics of the "I" and the meanings of the world as it is perceived. Three major functions of the self are involved in these transactions: the perceiving and interpreting, the self-appraising, and the intentional and motivational. Inner dissonance arises when these functions conflict in response to a particular problem of living. If the person cannot depend on prior problem-solving methods or secure help from others, he must distort, deny, or subdue any or all of these functions in order to assuage the distress of dissonance. Over time, these maneuvers evolve into ineffective patterns of adaptation. As these patterns are enacted in the person's social field they come to be judged in accordance with the needs, processes, and structure of the field. If this behavior is defined as problematic or disturbing, it is possible that the person will become known to any of society's institutions of palliation, remediation, or control. In these circumstances, he may be considered a deviant and defined and treated accordingly. Because his role is recast by others, the individual must now attempt to work out other modes of adaptation.

The limits of this work restrict the pursuit of the ethical, moral, and political questions that bear on the issue of social control. Explanations of the plight of the individual in conflict with his social order are only one side of the equation. What about the rights and needs of others who are violated or offended by the person's marginal adaptations? When is it proper and advisable (and who decides) for society's agents to enter into the life of its citizens and assume responsibility? Are there boundaries and limits to one's rights to self-determination? Is it possible to blend the humanistic and legalistic components of social control, or must they stand in tension because of their disparate orientations? Are there other political alternatives to this dilemma? In leaving these questions open, I hope that the committed human services worker will inquire further into their implications—or at least retain a cautious and skeptical view about easy solutions.[35]

PART THREE

The Process of Social Learning and Change

Chapter 7

Social Learning:
The Design of Change

The need for change is the obvious corollary of personal and social adaptation. Without some sort of intervention (whether by plan or by chance), personal or social maladaptive patterns will not only persist but become more intense, entrenched, and self-defeating. Given this perspective on adaptation, what is meant by the term *change?* Within the personal-social-societal configuration, where should change efforts be directed and what should be changed? *Webster's Third International Dictionary* offers a limited, somewhat tautological definition of the term, stating that change is "the action of making something different in form, quality, or state." This definition is value free; "something different" does not imply "better" or "worse" or "good" or "bad." But planned change *is* a value laden experience to the extent that the participants equate "something different" with something that is believed to be preferable or desirable. Change as a planned and intentional activity therefore suggests movement toward the attainment of a valued goal.

In our perspective involving the person in his situation, the valued goal is the enhancement of the individual's problem-solving strengths and abilities. If life is constantly in the making, the quality of life depends on the effectiveness with which the person contends with the expected and unforeseen problems of living. Whether change is aimed at achieving more autonomous forms of personal, interpersonal, or societal adaptation, the process itself must account for the committed and knowledgeable participation of those who will be affected by change. In its generic

231

sense, change, whether it is pursued individually or collectively, is an educative and learning process.

LEARNING AND PLANNED CHANGE

Among some scholars and researchers, it is recognized that behavior change is a learning experience that is not dissimilar to other educational enterprises. Learning occurs in any interpersonal and interactional experience that is directed toward planned change. Although London's observations are directed toward psychotherapy, they are cogent reflections on any experience that is concerned with changes in patterns of behavior, thought, and planning or in work with such systems as families and groups.

Because it relies on this most complex medium—the "higher processes" of language and symbol (sometimes considered the only uniquely human attributes)—psychotherapy is also a straightforward extension of education, which, in the perspective of our age, is regarded as the antithesis of control through coercion. . . . psychotherapy can always be properly regarded as a special case of educational treatment, though it is more often seen as a separate discipline which is not exactly the practice of medicine, not quite the same as teaching, more than just giving advice, and less than religious revivalism—but still a way of changing people's lives.[1]

In a similar vein, Hans Strupp comments: "Learning in psychotherapy, almost by definition, occurs within the context of the interpersonal relationship, in the course of which the patient typically becomes dependent on the therapist as an authority, teacher, and mentor."[2]

Jerome Frank's definition outlines in general the change experience. He asserts that the common denominator of all therapies is their ability to help the person reduce his suffering, smooth his social relationships, and improve his performance by fostering changes in cognitions, feelings, and behavior. The success of all therapies depends on the therapeutic alliance in which the individual accepts some dependence on the therapist based on the former's confidence in the latter's competence and good intentions. "The therapist uses his power to achieve three aims. The first is to enable the patient to discover new information about himself, both cognitively and experientially; the second is to arouse him emotionally, since emotions supply the motive power for change; the third is to

232

encourage him to change his behavior in the light of what he has learned and to practice the new patterns."[3] All forms of behavior change can be seen as promoting a new kind of experience that results in cognitive and experiential learning.

William Bennett and Merle Hokenstad suggest that the human services worker typically finds himself in an educative role. What distinguishes this worker from other kinds of professionals is his function of *catalyst*, that is, one who *shares* his knowledge with his clients as a means of enabling the client to help himself. The more "impersonal professions" (e.g., engineering, pharmacy, and architecture) use their respective bodies of knowledge as tools to perform the service, and there is no requirement for the client to partake of this knowledge in receiving the services he needs.[4] As a sharer of knowledge, the human services worker's role corresponds with the educator's. Both include catalytic functions to the extent that they create the climate and the cooperative effort in which insights and knowledge are shared to encourage the person to define his own needs and goals and take appropriate action to fulfill them.

WHAT IS LEARNING?

It is one thing to equate behavior change with learning but it is something more complex to say what learning is. Since learning stands for such a wide and varied range of activities it is almost universal in scope. It may be used in a concrete and definitive sense when learning refers to the direct acquisition of specific skills or knowledge. It implies more ambiguous and abstract meanings when it applies to the processes of mentation going on within a person which can only be inferred by others. Learning is not restricted to the human domain; most animals are capable of simple forms of learning. The domestication of certain breeds of wildlife and the work of experimental psychologists with laboratory animals offer ample evidence that even powerful instinctual patterns can be modified by the application of learning protocols. For that matter, plant life can learn; that is, if the meaning of learning is limited to the receiving and storing of information.

It is when we use learning to denote a particular human experience and activity that we find it difficult to specify what we are referring to. For the concept of learning to have any meaning whatsoever it must be linked with some referent or take account of the context in which it is occurring. If I phone a friend and inquire about what he is doing and he replies, "I am learning," I would probably be perplexed unless some additional information was forthcoming. If I did not have some foreknowledge about his current interests or activities, I would need to find out what he was learning, why, and for what purposes. This leads to the first basic premise about the learning experience: for the concept to have any meaning it must be qualified by certain conditional and situational forms of information. In sum, it is necessary to know *who* is learning *what, where* it is taking place, *under what conditions, in relation to who or what else,* and *for what purposes.*

The looseness with which the term is employed in ordinary discourse constitutes another problem of definition. Common expressions such as "He is going to have to learn to be a better husband" or "I really learned who my friends are" use "learning" as a synonym for "awareness" or "discovery," or the exposure to some sort of new knowledge. This basic level of awareness is the necessary first step in the learning sequence from which the more intricate problem-solving activities follow. However, the ambiguous way in which the term is used in these cases does not suggest necessarily that these stages of learning will ensue. Thus the statement "I really learned . . ." is far more exclamatory than it is explanatory.

The cloudy implications of the concept are nowhere more in evidence than in the very programs and settings where education and learning are the primary objectives. Here what is called "learning" all too often turns out to be a euphemism and the source of the public outcry about the decline of competency in literacy and the other skills that the institution purportedly teaches. Learning, in this case, may actually represent a number of other diversions: the ability to endure or comply with imposed requirements, the ability to ingest and feed back data, and the ability to assume the student role without becoming a learner. Obviously something is learned, e.g., how to succeed with short-term memorization, how to pass an examination with minimal knowledge, and how to muddle through. But these outcomes are only perversions of what incisive learning should involve.

Even if these semantic problems were resolved and the concept of learning (used either as a verb or noun) referred to a particular problem-solving experience, certain definitional questions would remain since the

234

concept can represent diverse processes and a wide range of objectives. I am not referring merely to the apparent differences between learning how to cook and learning about birth control measures. Even these tasks call for quite different types of motoric and mental processes. I am alluding to the different functions that learning serves relative to the way people adapt to and carry on their business of living. There are three broad categories of functions: strategic, tactical, and adaptive.[5]

Strategic Learning

Strategic learning can be understood as a deliberate activity or problem-solving venture enacted to achieve a more or less preconceived objective. It could involve acquisition of knowledge and data for decision-making purposes, improvement of technical or motoric skills for performance purposes, mastery of steps or procedures to achieve greater effectiveness, control, or responsibility, or development of wisdom to enhance self-esteem or motivation. In any case, learning expresses a particular intent, narrowly or broadly conceived.

Tactical Learning

Tactical learning involves the maneuvers required to adjust to unexpected contingencies of living. It is in some ways more responsive or reactive than strategic learning, inasmuch as it concerns chance happenings that interfere with plans and intentions. A person calls upon his practiced techniques for problem resolution to arrive at proper decisions, to find other alternatives, or to determine what other information might be needed for a short-term solution.

Adaptive Learning

Adaptive learning refers to an overarching form of learning and can be used interchangeably with *social learning* and *existential learning* since all three terms connote the involvement of self, its construction of reality, and the implications of learning for the person's present and future place in his world. Adaptive learning serves as a nexus, i.e., an experience that affects the individual's interactions with his environment as his perceptions of his past are linked with his projections of his future. This learning is integral to making choices and decisions, to the quality of relationships with others, and to the kind of planning that shapes future conditions. It

235

is employed in the seemingly minor decisions that are part of day-to-day living and in the rare and serious moments when more radical determinations need to be made.

The critical relationship between learning and personal and social evolvement has been clearly recognized, particularly among certain thoughtful educators and educational theorists who see formal education as considerably more than just training or conveying specific knowledge and skill. Anderson and Gates are quite specific about the relations between learning and adaptation. To them learning is the means by which man acquires new ways of behaving or performing in order that he can make a better adjustment to the demands of living.[6] Woodruff refers to learning as the vehicle by which the individual is changed from a bundle of potentialities to an acting organism having ideas, habits, skills, preferences, and other distinguishing personality characteristics.[7]

Perhaps the most fundamental approach to the clarification of what learning is all about is taken by Garry and Kingsley who stress that learning is a basic process of living: "Through learning the individual develops modes of behavior by which he lives. Whether we look at life in terms of culture, community, or the individual, we are confronted on every side by pervasive effects of learning . . . customs, laws, religions, languages and social institutions have been developed and maintained as a result of man's ability to learn."

This statement reflects many ideas of John Dewey, Harry Stack Sullivan, and Alfred Adler. Garry and Kingsley go on to suggest that this notion of learning also poses serious implications for personal and social change: ". . . to understand behavior, actions, interests, attitudes, ideals, beliefs, skills and knowledge which characterize any human behavior, we have to understand the learning process because learning and maturation comprise two major influences affecting behavior."[8]

OUTLINE OF SOCIAL LEARNING

Learning, in its fundamental sense, is change in behavior resulting from experience. Learning occurs when a person's response to a situation produces a new or changed kind of performance which then becomes part of his repertoire of behavior. This basic definition can apply to all levels of learning: for example, the awareness or conditioning arising from the discovery that cooked potatoes cool slowly, the complex motoric patterns sharpened in learning how to dance or engaging in sports, or the thinking required to solve an algebraic problem.

Social learning is a higher form of learning occurring in a social context for the purpose of personal and social adaptation. This definition differentiates between types of learning that do not require the participation of another and social learning that depends on interpersonal relationships. It calls on the use of abstract symbols and involves factors of affect, value, and motive; hence it is a higher form of learning.

Social learning and socialization are in some cases overlapping but not always identical processes. Socialization may be considered as social learning insofar as it is aimed at the acquisition of behaviors and attitudes that conform to existing social norms and expectations. But social learning can also have rather contrary purposes when the experience is largely individualistic and the person's pursuits may have little to do with or conflict with established standards.

Social learning occurs when a person's response to a situation is in some way influenced by the perceived presence of another or others, and this response becomes integrated into his repertoire of social behavior. The perceived presence may be real or imagined, intentional, accidental, or inferred.

Social learning is a goal-directed experience. People tend to engage in learning activities that have meaning for them in terms of some immediate or future purpose or reward. This does not suggest that all learning is deliberate or planned; adventitious events may offer gainful experiences provided the person is open to change or discovery and can envision some kind of positive outcome. There are obvious implications for the planned change experience since its intent can scarcely be realized if the participants cannot see that anything useful or personally desirable will come of it.

Social learning is a value experience. If learning is to occur in the first place, its value needs to be recognized and may need to take precedence over or be accomplished at the expense of other values. Value strain or dissonance arises when personal or social change is viewed as desirable, but to fulfill this intent other valued patterns must be relinquished.

The learning experience may express the person's instrumental or terminal values. Learning is the enactment of instrumental values when it is the means used to achieve certain outcomes that correspond with the

237

person's preferences and priorities. As a terminal value, learning becomes an end in itself, particularly as the person is committed to learning for its own sake.

Social learning is an experience that depends on the use of symbols. Learning is in many ways a uniquely personal experience. Even in those instances where the plan is to master such specific things as facts, categories of knowledge, and specific skills and procedures, it is likely that these matters will be interpreted in somewhat personal and figurative terms that may or may not have anything to do with the project. However, where learning is concerned with such abstract and intangible experiences as love, caring, relations, power, or vengeance, the probability is greatly increased that symbolizations of a more idiosyncratic nature will occur. Although certain generalizations about the process of learning can be made, within these generalizations it is necessary to take account of the symbolic characteristics of the learner and the specific style in which he tends to represent his reality.

Social learning that affects adaptive patterns can result in periods of personal or interpersonal disruption. The changes that accompany or are the consequence of learning can be expected to disturb the balance of the self and/or the familiar patterns of relationships. Even when the learning experience anticipates positive products or rewards, the process may involve certain transitions that prove to be distressing and painful particularly in the period when habitual patterns, symbols, and values begin to erode and are not yet replaced by proven and reliable new styles. Obviously the amount of disruption felt would depend on the nature and purpose of the learning experience and the extent to which it intruded into others' modes of living. For example, the active intent to learn to become more assertive within a well-established relationship is likely to be more unsettling than trying to understand the steps of assertiveness training by reading a "how to" book. Discomfort is more related to the extent to which aspects of the self or the system are at stake in the undertaking than to the objective nature of the learning event.

Social learning typically involves transactional processes. Learning occurs in relation to others in the person's environment. The changes accruing from the experience are not unidirectional: any actions that affect the environment will elicit a response that will generate yet other reactions. These responses may confirm, neutralize, or invalidate the learned behavior and serve as corrective measures insofar as they inform the learner about the value, desirability, or implications of his actions.

With regard to planned change, transactional characteristics should be especially considered when it can be predicted that the process or product of learning will impinge on significant social relationships. Typically, changes in the learner's patterns of adaptation are accompanied by implicit or explicit requirements for others also to change so as to accommodate to these new patterns. New learning may have the function of realigning the existing balance of relationships and may be disruptive. Such systemic implications are clearly evident in work with families and groups where it is as necessary to attend to the balance of the system as it is to the changing needs of its members and to achieve a measure of correspondence between the two. Similar approaches are also relevant to types of social action that aim to help people learn how to redefine their status in and their expectations of their larger community. A critical part of their learning would involve predictions about the kinds of reactions that might be evoked and preparations for dealing with them.

Social learning involves the interplay of cognition, emotion, and behavior. The importance of personal values and symbols requires attention to the emotional as well as the thinking and acting aspects of learning. Piaget and Inhelder observe:

As we have seen repeatedly, affectivity constitutes the energetics of behavior patterns whose cognitive aspect refers to the structures alone. There is no behavior pattern, however intellectual, which does not involve affective factors as motives; but reciprocally, there can be no affective states without the intervention of perceptions or comprehensions which constitute the cognitive structure. Behavior is therefore of a piece, even if structures do not explain its energetics and if, vice versa, its energetics do not account for its structures. The two aspects, affective and cognitive, are at the same time inseparable and irreducible.[9]

Any approach to learning must extend serious consideration to the links between motivational energies and the active processes of cognition.

A significant element of the learning experience is its climate of and potential for support. As it pertains to intentional change, the context of learning is typically a dyadic relationship, a group, or other collectivity. Effective learning requires an atmosphere that offers the kind of relationship and support that compensates for the distressing and disruptive aspects of change. It should also provide the opportunity to anticipate certain obstacles and the occasion to rehearse possible remedies. The conditions of learning are no less important than the process itself.

Social learning can be a group as well as an individual experience. Although learning is a personalized and symbolic event, it is also possible for numbers of people to share in the experience. It is important to differentiate between an aggregate of individual learners (as in a classroom) sharing the space and a group comprising people who are conscious of mutual values, perceptions, and agreement about the goals they are seeking. This does not discount the possibility of conflict and disagreement. In the working group, there may be discord about content or process issues but usually not about the value and aims of the group. Members can learn from others' thoughts and experience and can profit from the intragroup relationships that foster and offer the impetus for learning.

Under certain conditions, learning may evolve into a creative experience. The purpose of learning usually is to find productive solutions to problem situations. These solutions may be novel and original but largely utilitarian and problem specific in nature. Less frequently there are those occasions when the learning process, carried beyond its more functional purposes, may result in bringing into consciousness certain personal visions and potentials, forms of artistry that were never before recognized. It is this sort of undergoing that ruptures the boundaries of conventional reasoning and action and thrusts the learner into alien and unexpected realms of awareness. And beyond the intrinsic value of the experience itself, these extraordinary realizations may contribute to one's self-esteem as well as to the excitation of other potentialities for more creative living.

LEARNING AND HUMAN PURPOSE

Although an outline reveals the elements of a phenomenon, it can only hint at the qualities of the whole. Learning is experienced as a unitary event, an existential act that is inseparable from being and becoming. It is never finished or consummate; even as a simple task is resolved, other opportunities are disclosed or the doer realizes something more about his strengths or lacks that may be pertinent to other projects. Learning itself is not intrinsically "good." The process of learning is equally capable of producing negative or positive outcomes. Though learning is essential to human development, it does not assure that this development will be authentic or beneficial. Maliciousness and exploitiveness are as much products of learning as are the more loving and generous traits.

Most often, learning is a reactive experience. As problems of living arise, the person responds by attempting to devise solutions that will allow him to go on with his usual business of living. Learning can also be self-initiated without reference to any immediate questions or problems. Because the mind can anticipate and create images of what the future may be like, the person can create valued goals and at the same time foresee and prepare for the possible obstacles that might emerge.

The consequences of ordinary learning and problem solving related to the unexceptional difficulties getting in the way of the routines of living are usually not very noteworthy. As these problems are resolved in one way or another, scant attention is given to the experience as the person moves on to other activities. Even if failure is the result, very little may be lost—particularly if the person feels relatively secure and competent. He may also have the opportunity to attack the problem a second time and even if this is not possible, his self-esteem may be generous enough to grant him the kind of rationalization that will allow him to overlook his error. However, these seemingly commonplace events do become significant when they are understood as expressions of a general pattern of adaptation and learning rather than a series of discrete and unrelated episodes.

In the final analysis, the attempt to explain and characterize the concept of social learning is best achieved by showing its relevance for some particular conditions of living.

Maturation, Development, and Learning

Perhaps the most familiar periods in which problem solving and adaptation are essential are the fairly predictable phases of human development. Although the organism matures in an uninterrupted fashion, for a number of reasons these stages of living are marked off in terms of infancy, childhood, puberty, adolescence, the various phases of adulthood, and old age. These stages can be defined and explained by a number of frameworks (psychosexual, psychosocial, epigenetic, or cognitive).

Where these frameworks are useful for denoting the progression in the development of the individual per se, the concept of *social role* more closely complements the concept of social learning as a transactional experience. The idea of a social role captures the personal as well as the interpersonal strains that arise as persons leave one developmental phase and enter the next. Social roles are acquired in learning experiences that shape the beliefs, values, and behaviors supporting the person's attempts to become an active and effective member of his family, groups, and society. Such roles are the unfinished products of the transactions between self and environment involving the impact of socialization, the opportunities to observe and model after others, and sought or imposed guidance.

A person does not need to go beyond his personal experience to appreciate the fact that social roles are not worked out with any amount of ease. This strain does not arise out of any lack of prescriptions or images relative to questions about how to be, think, act, or feel: society and more intimate groups are overly generous in extending guidance. In one respect, these prescriptions are not easily ignored since their acceptance elicits rewards or avoids the penalties that attend their rejection. Yet, these invitations to think and act in conventional and approved ways cannot fully be assimilated without some loss to autonomy and individuality, because in important ways each individual must preserve his exceptional qualities. This strain arising between inner and outer standards and values creates an impetus for learning.

Social role learning is also confounded by the number of contradictory expectations encountered. Each person is an amalgam of a number of roles—gender, marriage, occupation, friendships. These roles frequently collide, particularly when a person struggles with questions of the priorities of needs and values. This conflict becomes even more distressing when contending with demands coming from outside sources that are irreconcilable. The woman who seriously strives to fulfill her roles as a single parent and an employee faces such a dilemma. At work, she may be expected to behave in a subordinate or dependent fashion, carrying out her duties in a prescribed manner as they are assigned. At home, society assumes that she will be dominant, independent, and self-sufficient, that she will care for her children and household effectively. On any given day she must accommodate to both sets of expectations as incongruous as they are. Similar absurdities abound in other situations: the unemployed father who is maligned because he is not more independent and self-assertive and yet excoriated because he will not accept a low-paying menial job, or the adolescent who is pressed to act in a more mature fashion but condemned because he will not abide by other's definitions of maturity.

Despite antagonisms and contradictions, the average mortal is able to appropriate a number of roles and muddle through a particular phase of his existence without severe loss to his self-concept and aspirations. The extent to which the person is able to meld and complement these roles offers a relatively dependable foundation for adaptability and a sense of personal continuity. From the fusion of these roles emerges what Orville Brim calls the "I-Them," "They-Me," and "I-Me" relationships that embody the expectations and appraisals that I have of others, those that others impose on me, and the ideals and standards that I hold for myself. [10]

There are times when familiar roles can begin to lose their effectiveness and their value appears doubtful. If the fit between others' and the individual's role expectations was loose, the gap grows wider resulting in confusion and uncertainty. Typically, these times are the transitional periods in normal growth and development or in the various phases of adulthood marked by the need to redefine questions of behavior, responsibility, relations, and goals. Movement into the successive stage of development is usually accompanied by the decay of former roles and the security they provided. At the same time, demands arise for the person to take on new behaviors and responsibilities and to alter his outlook on the world. These demands are voiced most stridently in the "They-Me" relationships, particularly if the transition is not accomplished with proper dispatch. They are expressed in such terms as "Quit acting like a child!" "Can't you realize that you're married now and that you just can't do what you want?" "Why can't you just settle down and accept that you're retired?"

Effective social learning in periods of transition eases change somewhat and allows for more wholesome growth and adaptation. Upon moving from familiar and well-tested social roles into alien and uncertain realms of being, the individual needs to attend to new factors and data, reconceptualize many issues and questions, and reconsider his categories of reality. The obstacles that learning and problem solving strive to overcome are at once common and unique. There are the usual impediments in attempting to secure a sense of role comfort: inconsistencies of personal and social expectations, ambiguities accompanying readjustment, and the difficulties in finding the freedom, room, and opportunities to rehearse and try a number of new roles. The unique impediments are harder to define since they are contained within the symbolic images, ideals, and self-definitions, and they touch on questions of dignity and self-esteem. In the end, the major obstacle is the matter of balance and proportion, which is the attainment of a degree of harmony between personal and social expectations in a way that does not discredit autonomy or result in alienation.

Existential Dilemmas and Learning

Conditions prompting social learning can be focused more specifically on the unpredictable nature of human existence—the *contigencies* of living, the unforeseen and unexpected events that arise to thwart complacent movement into the future.

Existential philosophy maintains that no matter how diligently man strives, plans, and manipulates in the final analysis he has little control over how his future unfolds. [11] Neither nature nor history can determine man's destiny, and faith alone offers little assurance about how life will work out. Living is thus an experience of being cast into a world of contingencies in which existence or even survival cannot fully be planned or predicted. Even if an individual accepts the future as incalculable and attempts to look ahead with caution and readiness, he discovers that he cannot know all that needs to be known in preparation for the unexpected.

The future as imponderable does not relieve the person of options to choose and act. He may take the inauthentic course and deny that life is indeed beset with unreckonable contingencies. Any number of self-deluding tactics may be used to avoid this reality. Or he may choose to confront uncertainty, to decide deliberately and consciously to "be in the world" as fully and honestly as is possible. Within the existential scheme, anxiety is the product of either choice.

Although each individual inevitably contends with the anxiety accompanying movement into the future, there is a marked difference

244

between the nature of anxiety resulting from each of the options. Should he choose to turn his back on the contingent nature of his existence he will experience a "neurotic" anxiety in the form of a sense of personal powerlessness and estrangement. He becomes demoralized as, to him, his world is formidable and obscure. However, should he elect to confront the ambiguities of living, he must deal with the "existential anxiety," the natural sense of disquietude and tension that accompanies such a choice. For the will to accept the realization that "I cannot fully control" generates a painful paradox. Although an individual is aware that he cannot regulate his existence, this awareness does not permit him to lessen his intentionality and planning. He knows that he cannot become a passive voyager enduring whatever fate places before him; rather, he feels obliged to confront the unexpected and at each point make the decision that allows him to move forward in an authentic and responsible fashion. In many respects, this choice reflects the needs that are involved in the attempt to create harmony between self concept and intention so as to preserve the integrity of the self.

How does social learning fit into this existential scheme? First we must consider the effects of the more pragmatic functions of learning, those that relate to the acquisition of special knowledge and skills to enhance competency. If we are able to become more effective in how we deal with the more mundane aspects of living in the present, we are able to reduce the risks and uncertainties of the future. Moreover, these abilities permit us to create a sense of order and find that there are aspects of living that do fall within our control. Yet, we are still bound to come upon exigencies that defy our most forward-looking motives. The decision to choose to act and the choice that is made at that point depends on the confidence we feel in our problem-solving prowess—the ability to attend to and be conscious of the details of the challenge, to manipulate symbols, judge, reappraise, and to some extent, predict. We may feel free to employ perceptual processes in a variety of ways, to apprehend the event on many levels of consciousness and permit ourselves to "see" and comprehend it in terms of its many possible meanings and implications. Simply put, my choice will be far more authentic and meaningful when I permit my full-blooded self to enter into the experience, not foolhardily, but with the tested assurance that I can wrestle with it. And if I fail, I am not destroyed for I am capable of contending with the failure.

245

Crisis Events and Learning

A field of social science knowledge called "crisis theory" offers what might be viewed as a more pragmatic approach to the understanding of the way people respond to the unanticipated emergencies of living. [12] Gerald Caplan defines a crisis in terms that correspond in many ways with Dewey's formulation. He states that crisis is a state "provoked when a person faces an obstacle to important life goals that is, for a time, insurmountable through the utilization of customary modes of problem solving. A period of disorganization ensues, a period of upset, during which many different attempts at solution are made. Eventually some kind of adaptation is achieved which may or may not be in the best interest of the person and his fellows." [13]

This definition fits the notion of problem solving as a means of contending with an obstacle by engaging in some sort of learning. In the case of the crisis, this process is qualified by the compression of time and the intensification of distress. Sudden threats to personal stability coming from such unexpected catastrophes as natural disasters, the death of a loved one, severe illness, or economic collapse are experienced as sharp and poignant intrusions that demand immediate resolution if any relief is to be felt at all. But the precipitous nature of the crisis event imposes two handicaps on the attempt to find a solution. First, because the occurence is so sudden and unexpected, its meaning is often obscured or it is clouded by intense feelings. Consequently, the ability to identify and make sense of at least the vague shape of the emergency is aborted. Even if the victim could grasp the essence of the crisis, the means of coping with the problem would elude him since by definition a crisis reveals the ineffectiveness of existing adaptive techniques.

A crisis calls for new forms of learning and the modification of accustomed patterns, and the outcome of the experience may vary. Learning may be inadequate and the consequences debilitating, diminishing the victim in many respects. His conception of self as an able and effective human being may be shaken by the realization of his failure to cope, and his world view may take on dismal proportions. The crisis can come to stand as a symbol of personal ineptitude leading to a sense of powerlessness in the face of the demands of living.

Perhaps more commonly, the outcomes of a crisis tend to follow the

246

principle of homeostasis. The individual merely learns to endure the event by devising patterns that allow him to deal with the obstacle in a way that permits him to return to his normal lifestyle relatively unscathed. The emergency is perceived as a temporary intrusion compensated by strategies that serve to reduce anxiety and disorganization. Once normality is again achieved, the crisis is relegated to memory where it remains as a milestone of sorts or perhaps as a referent that he can use to justify something about his actions or outlook. The crisis does not effect any appreciable loss to the person's self-concept but neither does it generate significant gains.

Another consequence of the experience might be an acceleration in the growth and realization of the self. Although the victim may emerge from the catastrophe scarred, the extent to which the crisis is seized in terms of the meanings it holds can lead to a richer consciousness and maturity. Apart from its pernicious qualities, the adversity also can be understood as something that succeeds in undoing major values and aspirations and the means that are commonly used to fulfill them. Rationalizations are stripped away leaving him open to the risks of reconsidering his cherished styles of living. If these risks can be confronted, new learning in its most creative and ambitious sense is possible and can lead to new visions of being, values, and goals. The existential crisis of the person who suffers a serious heart attack has become virtually a cliché. Other crises are exemplified by the implications of the rupture of a once fulfilling marriage or the realization that a career has reached a dead end. Comforting illusions are ruined, and the crisis destroys misconceptions that lent credence to the motives and self-conceptions they supported.

The intense and overwhelming emotions that arise are not merely corollaries of the crisis event, they are formidable expressions of the elemental self, affective statements that no longer can be contained by habit or conventional rationalities. Whether or not these potent feelings are particularly accurate or even justifiable is not important, but they can serve as a bridge to a deeper and more authentic consciousness. However, a person must be willing to defy the natural tendency to disclaim the meanings and messages that these emotions are expressing. It is also difficult to resist the blandishments of well-meaning others who, in trying to insulate themselves or the person from the anguish of the

247

experience, press for the suppression and control of these revealing emotions.

The expressive learning that may be gained from an ordeal is not restricted to the individual. Opportunities for the discovery of new means and goals also come to collectives of people. Few people remain unaffected by the news of families, neighborhoods, or entire communities that not only are able to survive a catastrophe but emerge with remarkable hope and ideals about rebuilding their lives and their futures. Verta Taylor, in her review of studies by the Disaster Research Center of Ohio State University, notes a challenge to conventional wisdom that emotional breakdown and pathological behavior follow catastrophe:

> Most specialists in disasters point to the high morale usually found in communities after a disaster. To meet urgent problems, people put aside their own suffering to help others. In a disaster, suffering isn't an isolated personal experience. . . . Researchers suggest that a heightened sense of community serves as a type of therapy that offsets some of the personal tragedy and loss. Put another way, damage, loss, and destruction follow disaster, but so do heroism, altruism, and rebuilding. . . . Perhaps the experience of coping with and mastering the many personal crises associated with the disaster might even enhance a person's psychological well being. [14]

Significant Interpersonal Relationships and Learning

Social learning refers to a process occurring within a significant involvement with another or others. Learning is understood as an *interpersonal* experience influenced in important ways by the nature and quality of the interchange between people. This interchange also has a *transactional* character; within it, a dialectic is enacted where one person's response affects the reaction of another, generating another rejoinder, and so on. Social learning is also *situational* since it is experienced within an environment consisting of normative, cultural, and attitudinal conditions that affect the learning event in important ways. Learning can be a group phenomenon within which shared beliefs, values, and patterns may serve as an impetus for learning and change.

The stages of human development imply the notion of a progressive, linear sequence of events. The idea of adolescence, for example, suggests the influence of the preceding prepubescent period and the implications of the present stage for the phase of adulthood to follow. When it comes to perceiving the contingencies and crises of living, they seem at first to be

248

marked by their irregularity, acuteness, and apparent unrelatedness to prior events. Yet these critical episodes find their place in the serial flow of living once they are over. At some point they become part of the evolving biography of the person as he moves on to the next episodes of living. These experiences are not forgotten or disposed of with any sense of finality. If the crisis was not resolved or did not contribute to the further growth of self, it may linger as a piece of unfinished business within the stream of existence.

We may also think about close and intimate relationships as if they had definite beginnings and endings at certain points in our histories. But these recollections are merely intellectual and descriptive; as they are actually experienced, they do not end even in the case of geographical separation or death. In Robert Anderson's play, *I Never Sang for My Father*, the protagonist broods over the recent death of his father:

> Death ends a life . . . but it does not end a relationship, which struggles on in the survivor's mind . . . toward some resolution, which it never finds. Alice said I would not accept the sadness of the world. . . . What did it matter if I never loved him, or if he never loved me? . . . Perhaps she was right. . . . But, still, when I hear the word "father" . . . (He cannot express it . . . there is still the longing, the emotion. He looks around . . . out . . . as though he would finally be able to express it, but he can only say . . .) It matters. [15]

Even as life ends, the relationship persists in the minds of the survivors as it does when the maturation of a child, divorce, or physical separation divide caring people. So much is invested in the inimitable intimate relationship as the partners come to disclose and discover fragments of self that were otherwise hidden or even unrealized. A flourishing relationship depends on the extent to which its members can break through the boundaries of the integral and solitary self and open themselves to the spirit and substance of the experience. The meaningful relationship stirs the self-extending aspects of the self, those that risk reaching out to fathom the other's values and ideals. Such affectional ties, loyalties, and identifications become a powerful impetus for learning and realization. These potentialities are captured in the *I-Thou*, Martin Buber's archetype of human association:

> Through the *Thou* a man becomes *I*. That which confronts him comes and disappears, relational events condense, then are scattered, and in the change consciousness of the unchanging partner, of the *I*, grows clear, and each time

stronger. To be sure, it is still caught in the web of the relation with the *Thou*, as the increasingly distinguishable feature of that which reaches out to and yet is not the *Thou*. But it continually breaks through with more power, till a time comes when it bursts its bonds, and the *I* confronts itself for a moment, separated as though it were a *Thou*: as quickly to take possession of itself and from then on to enter into relations in consciousness of itself.[16]

It is this consciousness that presses for more and continued knowing because within it the self increasingly is cut adrift from its seemingly secure and familiar convictions. Only as a person is able to maintain his separateness by keeping a safe distance from others can he continue to nurture the myths that he clings to and elude challenges to his cherished ideals, beliefs, and hopes. When he risks entry into a serious compact with another, his basic premises become vulnerable—particularly when he beholds that the prized other's realities and perceptions contradict his own. The individual's option in this case may involve retreat to his own comfortable beliefs; although the former self then remains intact, nothing is learned or gained. But if retreat is resisted and entry permitted, learning about that most elusive phenomenon—the self—becomes possible. And learning of this kind equates with the discovery of new meaning and purpose in the person's existence.

Social learning is not at all restricted to the intimate confines of the *I-Thou* or any other dyadic relationship. Even a political movement may offer the bonding experience that can release the potential for the discovery of a person's affirmative values and the means by which they may be expressed. A report on the National Women's Conference of 1977 stated:

What happened, particularly for the 14,000 who attended the Houston meeting, was an end to the psychological isolation that had constrained their activities and ambitions. They learned that many of the middle-of-the-road, American-as-Mom's apple-pie women shared with them a sense of second-class citizenship and a craving for greater social and economic equality. . . . A new-found confidence visibly emerged during the conference; women were suddenly put together with others sharing their views, hopes, and anxieties. Alliances were forged for the battles that lie ahead. The women knew that their political skills were on trial, and they passed the test with flying colors.[17]

The meaningful relationship is also a critical variable in the process of planned change. The encounter between the client and his counselor or

250

the person and his group depends on the quality of the relationship if learning and change is to unfold. (This is not a mystical or ephemeral experience as often portrayed!) As openly and as authentically as possible, the worker attempts to create a climate wherein the client can begin risking the giving up of needless control and grant the worker a measure of direction. Beliefs, values, and basic premises about the nature of reality emerge into openness, creating a hiatus of sorts that can only be resolved by a mutual search for other potentials.

THE SOCIAL LEARNING EVENT

Learning was described as a *process* that involves *someone* mastering *something* for some *purpose* within a particular *situation*. What makes it a social learning event are its interactional and social characteristics and purposes. The critical concepts that signify the learning event are process, person, content, intention, and environment. These are not discrete concepts since their meaning and import depend on the peculiar way they stand in relation to the nature of the particular obstacle that evoked the learning event in the first place. Figure 4 clarifies this phenomenon by showing a person in a situation in progress toward the attainment of a

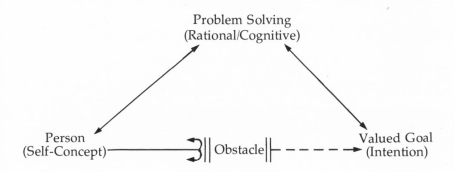

FIGURE 4. Problem Solving

desired objective, his path blocked by an unyielding obstacle. The rational/cognitive functions act to give meaning to the goal and the obstacle, and they are the means by which some sort of solution is reached. Each of these interacting elements has an important role in each learning typology.

The Situation

Situation refers to the social and physical setting where the learning episode occurs and includes the weight of interpersonal, societal, emotional, and facilitative conditions that may possibly influence the event. The conditions and their implications may be perceived quite accurately by the person or they may be ignored or misconstrued. Some of the more specific aspects of the situation impinging on learning include:

1. *Availability of resources:* The required materials, tools, commodities, equipment, and expertise of others and the extent to which they are accessible;

2. *Availability of information:* Access to necessary facts, data, knowledge, procedures, guidance, rules, and direction;

3. *Evidence of opportunity:* Clear indications that the setting does encourage or will not hinder problem-solving attempts;

4. *Evidence of alternatives:* The extent to which the setting offers or encourages other options for action or other desirable goals;

5. *Conventions:* The tacit or explicit assumptions about how one ought or ought not to pursue solutions; and

6. *Climate:* Intangible emotional, relational, and atmospheric conditions that say something about the presence of consistency, support, and freedom to experiment, and intimations of encouragement, hope, and reward that may animate or depress aspirations for success and change.

This is not to suggest a clear-cut, cause-effect relationship exists between the quality of the learning environment and the effectiveness of learning, although in a probabilistic sense the richer setting ought to effect better learning. Perception plays a pivotal role because the setting may be saturated with inducements and opportunities that are ignored by the learner, or the absence of opportunities may be perceived by the

252

person as the challenge he needs to rise up and overcome these conditions.

The well-planned school classroom is an example of the attempt to create an atmosphere to facilitate learning. The educator seeks an attractive and stimulating atmosphere where detractions are minimized, the necessary control and discipline are imposed, and learning aids are made accessible. Other settings are designed for planned personal and social change. The typical counselor's office is quiet and comfortable and is protected against intrusions. It may display diplomas and certificates to assure the client about the counselor's qualifications. Any perceptive worker is sensitive to the differential implications of the surroundings wherein he is attempting to foster learning and change. In working with a family, he is aware that the process will take on different proportions, depending on whether he is seeing them in their own home or in the confines of his office. There is a difference in working with medical patients within the hospital or in the open space of their community; with employees on the job or in the union hall; or with administrators in their own office or in another's. Each setting poses certain advantages and disadvantages as far as progress is concerned. Each admits important implications for the direction, content, and overall character of the learning event.

The Obstacle

An obstacle is the intrusive condition which by its *felt* presence, bars movement forward to the individual's goals and thereby compels the need for some form of learning. The obstacle may be "real" or a purely personal construct that has no recognizable referent in the real world. It can exist as an actuality outside the person, somewhere in his environment, or it can be something that the individual experiences within himself. Some of the characteristics that the obstacle may acquire are: 1) *clarity and definition*—the attributes that affect the extent to which the nature of the obstacle lends itself to identification and recognition; the qualities of the stimulus also apply; 2) *Intrinsic importance*—a call for judgment or a determination about the value of the goal in relation to other values;[18] 3) *Intrinsic difficulty or complexity*—judgment about the reasonableness of the task; and 4) *Intrinsic meaning and implications*—the possible ramifications of the obstacle.

253

The Person

The characteristics of the problem solver will dominate the nature and process of the learning event. The more apparent personal traits and characteristics include: 1) *health and vigor*—the level of energy, state of well-being, stamina, and endurance required to initiate and follow through on the problem-solving venture; 2) *intelligence*—in its generic sense, a wide range of functions, each having differential implications;[19] 3) *behavioral traits*—the more distinctive styles of conduct that the person uses in a characteristic fashion in his approach to the world; and 4) *knowledge and skill*—the wisdom and the capabilities acquired over time and their relevance to the task.

These characteristics will affect the style and the vitality with which the individual approaches the learning event. They symbolize the personal mark that is insinuated into the experience.

Complementing these traits are the following dispositions that stand for the subjective motivational and intentional forces revealing the needs and commitments of the learner: 1) *bodily image*—the person's appraisal of himself as strong or weak, attractive or undesirable, healthy or sickly influences his manner and determination; 2) *self-identifications*—the extent to which the person is identified with the beliefs and ideals of certain groups or a culture will have considerable bearing on his attitude and approach to the problematic event; 3) *self-image*—beliefs and feelings about one's essential esteem, competence, morality, and goodness dominate the cast of the learning venture; and 4) *reflectivity*—the ability of the person to stand apart from himself in a figurative sense and contemplate his motives, judgments, ideals, and methods.

Another dimension of the self is the self-determining function that directly involves the intentional and motivational incentives. *Self-enhancement* comprises the needs felt to be essential to a substantial existence and which impel the person toward goals that he wishes to make part of his being. *Self-extension* is a higher order of intentionality that impels the individual to break out of himself and become part of other aspects of the world. *Propriate striving* is the determination to place the self at risk in order to seek idealistic, vitalistic, or creative ends.

What the individual has at stake in the learning event has a great deal to do with how he enters into and performs in the learning experience.

254

Whether his motives are egocentric, concerned with social well-being, represent compelling creative drives, or whether the goal appears to prosaic, exotic, or perilous, the common underlying need is the need for a sense of wholeness and the evidence that he is, indeed, of some worth.

Goal/Purpose

In teleological terms, a goal is an abstraction, an idea, or a vision in the mind of the person of something standing "out there" toward which he is moving. Purpose conveys the meaning of the goal and represents the rationale for learning and the force that energizes the process. Whether the goal is something objective or intangible, its symbolic content reveals its implications and significance for the goal-seeker. Some types of goals are as follows:

1. *Concrete goals:* material things that may be valued for their intrinsic attributes alone or as a means of achieving yet other types of goals;

2. *Competency goals:* achievement of certain skills and knowledge or the fulfillment of personal talents for practical purposes or for self-realization;

3. *Restorative or palliative goals:* real or imagined goals that are believed to be the means of reducing pain, anxiety, or unhappiness or that might allow the person to return to a normal state;

4. *Status or security goals:* certain valued ends that one assumes will provide a measure of shelter and protection or will possibly enhance one's social position;

5. *Social and interpersonal goals:* objectives that involve affiliation with others and the rewards accruing from close relationships; and

6. *Idealistic goals:* the personal and transcendent visions that resist simple definition but involve a commitment to a set of exceptional values, a prime achievement, or a select lifestyle.

In reality, relatively few life goals fall into such neat or discrete categories. Even the pursuit of basic commodities that are needed to insure biological survival may suggest the presence of some higher goals. Merely naming the goal provides only a superficial notion of the goal-seeking experience. It is necessary to be aware of the felt purpose of the goal in order to appreciate why it is selected instead of another. It is also important to understand why goal seeking is not always a reasonable enterprise, particularly when it appears that the person is deliberately denying himself more attainable gratifications or is rushing pell mell toward an obviously quixotic end. What may be basic to most serious goals is expressed by Ernest Becker: "Each person wants to have his life make a difference in the life of mankind, contribute in some way toward securing and furthering that life, make it some ways less vulnerable, more durable.[20]

SUMMARY

Social learning is initiated when a person's movement toward a valued goal is blocked by a perceived obstacle that will not yield to familiar and tested methods of resolution. The person must resort to developing new solutions, and learning is set in motion. Learning is essential to human adaptation and evolvement.

Each learning event is characterized by the personal, social, situational, value, and emotional variables and their relationship. Social learning is part of everyday living and is relevant to the acquisition of new and more effective roles over the entire course of living. It is necessary when a person confronts the contingencies of living and needs to come to terms with the realization that he has only limited control over his destiny. It is central to the development of coping abilities when people are faced with a crisis. Social learning can encourage the kind of growth that becomes possible when people enter intimate human relationships. In sum, learning is ineluctably tied to the basic human purpose of more conscious and competent mastering of the problems of living.

Chapter 8

Discrimination Learning:
Impressions of Reality

The concept of social learning provides an explanation of the way people resolve problems of adaptation to their varied experiences of living. In its active form, it can be understood as a problem-solving venture that, for purposes of analysis, can be described as a logical and progressive series of stages. Each of these stages must be accomplished before the next can be attempted; each involves certain functions of perception and the accompanying processes of thought and action. These stages include:

1. *Discrimination learning,* the initiation of the learning event directed toward raising of consciousness and the sharpening or broadening of attention. The objective of this form of learning is greater awareness or selectivity about the problem, obstacle, and the personal, social, or environmental conditions that need to be discerned.

2. *Concept learning,* the transformation of gained impressions or feelings into personal symbols or concepts in order to enhance the person's ability to make sense of and manage obstacles to learning and change. This stage of learning is concerned with the person's basic premises and cognitive styles that serve to organize his reality and provide a basis for his behavior.

3. *Principle learning,* movement beyond knowing to include the influence of personal values. What the individual learns about self, others, or his environment needs to be blended with or balanced against his system

of values if this learning is to be translated into consistent, personally meaningful, and autonomous behavior.

4. *Problem solving*, the systemic whole of adaptation or the general style with which the person enacts and validates the learning experience.[1]

As life is actually lived, human learning and problem solving are typically more erratic than this logic indicates. Any number of factors, both personal and situational, assure that the learning event will not unfold in the neat sequence described. Certain stages may be overlooked for the moment, seemingly valid solutions may lead to a dead end, or the person may realize that he needs to retreat for a time from an effort that appears to be fruitless or frustrating. Although the course of learning may have to be spasmodic or repetitive, the successful learning experience will, over time, involve an adequate completion of each of these stages.

In this perspective on learning and change, the human services worker assumes the role of educator. This is not a pedagogical or didactic role; rather, it is an active and collaborative role consciously enacted in accord with clients' values and premises to increase the possibilities and opportunities for effective adaptation. I will show that as an educator the helper manages the learning experience in a sensitive and responsive fashion to assure that it evolves in relation to the needs and best interests of his clients.

DISCRIMINATION LEARNING

Discrimination learning is primarily focused on the perceptual functions of consciousness and attention to enable the individual to become more sensitive and responsive to those aspects of his experience that, for some reason, remain obscure. These aspects may include hidden emotions, subtle behaviors, or special qualities of the environment. In any case, it is assumed that the person cannot begin to tackle his problems of living until he is fully conscious of all of the elements that somehow bear on the problem.

The intent to amplify the idea of discrimination learning creates a dilemma of sorts: How is it possible to describe a human experience that is primarily nonverbal and often nonrational in verbal and rational terms? In this first stage of learning, the discriminations that are made are essentially *pre*conceptual; they involve images, sensations, and feelings

258

that await transformation into conventional words and concepts. The kind of "knowing" that is generated is largely metaphorical and synthetic, much like the products of right hemispheric perceptions. As these impressions appear in the mind, they are not readily communicable. Only when they are analyzed and converted into articulate words by the left hemispheric functions of the brain can they be imparted to self or others. But what can be communicated once this transformation occurs can only be an abstraction, an incomplete representation of a total experience.

One way of solving this dilemma is the use of examples that show the incongruities that arise when deficiencies and gaps in this stage of perception interfere with the individual's ability to deal with his problems of living.

Henry had been seeing a counselor for awhile, having first sought help for what he only could describe as vague but unsettling feelings of anxiety. He and his counselor sorted through many aspects of his life—past events, his dreams and fantasies—but nothing related to his present state emerged. And as far as his immediate life was concerned, Henry spoke about everything being more or less as it should. Somewhat at loss, the counselor suggested that they ought to give a closer look at the details of Henry's life style and asked Henry to tell him what he did on a typical day—a moment to moment account. Henry protested: "That won't do anything. Considering what all this is costing me in time and money, it'll just be a waste. I already said that there's nothing unusual about my life!" The counselor persisted and so Henry gave in and glumly recited the following account: "Let's see . . . I usually get up about 7:30, head for the john for a shower. Then I get dressed and make the bed. I guess it's about 8:15 by now. Then I make breakfast . . . cereal or eggs of some kind. Then I eat, read the paper, throw up, get my stuff ready for work. . . ."

Some practitioners will see more than humor in this fiction and find the kind of incongruity that is not far removed from their own experiences in working with people. Another example is similar, except that it is drawn from an actual event.

Some years ago I counseled with a woman called Ann, who was in her late thirties, married to a relatively successful chemist, and the mother of five children. She had sought help on her own because she was unhappy and had doubts about herself as a wife and mother. In most respects, life to her was less than gratifying. She was a remarkably open and expressive person who attempted to grapple with a number of painful past experiences. We spent a good deal of time exploring curious and intense regions of her existence. I thought that I knew Ann to the extent that it is possible to know another; there was little of her being that escaped our attention.

In time she resolved many of her questions and doubts and felt considerably more secure about herself as a person. In our last meeting, we reviewed the counseling process, and with some assurance, she described the many changes that had been made in her household. She mused a bit about her husband and almost as an inaudible aside wondered if "maybe someday he will even eat with all of us at the dinner table?" Was I hearing right? What was she talking about? She had referred to John in many ways but had never said anything about this matter. Responding to my bewilderment, she said, "Oh? I guess I never mentioned it, did I? Why, when John comes home from work he always locks himself in our bedroom. When it's time to eat I bring him his dinner on a tray, and I go ahead and eat with the kids. Never really looked at that. I guess it is important, isn't it?"

Certainly Ann's senses made it possible for her to register her husband's mealtime patterns; after all, she had accommodated to this plan night after night over many years, but she really did not "see" what was going on. She was able to exclude large sectors of a critical reality from her conscious awareness.

Such gaps in awareness are perhaps more jarring when they are encountered in the context of psychotherapy since such exclusions stand in vivid contrast with the other esoteric content that is dredged to the surface. A person searching for the intricate and profound mysteries of his existence, meanwhile ignoring some rather obvious aberrations in his ordinary living, appears rather absurd. Why does Henry overlook his morning regurgitations in favor of the search for something that will ease his soul? How can Ann delve into the many vagaries of her relationships yet ignore her husband's hibernation? Clinical procedures that attend more to the mysteries of the past than to the more prosaic qualities of the present tend to divert the client's attention. Yet this alone cannot account for such curious behavior since problems in discrimination are equally a part of other forms and purposes of planned change. There are eager, young community workers who are dismayed and frustrated when the residents they are trying to help do not recognize and are reluctant to act on the injustices or deprivations so painfully apparent to the workers. Anyone who has worked with groups of any kind no doubt is cognizant of the ability of people to share a common insensibility to conspicuous facts. Within the more ordinary spheres of living, this hiatus is the repeated source of breakdown in communications between parents and children, husbands and wives, employers and employees, legislators and their constituents, or any pair or group in which people employ incompatible filters to screen their impressions of reality. Human relations workers whose stock in trade is sensitivity to the nuances of reality are no less immune to this sort of discriminatory defect. It is most apparent among those workers whose practices have become routinized, who see their clients as a sequence of "cases," or who insist on regularizing their clients by fitting them into a uniform framework of theory and method.

In a more direct sense, discrimination learning involves those aspects (consciousness and attention) of the perceptual process by which the person grasps and distinguishes the subtle characteristics of his inner and outer reality. Discrimination embodies a wide range of abilities and perceptual powers that are probably boundless. They involve the capacity for exploring the physical world in terms of discerning variations in color, sound, temperature, mass, and contrast; they shape the aptness for reading the moods, feelings, and bodily sensations that come from a person's inner world; and they affect an individual's sensitivity to his social world insofar as they bear on his responsiveness to communications, others' state of being, the quality of interaction, the emotional climate, and needs. Discrimination learning is limited to the elemental processes through which man attempts to achieve some level of fusion with the nonself. It is the process that forges the first critical link in the growing chain of meaning.

CONDITIONS OF LEARNING

Since learning is a human act occurring in a particular context, the quality and nature of each stage of the experience will be affected by certain personal and environmental influences. Planned change that is directed toward effective learning is as concerned with the climate of the event as it is with the methods that are used. Therefore, it needs to take account of certain important contingencies.

Situational Conditions

Outstanding among the many environmental factors that bear on learning is the extent to which there is the climate and the opportunities for the person to explore himself and his surroundings. If discrimination learning is to be fostered, incentives and freedom to discover the minutiae of the person's field must be present. The significance of these conditions has been underscored by many investigations coming from the field of education. [2] Researchers note that a disproportionate number of children coming from lower socioeconomic backgrounds persistently fail in their school programs. Although socioeconomic status alone is questionable as a causal factor, these studies show that the homes of many of these children typically lack incentives for the child to discover his world by becoming aware of its diversities of sound, color, quantity, and form— awarenesses that are thought to be an essential ingredient of normal development. The children of these environments confront other defeating handicaps. They are likely to receive less attention than they require inasmuch as most educational methods and programs are designed for the middle-class child, whose discriminatory abilities are assumed as givens. Moreover, teachers tend to be more comfortable working with children from middle-class families who have already prepared their children to learn. [3]

These findings are applicable to the field of planned change because depressed situational conditions would also have a serious effect on the client's ability to understand and participate in the change procedures. This plight is shown in the findings of Salvador Minuchin and his associates, one of the few studies of practice with disadvantaged families that have been undertaken within the human services. Minuchin's investigation of the lifestyles of a number of these families emphasizes the relation between the quality of the home and the reaction and learning patterns that are fostered: "One essential feature of the family and home environment is its impermanence and unpredictability. These characteristics make it difficult for the growing child to define himself in relation to his world. . . . The geography of the home and its arrangements impede the development of a sense that "I have a place in the world." [4]

This study also confirms earlier observations that were made about the role of the stimulus in the perceptual process. If discriminatory abilities are to be refined, the stimulus should be accessible to the perceiver as something that is relatively clear, constant, and vigorous. But Minuchin finds that the disadvantaged home may be characterized by a deficiency of these conditions: "This kaleidoscope of moving and shifting stimuli hinders the ability of the child to develop the object constancy essential for keeping hold of an object in thought. . . . [the child] remains relatively unexercised in the use of focal attention for observing himself or the specific characteristics of the situation."[5]

It seems apparent that adults and children who come from homes lacking what is necessary for discrimination learning would enter the human service setting with some serious handicaps. Although this problem may be found with greater frequency among the disadvantaged, it cannot be assumed that it is restricted to this group. It may be an attribute of more affluent families that strive to create a household replete with all sorts of incentives to learning, containing musical, literary, and intellectual inducements available to the child. A surfeit of incentives may have effects similar to a lack of incentives. The child is overwhelmed by the abundance and variety of stimuli and may retreat into his own less complex world. This sort of coping mechanism will likely invite other problems inasmuch as the child's withdrawal will threaten or thwart his parents' well-meant intentions. Moreover, there is the risk that a human services worker may be oblivious to this confusion. To the extent that he shares a middle-class value system, he might applaud the presence of these amenities, accept them as givens, and overlook the fact that the existence of incentives to learning does not assure that learning will occur.

In many instances, the client finds himself in an environment created by others ostensibly for the client's welfare, e.g., residential treatment centers, mental hospitals, day treatment centers, and correctional institutions. Such settings should be designed to encourage this basic form of learning, but this is often not the case. There are hospitals and institutions where seemingly genuine efforts are made to assist patients or residents in achieving greater self-awareness, an understanding of social relationships, or more productive social roles. Inmates may be the beneficiaries of intensive therapy, group therapy, occupational therapy, or other services offered to enhance improvement. But the potentials of these programs are often eroded by the kind of institutional environment that devitalizes the resident by its insistent drabness and monotony. The individual, apart from the therapeutic projects, languishes in a climate devoid of stimulation.

Perceptual Conditions

Discrimination learning depends on the perceptual functions of consciousness and attention. Consciousness refers to the various levels on which we can receive and experience impressions of the inner and outer world. The sensory level is the most familiar, since sight, hearing, taste, touch, and smell appear to make our impressions somewhat more verifiable and objective than those captured on sentient, behavioral, or imaginal levels. Attention involves the readiness to receive impressions and the focusing and selective functions of discrimination.

Optimally, consciousness and attention complement each other in shaping the primary perceptual impressions. But at times it appears as if one function is operating to the exclusion of the other. A person may be adequately attentive to what is going on but not really conscious of the experience. This disparity is evident in the examples of Henry and Ann, which show how people can be attentive to parts of their routines of living yet remain oblivious to their essential implications. On the other hand, we may be intensely conscious of an event but lose sight of its details and specifics. Having spent time with others, we may be deeply moved by the experience yet remain unaware of what actually occurred. Music or dance can also remove us from the material features of our surroundings. And it is not uncommon for the average client to come away from an interview with a certain profound awareness yet feel puzzled because he cannot describe what his counselor said or did.

Such perceptual discrepancies may be transient and related to the person's immediate priorities or the weight of self-consciousness, or possibly the presence of more pervasive problems. In either case, discrimination learning is concerned with bringing the functions of attention and consciousness into closer accord and enriching the acuity, depth, and resonance of these functions. More specifically, this form of learning involves:

1. The expansion or deepening of consciousness by (a) the enrichment or intensification of the appropriate level of awareness, and/or (b) a shift

264

from one level to alternate levels of consciousness, e.g., from sensory to sentient.

2. Focusing or generalizing attention by means of (a) sorting out specific details or general connotations of a phenomenon, (b) fostering sharper vigilance and the readiness to attend, (c) broadening the span of attention to allow for greater concentration, or (d) modifying attentional response patterns, e.g., from erratic to more systematic.

3. The attainment of better fit and harmony between consciousness and attention.

OBSTACLES TO LEARNING

As an extension of the concept of conditions of learning, obstacles to learning refer to the peculiar circumstantial and personal factors that interfere with the resolution of perceptual problems at each stage of learning.

Circumstantial Factors

It was noted that an empty, chaotic, or inconsistent environment does little to enrich or actuate discriminatory skills. Although the potential impact of such conditions cannot be minimized, we may still ask why the person caught in these circumstances appears unable to discern the seriousness of his plight and seems to accept these conditions as natural and unexceptional. The tendency to resort to causal explanations would lead to the hypothesis that the severity of environmental circumstances themselves depresses discriminatory abilities which, in turn, results in an impaired perceptual style. Because of this impairment, the individual is unable to detect the more serious impediments and the cycle continues. This appraisal may be valid in some cases and modifications in the person's environment may encourage the development of latent perceptual skills. In other instances, however, environmental change may be necessary but not sufficient as a support for discrimination learning. Even in the case of more fortunate people who are surrounded by incentives to sharpen discriminatory skills, there are some who remain unresponsive and insensitive to the nuances of their world.

Where environmental defects alone are not the obstacles to learning, other conditions within the person require attention. The most basic and critical concern the person's physiological state. Since discriminatory powers depend on the ability to apprehend impressions and sensations, the perceiver's sensory and neural faculties must be free of impairment. If any of the senses are flawed, the person is, to some extent, separated from certain aspects of his world and therefore unable to make proper discriminations. Contrary to popular belief, the person who suffers from an impairment of one sensory mode cannot always compensate for this loss by overdeveloping other faculties. There is considerable evidence that a single sensory defect will seriously disturb one's general discriminatory abilities. Myklebust and Brutten subjected a number of eight- to ten-year-old deaf children to a series of problems in visual perception and found that they performed at a significantly lower level than an unimpaired control group. The authors concluded that the deaf children's perceptual inferiority was linked to an impairment in abstract functioning, and that a single problem in sensory deprivation leads to more general organismic disturbances.[6] Even the less serious visual and auditory defects may contribute to the development of discriminatory problems, especially if undetected and untreated. Owing to mild disabilities in sight or hearing, numbers of children are judged to be "slow" or retarded only because they are unable to grasp what other children can. There is also the hyperkinetic child whose mental filters are not working well and is therefore overwhelmed by the barrage of stimuli coming at him.

Other circumstances involve the conditioning effects of constant exposure to the kind of repetitive and dulling lifestyle that succeeds in dampening curiosity and interest. The individual learns to inhhibit consciousness and restrict it to elemental levels that produce austere and depleted images of reality. Attention is also blunted, and the individual tends to limit his responses only to those aspects of his world that provide immediate gratification or that intrude into or threaten his security. Not rarely, these are people who, as a result of incessant deprivation, have exhausted hope or who have resigned themselves to an abject and meaningless existence.

The quality of the socialization process to which the person was exposed is also a condition that can enhance or hinder the emergence of discriminatory potential. Among the many studies of the relationship of socialization to the cognitive development of children, one is quite specific about the influence of parental attitudes on the development of discriminatory skills. Parents who have little time and energy to respond to the many demands of their children tend to reward behavior that is seen as less taxing. The child is praised and reinforced for staying out of the way, and as this pattern continues, the child's exploratory behaviors and curiosity gradually dwindle and can disappear. When these children become adults they turn out to be unreflective people who will often turn to an outside authority rather than to their judgments as support for their actions.[7] This study also suggests the reasons why children living in homes abundantly supplied with incentives for learning and explorations do not always benefit from these advantages. Anyone might react with apathy or renounce his personal enthusiasm when he senses that what may outwardly appear to be a well-intentioned benefit is really being used to control or deflect spontaneity.

Although environmental circumstances cannot be overlooked as an obstacle, they need not be the sole impediments to effective learning and adaptation. They should be considered in relation to the attributes of the person—what he brings into these circumstances and the peculiar way these personal and external factors interact.

Motivational Factors

The richness of one's discriminatory abilities depends largely on the extent to which one is open to his world of experience. The measure of the person's openness would seem to be the degree to which his attentiveness and consciousness are directed outward toward his milieu or inward in a self-preoccupied fashion. The term *outward* does not exclude an awareness of the inner self; it involves consciousness of self both as an entity and in its relation with the objects, events, and people apart from self. The person who is turned outward would be considered one who is sensitive to inner and outer realities.

The individual who is turned inward appears overly engrossed in concerns about the self. Matters of self-esteem, questions about appearance, or certain compelling needs seem to control his concentration. He is much more responsive to the tumult within himself than to the circumstances around him. This kind of self-consciousness may be a transient and natural occurrence, perhaps a reaction to a stressful event. Stage fright is a striking example of the type of self-preoccupation that excludes awareness of the person's surroundings.

Self-absorption can also be a chronic and pervasive pattern of accommodation to reality and can take any of a number of forms. When this pattern takes an extreme form, the virtual absence of discriminatory faculties can in some instances lead to the label of psychosis. In this state, the individual is prepossessed with the need to cling to even a fragment of something that he can recognize as a self and is thus inured to the actualities of what is taking place around him. What he does apprehend from the outside is likely to be twisted and distorted to conform with his chaotic inner being. This type of inwardness may not become problematic or even considered markedly peculiar as long as the individual is able to maintain a proper distance between himself and others. However, if thrown into continuous contact with people, his behavior may be seen as bizarre and possibly disturbing, particularly when his dogged preoccupation of self negates or distorts the presence of others and, of greater consequence, leaves him unaware of how he affects others. Thus, a self-destructive cycle is set in motion in which his garbled discriminations invite reproval that then leads to a further retreat inward, and so on.

Inwardness of another type also characterizes the chronically depressed person. Preoccupied as he is with his inner pain and self-loathing, he appears at times to be willful in the way he retracts his attention to and consciousness of his surroundings. But in addition to people obviously tormented by depression, there are those who occupy a grey world that to them is bereft of meaning or interest. Their depression is more difficult to discern since it flows into drab and pointless lifestyle, commanding little notice. They are often the bane of therapists and counselors who consider them poor candidates for help. Frequently they are dismissed because they "lack motivation." It is not mere recalcitrance but feelings of hopeless or nameless dread that leave them unattentive to anything in life that might be inspiring. They remain vigilant only of those conditions that might prove their worthlessness or the futility of attempting to better their existence.

This type of introversion can also be understood from another perspective having to do with the way the person defines his status in and relations with the social order. If he sees himself as passive rather than active, supine rather than erect, and reactive rather than assertive, he comes to accept an inferior and inarticulate role in society. If his troubles become overwhelming, he assents to the secondary position in the symbiotic helping relationship. Any inclination toward learning and growth is blighted by attentional processes constricted to avoid further evidence of his inadequacies. Likewise, his consciousness is attenuated, limited to simple sensory responses that allow him to pursue the routines of living. But this sort of self-deprecation can evoke just the opposite response: the person assertively protects his vulnerability by inventing all kinds of safeguards. What was referred to as paranoid ideation fits these tendencies. Attention is honed to a sharp edge utterly responsive to the smallest sign of threat or possible invasion. Consciousness leaps beyond any reasonable bounds, wildly transforming and distorting impressions and sensations into any form that will confirm his ominous beliefs about the world. Learning and change are blocked by overdetermined discriminatory processes that make certain that he will miss the entire point of his existence.

Motivational factors impeding the ability to make a fruitful contact with the actualities of living are curiously evident in many other aspects of living. A good many marriages often seem to be precariously balanced on the fulcrum of discriminatory powers. To the perplexed observer, a particular marriage is obviously scarred by stress and conflict, yet the partners carry on rather blithely as if nothing was amiss. One mate may flaunt infidelity; the other appears to be oblivious. Their children's obnoxious or destructive behavior may disturb the neighborhood or the school but is unrecognized by the parents. The monthly accumulation of bills clearly points to financial catastrophe, but irresponsible spending goes on unabated. We can say quite glibly that these folks are denying reality. But this explanation scarcely reveals the implications of their taking a closer look at the dismal nature of their circumstances.

The ability to discriminate and attend to the more critical elements of being involves much more than the mere intake of impressions. Sensitivity leads to thinking, thinking to meaning, and meaning to action. If the perceptual process can be aborted at the initial point, nothing needs to be done, and living, tenuous though it may be, can go on as it has. Hence, to understand the grotesque blindness of these families, we need to ask what they would have at stake in acknowledging their circumstances. What would the mate who admitted to her partner's infidelity need to do: Leave him? Punish him? Confront her failure? How would the parents of problem children need to redefine themselves? What can they do about their behavior? So again we find that obstacles to learning are not inert things blocking the path to more productive goals but very purposive means of coping and adaptation.

Blunted or muted discriminatory tendencies are not restricted to the more severe problems of living; they are also the critical means by which most of us can endure many of the common absurdities that intrude into our daily lives. If we were constantly alert to the foolishness, hypocrisies, and inconsistencies of our colleagues, friends, neighbors, and ourselves, life would be without comfort, and relationships would be continually dissatisfying or at risk. By the use of selective inattention and a practical sort of consciousness, we filter and sort, excluding the realities that may disturb the balance of our relationships and way of life.

CONDITIONS OF CHANGE

Discrimination learning has a significant place in the planned change enterprise, particularly at the point where the human services' client enters the change experience. It is here that he needs to grapple with a melange of unfamiliar impressions of the physical setting, the persons with whom he will be working, all sorts of unspoken expectations, subtle clues about his freedom, rights, and obligations, and notions about the general climate. If this initial awareness does not evolve either spontaneously or with the encouragement of the worker, the client remains impervious to the actual meaning and nature of the event. He will be unable to assume the client role and will go on being "resistant" or confused.

The term *strategy* is used here to refer to the interventive approach of the human services worker used to improve discrimination and the subsequent forms of social learning. It is important to distinguish between a strategy and a technique. Strategy is a general guide to action, or the principles of intervention devised in response to the worker's understanding of the problem. As a guide, it is ultimately translated into particular behaviors representing the worker's unique style, proper timing, and the needs of clients. A technique is a specific method or tactic that is part of the general strategy. A strategy connotes the intent to achieve a short- or long-term goal (e.g., to enable the client to be more aware of his behavior); techniques are used to bring about the intermediate and specific changes in the movement toward the goal (e.g., clarification and direction). The following strategies suggest possible approaches to special problem situations. How these strategies are to be employed will depend on the express nature of the person and his problem and the distinctive style of the worker.

Evaluation

Any strategic approach to planned change must be supported by careful assessment and judgment if it is to be a sensitive response and an effective act. The human services worker strives to find some meaning and order in what otherwise appears to be confusion or chaos. Formal structures of knowledge are essential to the task of understanding but in themselves are not sufficient for achieving a deeper awareness of the human event. The worker must trust his own discriminatory abilities. He must be aware of the idioms that color the client's vocabulary, the select terms that he uses, the words that are disturbing to him or are omitted from his speech. The timing of the client's pauses, lapses into silence, or sudden digressions from the topic may suggest certain attitudes or feelings that are only tangentially connected to the rational process. Gestures and posture ("body language") hint at the client's inner state. The use of these subrational impressions requires a penetrating mind and a readiness to respond to slight intimations that in ordinary social intercourse would be ignored.

Evaluation, as used herein, refers to an approach to understanding very different from that proposed by the traditional medical model. Evaluation is a process, a search for premises and meanings that proceeds onward, exploring the essence of each phenomenon as it arises. The constant vigilance for new implications suggests that there should be a readiness to discard former impressions no longer pertinent to the problem.

Ongoing evaluation will direct the worker's attention to the three major variables: (1) the influence of situational and environmental factors on the client's modes of perceiving, (2) characteristic perceptual processes and styles, and (3) underlying motivational energies.

Considering the first variable, the worker needs to be sure that how he is asking his client to peer into and sort out the elements of his reality somehow fits the usual expectations of his culture or region. For example, the setting was a metropolitan child guidance clinic that also served families living in the surrounding rural area. These families had little exposure to or interest in the modern psychology of child rearing. Their culture was simple and unadorned, and important matters were handled in concrete and basic terms. When one of these families was referred by the school to the clinic because of a learning and behavior problem of a child, the clinic routinely requested the entire family to come in for the exploratory session. As a typical rural family, complying with an authoritative request, they arrived and sat down in uneasy silence. Their attention was numbed by the unfamiliar and puzzling circumstances. The therapist launched into a series of penetrating questions attempting to get to the core of the problem. These inquiries degenerated into an exchange like the following:

THERAPIST: Can you tell me a bit about Johnny's first years?
MOTHER: Like what . . . what d'you mean . . . what about them?
THERAPIST: I mean . . . uh, was he an easy baby to raise? Any significant problems . . . easy to manage? . . .
MOTHER (pauses): No . . . no different than any of the other kids, I guess.
THERAPIST: O.K. . . . well, uh, how do you get along as a family? (Silence. The family members look at each other in a befuddled way.)
MOTHER (finally): All right, I guess.

If the therapist survived what to him was an unproductive session and proposed another, these rural families often did not return, usually without canceling their appointment or offering an explanation. How the clinic rationalized this failure is another matter; the point is that the therapist's lack of attention to some fundamental discrepancies between his and this family's customary modes of discerning the elements of their respective realities obstructed the first step toward problem solving. Serious conceptual conflicts were also generated by the meaning of such terms as *significant problems* or *getting along*. At any rate, the differential effects of cultural, ethnic, or regional backgrounds remain extremely important because (a) language, ideation, and perception are shaped in one's natural environment, and (b) each person is sufficiently convinced that his thought processes and language are comprehensible and assumes that others experience the world as he does.

To mention the second variable briefly, evaluation requires an appreciation of the client's accustomed manner of perceiving reality, in this case, inferences about questions of awareness and the particular ways the individual attends to his conditions of living. The worker should look for particular gaps and inconsistencies, e.g., shallowness, rigidity, the tendency to overgeneralize, and the difficulty of separating the important from the trivial.

The third variable, motivation, brings the immediate assessment of what is taking place at least to a tentative conclusion. The focus is on the meaning and purpose of observed behavior, the adaptive consequences of the particular way the person uses his discriminatory tendencies. The worker asks himself: "How does this outlook enable this person to hold on to a measure of self-esteem and security? If his attention was more precise and his consciousness more profound, what would be the personal or interpersonal consequences of this change?"

The rural family example helps to clarify the implications of these questions. Their viewpoint was an extension of the norms and styles of their familiar environment. This explains the "how" of their approach to an unfamiliar event, but it only partially explains the "what for" of their perceptions. If the experience was strange but unthreatening, they might survey the situation in their own terms and go on from there. But the occurrence was far from neutral: some authority sent them to this alien setting; it had something to do with a "problem"; and it was implied that the parents had something to do with the child's troublesome behavior. Hence, the peculiarities in their discriminations might well be expressions of protective and security-based needs; for example:

1. Lack of attention to the physical surroundings or reluctance to acknowledge or confirm the presence of the therapist could serve to camouflage feelings of ignorance and insecurity. By curbing attention and not allowing their discriminations to lead them to further investigation, they would not be placed in the uncomfortable position of having to admit their naïveté.

2. Inattention obviates the need to engage in any kind of assertive action. If they did not recognize the procedures, they were not in a position where they would have to request clarification of what the appointment was supposed to accomplish and what were their expected roles.

3. Blunted behavior provides a means of keeping a safe distance from the unpredictable and alien person who calls himself a therapist. It

273

preserves status quo by forestalling any dubious interactions among the family members. Uncertain about where the therapist's questions might lead, a cautious awareness headed off the risk of some unforeseen threat.

These perceptual devices ultimately are the defenders of self-esteem and the only available means of controlling what is controllable in an obscure situation. These reactions are representative of the learned patterns of adaptation that people resort to when confronted by a situation perceived to be uncertain or ominous; they are not the products of deliberate thinking.

Strategies of Intervention

The perceptions, inquiries, and hunches comprising the ongoing evaluative process should logically lead to tentative assumptions about appropriate interventions and the timing of their application. Another factor influencing the human services worker's strategies is the size and nature of the client unit. Depending on whether he is interacting with an individual, a family, a group, or residents of an institution, the worker must contend with somewhat different demands.

Work with families places a special demand on the practitioner. His activity is involved with the unique discriminatory patterns of each member, and he is simultaneously concerned with the way the family has organized itself to create the norms and rules that assure its stability. Part of these expectations includes unspoken precepts about which among the total set of conditions ought to be recognized and which should be disregarded. For example, some families subtly screen out anything that approaches disagreement or hostility. Although an observer may sense anger among the members, the family pictures itself as an oasis of harmony and accord. The worker's task is twofold: dealing with the collusive efforts of the family as a whole and enabling the individual members to open themselves to the realities of their experience. If the family persists in being oblivious to critical aspects of their lifestyle, the change experience will be stalemated on this beginning level, and frustration continues.

Not uncommonly the "family problem" is a variation on this theme. One member becomes the deviant who will not abide by the rules that govern perception. The maverick insists on seeing precisely what the rest of the family has tacitly agreed to ignore, for example:

SON: I heard Mom and Dad really getting into it last night! It was some fight. Mom started to yell and Dad . . .
PARENTS (in unison): Why do you say such things? You know very well we don't fight in this house! We were just having a friendly discussion about . . .
SON (frustrated): But I heard . . . I was awake when you . . .
FATHER: Never mind what you heard! You have this strange imagination, always making up stories. Now I don't want to hear anymore about it, do you understand?

The worker cannot disregard the child's perceptions because he would be playing into the family conspiracy. If he identifies with the child's perceptions, he will be violating one of the family's adaptive rules thereby threatening its security and balance.

The critical question concerns what the family has at stake in ignoring important elements of their existence. What sort of dissonance does this behavior mask? If the worker is at all sensitive to the purposes of this behavior, he can approach the problem either by focusing on the fears and risks themselves or by employing tactics that will induce the family members to confront the very conditions or feelings that evoke aversive reactions.

Practice with groups poses almost polar demands. The formed group organizes itself with little consensus as to desirable perceptual styles. Whether a particular group convenes for therapeutic, task-oriented, or recreational purposes, its members bring to the experience a wide range of ways of looking at reality. The responsibility of the group leader is to enable the group to find a common ground as a basis for pursuing its intent without severe loss to the perceptual integrity of its various members. Discrimination learning plays a major role since it calls attention to the nuances of conflict, rivalry, or affection in the group's atmosphere that would be politely overlooked in more ordinary social circumstances. Some group leaders will exploit the emerging dynamics of the group to assist the members in becoming more sensitive to the gradations of feelings and attitudes. Others introduce certain exercises and procedures to activate this process. Here a number of noncognitive tactics may be used: playback of videotape recordings of the group in

275

action, drawing pictures of one another, role playing, and splitting the group into sections of actors and observers.[8]

Practice in institutional settings must be mindful of the risks inherent in the environment. Safeguards must offset institutions' potential for blunting the attention and consciousness of the residents. The methods used vary because of the many functions of the institutions—correctional, custodial, remedial, educational, etc. The literature directly or indirectly proposes certain remedies for the stultifying quality of institutional life.[9] At the very least, such organizations can do something to encourage and support the perceptual vitality of their residents. The rules, policies, and routines imposed to maintain order should be reviewed to ascertain whether they smother perceptual acuity. At the same time, the rights, choices, and opportunities available to the residents should be accentuated. What must be recognized and prepared for is the possibility that the actuation of powers of discrimination might disrupt the routines of conformity and control.

The following examples may appear elementary and inconclusive because they describe only the initial stage of an ongoing and increasingly complex series of problem-solving activities. The modest expectations of this stage of learning are not insignificant. If clients do not acquire new ways and styles of scanning their inner selves and outer environment, any attempt at change becomes an exercise in futility. Unfortunately, some workers attack the heart of the client's problem, attempting to change "what's wrong" or "dysfunctional" well before the client has altered his primitive and adaptive impressions of what his world is all about. In its true sense, discrimination learning begins with regard for the client's essential impression of his reality. Only as he becomes cognizant of the limits and flaws distorting his perceptions can he start to move toward an appreciation of the formerly unrecognized portions of his existence.

EXPANDING/DEEPENING LEVELS OF CONSCIOUSNESS   The purpose of expanding levels of consciousness is to create conditions wherein the individual either becomes aware of his blindness to some facets of his experience or appreciates the nature of his situation with greater intensity. For example, the client is a woman who, many months after her husband's sudden death, remains frozen in grief and unable to reenter the living world. She says that part of herself died with him and that a silent anger suffocates even the slightest tremor of vitality. Her counselor listens with sympathy to her account of her life and her certainty about the futility of living.

COUNSELOR: So when it comes down to it, you see yourself wiped out . . . can't think . . . totally paralyzed it seems. The fact that you're even saying this must mean that there is a spark of something somewhere inside you that wants things to be different . . . like not wiped out . . . not paralyzed.

CLIENT: (looks up, suddenly alert, perplexed): Did I . . . I didn't say that . . .

COUNSELOR (avoiding debate): O.K. Whether you did or didn't . . . well, I'd like you to do something for me, Helen. Be quiet for a minute and think. . . . Look ahead, say to six months or a year from now . . . tell me about the picture that comes into your mind.

CLIENT: (a long silence—she stares at the floor): Uh . . . nothing, blank . . .

COUNSELOR: Wait, you're not giving it a chance. Let's say it's next November, it's cold, the first snow just fell, you're alone in your apartment, it's dreary. . . .

CLIENT (morosely): November . . . that's the time when I'd really get into planning for Christmas . . . if Robert was alive I'd be out buying . . .

COUNSELOR: But Robert can't be part of that picture anymore. . . . How does the picture change?

CLIENT: (crying): I know I'll be so terribly lonely . . . we had so much planned. (Long silence. She is grappling with something.) I don't know . . . I guess that I'd have to do something . . . can't just let Christmas go by. . . . It meant so much.

COUNSELOR (leaning forward): Good. But describe it, Helen. You want to do something . . . you're there, it's terribly lonely . . . but . . .

CLIENT: (raises her eyes slightly): Well, I . . . no; it's foolish . . . silly. (Counselor encourages her to go on.) Well, Robert and I always talked about getting a dog for me, a real lovable pet for Christmas . . . but, I don't know why, he never got around to it. Now . . . well, anyway . . . I live in an apartment that won't allow pets . . . but maybe . . .

A fragile yet meaningful movement from a stony state of being toward a flicker of hope has occurred. A sentient level of consciousness dominated her basic response to her circumstances. Notions of the present and the future were filtered through feelings of desolation and abandonment, ruining any sense of intentionality or the consideration of alternatives. The counselor first revealed to her the other side of the coin; in dialectical terms, any one belief or version implies an antithetical belief or version. Thus, her complaint that she was helpless is relative to the implied ideal of being capable. She cannot picture herself in any one state without an implicit reference to its opposite form. Evidence that she was not ready to deal with this possibility led the counselor to let it lie for the moment. Yet, indirectly, he capitalized on this awareness by asking her to do something for him, by appealing to a fraction of her desire to be "unparalyzed." Without ignoring her feelings, he urged her to create a vision (imaginal awareness) of some plausible future scenes and to envision what she might be doing within them (behavioral awareness). Her consciousness became unstuck, and she was torn between two levels that served to unbind her intentional self and activate vestiges of her self-enhancing desires. Even if her visions about her future cannot be realized, the strategy would still be valid. It is not the *content* of vision and consciousness that is most important but the *intent*, i.e., the emerging willingness to create a future of some sort rather than remaining fixed in an aimless pattern of the past.

FOCUSING ATTENTION AND DEFLECTING CONSCIOUSNESS   In focusing attention and deflecting consciousness to other levels the intent is to redirect awareness to behaviors about which the client has disclaimed any responsibility and to complement this vigilance with an altered awareness of the unrecognized implications and purposes of these actions. For example, the client is a ten-year-old boy who is constantly in trouble with his parents and school owing to his explosive and aggressive outbursts. At the very outset, Tom argues that he can't stop himself from blowing up and, "anyway, it's their fault. People are always picking on me—they make me do it!"

COUNSELOR: (after some discussion): You've almost got me convinced that you can't help it . . . just kinda happens to you, eh? Still . . . I don't know . . . there's still something coming off wrong because you always wind up getting the worst of it. Maybe you're not blowing up right. Tell you what, let's try some play acting and see how it works. Now you will be you and I'll try to act like your Dad . . . like how you say he acts when he gets sore at you. But here's the hard part. No matter what I do or say you are going to have to just sit there, hold onto your chair, and for right now don't do anything. Then let's talk about it and see what happens. O.K.?
TOM: Well . . . I dunno . . . it won't do anything . . . O.K., I'll try.
COUNSELOR: (takes a moment to create the mood; glares intently at Tom for a moment and suddenly shouts) I've had all I can take of your rotten behavior! Do you hear me? I want you to keep your hands off your little brother! Is that clear?
TOM: (grins but is growing rather uneasy.)
COUNSELOR (even louder): Don't you grin at me young man! You wipe that smirk off your face right now, you little punk!
(With this Tom jerks himself up, his hands clenching the arms of his chair, almost

ready to spring. The counselor, recognizing he is approaching the breaking point relaxes and sits back. Tom's fury abates and he sags into his chair.)

COUNSELOR: Say, we're a couple of good actors. O.K. Tom, what happened?

TOM (still surly): Nothing.

COUNSELOR (outwardly surprised): Nothing? Ah, come on, Tom. I really got to you just like everybody else can . . . You wanted to come out of that chair real bad. You felt like . . . I don't know . . . you wanted to do something to get me off your back.

TOM (mumbles): I wanted to get out of here.

COUNSELOR: Sure. But something went off inside of you . . . something exploded. . . . What was it; can you describe it?

TOM (almost in tears): I felt like . . . I don't know . . . you were mad at . . . well, not you . . . but like you were going to do something bad and I had to run but I couldn't . . .

This interchange could be carried on further to consider the frightful images that Tom entertained. But this excerpt shows a shift in attention away from "what others make me do" toward "what I feel like and what I am doing." This is a qualitative shift—enough to move Tom off the center of irresponsibility for his behavior. A change in levels of consciousness is also emergent. Previously, Tom's impressions of threat tended to by-pass rational or even affective levels of consciousness; incoming stimuli were processed by consciousness of a behavioral kind that further removed Tom from awareness of what he thought and felt. In terms of his discriminatory patterns, Tom and his world had formed an undifferentiated lump. He could not distinguish "what is me" from "what others are doing to me," nor could he differentiate the significant others in his environment and perceive them as anything more than a threat.

This counselor also resisted the temptation to engage in a pointless debate and settled for Tom's estimate of the problem. This marginal agreement allowed him to begin to explore the difficulty from Tom's perspective rather than from the position of an unwelcome and threatening intruder. He was able to use role play in a way that would force Tom to deal with his reactions in other than a behavioral manner. He created a state of tension in which the potential for action was sealed off, thereby forcing Tom to break the tension by other means. Although Tom *talked* about behavior (wanting to run) he reacted on an emotional level of consciousness and revealed the intensity of his fears and the imagery of the threatening others in his environment. If nothing else, Tom has learned (not necessarily in conceptual terms) that he is frightened, angry, and that in some ways his blow-ups are the adaptive substitutes for flight. Tom and his counselor have achieved a prologue of sorts to ways of working toward a solution.

DIRECTING AND FOCUSING ATTENTION   The example in this instance does not involve personal change; rather, the strategy is directed toward guiding group members' perceptions toward the apprehension of certain phenomena that seem to lie outside of their field of vision. It is assumed that cognizance of these conditions will allow for more thoughtful decisions and choices.

A community service center has received a grant to develop a program to improve housing and the appearance of a decaying inner-city neighborhood. The community workers decided that there would be more lasting gains if the residents themselves would take the lead. The participation of the beneficiaries might generate some hope and pride—attitudes that had disappeared with the degeneration of the area. The first meeting with a group of residents failed to show any interest. The workers decided to try again. This time they invited selected residents whose outlook seemed to represent the more positive end of the scale of indifference. After introductory discussion again failed to generate any participation, the community workers changed tack:

WORKER: It doesn't sound like anyone is against the idea of making this neighborhood a better place to live. But I guess you want us to do it. Well, that's one possibility. But we have to depend on you for at least one thing, we have to set some priorities. Maybe you could tell us where to start. What's *really* wrong with this neighborhood?
MR. A. (laughing): Nothing that a couple of bulldozers couldn't fix in a hurry.
WORKER (also laughing): Yes, but that would put me out of a job. We wouldn't want that, would we? But really, what needs fixing the most? Where do we start?

(This question sets some of the group to joking among themselves about Mr. A's yard, each trying to outdo the others in listing the kinds of junk that can be found there.)

WORKER: Great! Let's start right there!
MR. A.: Hey! Hold it! I ain't going to have a bunch of outsiders messing around on my property. Besides that stuff is valuable.

MRS. B.: Believe me, I wouldn't mess with that junk. Besides, there are more important things . . . like that row of houses on Burton Street. I feel so bad about the folks who have to live in those places.

MR. C.: What houses? I never noticed any houses. . . . I go by there every day to catch the bus.

MRS. B.: You know, the Simpsons . . . the house that caught fire last winter . . . all those on either side.

MR. C.: You're right . . . I guess I never did notice how bad they are.

MR. D.: You talking about the Simpsons reminds me. I've watched these kids playing out in the street . . . they don't have any real place . . . what I mean is that a playground wouldn't be a bad idea.

WORKER: If nothing else, we got Mr. A's yard to work on . . . but so far you think the houses on Burton Street could do with some repair . . . and the idea of a playground, a great idea . . .

The process is somewhat self-evident. The worker assumed that involvement in the proposed project would not be forthcoming until some of the more motivated residents could begin to discard their habitual perceptions of the neighborhood and take a fresh look at what had become dulled by familiarity. He accepted the initiative not to command but to evoke their knowledge and to direct their attention to what they already know. As members of the group responded, the worker accommodated to their style and ethos and encouraged the members' observations and associations. Two levels of attention came into being: one was more generalized, encompassing a wider scope of neighborhood problems; the other narrower, focusing on specific problems.

Filtering occurred as a few of the group members sorted out the special and more acute problems from the range of conditions (e.g., the Burton Street houses and children playing in the street). There were also significant signs of increased *vigilance*, or a mental set that became somewhat more attuned to conditions that had been ignored. Moreover, there were indications of an extension in *span of attention*, apparent in the members' willingness to contemplate issues that had been dismissed as inconsequential.

Discrimination learning deals with rather primitive and preconceptual dimensions of thought, suggesting that the worker needs to turn to somewhat unconventional methods to encourage learning. His ingenuity may be his most effective tool.

THE CLIENT'S LIFESTYLE   Requesting a detailed accounting of the client's lifestyle informs the worker about the typical patterns and systems of the client's life. In addition to its practical values, this approach directs the client's attention to conditions and events that have become obscured by mindless routine and seem to be inconsequential. It also may be fruitful to inquire about the details of a particular interactional episode, especially one where the client has already arrived at some definite conclusions. For example, a cleint states that "I had a long talk with my wife about my taking that new job, but she really doesn't want me to get ahead." Careful questioning about what was actually said, and in what sequence, may validate or invalidate this conclusion; in either case, it offers a more reasonable basis for further planning. It is advisable to act on the principle that the aspects of the person's life that deserve the most attention may be those he has dismissed as insignificant or irrelevant to his difficulties.

CLIENTS IN THEIR ENVIRONMENT   Working with clients in their own environment could include home, neighborhood, place of employment, and recreational center. It should disclose conditions and paterns that usually are not reported or described with accuracy because they are so commonplace that they do not warrant the individual's special consideration. Everyone naturally becomes inured to the peculiarities of the space he occupies over a period of time. The most immediate example of such blindness to the character of a life space is apparent in the ordinary family. The rules that govern family living are so thoroughly absorbed into day-to-day operations that they escape the family members' attention.
      Practice within the client's milieu is a practical alternative when the worker finds himself somewhat alienated by ethnic, cultural, racial, or socioeconomic differences. Only by entering the reality of the client's existence can the worker appreciate the conditions that shape his own and the client's perceptions of the world. Not being a part of that particular culture, it is doubtful that the human services worker can "see" reality in the same way. However, he will recognize the boundaries of his own frame of reference and be more amenable to points of view that would otherwise seem aberrant.

"UNCONVENTIONAL" IMPRESSIONS   Heightened consciousness can create rather curious impressions, the kind of "knowing" or "feeling" that does not seem to fit rational ways of thinking. These impressions might be the sudden awareness coming from the penetration of a formerly opaque event, a vivid intuition, or the realization of a "truth" that cannot be empirically verified. Ernest Rossi calls this awareness an "original psychological experience" and sees it as the starting point for "breaking out of old habits to discover a new world of understanding."[10] This starting point does not often materialize because these impressions seem to be out of line with the conventional reality and also because they cannot be communicated in a language that has shared meanings. This being the case, the individual has few options. He might suppress his impressions or use them as proof of his peculiarity. He can allow his rational faculties to censor or distort them. Or he might reject them entirely. In any case, he succeeds in separating himself from potentially valuable insights.

In the process of discrimination learning, the task of the worker is to assure that the interactional climate is sufficiently open and supportive to allow these impressions to come forth without fear of penalty or threat. A direct approach involves the worker's inquiry at a pause in the flow of discussion about the client's thoughts, feelings, or visions at that moment. Indirectly, the worker might offer his own associations and impressions as an invitation to the client to express his own. Regardless of the approach, it is not the content of the client's impressions that are of prime importance at this point in learning but his opportunity to realize and experiment with new modes of awareness.

WRITTEN AND RECORDED IMPRESSIONS Diaries and journals can be used to evoke alternative levels of consciousness. Not all clients would be receptive to this medium, but this possibility should be investigated.

The client can be asked to record his thoughts and perceptions with as much freedom and openness as he can muster. Even if he does not share his impressions with the worker, they still remain a source of valuable intuitions that normally would be forgotten. Entries need not be done in any special or systematic way; spontaneity of expression is the goal. Content is not the central issue inasmuch as the aim is to encourage sentiency and sensibility.

The usefulness of journal writing is not restricted to the planned change event. A journal offers the opportunity to grapple with musings and questions about any human event, to explore the issues of living, and to anticipate probabilities. Administrators, planners, researchers, and practitioners find the journal a valuable tool for recording immediate impressions and insights that may have some future bearing on their work.

HOMEWORK AND EXERCISES   The prescribing of homework or exercises was developed and refined by Albert Ellis in Rational-Emotive therapy.[11] He believes that assignments are especially indicated with people who are inhibited or withdrawn. This approach serves to direct and sustain attention and create opportunities for the expansion of consciousness. The time actually spent in deliberations between worker and client constitutes only a fraction of the latter's total experience. The extent to which the worker can encourage a refinement of discrimination in episodes of the client's life can maximize the effects of the change process. For example, an adolescent may be requested to observe and record features of his school experience or family life and report what he believes occurred; or a group of citizens, troubled about their inability to change certain conditions, could be asked to attend a local legislative session to make them more sensitive to the political aspects of decision making.

Efforts to strengthen and refine discriminatory powers are not limited to the confines of the formal, planned change encounter. Many opportunities for enriching levels of precognitive and cognitive awareness are available, but some resourcefulness and curiosity may be required to locate them. Dancing and other forms of body movement provide access to kinesthetic awareness and sensitivity to movement and rhythm. The discipline of quiet listening and observing can unleash a person's senses, allow imagery to arise, and open a world largely unregarded. This sort of vision is epitomized by Annie Dillard in *Pilgrim at Tinkers Creek*,[12] which contains her reflections on nature. The major value of nature walks and tours of ethnic neighborhoods is the opportunity to soak in the experience of difference and contrast and experience the other side of reality.

Meditation, according to Ornstein, can help "to increase one's capacity for experience and self-understanding."[13] It engenders an alteration in a person's usual approach to his world and offers a glimpse of consciousness not yet achieved; it does *not* connote a lapse in attention.

It should be evident that discrimination learning has few discernible boundaries. The parameters of human attentiveness and consciousness are inconceivable. Discrimination learning depends only in part on deliberate or formal procedures. It is most responsive to unusual opportunities—those that are inventively fashioned and those that arise spontaneously. It seems that the perceptiveness and ingenuity of the worker become the major conditions of learning and change. They may take any number of forms: his sensitivity to the flaws that impede his clients' awareness, his ability to invent an atmosphere in which sensibilities can be nurtured, and his keenness in discerning and grasping fleeting opportunities. Basically, he should be comfortable in dealing with ambiguous perceptions and be able to use metaphors and analogues as representations of reality.

SUMMARY

Discrimination learning, the first of the operational approaches to problem solving, involves the enhancement of attentional faculties and levels of consciousness to enable people to expand their apprehension and differentiation of their conditions of living. It constitutes the beginning phase in the more elaborate scheme of learning and problem solving. If gaps and deficits are not resolved at this stage, the probability of success in the development of effective adaptation will be in serious doubt.

The concept of conditions of learning refers to the factors that have direct bearing on the quality of discrimination learning. These conditions include the person's sensory attributes, the climate and the opportunity for learning, and special perceptual and motivational factors affecting the learning task. Careful and ongoing evaluation of learning patterns, deficits, and purposes is basic to the effective use of strategies of planned change. Evaluation depends not only on the worker's intellect but also on his unconstrained use of his own discriminatory skills. The worker must use various direct and indirect strategies to focus or broaden attention, to encourage expansion or shifts in levels of consciousness, or to bring consciousness and attention into harmony.

Chapter 9

Concept Learning:
The Construction of Meaning

Wittgenstein's declaration, "The limits of my language mean the limits of my world," sets the theme of this series of chapters concerned with the way people use language and symbols to create their worlds and to respond to the worlds that they have created. Language is the product of conceptualization or concept formation, a mental process defined as "forming ideas or abstractions or grasping the meaning of symbols representing such ideas or abstractions."

Discrimination is the function that links subject with object and generates certain impressions. If the impressions that are sensed or felt are to be at all useful for organizing and managing reality, they must be named, categorized, or related to other known experiences. If problem solving and adaptive abilities are fairly intact, this type of abstracting and symbolizing follows in a relatively natural fashion. If these abilities are deficient or distorted for some purpose, concept learning is necessary.

CONCEPT FORMATION AND CONCEPT LEARNING

The etymological derivation of the word "concept" is the Latin *concipiere* meaning "to take together, to contain, to gather, notably *concipiere semina* (of a woman) to gather a male seed, to conceive."[1] Archaic meanings still pertain, both literally and figuratively. In conception of a child or an idea, something is gathered together to give life to something that did not exist in its immediate form. Seen in this way, concept formation is an act of creation as the mind works to transform crude images and impressions into an abstraction or symbol that produces a new awareness of self or the world that the person inhabits.

Robert Gagne, a learning theorist, defines concept learning as the ability to put things in a class and to respond to the class as a whole.[2] Although his description of the steps of learning concerns the formal educational experience, these steps appear to be germane to learning in general. Basic to concept learning is the individual's ability to use his discriminatory skills to make proper distinctions among things that make up his environment. "Stimulus objects," things that need to be named, related, and categorized, should be presented to the learner simultaneously. The teacher attempts to elicit from the learner what the common link is that indicates the various items belong to the same class. Positive reinforcement is offered in the form of confirmation and what is learned is then transferred to other problems. This sequence is typical of the more practical learning event as when children discover that objects as different as apples, bananas, and oranges all fit into the concept "fruit" or when older students learn that terms such as dictatorship, tyranny, and fascism may be subsumed under the term "totalitarianism." This sequence is also a part of the critical phase of the planned change event. For example, an employment counseling interview concerns a client who cannot hold a job for any period of time because of his impulsive and aggressive behavior. Although the planning and sequence of the steps are not as deliberate as in a structured learning situation, they are used in this attempt to create meaning from a confusing event:

CLIENT: This was the third time I got fired this year. . . . They've just got it in for me.
WORKER: The third time? What happened the other times? (Discrimination learning.)
(Client at first denies any responsibility for the firings. Worker quietly asks him to detail the events leading up to the loss of the client's job. The latter responds by describing a number of untimely arguments, e.g., "So I got mad, blew up . . . told my boss where to shove it!")
WORKER: O.K. But what was going on at the time? Could you tell me about the things that got you mad? (Identification of stimulus object.)
CLIENT (after trying to avoid the question): Well . . . you might say it's when I want to do things my way and they won't listen, or they try to stop me.
WORKER: These the only times you get sore? Does "they" mean others are bugging you too?
CLIENT: No. Well, I really get pissed off at my wife when she starts in on her bossing

. . . but I just clam up and won't talk with her. Yes, there's my neighbor. . . .
(Identification of stimulus objects.)
WORKER: Your boss, your wife, your neighbor . . . so what's going on? Does this tell
you anything?
CLIENT (after a silence): Yeah, I guess I just can't stand being told what to do.
(Discovery of a common link.) I guess (quietly) I'm a pretty stubborn, angry son of
a bitch. (Concept.)
WORKER: Maybe you're right. It looks like you've put your finger on part of the
problem. (Confirmation.) Maybe you got something to be angry about, I don't
know . . . but since you seem able to figure things out, maybe we can work
together to see if we can find better ways of your working things out without
always getting canned.
(Reinforcement and extension of problem solving to other aspects of problem.)

These learning increments are not restricted to the thought processes
of the client alone. The worker is also engaged in concept learning as he
attempts to unravel the muddled nature of the problem. He searches for
the common denominator that can transform what appears to be unrelated into a gestalt that tells something about the motives or causes of the
persistent difficulty. How he will conceptualize the essential link will
depend on his particular theoretical predisposition. If he is dynamically
oriented, he might define the problem as "conflict with authority." If he is
psychoanalytically inclined, he could see the problem as a symptom of an
"unresolved Oedipal struggle" or perhaps an "anal fixation." He might
take a more descriptive approach and call the problem a sign of "imma-
ture impulsivity" or a "characterological defect." If the worker is comfortable with a telic, purposive view of behavior, he might understand his
client's actions as a self-defeating attempt to preserve something of the
self (integrity, self-esteem, or self-enhancement). In any case, the immediate product is a concept that provides a modicum of sense and order.

The client's new ability to reconceptualize his behavior and redefine
himself in some ways enables him to modify his view of himself as a
helpless victim of incomprehensible impulses. The shift from the conception of "I am helplessly mad" to "I am stubborn and angry" connotes a
change in orientation toward self from passive to active. Even this slight
awareness is a step toward a greater sense of personal responsibility for
the changes required. The worker's conceptualizations grant him a
greater measure of direction and control. The ability to name and explain
the problem should increase his confidence and suggest possible avenues

for problem resolution. Optimally, the separate experiences in concept learning will converge and create the basis for a shared endeavor.

Ralph Garry and Howard Kingsley note that concepts may be learned both in systematic and informal ways.[3] Deliberate learning occurs when someone is taught the rules, principles, and schemes that lead to the understanding of concepts of increasing orders of complexity. Systematic learning, involving the exposure to knowledge and the discipline required to manipulate and transform symbols is indispensable to effective living. Thomas Jefferson wrote: "Whenever the people are well informed, they can be trusted with their own government." But to be informed, people need to have access to the major concepts that signify the legal, political, scientific, and economic realities of their time. Some of the difficulties in living that disenfranchised and disadvantaged people face are rooted in their unfamiliarity with the concepts requisite to negotiate the obscure paths of daily living. The ramifications of such concepts as "due process," "in loco parentis," and "ombudsman" and the endless stream of bureaucratic jargon are extremely complex when translated into serious injunctions and prescriptions. Unfamiliar with these terms, people are lost and powerless when confronted with certain issues that bear on their existence.

Some important concepts may also be acquired in more informal and casual ways. To maintain a steady state while coping with life's contingencies, people are in a constant process of creating, shaping, and revising their conceptions of reality. Although this process unfolds in an apparently unpremeditated fashion, it is doubtful that informal learning of this type could occur without prior exposure to more systematic forms of concept learning.

It is obvious that before an individual *can* learn he must learn *how* to learn. This is the objective of any worthwhile formal educational program at any level. Imparting knowledge or training is in some respects always secondary to enhancing essential learning skills and interests. John Dewey stressed the meaning of excellence in learning. He asserted that: "the problem of *method* in forming habits of reflective thought is the problem of establishing *conditions* that will arouse and guide *curiosity*; of setting up the connections in things experienced that will on later occasions promote the flow of *suggestions,* create problems and purposes that will favor *consecutiveness* in the succession of ideas."[4] Jerome Bruner

289

urges that "a theory of instruction should specify the experiences which most effectively implant in the individual a predisposition toward learning—learning in general or a particular type of learning."[5]

It is safe to assume that many of the people entering the various human services systems have not benefited from or have been deprived of opportunities to develop basic learning skills. Some are overwhelmed or victimized by a baffling and impenetrable social complex. Yet, the kinds of assistance that these human service systems provide are largely educative. Although these programs may refer to the help they offer as "treatment," "support," "rehabilitation," "provision of personal services," or "protection," what they often hold in common are the opportunities they extend to their clientele to engage in deliberate and systematic forms of learning.

One of the basic services provided by community social welfare services is *information and referral*, an attempt to link people with such resources as housing, health care, legal aid, and services to children and the aging. If this service is effective, it accomplishes something more than merely steering people to the proper agency or organization. They may learn something about how bureaucracies function, how personal needs might best be expressed, and how to deal with agency protocols and authorities. If fortunate, clients may learn certain *situational* concepts that will enable them to deal more effectively with the systemic and procedural conditions bearing on their personal needs. To the extent that these new concepts are assimilated and become part of a person's understanding, they add to his ability to manage other aspects of his encounters with society.

The group experience calls for the learning and development of a shared set of concepts that will enable the participants to interact, exchange points of view, move toward a mutually defined goal, and otherwise partake of collective action and outlook. Both situational and operational concepts are acquired in the group setting, concepts that represent ideas about "who we are," "what we are doing," and "where we are heading." Only as these concepts are integrated, owned, and shared by the members can the group proceed toward learning that is informal—arising from spontaneous interaction.

The field of psychotherapy has a rich and varied assortment of learning experiences. Arnold Goldstein observes, "whatever else it is, psychotherapy must be considered a learning enterprise, . . . it may be specific behaviors or a whole new outlook on life, but it cannot be denied that the intended outcome is a change in the individual that can only be termed as a manifestation of learning."[6] The individual needs to learn something about his role as a "client" or a "patient" and the expectations that shape this role. Although he may have some vague notions about the implications of "treatment" or "therapy," he will quickly have to revise his conception to fit the particulars of the specific experience. He also needs to grasp the language and idiom that expresses his therapist's special theoretical orientation. These learning requirements are most challenging and difficult since they involve the mastery of concepts that are of a rather high order and have relatively little application to the business of everyday living. The conceptions and abstractions of psychotherapeutic discourse often refer to phenomena that have no observable referents. Concepts that allude to such states as "defense mechanisms," the "ego," or "repressed feelings," are actually reifications—verbal symbols of a nonmaterial, nonexistent something.

The client would have to be at least marginally comfortable in dealing with the abstract world of ideas if he is to manage this form of learning and benefit from therapy. Therapeutic concepts are often irrelevant to conditions in ordinary spheres of living. Their irrelevancy complicates learning because concepts are most readily learned and assimilated when the person can apply them to a broad range of personal situations. These learning demands explain why traditional psychotherapeutic methods have such limited success with the poor, the working class, or others who are seen as being "psychologically unsophisticated."

The incoming resident of an institution needs to integrate a number of situational concepts that represent the rules, procedures, and proscriptions of the particular setting. Such learning implies something more than mere memorization of the major protocols. If the resident intends to become a vital and active member of the institution, he needs to discover some personal value and meaning in these conceptions. How do they help him in getting along, fitting in, or finding a meaningful place in an impersonal and unfamiliar environment? For example, an inmate soon comes to learn the concept of the "pecking order" of the institution, if he is at all observant. He may find this idea repugnant and dehumanizing, but it can become an effective tool for survival.

291

Meaning and Explanation

Concepts are something more than literal images of reality; they are also the bearers of *meaning*, the personal and idiosyncratic inferences that these images generate. A concept has an explanatory function insofar as it is employed to make things comprehensible and manageable. But a concept can also reach beyond explanation and enter the realm of meaning. An explanation states what a thing is; meaning is synonymous with intent, purpose, significance, connotation, and denotation. Joseph Rychlak states: "Meanings therefore always reach beyond the specific and suggest, imply, connote, or clearly signify something beyond simply the given. This means that a *relation* or *relationship* is being emphasized whenever we speak about the meaning of anything."[7]

The root of many personal and interpersonal conflicts is confusion or differences about the essential meaning of particular concepts. An example of marital strife shows the kind of struggle that can occur in any human relationship when people disagree about the meaning of a critical idea. Ella and Tom are a couple of their late thirties. On its surface their marriage of fifteen years was devoid of serious problems since Ella seemed to agree with Tom's definition of their relationship and how it ought to work. When Ella began to develop various physical ailments that appeared to have no specific organic basis, her physician referred her to a psychiatrist. She came away from this experience with a markedly different outlook, one that abrasively rubbed against Tom's convictions. The result was strife that increased to a point that they felt compelled to see a marriage counselor. The following excerpt, taken from one of the early joint interviews exemplifies a sincere struggle over meaning. Ella and Tom had been accusing each other of willful misinterpretation of the "facts" of a particular event. The counselor, responding to their opposing versions poses the central question:

COUNSELOR: Well, maybe that's the whole issue—the matter of trust. . . . Do you think you trust each other?
ELLA: Well . . . no. . . .
COUNSELOR: Do you trust her, Tom?
TOM (assertively): I trust her that she's moral.
COUNSELOR (confused): Does that mean that the only time . . .
TOM: No, that has too many ways of meaning. . . . I don't know . . . if you mean can I give myself to her . . . no . . . because I don't feel accepted as I am with her.

(He ruminates about his own feelings of inadequacy, his inability to change her and then goes on.) I don't understand what you mean when you say, "Do I trust her?" I really don't understand what you mean. Are you saying, "Do I have confidence in her?" Is that part of trust?

ELLA (breaks in before counselor can respond; she attempts to explain): In other words, do we have a relationship that is solid enough that no matter what we do we can't possibly ruin it . . . we have an emotional stability, a tie between us . . . that's trust . . . is that correct? In other words . . . an emotional tie, no matter what we do, what I say to you, I feel I'm loved.

COUNSELOR: When you say "love" and "trust" tears well up in your eyes. Does what Ella says make any sense, Tom?

TOM: It makes sense, but I . . . I guess I don't trust Ella, then, if you put it in that term . . . if that's what trust means. I don't feel that whatever I am, I can be loved.

Both Ella and Tom are intelligent adults who in ordinary circumstances would have little difficulty explaining and defining "trust." Their occupations (Tom, an insurance broker and Ella, a teacher) require them to be able to use "trust" and other abstractions with considerable facility. At this unsettled point, the root of the controversy is not the *explanation* of the concept but the varied *meanings* that it implies. Ella sees trust in relational terms akin to a sense of intimacy. It is an unrealized ideal that she longs for in one way; she also feared this ideal since trust somehow is connected in her mind with surrender. To Tom, the notion of trust stirred a number of very different meanings. Tom was first of all caught up with questions about his own self-esteem since the image that he held of himself required him to be able to answer any question with precision and certitude. More important, Tom understands trust in a rather unilateral "I" rather than in "we" terms—something that "I" feel rather than what "we" share. Trust is also equated with frustration and anger derived from the rejection he feels because his wife violated their compact.

On a lexical and explanatory level, Tom and Ella are able to agree about the definition of trust and other concepts; the meanings that they ascribe to the concept, however, are painfully at odds. The implications of this kind of dissonance are far-reaching. Each one's beliefs about reality are offended by the other's beliefs, as are their essential assumptions about how their estrangement might be resolved.

A term may have *sign meanings* and/or *symbolic meanings*.[8] A sign meaning is a collection of letters, numbers, and the like that stand for something else. It is a formal designation that acts to objectify a particular referent in a manner that is communicable and understood by most people. It is also stated in third person terms (e.g., "That is a . . .") and has no purpose other than to classify and to create a link between a given and the thing to which it points. In this sense, even a term as soft as "trust" could refer to a specific action that is observed: "Jack is showing trust since he loaned Bill a large sum of money without asking any collateral."

Symbolic meanings are the products of thought and reflection. As expressed in a concept, they involve the introspective, subjective view. Such concepts do much more than merely point to or identify something. They are indicative of personal cogitations, and the new and unique interpretations of a particular reality. As first person expressions (e.g., "I believe, know, or think that is a . . ."), symbolic meanings are also teleological because they intend something or purport to express something. What is perhaps most striking about concepts connoting symbolic meanings is that they are relational (or what Rychlak calls bi-polar) insofar as they reveal the link between the perceiver and the referent. If, for example, I happen to be driving with you and happen to point to a building and say, "There is a new house," I am using a sign meaning that identifies something and reveals very little about myself other than the fact that I am able to differentiate between a new house and an old one, or between a house and barn. If, however, I point to another building and say, "Now there is my dream house," I am expressing a symbolic meaning. If you appraise the house and hear my words, you now know something about my aspirations, my ideals about what a home should be like, my aesthetic sensibilities, and other facets of my self.

The idea of bi-modal thought assumes that reality can be shaped by either hemisphere of the brain. If each hemisphere is capable of creating vastly different impressions of the same stimulus, the concepts that are ultimately produced to declare these impressions are also of different orders. Sign meanings appear to be the product of the logic, objectivity, and language that is believed to characterize left brain thought. Symbolic meanings containing figurative and allegorical connotation represent right brain thought.

Although Paul Watzlawick and Joseph Rychlak discuss the question of meaning from somewhat different perspectives, their conclusions are remarkably similar. Watzlawick speaks of "two languages."[9] The first is what he calls *digital*, a term taken from mathematics. Digital language is objective, definitional, cerebral, logical, and analytic. Digital concepts are arbitrary since they have no relation to the thing that they represent (e.g., the word "dog" has nothing to do with an actual canine; it is the designation used arbitrarily to refer to what is being spoken about). Digital concepts also are conventional since they are terms that can be exchanged in ordinary communication with the assumption that the listener will understand their meanings. The second form of language conforms to the idea of symbolic meanings in that it embodies imagery, metaphor, and symbols. Watzlawick calls this language *analogic* since it can take the form of images, pictorial signs, dreams, or onomatopoeic words suggesting the sound of things. The two languages have separate functions: digital—analyzing and dissecting; analogic—grasping the whole of what it attempts to represent. They also create two different world images that either correspond to and enrich each other or stand in conflict.

The two languages are products of the unique functions of each of the two hemispheres. The left hemisphere is typically dominant since its province is the translation of perceptions into logical, semantic, and phonetic representations or concepts of reality and the means of communication with the outside world. The right hemisphere can grasp complex relationships and the patterns, configurations, and structure of an event in holistic, all-embracing terms. Moreover, it is able to recognize the totality of a phenomenon on the basis of one essential detail. For example, perception of one facial feature can evoke recognition of the total person.

. . . the right hemisphere is competent for the construction of logical classes and therefore for the formation of concepts—two abilities without which our perception of reality would be a kaleidoscopic chaos. This is to say that when we use concepts (like "triangle" and "table" for instance), we mean abstractions which do not exist *as such*. Rather, we mean their quintessence (the logical *class*), so to speak, of all existing or imaginable triangles, tables, and so forth. Without this ability to order the chaotic complexity of the world into logical classes, both human and animal existence would be impossible.[10]

That human beings are of two minds (in itself, an accepted figure of speech) is a familiar and unexceptional theme in a good many literary, philosophical, and theoretical works. In fact, it is not unreasonable to suppose that the very idea of the bicameral brain possibly originated in right hemispheric cogitations, its verification coming from the logical-analytic functions of the left hemisphere.

Observations and Implications

The etymological roots of concept that imply "gathering together" and "creating" are as pertinent as any definition we might settle for. When we refer to something called a concept, we are, for all intents and purposes speaking both of a *process* and a *product*, a mental activity and a symbol that serves the human need to manage reality by evolving representations of that reality. Our concepts provide us with the conventional means for communicating and establishing intelligent contact with other human beings. We are also able to devise conceptions of reality that are not confined by convention and logic and that to others may seem to be out of touch with reality as they know it.

It is apparent that discrimination learning and concept learning are interdependent in the way they contribute to the nature of an individual's basic images of and premises about his world. The richness or poverty of impressions derived from faculties of consciousness and attention inevitably influence the signs and symbols—the concepts that embody the form and meaning of these impressions. At the same time, the ability to ascribe form and meaning to these incoming impressions depends on the store of concepts or the ability to create new conceptions. In one respect, the ability to conceptualize may be impaired because of rather barren discriminatory skills; in another, valid and meaningful impressions may be ignored or discarded because the person lacks the necessary conceptual structure in which to organize them. In either case, the person's adaptive potentials will suffer since these deficiencies will impede the use of effective judgment, knowledge, and understanding and will lessen his ability to infer others' needs, motivations, and intimations.

The idea that concepts can express both literal and symbolic meanings also has certain implications for the effectiveness of adaptive styles. Normally, one employs or turns to either of these levels of meaning as the situation requires. An individual might entertain a distinctly personal image of an event while communicating his thoughts in conventional and socially comprehensible terms. This is sometimes called "politeness," "etiquette," or "discretion." Some people lack this sort of mental ambidextrousness and have a difficult time sorting the two in an appropriate fashion, inviting certain social penalties.

It is not uncommon for a person's conceptual style to be mired in either the literal or symbolic mode. "Literal" people are overly intellectual and analytical and place little trust in the metaphorical images of their experience that arise in their minds. They are often quite oblivious to others' feelings and to the sensations and the relationships of things that fall somewhere outside their fixed system of logic. The worlds of "symbolic" people are largely allegorical and defined by a figurative language that is comprehensible only to themselves. Under good circumstances they may be thought of as lively, curious, and entertaining and as exciting diversions at dull cocktail parties, or as fanciful poets. Under bad conditions, they might be tendered a pathological label of some sort. Other problems also arise from the literal-symbolic confusion when a person is able to think both in literal and symbolic terms but becomes riven with self-doubt and indecision when he finds the two in conflict.

Together, the language, idioms, and symbols that people use to decipher and express their reality contain their unique premises about the nature of the world that they inhabit and reveal their personal definitions of their role and purpose within it. The implications of these tendencies for social learning and change are clearly apparent. As Watzlawick proposes, "the search for premises" is the medium by which change can be accomplished; as an individual's basic premises about the nature of his reality are disclosed so are his "values, hopes, fears, prejudices—in short, his world image."[11]

CONDITIONS INFLUENCING CONCEPT LEARNING

Situational and Cultural Conditions

The quality of one's environment including the opportunities, incentives, and support that it offers is a major influence on any stage of the learning process. Impoverished, chaotic, or inconsistent environments tend to retard or overwhelm discrimination learning and affect the process of concept formation. Although some individuals can surmount these handicaps, many feel the effects and rely on a rather crude and restrictive repertoire of explanatory concepts. The individual appears to have a rather gross and undifferentiated view of his experiences since they tend to be expressed in frugal and ambiguous terms.

It is not uncommon, for example, to hear the word *thing* used to represent any number of objects or events that a person cannot properly conceptualize, e.g., "I saw a thing the other day that. . ." or, "things just always get in the way." The more intangible qualities of relationships are also lost to this person who either fails to see important connections or else lumps together those aspects that should be perceived as independent. A common form of this trait is the adolescent who persists in referring to his parents as "them" and cannot adequately describe his mother and father as unique and separate beings.

It is not the environment itself that causes learning deficits, but its transactional characteristics that set the stage on which such deficits may be fostered. Depleted conceptual skills are not the sole property of a particular class of society; language fads and the deterioration of communicational styles have impoverished contemporary speech patterns.

Another attribute of the environment is the extent to which it allows the individual to experiment with symbolic meanings and the freedom to release his thoughts and images in language that is less commonplace. The license to delve into metaphor and simile is a creative step that can lead to more poetic truths. Encouragement of this kind of analogical and metaphorical expression is often not forthcoming because it tends to produce insights that may subvert what is accepted as conventional wisdom. Expectations are frequently imposed on young children. For a time the child's primal visions of his world—his creation of imaginary friends or the way he gives life to inanimate objects—may be intriguing. Yet at some point he is expected to "grow up," discard these fanciful thoughts, and approach his world in a more "realistic" and "logical" way.

Group or family approaches to problem solving can have the effect of nurturing peoples' inclinations to unfreeze their imagery and symbolic conceptions of experience. If the group is encouraged to develop an ethos in which verbal restraints are diluted, its members may try their analogic modes of thought which ordinary convention and social self-consciousness prohibit. Moreover, the kind of contagion that a group generates may stimulate the association of ideas that would be improbable in other settings. The stability of the family depends in large measure on mutual agreements about language that is permissible and unacceptable. Persistent patterns can hardly change if the family cannot respect the very personal ideations of certain of its members that contradict their collective reality.

Culture has enormous effects on concept formation. As Silvano Arieti asserts, "Most concepts which affect the individual are learned from others, either private persons or social and cultural institutions. . . . Culture, with its systems of knowledge, language, beliefs, and values, bestows upon each person a patrimony of concepts which become part of the individual."[12] The concepts bestowed by culture color and shape the individual's general orientation to his life space. The definitions proffered by a particular culture tend to affect the way a person comes to understand the meaning of quality of life, the problems that arise in relation to this meaning, and the solutions deemed to be practical and desirable. These beliefs are inclined to be transformed into ideologies and "truths" which, in their final effect, obviate the need for reflection or question.

Cultural differences account for a significant variable in the planned change event—particularly when worker and clients represent distinctive classes, backgrounds, national groups, or races. It is a variable that is rather elusive, one that cannot be objectified because it is so securely rooted in fundamental and unquestioned belief systems. The worker, himself, is often an unwitting product of his own cultures. Even though he may entertain an intellectual awareness of the concept of cultural diversity, the implantation of his own cultural beliefs may well override his knowledge when he confronts persons whose vernacular and outlook contrast sharply with his own. I recall as an example the foreign-born psychiatrist who wanted to hospitalize his American patient because he was certain she was having delusions when she mentioned that she felt like "I have butterflies in my stomach."

Perceptual Conditions

A prerequisite of concept learning is the presence of at least a minimal awareness of the stimulus, the discriminatory ability that allows the individual to sort out the object, event, or state of being that is to be conceptualized and understood. The individual must be conscious of and attentive to the event before he can go on to classify and attach meaning to it.

The second prerequisite for concept learning is adequate maturation and development. Piaget points out that in the normal development of children the ability to deal with abstractions and concepts in a formal and organized fashion does not take place until the mid-teens and represents the last stage of cognitive maturation. [13] This ability includes the use of symbolization and models and the capacity for classifying events and engaging in problem solving on an abstract level. Effective practice with children appreciates the limits of their conceptual skills when it employs the kinds of media that minimize the need for conceptual language, e.g., play therapy, games and sports, vicarious experiences, and exposure to models of activity.

It would be foolish to assume that chronological and conceptual development proceeds at an even pace. Studies and other research show that the quality of experience has much to do with the rate and effectiveness of cognitive development. [14] This premise can be extrapolated to adults as well. People who spend a good part of their lives in depleted environments and are deprived of an exposure to a wide and assorted range of experiences are likely to have much difficulty grappling with the many abstractions that refer to things having little to do with their confined lifestyles. For that matter, the need to deal with reality on an abstract level may prove to be discomfiting.

The third prerequisite is a corollary of the first two. If the individual's discriminatory and/or conceptual functions are blunted, his ability to engage in concept learning will also be impaired. Lacking an ample store of personal conceptions of the world, this person would have difficulty in making inferences, classifying, or generalizing. The implications for planned change are apparent when considering the essential nature of the typical human services establishment. For the most part, there is very little that is concrete or definable about such establishments. The services and programs, technology, jargon, procedures, and policies are massive and intricate formations of abstractions that often defy comprehension even by the functionaries of the organization. A client's estrangement is not insurmountable, and he can be helped to find his way through the maze. A serious problem will arise, however, when the client's conceptual limitations are hastily mislabeled as evidence of intellectual or mental defects or his attempts to hide his ignorance and protect his integrity are misconstrued. Such mistakes establish a barrier between worker and client, forcing a kind of accommodative behavior on both their parts.

This type of accommodation is satirized by a social worker employed in a state agency designed to meet the medical, social, and psychological needs of seriously ill people. The following account is sardonic and caustic and expresses the writer's disenchantment with the staff's inability or reluctance to respond helpfully to patients' special needs.

Our patients also have classifications. Our first category is the HPP (Humble Person Patient) I, II, III. Second, we have the PPP (Pleasing Personality Patient)—III only. And last but not least, we have the Ingrate I, II, III.

There are of course varying degrees of requirements for each position. To qualify for HPP I, one must thank the clinic personnel for the privilege of waiting for hours in the crowded waiting rooms, bask in the radiance of our physician's knowledge, and answer willingly and honestly all questions on our application form. HPP II positions require even greater endurance. And qualifications for HPP III include showing no outward dismay when the attending physician invites non-medical people to witness his taking a Pap Smear of the HPP applicant. No one with less than three years' experience as an HPP II can qualify for this position. The easiest position to qualify for is the PPP III. There is only a grade III classification in this position because a lesser grade in being pleasant is not acceptable to the program. PPP IIIs smile a lot, ask about your children, tell you how sweet you are, and bring you fresh vegetables from their gardens because you have been "so sweet" to them. (People who have skin burns from chemotherapy usually do not qualify for PPP III, although they can qualify for HPP II if they are willing to accept the burn as God's will.)

We have very few Ingrate I, II, and III positions allowed, so the competition for these slots is pretty stiff. To qualify for Ingrate I, the applicant must ask the name of the drug he is expected to take. An Ingrate II must refuse to answer questions about education, religion, and the number of rooms in his home. An Ingrate III must do all the things the other two do but, in addition, must demand the right to know and decide upon what is going to be done to him. There is a big turnover in our Ingrate III positions because so many of them die.

We have another category called PP (Plain Patient) which is used to cover those positions held by people who are too sick or in too much pain to say enough to the staff for them to decide which category they fit into. Ingrate IIIs are often demoted to this position when staff can make an allowance for their ungrateful behavior due to this patient's severe pain or the imminence of death.[15]

This might seen an unfair representation of what psychological and social services are really like. It can be hoped that these travesties portray the exception rather than the rule of human services, but the risks and penalties of misconception and misinterpretation cannot be exaggerated.

Martin Luther King observed: "Nothing in all the world is more danger-ous than sincere ignorance or conscientious stupidity."

Cognitive Styles

The individual's cognitive style and the characteristic way he inter-prets and makes sense of his reality powerfully affect the design and process of concept learning. The convergent thinker who tends to depend on digital language can be expected to be more at ease with concrete and circumscribed ideas as he deals with the learning task. The divergent thinker, on the other hand, will feel free to generate all sorts of meanings and associations as a result of his comfort with analogic language.

As a preexisting mental set, the schema will forecast the nature of the learning event since it embodies the person's knowledge and beliefs, his values and preferences, his expectations of what will or ought to be, and his proclivity to adopt or exclude certain orientations to living. Consider, as an example, the implications of the beliefs and expectations that are ascribed to the term *control* as it refers to the issue of autonomy and self-determination. As long as the term is restricted to its sign meanings, it presents few problems in ordinary discourse. It is when its symbolic meanings come into play that understanding can become obscured. These meanings arise when the person ties the concept of control to his personal presuppositions about his capability for deciding upon and acting on certain critical issues of living.[16] When confronted with a particular challenge, a person might respond, "I know exactly what I want and what I am able to do about it." Another might say, "I will do whatever you or others think is right." Yet another: "It makes no difference what I do. It's all a matter of fate anyway." These are not casual responses; they are deeply rooted beliefs that disclose the person's orientation to his control of reality.

These three perspectives on locus of control were the focus of a study of hospitalized mental patients.[17] The researchers called these perspec-tives *internal* (e.g., "I know what I want to do."), *control by powerful others* (e.g., "I'll do whatever you think.") and *control by chance forces* (e.g., "It makes no difference."). As a descriptive study, it attempted to determine if there is any difference between the way psychiatric and nonpsychiatric patients think about the locus of control, whether differ-ent diagnostic classifications are related to the concept, and if patients change their expectancies of control as they improve clinically. The assumptions of this study were derived from Rotter's hypothesis that people who view reinforcements as contingent on their own behavior (the internals) are better adjusted than those who see reinforcements as determined by powerful others or by fate or chance.[18] Research procedures involved self-report measures that contained patients' positions about controls affecting their lives.

Patients classified as neurotics and normals showed some significant differences as they were less likely to believe that they were controlled by chance or powerful others. Patients having long-standing problems believed they were controlled by chance or powerful others. It was found that these well-entrenched orientations to control were not affected by hospital treatment; at the time of discharge, patients' beliefs that control of their lives is in external sources were scarcely changed. (Institutionalization itself, however, might be the critical variable that reinforces the reference to outside control.)

The premises in an individual's schema about the question of locus of control is but one of the beliefs that has a powerful influence on how he comes to shape his conceptions of existence. Presumptions about love, passion, power, desirability, competence, goodness (and their opposites) will affect his values, choices, and approach to problems of living.

As a condition of learning, the influence of the individual's schema becomes central to the practitioner's understanding of the way the client's world view is shaped. This understanding staves off the impulse to judge the client's behavior by normative standards of pathology and assign him to a closed diagnostic category. (Impressions of strangeness fall away as the person's frame of reference becomes meaningful.) More important than understanding is the affinity that is fostered by *willingness* to understand and the implied caring. Even a rudimentary awareness of the client's perspective leads to a deeper level of understanding of the adaptive purposes that the frame of reference serves. There is a telic function to concepts and the meanings ascribed to them. Conceptions of reality exist *for the sake* of something: to make sense of living in the world; to preserve self-esteem; to maintain stability of the self; to cling to a vestige of control; and to preserve relationships. As purpose is appreciated, affinity and understanding develop, and comprehension of the purpose of an individual's presuppositions begin to suggest the potentialities for change. If premises and purposes can be reconceptualized, the client's outlook and behaviors alter accordingly.

Reconceptualization, rethinking, and reevaluation of premises are the dynamics of conceptual learning. Concepts are shaped through learning in experience; conceptions can be changed through relearning in other experiences. Rychlak states: "When Einstein later challenged our popular conceptions of space and time he did something Kant felt any person could do—that is, 'in principle' look at the other side of any meaning-affirmation and thereby propose an alternative . . . no person is frozen into his conceptual equipment one way because he can always think to the opposite of what this portends—and to the opposite of this opposite *ad infinitum*."[19]

OBSTACLES TO CONCEPT LEARNING

Such conditions as quality of environment, cultural forces, cognitive styles, and frame of reference can also be seen as impediments blocking the attainment of a productive conceptual grasp of reality. Defects in *learning skills* can also stand in the way of effective learning. These skills involve *cognitive ability*, the person's store of knowledge that can be generalized to the solution of the problem, and *cognitive flexibility*, the person's readiness to rework this knowledge in accordance with the needs of learning.

Obviously, the individual is likely to encounter a wide variety of problems in his movement toward a goal, problems capable of evoking any of a number of responses. Mathis and his colleagues identify five types of conceptual conflicts that might arise as responses to an inexplicable event.[20]

1. There is *surprise* when a person encounters a phenomenon that appears to be contrary to his convictions and beliefs;

2. *Doubt* arises when a person is torn between belief and disbelief about an occurrence;

3. *Perplexity* occurs when the problem appears to have several solutions but only one is correct and that one is not known;

4. There is *bafflement* when the particular problem seems to pose irreconcilable demands; and

5. There is *contradiction* when what is known about the problem is apparently incompatible with its reality.

Although each conflict may call for specific adaptive tactics, all require the application of some basic learning skills: e.g., the ability to rethink the problem, to generalize from past experience or determine the kinds of new knowledge that needs to be sought, and to trust the intuitions about possible solutions that cannot be immediately verified.

A special obstacle concerns the responses of perplexity and bafflement. The person feels certain that he has a fairly adequate conceptual grasp but discovers that this knowledge is irrelevant to the unique demands of a particular problem. A case in point is the learner involved in educational preparation for practice in any of the human services fields. As he strives to master as many theories and techniques of his craft that he can in the prescribed period of professional education, he is likely to become discouraged when he finds that his learning is insufficient because it does not permit him to fulfill his ideal image of the complete and competent helper. Signs of professional maturity begin to appear when he reconsiders the peculiarities of the human state and accepts that it obstinately refuses to conform to existing models and frameworks of knowledge. Perplexity and bafflement may persist, not as obstacles, but as incentives to ongoing learning if he appreciates that each new encounter with his clients provides the opportunities for continued growth as a professional.

Another conceptual difficulty arises when knowledge is acquired but the central ideas cannot be related to any referent in the person's field. A striking example of this sort of discrepancy is the prodigious stream of terms that deluge the public daily. The press, radio, and television babble about detente, coalitions, "summitry," and other geopolitical cant. Technology, advertising, economists, and bureaucracies endlessly spurt slogans, acronyms, neologisms, and jargon. Whether or not the ordinary person understands these terms (or whether the terms even have real meaning) usually makes little difference. However, there are instances when the discrepancy between the concept and its referent in reality is problematical.

It is not infrequent that people are intellectually aware of a particular condition but cannot appreciate that it has any meaningful implications for their life circumstances. This gap can hamper the well-intentioned preventive efforts of the human services when people who might benefit from these efforts cannot relate what they know to critical aspects of their lives. A cogent example concerns the attempt to circumvent the predictable disabling emotional and relational consequences of a potentially fatal disease. A preventive project was aimed at the spouses of patients scheduled to undergo renal dialysis for kidney failure.[21] It was common knowledge that dialysis patients undergo a series of adjustments to the radical medical regimen, which places enormous demands on family and marital life. Conventional group psychotherapy aimed at preparing patients and spouses for the rigors of treatment had only meager success. It was then decided to form a "psychoeducational" group for the purpose of offering the spouses an intense, in-depth educational experience focused on what they needed to know to adjust to the demands of hemodialysis. The group would be encouraged to deal with the critical knowledge about the disease and its treatment, and the emotional and relational problems that are bound to accompany therapy. The results of this project were less than successful. The project leaders concluded "that the patients and significant others are virtually inaccessible" as far as preventive intervention is concerned. The "massive denial used by the patients and the anxious worry, pity, and sympathy on the part of the significant others render both of them poor candidates for a prophylactic intervention program." Apparently recognizing that there had to be a measure of congruence between knowledge and experience, this study recommended that this group project be introduced after dialysis was started, the point when what needed to be learned could be connected with the actual referents in the adjustment experience.

Existential threats that arise when an individual is faced with the need to reconsider his personal conceptions of truth or fact form significant obstacles to concept learnings. Within the critical realms of living, the need to revise or admit to the error of a central belief can evoke powerful feelings of loss. Within an uncertain and undependable world, a reliable conviction must be relinquished, possibly leading to doubts about other worthwhile beliefs. It is not merely the changes in conceptual truths that are painful. Changes in the person's familiar approach to living that follow redefinition are also a source of anguish.

A student in a counseling class expressed her bewilderment about one of her clients, a woman who had been a chronic alcoholic most of her adult life. This woman was now able to acknowledge that a feeling of *powerlessness* had driven her to devote herself entirely to looking after others' needs. If she now recognized this fact, the student wondered, why didn't she want to change? The student was asked to consider the implications of this new concept. Certainly her redefinition of herself as "powerless" was a revelation that was no doubt disturbing. Yet, what more would be involved should she consider the attempt to change this state? She would now have to think about assuming some power. Given her long-standing doubts about her intrinsic value and her tendency to retreat to the security that alcohol provided, what kinds of meanings might she ascribe to "being powerful?" How would she have to act? How would she need to counter her husband's definition of her as a confirmed alcoholic, his comfort with the control that he had assumed over the years, and her children's dependence on her. How would she begin to change the system (her family) that has developed around her role as an habitual drinker? These questions suggest that although concept learning can expand boundaries of comprehension and meaning, it can often evoke serious existential strains that require as much attention as the basic learning itself.

SUMMARY

Concept learning is a dynamic of change that is central to the development of effective modes of adaptation and problem solving. As a blend of skill and art, it is the means by which people create their definitions and meanings of reality in order to better manage and cope with the demands of existence. The ability to abstract perceived reality by creating conceptual forms also shows how basic premises of self and world are constructed.

This form of learning helps define the key processes of planned change. All approaches to personal, interpersonal, and social change depend on the use, manipulation, and change of concepts. At some point (if not at all points) in the process, important changes in cognition must occur.

There are two dimensions of concept formation, the literal and the symbolic (or what are also called the sign or digital and the analogic respectively). The literal dimension is essentially explanatory and descriptive since it orders, classifies, associates and therefore tells what something *is*. Literal concepts are generally communicable since they conform to conventional definitions. The symbolic dimension is often idiosyncratic and telic, representing what the perceiver believes something means. The derived symbol is therefore less communicable as it represents distinctly personal meanings. The difference between the two conceptual levels is crucial to the understanding of the client's fundamental premises about the nature of his reality.

The general conditions bearing on concept learning include such situational factors as the opportunities offered by the environment for free expression and the exploration of symbolic possibilities. Perceptual conditions involve the person's cognitive style (i.e., the dependence on convergent or divergent cognitive modes), and the restraints and orientations of the schema. Obstacles to learning might be difficulty in the ability to generalize, the irrelevance of the person's cognitive structure to the demands of the problem, the inability to relate the concept to the thing it represents, and the existential strains to follow cognitive change.

Chapter 10

Concept Learning:
The Study of Transactional Factors

Social learning is essentially an interpersonal experience. The exchanges and transactions that foster learning and change may be enacted in the dyadic relationship or in the more complex, multiple relationships that characterize families, groups, or other collectivities. Something more than the mere exchange of information occurs in these interpersonal contexts; impressions, meaning, and intentions also need to be discovered and brought into the open.

The progression of transactions that constitute concept learning occurs on both literal and symbolic levels. The literal level represents the pragmatics of the learning experience and involves the interventions and reactions based on judgments about the requirements of the learning task. Assuming that they are sharing a common idion, the participants should be somewhat aware of what is taking place on this level of exchange. The symbolic level is far more ambiguous since it concerns the inferences and images that infuse the experience with rather private and sentient meanings. These meanings may correspond to or diverge from the expressed ideas about the purposes and goals of change. In either case, the personal meanings of the participants often enclose their personal premises and questions about mutuality, process, and expectations that have considerable bearing on the flow and outcome of the learning experience.

PERSONAL PREMISES

The "search for premises"[1] best characterizes the attempt to understand and find meaning in the client's conduct. The term *verstehen* also applies since it tries to capture the motivational and valuational aspects of behavior. However, both terms imply that one person's understanding of another is inevitably partial and inconclusive—the "truths" devised about another's inner reality, if they are at all valid, can be trusted only for that moment in time. The vulnerability of "knowing" and understanding is a result of the act itself. The intent to enter into and comprehend another's subjective world tends to contaminate the integral nature of that person's reality since his conceptions were, to the point of the intrusion, without audience and relatively intact. His awareness of an audience has the effect of altering something in his frame of reality, regardless of whether the audience happens to confirm, condemn, or ignore his particular persuasions. The individual may be pleased to find confirmation or may wish to defend his premises; in either case, the premises that were first understood have now changed if only in qualitative terms.

The subjectivity of the observer also confounds his desire to understand another's assumptions and versions of his world. Irrespective of the observer's protests about his wish to be objective and impartial, he remains bound by the constraints of his language, his entrenched values, and his personal frames of reference. He cannot strip himself entirely of his essential convictions and moral beliefs; were he able to do so he would come to be seen as something more than human. However, the observer's thoughtful awareness of his tendency to impose personal judgments on others' conceptions leads to the realization that what can be known and understood is to some extent equivocal. Awareness can result in greater openness, a willingness to step outside of our cognitive boundaries and attempt to receive the other's symbolic reality as it is and not in terms of what we think it really ought to mean. Whether this openness is called "empathy" or "sensitivity," the "knowing" that is gained is understood as only an approximation of the other's inner experience.

NEED FOR MUTUALITY

Each planned change encounter is unique in many ways. Moreover, the nature of the experience changes in quality and character with the

310

passage of time. Yet, beyond its situational, relational, and temporal attributes, there is a common denominator as far as *intent* is concerned. What people basically seek in an interpersonal relationship is a sense of mutuality or community. Mutuality does not necessarily mean agreement. Although harmony is gratifying, mutuality may also develop from the appreciation of differences or even the agreement to disagree. Mutuality is the deeper experience of confirmation of self, the validation and acceptance of that which makes the other exceptional. As the client begins to feel that he is confirmed, the way is opened for him to begin to risk disclosing his inner versions of his reality.

A measure of mutuality is more readily obtained when the client is someone who feels troubled and voluntarily seeks the assistance of a professional he believes can help him find a solution to his problem. Initially, the client and his worker assume that they have a valid basis for mutual understanding insofar as they agree that asking for and receiving help is commendable. If all goes well and they are able to reach a collaborative understanding about the nature of the problem and what needs to be done to resolve it, their respective initial assumptions will be validated. Mutuality may then continue to deepen, particularly as the client confirms his worker's worth as a helping person and the worker authenticates the client's role and activity.

Mutuality becomes a thorny issue when the client appears unwilling to acknowledge a problem and is compelled by others to seek help. In these circumstances mutuality becomes the prime issue, and the apparent problem needs to be put aside temporarily. The temptation to engage in debate about the severity of the problem, its consequences, or the value of help should be resisted. Such debates result in a stand-off or a polarization of feelings that serves only to justify (a) the worker's doubts that this resistant person can be helped, and (b) the client's belief that he is right in not getting involved in whatever this experience is supposed to be. The worker's alternative is a search for a common ground as a basis for the beginnings of understanding and reciprocity. The intent is to see the client as a unique individual and not merely as the bearer of a problem. The worker needs to discover what is at risk as far as this client is concerned—what aspects of the self related to motive, esteem, or perception appear to be in jeopardy. The intent is in itself an act of confirmation and authentication.

CONTENT AND PROCESS

The relational component of concept learning can be understood from another perspective involving the literal and symbolic levels of interpersonal communication. Literal meanings are typically represented in the conventional forms of language employed to convey information and maintain a measure of rationality. These meanings are part of the *content* of communication and include matters of topic, focus, and intent that shape the substance of the event. Symbolic meanings are consonant with the idea of the *process* of interpersonal exchange or what the interaction theorists prefer to call *metacommunication* or "communication *about* communication."[2]

Process refers to the undercurrent of symbolic experience and represents what is *really* going on in a specific case of human interaction. But what is *really* happening can only be inferred inasmuch as the underlying premises of the participants are often obscured. The symbolic meanings that do find their way into open discussion begin to take on narrow literal meanings as they are forced into the logic of language and syntax. The moment an individual translates his visceral feelings and images into words such as "anxiety" or "depressed" the deep-felt meanings of his inner experience become diminished by the syntactical limits of these terms. Certainly the emotions that accompany the words add a great deal to the understanding of the person's inner experience. Yet some part of this experience is lost in the process of communication and must therefore be inferred.

Process is also an inferential experience because of the very nature of that to which it refers. The concept represents something that is scarcely objective; rather, process embodies a fluctuating, flowing, everchanging current of thoughts and impressions. The moderating effects of feedback and the chain of inner associations of thought assure that whatever the notion entertained a moment ago, it has already been qualified or elaborated by a consequent impression. In this view, process appears to correspond to what Bergson called the "prime reality" or the state of flux, change, evolution, and perpetuity that exemplifies the actual nature of human experience.[3] This experience has no beginning or ending and cannot be truly captured in an arbitrary temporal frame. Moreover, the attempt to apply the rational intellect succeeds only in freezing that which

312

is essentially fluid and fragmenting that which is essentially whole. Bergson proposed that the prime reality of experience can be known only when a person can free himself from the intellectual constraints of reason and logic and allow himself to enter the flow of the experience actively and symbolically. What he grasps intuitively and inferentially enables him to gain some of the meanings of the process of human interaction; how he ultimately makes sense of these impressions by translating them into useful concepts enriches the content of interaction.

Therefore, the search for premises in the phase of concept learning requires involvement with the literal and symbolic dimensions of human exchange and calls for the unconstrained use of the human services worker's perceptual talents. The concepts of communication and meta-communication offer a useful means for reaching a measure of understanding of the client's underlying premises and how they bear on his understanding of self, his relationships, his environment, and other aspects of his existence. In more specific terms, close attention to the client's language (and the accompanying qualifiers of tone, feeling, posture, and timing) offers entry into the following dimensions of his being.

1. *Cognitions.* What the client knows and understands about himself and his life situation, and what he communicates not only tells something about his store of concepts and knowledge but also the gaps, omissions, inconsistencies, and distortions that may block effective problem solving and adaptation. This point is so patently obvious as to be overlooked in many instances: the practitioner's eagerness to get down to the "real problem" or "deeper feelings" may ignore the simple possibility that the client just does not know what he needs to know to deal with his problems or, more typically, what the worker assumes he does know. An example: young mothers complain that they are overwrought with feelings of failure because they can't manage or understand the defiant behavior of their toddlers. The problem is not incompetency or rejection, but a lack of knowledge about the negativistic phase that two- and three-year olds usually go through. Simple developmental information provided what these mothers needed to recapture the role of the effective parent.

2. *Symbolic assumptions.* The language a person uses, especially during

moments of stress, reveals certain facets of his more primitive conceptions of reality. Watzlawick observed that language often betrays the sensory modalities with which the person primarily perceives his world, whether by purely visual or proprioceptive modes.[4] Typical language patterns may also reveal something about the level of consciousness being used. For example, the person who tends to use such phrases as, "I can see that . . . ," "I know . . . ," or "I understand that . . ." might rely on sensory or literal levels of consciousness. Another who qualifies his statements with terms such as "I feel that . . . ," or "It tears me up to find that . . ." may be indicating his use of the sentient level. Others may resort to a kind of behavioral consciousness by the dependence on body language to report their inner conceptions. There are some whose expressions disclose powerful imaginal and metaphoric forms of consciousness revealing the extent to which they are able to capture reality in almost poetic terms. These patterns serve only as clues that can alert the worker and stir his curiosity about the client's general perceptual style.

3. *Cognitive style*. Communicational patterns are good indicators of the manner in which the client thinks through his impressions and gives them meaning. Some people who are more comfortable with convergent styles of thinking are baffled when content questions call for abstract responses; for example:

WORKER: Did our last talk stir any new ideas in your mind?
CLIENT: Uh . . . what do you mean?
WORKER: Did you have any special reactions? Anything cross your mind?
CLIENT: Oh. Yes, I wondered whether I would be able to use the car for this appointment.

Conversely, the divergent thinker will attack any topic from any of a number of vantage points and consider its many ramifications.

4. *Personal responsibility*. Language can disclose questions about locus of control and where the client sees the source or cause of his circumstances. It makes some difference whether the individual generally uses "I" sentences ("I believe . . ." or "I always . . .") or "They" or "it" sentences ("They make me . . ." or "It always happens . . ."). It is quite possible that these language patterns may be learned or habitual modes of speech. They may also reveal where the individual wants to place responsibility for the significant events that affect his existence. Language

also shows whether the client basically believes that he has something to do with or can do something about these conditions or whether he defines himself as a victim of forces beyond his control.

5. *Self Concept.* The individual's statements, particularly as they relate to a serious challenge or a problem, suggest something about his estimation of self, e.g., whether he sees himself as active or passive, able or helpless, competent or inadequate, or at some state in between. Disclaimers such as "I feel ready to give up," "There's just no use," or a passive silence serve to disqualify self as an effective actor on one's own behalf. Statements reflecting the person's self-esteem say a good deal about his role within significant relationships and what he believes he deserves from others. Similarly, these words offer the listener an idea about his critical value positions and commitments and if and how he proposes to defend them.

6. *Personal history.* The manner in which the client verbally recreates a profile of his past is most revealing. Anyone's autobiography is not a succession of verifiable facts but a concoction of personalized impressions of particular episodes, hurts, joys, successes, and defeats. How these are reported can provoke a number of penetrating questions. How is the past incident related to conditions in the present, e.g., does it say something about what he feels he is or is not able to do? What purposes are served by what the person reports and what he ignores? Why does he select one set of events and not others? Why does he choose to interpret them in one way and not another? How does this account vindicate or explain his current actions? How is he attempting to persuade the listener? To paraphrase Emerson: Is this client "mortgaged to yesterday" and therefore "not free to use today, or to promise tomorrow?"

The range of possible modes by which people may reveal their sheltered conceptions of their I-world relations is extremely broad and the subject of study by the emerging field of interpersonal communication.[5] Sensitivity even to the most prosaic content of communication tells much about the fascinating and unique fashion by which a person simultaneously frames and validates his special version of reality. In his participation in the content and process of communication, the human services worker does not need to renounce his own style of expression and adopt the client's language, but the extent to which the client's vernacular is accepted reduces the need to socialize the client into the unfamiliar realm of professional jargon. The willingness to enter into the client's idiom tells the client that the worker is willing to enter into the client's world of experience as he sees it.

EXPECTATIONS

What people elect to talk about in the change relationship is not always deliberately or consciously planned, but it should not be seen as aimless or random. Although a number of incentives bear on the choice of content and focus, the person's expectations (how he assumes things will work out, what he thinks the other will do next, or what he anticipates will be asked of him) are also critical aspects of the content and process of interaction and communicational behavior. The role of expectations in the experience of learning and change (and ordinary living) cannot be overstated. There is convincing evidence from research in the field of psychotherapy that client expectations have a direct correlation with the success or failure of the enterprise.[6] If, as Rotter stated, ". . . one of the major predictors of behavior is the subject's expectancy regarding the outcome of his behavior in a given situation,"[7] awareness of his expectancies reveals much about his perceptions of self and his immediate circumstances. Perception and expectancy are both interdependent and reinforcing. A person's expectations about a particular episode will direct and focus his attention; his attention will tend to screen out those conditions in the environment that do not conform to his expectations. The dialectics of expectancy and perception explain the unyielding persistence of personal bias, prejudice, and stereotype. They also explain some of the odd misinterpretations that arise in the change relationship; for example, the client who is hostile and resistant because he anticipates a punitive lecture is clearly oblivious to the warm and well-intentioned attitudes of the worker.

The qualities of the typical helping relationship have a number of implications for the expectancies of the client. In his ordinary life situations (family, work, or social relationships) the question of expectations is usually fairly well resolved. As these relationships develop, their rules, procedures, and roles are determined, and members learn how they are supposed to behave and what they might expect. This measure of certainty does not exist in the change relationship.

There are few human relationships that are as ambiguous and as subject to misconception as one in which a human relations professional is trying to help an individual (or group) fill some need or resolve a problem.[8] What is perhaps most perplexing for the client coming into the change setting is the absence of clear-cut rules of behavior. Whether the focus of help is on personal troubles, the lack of necessities, or social grievances, there is relatively little clarity about who is supposed to do what, under what kind of conditions, when, and for what purposes. Some general guidelines and policies may be communicated, but they set only the more superficial parameters of the enterprise. The client first discovers that he is expected to "define" his goals and what he believes may be the best way to achieve them. Implicitly and explicitly, implications about the importance of self-determination enter the discussion to underscore the client's right and need to express his own expectations and ambitions. But the client would have to be rather unthinking or oblivious if he did not recognize that he was sharing the immediate space with an expert who must know something about how to proceed and which goals are preferable.

The client could be bewildered about questions of power and control and where they are located in his interactions with the worker. Even if the human services worker assumes a nondirective orientation to change he would in many ways need to be directive and controlling in attempting to create an atmosphere in which the client could assume some responsibility for change. Even in a seemingly benign and permissive change setting, the new client is likely to be conscious of the unspoken authority of his worker. How would the client know whether or not the worker will withhold what the client needs, be critical of his thoughts and actions, or reject him as a person. In clearly authoritative settings (prisons or hospitals), the client may be subject to even more ambiguous and conflicting messages about what is expected of him. He will be given rules and constraints controlling his conduct and the penalties that infraction will bring. Concurrently, the client may find himself trying to integrate contrary messages about his rights, the importance of his values, and the intent of the worker to help him become more independent.

This preliminary confusion does not necessarily diminish when the worker moves on to establish what he hopes will be an open and productive relationship. The desire and expectations of the concerned and committed human services worker would be for his clients to express themselves in the most authentic way possible, without fear of retribution of any sort. This expectation is essential if the learning experience is to evolve in helpful ways. But, ironically, it would be difficult for a good many clients to behave authentically simply because the typical professional setting is not authentic to these clients. An office, hospital, prison, or other organization is quite unlike anything the client has experienced in his conventional relationships. Moreover, the professional with whom he is dealing does not resemble the other professionals he may have dealt with previously. This professional does not usually employ a particular technology or provide specific data or solutions. Unless the client is requesting material aid, he will probably depart from the first interview empty handed and his mind filled with questions. If things work well and both worker and client are able to resolve these expectational dilemmas, a measure of trust and a willingness to test authentic expressions may evolve. In the meantime, the client needs to resort to a variety of symbolic maneuvers to cope with the uncertain and perplexing nature of the relationship.

The worker should strive to reduce ambiguity and to make the experience as intelligible as possible. Yet, the absence of a visible technology, data, or solutions makes it inevitable that some uncertainties and misconceptions will persist. The worker's ability to enhance his client's faith in the experience may succeed in getting the client through this tenuous phase, but it is apparent that careful and sensitive attention to the ambient meanings and expectations will begin to reveal something about the client's symbolic conceptions. If the client can be helped, urged, or persuaded to voice his expectations without fear of ridicule or penalty, the respective presumptions underlying the behavior of worker and client will come into somewhat clearer view. The participants will have a better idea of whether or not they are anywhere close to sharing the same wavelength.

The need to elicit latent expectations may, in practice, appear to be less urgent with the voluntary client than with the coerced or captive client. The former initiates a request for help with hopeful expectations, and his anticipation of relief or a positive outcome permits him to endure the uncertainty of the first exploratory stages. Nevertheless, it is necessary to open the client's expectations to view, if only to rectify the natural misconceptions that would hamper the development of the learning enterprise.

With the involuntary client, the major focus of the beginning phase of treatment should be to make clear both the worker's and the client's expectations. Because the meanings and implications of this venture are not understood, the involuntary client will not feel a sense of optimism or hope. Though help may be extended to him, this offer might be interpreted in diverse ways—as a symbol of his personal failure and incompetence, as an indication of loss of control over his life, or as a requirement that he be dependent and submissive. He may voice very genuine protests, which the worker needs to hear and regard if he wants to clear up the client's misconceptions. It is more likely that the client will resort to certain devious tactics in order to cling to a vestige of control—silence, obsequiousness, false resignation, or aggression, for example. As expressions of his apprehensions and fearful expectations, his behavior should not be judged or patronized; it should be understood as a statement of how the client is looking at his reality.

At the same time, the worker must appreciate that the primal impressions and expectations that evolve during the early stages of most human relationships tend to persist even in the face of clearly contradictory facts. Understanding of the power of these underlying premises offers the worker some guidance about how he ought to proceed—e.g., what assumptions should be confronted, overlooked for the moment, or expanded. At the very least, consciousness of the purposes that these premises serve for the client may forestall his reversion to more serious maladaptive behaviors.

THE LIMITS OF UNDERSTANDING

In his quest for meanings, the human services worker is not, of course, a neutral receptor. Restrained as he is by the boundaries of his own perceptual system, how does he know that he really knows? Can he justify and validate his impressions and interpretations of another's needs, motives, symbols, and behavior? In traditional approaches to human problems, the practitioner solves this dilemma by testing his assumptions against a preexisting framework of knowledge—such as a particular personality theory or a clinical taxonomy of mental disorders. Reliance on this type of framework can result in highly generalized and abstract inferences that are often only remotely related to the actualities of the problem.

We have considered certain methods of understanding that more closely approximate the realities of a human experience. The *phenomenological* approach to validation involves the concepts of mutuality, content and process, and expectancy. These refer to what is taking place in the "here-and-now" of the human event and the immediate meanings that are contained within it. The *transactional* mode of validation emphasizes the interpersonal processes of exchange—the idea that behavior becomes meaningful when it is understood in relational terms. The *telic* view embodies the purposive and "for the sake of" implications of behavior and the expectancies that people hold about themselves and their circumstances.

These modes of inquiry and understanding contribute to the accuracy of impressions in two ways. Although the worker must abstract his impressions in order to conceptualize his observations, these abstractions are less subject to error because they are not too far removed from the event they are intended to represent. The worker also has the option of feeding back and testing what he believes he understands about the client's motives and premises. This option not only tests the accuracy of his assumptions but also measures their relevance for the process of learning and change.

Despite the potential efficacy of this "common sense" approach to the understanding of the human state, the thoughtful human services worker can remain troubled by the possibility that his impressions may still be biased by some of his deeply ingrained and unquestioned beliefs about the nature of things. How can he be sure that his perceptions are not too greatly slanted by the effects of his own experiences and his accustomed frames of reference? He cannot be sure, and in fact would have to assume that his outlook is indeed prejudiced in some ways. As a member of Western society he is ineluctably influenced by pragmatism and existentialism—the dominant philosophic frameworks of logic and ethics that shape this culture's orientation to reality.

Pragmatism is a distinctly American philosophy with its roots in the ideas of William James and John Dewey. Its implications for the human services worker are evident in situations where an individual is faced with a choice of radical alternatives or "live options."[9] A pragmatic choice would be one that appears to bring the greatest benefit to the person, and in choosing one option, the others are disregarded. This philosophy is consonant with the ethos of hard-headed realism and a down-to-earth approach to personal and social problems. It is primarily concerned with "what works" in order to achieve a specific result. Implicitly, pragmatism suggests that there are certain norms for "goodness" and "rightness" and therefore takes account of the social expectations that shape these norms. In work with clients, a pragmatic approach is expressed in impressions and judgments about conduct and outlook based on prevailing social standards of effectiveness. It is most evident in such polar judgments as functional and dysfunctional, appropriate and inappropriate, and adjusted and deviant.

The existential position can only loosely be called a philosophy inasmuch as it encompasses an extremely broad range of ideas. Kaufmann states that existentialism is more of a revolt, or a number of different revolts, against traditional philosophy than a philosophy in its own right.[10] Among others, it is identified with Kierkegaard, Jaspers, Heidegger, and Sartre. Although the existential view also sees the person in a crisis caught between live options, it argues that any choice that is made will contribute to some degree of anguish and loss. In choosing one option, the others are lost and remain unfulfilled. If a person chooses married life, he must contend with the loss of whatever benefits he sees in the single life; if he chooses one career, he gives up the opportunity to pursue others; if he decides to assert himself, he rejects the security of compliance. The existential perspective, therefore, gives more attention to the personal meanings and consequences of a particular choice than to questions of effectiveness, product, or "cost benefits." Clients' conduct and aspirations are understood in their relation to personal values, autonomy, self-esteem, and the extent to which they conform to social norms. At the risk of oversimplification, pragmatism is concerned with effectiveness and results; existentialism centers on the meanings and implications of choice for the individual's ongoing existence.

As the human services worker conceives certain impressions of his clients' behaviors, he should pause and examine not *if* his personal orientation biases his understanding but *how*. A purely pragmatic frame of reference will exclude awareness of the despair and other deeply personal meanings that are bound to follow a critical choice. Placing total

321

stock in the existential frame, however, could obscure the reality of the person's social situation, its normative requirements, and the idea that most choices involve questions of social as well as personal well-being.

TRANSACTIONS IN HUMAN SYSTEMS

A human system can be viewed from a number of perspectives. In structural terms, it refers to a unique arrangement of people relating, assuming special roles, and participating in certain subsystems. In purposive terms, a system can be characterized by its major themes. These themes represent the composite of values, goals, and beliefs that give the system its distinctive and vital human qualities. In maintenance terms, a system is defined by its complex of patterns, rules, and expectations that serve to sustain and perpetuate its integrity.

If maintenance is a major function of the human system, it appears that this function would override the singular needs and goals of any one of its constituents. In most cases, an individual's membership and integration in a system depends on his willingness to adhere to the system's normative requirements. Deviation from these norms may be perceived as a threat to the security and the symmetry of the whole and lead to strain, penalties, or ostracism. The tension between individual needs and system requirements has been studied by many theorists in the field of family treatment, and their constructs help differentiate the many dimensions of person-system transactions; for example: *family homeostasis* (Jackson and Weakland)[11]; *undifferentiated family ego mass* (Bowen)[12]; *family networks* (Speck and Attneave)[13]; and *thinking, operating,* and *emotional systems* of the family (Fogarty)[14].

Basic to any perspective on the human system is the nature of its communication patterns and networks. Communication is the medium by which members are informed or persuaded. For this reason it has significant implications for the process of concept formation and learning in all human systems.

The Family

Observation of any family reveals that it has characteristic themes or scenarios that are reiterated and elaborated over time. Ordinarily, these themes may escape notice when they blend into the usual flow of living. It is at points of dissension and strain that their intensity is most evident.

Some of these themes are generic in nature, touching virtually every segment of family life. A power motif, for example, might contaminate every issue from questions about who will carry out simple chores to the major decisions that bear on the existence of the family as a unit. Other themes may be narrower and germane to special aspects of family living, e.g., patterns of money management, discipline, or sex.

The concept of a family theme assists the observer in understanding the meaning and purpose of recurrent patterns of interaction. The observed family, however, would be surprised by the notion that it is guided by special motifs. Because family patterns are expressions of generally shared and ingrained beliefs, values, and constructions of reality, they are accepted as "natural" ways of being. The bewilderment or hostility that is provoked should the observer question the family's purposes is a clear index of the deep-seated, self-evident nature of their theme.

Family themes are transmitted to and assimilated by most of the members in much the same way that cultural influences permeate a social group. The restriction to "most of the family's members" is necessary because (a) if the majority of the family do not share basic values and beliefs about family life, increasing conflict and disintegration occur, and (b) when dissonance arises in family living, it often comes from a minority who refuses to accommodate to the prevailing theme for personal reasons. In small or large ways, the family's belief system will affect how each member comes to conceptualize his own version of reality. Close attention to the way the family expresses itself reveals the reiteration of language and concepts that encourage, ignore, and discourage certain actions. One family may appear to be preoccupied with "achievement," "getting ahead," or "making it"; another may be concerned with "minding," "not making waves," and "toeing the line"; and still another may be bogged down in "nothing works," "why try," and other expressions of futility.

As an interactional concept, family theme directs attention to the manner in which the members live and whether it tends to enhance or harm the quality of life. As the functional attributes of patterns become apparent they suggest the kinds of intervention that may be required and where they are best directed.

A thematic study of the family could lead to the following questions:

Who has most at stake in the perpetuation of the style of the family's patterns? If this person can be identified, what is the basis of his commitment to these patterns? Is it simply a product of learning, a recapitulation of this person's own family experience? Is it a need to maintain control, to preserve self-esteem, or to cling to a particular role definition? Does this insistence relate to some sort of inner dissonance— the conflict between self-concept, intention, or perception? How is the theme promulgated? Is it by a collective process involving the participation of most members, or the autocratic imposition of control, or by an insidious kind of collusion by a subunit of the family?

These questions would probably direct attention to one or both parents as the source of control and direction, but this is not always the case. Although a parent may retain his formal role, one of the older children might displace his authority over time, an occurrence that is fairly common in cases of the single parent family. One or more of the children might also succeed in tyrannizing the rest of the family. Other important questions: How does the theme come to be enacted within the family? Is it spontaneously expressed or does someone assume responsibility for its initiation in certain circumstances? Are its boundaries rigidly fixed or is there some freedom for individual interpretation and occasional deviance? Is it expressed with a degree of consistency or are the family members perplexed? Can any assumptions be made about the possible costs and outcomes of change if the theme is altered in any way?

Obviously, there is a need to know something about the strength or fragility of the family system, the extent to which its stability is dependent on maintaining the pattern in question, and the other existential purposes it serves.

Family Communication

These questions direct attention to the specific communicational patterns used by the family to enact its affairs of living and relating. The family interaction scale developed by Riskin and Faunce delineates six communicational characteristics:[15]

1. Clarity—the distinctness and intelligibility of the way people speak to one another.

2. Topic continuity—the ability to stay with one topic or the tendency to shift topics.

3. Commitment—the extent to which family members take direct stands on feelings and issues.

4. Agreement and disagreement—the extent to which family members confirm or disagree with others' positions.

5. Affective intensity—the amount of affect and its variations in the way people communicate.

6. Quality of relationship—the extent to which members are friendly or attacking.

Research into these categories of family action revealed some significant differences in the patterns of adaptation of various types of families. The multiproblem families were very unclear in their communications, shifted topics frequently, were strongly opinionated, tended to disagree most often, and were assertive, unfriendly and nonsupportive. Families with child-labeled problems were fragmented and quite unclear, assertive without being cooperative, displayed disagreement but little other affect, and hinted at the presence of an underlying power struggle. Normal families (ostensibly problem-free) were only moderately clear, because of the absence of the need to be compulsively rationalistic. They were free to use humor, sarcasm, and irony without fear of retribution, and showed much spontaneity, information-sharing, and cooperation. But these normal families evidenced a low commitment to their members' feelings and ideas. The researchers surmised that there was little need to preserve individual autonomy because of the reserve of good will and the greater interest in the task at hand.

Another dimension of communication concerns the tendency to resort to *double-bind* mechanisms. [16] This is a devious technique because the user can clearly deny responsibility for his actions. It is employed for a variety of self-serving purposes including the control over another and the intent to punish without having to take direct or assertive action. A double bind occurs when a message is given that is so structured as to assert one thing but at the same time assert something else that denies or contradicts the first message. The receiver hears a message that in literal terms appears to be straightforward; yet implicit in this message is an assertion that contravenes what the message seemed to intend. No matter how the listener responds to the message, he will be wrong. If he responds to the literal message he can be charged with missing the point; if he responds to the implied message he can be charged with all sorts of things including being malicious and wrong.

The devious and controlling qualities of double-bind communications can be illustrated by a family referred for counseling because of twelve-year-old Bill's school problems. He had always been rather passive and withdrawn and now these patterns were clearly getting in the way of his learning. From the outset of the family meetings, the undercurrents of unexpressed anger and resentment were striking. If these feelings were touched on in any way, the father would deny vehemently that there were any ill feelings in *his* family. When the discussion did not go his way his face would become sullen and hard. Asked if he was angry about something, his eyes would narrow, his jaw would thrust outward, and in a measured cadence he would respond: "I never get angry." Then quickly, "I get *irritated!*" Bill would twitch for a moment, ready to say something, and then sink back into glum silence. If his father noticed Bill's behavior at all, he would shake his head hopelessly and would say to no one in particular, "See, all this kid can do is clam up." And to Bill, "Speak up, son, no one is going to bite you." This performance repeated itself many times.

After a number of incidents where the counselor's reaction to the father's assertion was clearly less than believing, it was suggested that he was pretty angry. His reaction was almost violent. He beat on the arms of his chair with his fists, furiously shouting, "Goddamn it! I told you I never get angry! I get irritated!" Immediately, the mother, Bill, and the other siblings burst into unconstrained laughter. The discrepancy was now transparent: the peculiar gap between the literal concept and its symbolic message was closed and its absurdity revealed. The double-bind message "I never get angry but if you disagree with me or displease me I will get angry" could no longer be denied.

A convergent orientation reduces the nature of reality (in this case, emotion and anger) to singular, literal, and concrete concepts and renders that version of reality invulnerable to criticism or change. The utter simplicity of convergently formed concepts (e.g., "Children should never see parents fighting," or "A good mother stays home where she belongs with her children") gives these concepts a kind of sanctimonious aura and suggests that they are indisputable truths. The conceptions that arise from divergent reasoning are immensely vulnerable since they are not committed to a final, resolute meaning and may invite other interpretations.

When arguments arise in families, it is the convergent thinker who must "win" if for no other reason than his definition of reality ultimately turns out to be a *non sequitur* that stifles the possibility of the further pursuit of meaning.

The study of the way conceptions of reality are shaped and transmitted in families questions ends and means. The ends are represented in the family's themes, the telic aspect of the system's patterns of relation and adaptation that seek particular states of being. The means are expressed in traditional communicational patterns, the conceptual transactions that are designed to fulfill the ends. Together, ends and means begin to reveal the *what* and *what for* meanings in systemic behaviors.

The Group

The conceptual patterns of individuals and families obviously apply (with some qualification) to the group as a human system. The behavior of the individual in the group must be observed if only because individual roles, needs, and patterns sometimes are lost in the midst of the excitement of group interaction. There is a tendency to forget that the term "group" is merely an abstraction used to refer to two or more individuals in relation who happen to be transactionally involved in a collective activity. In that these people are in relation, are transacting, and shape a collective makes them a group rather than a mere aggregation of independent individuals.

A primary or natural group can be characterized by a shared history and by the patterns and themes that have developed over time. The formed group, composed of people whose backgrounds, values, patterns, and conceptions are different, faces the task of developing shared patterns and themes. The study of the primary group is concerned with the effectiveness and existential consequences of its ingrained patterns; that of the formed group is directed toward questions of the emergence and evolvement of these patterns.

As is true of any human system, the durability and coherence of a group depends on the extent to which its members share a common bond of agreement about something of value. Whatever this agreement is about, this unanimity can be called the group's theme or motif. This theme may be clearly conceptualized, as if often the case with task- or goal-oriented groups formed to achieve specified ends. The theme may be spelled out in the charge given to the group, in the shaping of agendas, or in the definition of the task. Possibly, various group members may disagree about many peripheral issues (e.g., priorities, methods, and assignment of responsibilities); yet as the collection of individuals becomes a group in the full sense of the term, these disagreements become overshadowed by the shared commitment to a central theme and purpose.

Other groups formed to achieve less definitive goals (e.g., personal change, role development, and recreation) are not characterized by the same degree of thematic clarity because methods and outcomes cannot be specifically defined at the outset. The members find it difficult to find something in common other than their mutual questions or uncertainties about the experience. The development of shared motifs that contribute to the group's integrity is scarcely a natural or straightforward process. Tension, ambiguity, and misconceptions are bound to arise when a number of strangers convene for rather obscure purposes and rewards. As the members struggle with their uncertainties, the beginning stages of the group's emergence follow what appears to be a meandering course that at times seems superficial, pointless, or even counterproductive. A transient theme emerges, takes on importance, and is then discarded in favor of another idea. For a time, the members may be preoccupied with the search for how they are alike, inquiring about where the others come from, their employment, or their interests. If these queries succeed in revealing that the members do have something in common, the members might risk more personal questions about religion, political preferences, horoscope signs, or more intimate matters.

The literal content of these elementary transactions can provide the members with substantial bases for identification. These interpersonal processes also contain a number of symbolic implications for the continued development of the group. They can build toward: 1) group cohesiveness—relational qualities of trust, openness, and caring and commitment to loyalty, fraternity, and mutual support; 2) group integrity—development of themes, norms, and procedures; 3) group objectives—ascription of value and purpose to the group's goals; and 4) group learning—freedom to borrow, share, and experiment with alternative conceptions of reality.

As the group comes into its own, all of these attributes may coexist at any given time. The members of a community action group, for example, organized to achieve certain political ends, may come to enjoy the growing spirit of cooperation and learn something about the effective use of power. Ultimately, the feeling of brotherhood and mutual regard that evolves could encourage the group to continue even after its original purposes are achieved.

The group leader's role in this convoluted process is of considerable importance. His personal commitment to the value and benefits of the group experience serves to persuade the various members to discover what might be of special value to themselves. The leader's commitments provide a measure of support and reassurance that can be borrowed until such time as the group itself comes to take on significance in the perceptions of its members. As the series of thematic concepts develops, the leader must be able to recognize and be ready to deal with symbolic and literal content, and also be flexible enough to shift between the two as required. In these early stages he probably needs to offer a fair amount of clarification and interpretation in attempting to bring into cognitive awareness the kinds of issues and obstacles that may be blocking progress. He must be aware that he does not stand in the midst of the transactional ferment as a detached observer watching an embryo taking on its own life. His very presence is drawn into the members' struggle to discover coherence and purpose in this endeavor: His conduct, values, manner of relating, and other personal attributes become influential factors affecting not only how the group's themes and purposes develop but what they develop into.

GROUP COMMUNICATIONAL PATTERNS   Despite the differential functions of the two systems, the framework used to study patterns of interpersonal communication in the family also can be applied to the study of communication in the group. This framework is applicable to any stage in the life of the group but is most relevant to the early, developmental phases when the group is developing patterns and systems of communication that endure and come to characterize the effectiveness with which the group grapples with critical problems. It is incumbent on the leader to be alert to modes of communication that are likely to undermine productive and gainful interaction. Study of these modes should distinguish between those that are indicative of personal deficits in communication and others that are more purposive or manipulative in intent (e.g., to control, avoid self-disclosure, and maintain distance).

Clarity of communication is perhaps most critical for the group's development. Lack of clarity in verbal family interaction may not be quite as important since members learn to adjust to others' ambiguous expressions or depend on the nature of the particular situation or qualities of tone and posture to understand the message. The beginning group does not share this luxury. Unfamiliarity with other group members' styles of self-expression means that understanding will be based on the literal content alone. Whether the speaker is basically unable to clarify his thoughts and feelings or is intentionally vague to avoid taking a stand, the implications of his words will be lost to the rest of the group. Despite the self-evident importance of clarity in interpersonal communication, it is often overlooked, perhaps because of the reluctance to challenge another's ambiguity, or the unwillingness to admit the lack of understanding.

The matter of *commitment* to one's convictions can be expected to pose special problems concerning the growth of group solidarity. It is likely that incoming members will sense that their essential beliefs and points of view are in some ways different from those of others. Should these members become preoccupied with protecting these differences, factions will emerge and group spirit will be diminished. If, on the other hand, personal commitments are disclaimed to avoid the discomfort of conflict, then a spurious quality of rapport would follow. In this case, the members would be bound by a tacitly shared norm that prohibits anyone from "rocking the boat." The members' task at this early stage is to learn that *agreement* does not always connote harmony and that *disagreement* does not need to result in rejection or disconfirmation. This task is more challenging if the group members are well-socialized citizens who have learned the rituals of accommodation that neutralize discord. The leader's task is to enable the group to appreciate that authentic communication, although risky, will generate more rewarding relationships. This task is best accomplished by the open and self-disclosing group leader and by the focus on what appears to be at stake when a particular disagreement (or the reluctance to disagree) arises.

Although *topic continuity* is a necessary component of concept learning and effective problem solving, it rarely develops easily and spontaneously. The more obvious effects of socialization are the tendencies to be "polite" and to defer to others' interests or to voluntarily change the subject when it becomes uncomfortable to self or others. A deeper reason concerns the threat to long-standing adaptive patterns that would result if a particular topic was pursued to its logical implications. The exploration of a pattern, habit, or outlook strips away its self-serving conceptions thereby revealing the precarious premises on which they are based. Felt vulnerability to this sort of exposure would in itself press the individual to terminate the discussion or switch to less disturbing matters. In this case, the worker is called upon to establish a balance between self-disclosure and self-protection. Though, as group leader, he strives to encourage exploration and testing of basic beliefs, he must also be sensitive to questions of readiness and to the issue of what is at stake in the revelation or the shielding of these elemental premises.

To a great extent, the *relationship* qualities of a group encompass the various characteristics of communication. Freedom to state differences, express a particular commitment, or follow through on a serious topic is contingent on the emotional and cohesive attributes of the group. A relational state that encourages learning and change also depends on how similarities and differences in the cognitive styles of the group members are resolved; what members attend to, how they reason, and how they interpret the same reality will clearly affect interdependence and unanimity. For example, the convergent and divergent thinkers in a group are likely to disagree about the implication of a particularly important topic. Even the matter of the sense of disagreement itself will be subject to diverse definitions. The convergent thinker may feel immediately that severe difference of opinion is a sign of "unfriendliness" or perhaps "hostility." The divergent thinker may repudiate this notion and welcome disagreement as a way of getting to new and more stimulating ideas. These differences can be helpfully exploited; the transactional climate of the group offers its members the unique opportunity to become more sensitive to the meaning and impact of their perceptual approaches to reality.

At times people resort to the use of *double-bind* maneuvers, particularly within the precarious confines of the personal change group. In fact, a function of this type of group is to provide an arena where habitual maladaptive and manipulative patterns can be enacted and subjected to scrutiny. Even the more pragmatic task-oriented group is not entirely immune to the double-bind gambit. Any veteran of task force or committee activities is aware of the subterfuge, the hidden agendas, and other political machinations that characterize the group's efforts, e.g., exploitation of democratic processes for autocratic purposes, support of resolutions and policies that are patently unfeasible, and the use of "frankness" and "candor" to stifle opposition.

The study of the group as a human system concerns the manner in which a number of unrelated people join together in a loose aggregation and, by negotiation and transaction, shape this structure into a working, effective, and interdependent group. These transactions include the development of consensual values and themes and certain normative patterns of communication. Though the bonding characteristics of the group tend to stabilize once functional patterns are worked out, the group still continues to undergo change. Both in its inceptive and maturing stages, cognition and the processes of concept learning and formation are the channels through which rules, norms, patterns of exchange, and goals are elaborated. The literal and symbolic conceptions of the experience give a special reality to the group as it is defined and shared by its members.

The Institution

Unlike other systems that are not distinguished by a palpable structure, the idea of an institution may prompt a mental picture of some sort of building that houses a number of people for a specific purpose. In the case of human services programs, the purpose would be related to a particular social problem. This view offers only a structural perspective on the institution as a system and overlooks the organic attributes that allow the institution to be understood as a human system.

Institutions are administered by and serve individuals and therefore articulate individual needs, actions, conceptions, and values. The individual served is most often part of a family; progressive institutional policies consider that the person is temporarily on leave from his family and treat him accordingly. Temporary "families" sometimes form among the residents to fulfill the affectional and relational needs otherwise unmet in the institution. Groups, the core of institutional life, are deliberately or spontaneously formed among the residents and the administrative and staff personnel. In this view, the institution can be seen as a *suprasystem*, embodying many of the structures and functions of other significant human systems.

Institutions are also defined by their special themes bearing on concept learning, as are families and groups. However, the incoming resident faces problems more demanding than those confronted by family or group members. The new resident has not participated in the formation of these themes and would be unaware of their implications. His task, then, is to discover what they are so he can survive the experience and profit from it. Familiarity with the language and symbols used by the institution to identify, maintain, and perpetuate itself is the primary means by which he can come to learn his role and status in the setting. [17]

Perhaps the most critical concept that is used by an institution is the formal and/or informal term employed to designate the role and standing of the resident. This designation is usually applied when the person is admitted and since he is likely to be quite impressionable at that time, the title can be readily assumed. The formal designation (or sign meaning) may be "client," "member," "inmate," "patient," or "resident." The informational value in these terms tells the individual something about his status and where he stands in relation to others.

The resident must then reckon with the official classifications or other descriptive forms used by the institution to categorize or explain his disability. Formal classifications of this type are best represented by the *Diagnostic and Statistical Manual of Mental Disorders* of the American Psychiatric Association. Certain behavioral classifications and descriptions, intelligence quotients, levels of mental retardation, and other systems might also be employed.

The informal (or symbolic) meanings of the title may take a little longer to learn since they are products of ongoing interaction. For example, the "inmate" might first assume that he is merely a passive ward of the institution but through association with more knowledgeable others find that he can be somewhat more independent and assertive.

Conversely, the "patient" might expect to receive professional treatment but learn that he will get only custodial care. Because of the rather confining space shared by staff and residents, another set of designations will often emerge—the symbolic impressions of the others' idiosyncratic traits and dispositions (e.g., "clown," "cool guy," or "loser"). The residents also devise their own favorite terms of reference for the various staff members.

The institution's legal or social mandate determines the type and limits of control that it can impose on its constituents. The constituted authority is probably of less significance than the extent to which its conditions are clarified and made accessible to the residents and to their families and guardians having some say about their well-being. If the resident does not learn about his rights and obligations, what he is entitled to in terms of service, and the nature of his future prospects, he will undoubtedly languish in a timeless and pointless existence. Correctional institutions are more explicit about matters of control and length of incarceration—terms usually set by legal mandate. Mental hospitals, once notoriously vague and arbitrary about these matters, have been forced by recent civil rights legislation to become more precise and informative about patients' rights to treatment, due process, length of stay, and other privileges.[18] Subtle and informal methods and procedures can nullify or distort legal and moral obligations, however, and in certain settings (e.g., child care and aging), the issue of civil rights is somewhat cloudy, and the need to inform may be totally ignored.

Some general observations clarify these implied criticisms of institutions. First, although institutional living is not all that uncommon, it is, in many ways, an unnatural experience. There is no question that it is a necessary and probably helpful resource for those who cannot remain in their natural community for reasons of dependency, incapacity, or extreme deviancy. Despite this social reality, the typical institution is at best a synthetic substitute for the intimate groups that ordinarily minister to and support human needs. At worst, it can be a depository for human misery and impairment. The institution is also a product of the larger culture and simultaneously an architect of its own culture. As such, it expresses the shared beliefs and convictions of the society that sanctions its existence and the beliefs that are generated by the internal system itself. These beliefs, whether congruent or not, take on meaning as they are molded into concepts (expressed in policies, procedures, and programs), which are then transformed into actions. Society creates social formulas assumed to be rational; the institution also generates policies, regulations, and programs which it assumes to be rational. Yet the internal culture is the intermediating force that affects how these seemingly logical precepts will be interpreted and diffused throughout the system.

These precepts are filtered through the human system and subjected to personal interpretations. They emerge somewhat altered or even warped. In some instances, distortion is beneficial to the institution's members, particularly when mechanistic regulations are converted into more humanistic applications. But protective policies may also be subverted to the detriment of the client. Despite the formality of its structure and the clarity of its official policies and procedures, the institution is as subject to the vagaries of human motives as are other less formal human systems.

SUMMARY

Effective concept learning requires careful evaluation of the purposes and meanings of language and communication. This evaluation can also be called the search for premises. The literal and symbolic design of language is best observed in the transactions of interpersonal relationships where people attempt to resolve their needs for mutuality and confirmation. Personal expectancies also have a significant role in these relationships as they tend to predict behavior and outcomes. The communicational transactions in human relationships can be understood in content and process terms. Content refers to the literal and rational dimensions of communication that are concerned with matters of topic, focus, and direction. Process involves the inferential flow (or metacommunication) containing the personal symbols of need, intention, and expectation.

The study of these transactional factors calls attention to the special attributes of the various human systems. Each system develops what can be called a conceptual theme encompassing the recurring and purposive set of values, beliefs, conceptions of reality, and norms that typify the particular system. Such themes are expressed in characteristic patterns of communication. The family is a natural or primary group that has elaborated over time its special themes. These themes may enhance or inhibit the learning process. The formed group, composed of a number of relative strangers, must learn to shape its own themes if it is to create a climate that is conducive to learning. Among its other attributes, the institutional system is also marked by themes that express its policies, procedures, and formal and informal attitudes. In this case, the incoming client or resident must actively learn these themes if he is to become a functioning member of this system.

Chapter 11

Concept Learning:
Strategies for Change

We have considered the importance of careful study of the way people express their premises about their realities—particularly in social and interpersonal settings. The conclusions gained should lead to at least tentative assumptions about the timing and nature of interventions that will encourage change. Study and intervention are distinguishable only as abstractions in a theoretical space; in the actualities of human interaction they become reciprocal and inseparable. Together they represent a cyclical and recurring flow of activity within which a perceptive understanding of another's patterns should lead to a helpful act. Yet even a seemingly modest intervention may have the effect of modifying the other's prior state of being or relating if only in qualitative terms; thus, the helping person must be ready to reassess these changes before he can respond again. Study and intervention should therefore be seen as a dialectic scheme in which the helper as well as the client is constantly engaged in the process of reconceptualization: he searches for meaning, acts, appraises the implications of his actions, revises or reaffirms his initial impressions, and acts again.

The interventive strategies that are germane to concept learning have three major objectives: to create or modify a climate within which effective learning can be enhanced; to surmount the obstacles of thought and feeling that impede rewarding learning and change; and to enable clients to renew, revise, or amplify their premises and conceptions of reality as a critical step toward useful problem solving.

The Client System

Learning and growth are likely to be retarded when people live in a social environment that is marked by serious deprivation or disorganization. In many cases, the existence of one of these deficiencies is the condition for the other. Particularly in the case of deprivation, the kind of reasoning and thinking that is called for in the process of concept learning might appear to be an unaffordable luxury to individuals and families who are suffering from the lack of basic needs. Maslow's scale of primary human needs supports this notion, as he argues that people cannot contemplate such abstractions as affiliation or aspiration until primary biological and security needs are met. [1] Although the incremental nature of this thinking can be questioned, it is apparent that the human services worker is obligated to assure that deprived clients do have access to the commodities and resources they require.

Provision for vital needs is a necessity, but does not in itself nourish the total person. The suffering of people undergoing deprivation or felt oppression involves something that can be more damaging than the physical penury itself: hopelessness and the absence of alternatives. Impoverishment can be endured in cases where people perceive it as a transitory state and can preserve a vestige of hope for better times. But when all other options are closed and the individual feels bereft of more promising alternatives, the inner self begins to wither. It is not, as Maslow suggests, the absence of basic needs that *causes* the person to be incapable of respecting and pursuing his more expansive human qualities, it is the consequent feeling of hopelessness and self-degradation that isolates him from his potentialities.

Individuals and families who are basically self-sufficient and capable but who have, for some reason, fallen on hard times may require little more than the commodities and practical services that will enable them to return to a more comfortable level of living. Those who chronically endure a marginal and depressed existence require something more than this type of aid and certainly better counsel than the kind that is often dispensed as an adjunct to this assistance. The help that is extended to the dependent client is sometimes irrelevant and possibly counterproductive because (a) it can be interpreted by the recipient as merely a condition he must put up with in order to get what he needs, (b) such help may increase the sense of dependency, and (c) it may suggest that the client's best hope is to resign himself to his wretched circumstances.

Clients who feel trapped by privation need to be helped to reconsider their claim to a more humane way of life—a claim that takes on meaning only when their enduring sense of despair and hopelessness is challenged. Rather than smothering anguish with some momentary aids, the human services worker needs to seek and arouse the traces of outrage that still linger within his client. Of greater importance, he must inspire the client's right to entertain such sentiments in the first place. This is by no means a pleasant task since few people are comfortable in the presence of hostility and outrage. Yet it is clear that outrage can be the only healthy response to any kind of inhuman deprivation; resignation or the exhausted acceptance of this state is inevitably crippling. Only when such feelings can be ventured can the client begin to see that he has the right and the obligation to contemplate other alternatives to his plight—even though these alternatives may for the moment appear to be beyond reach. The search for other options may also pose painful risks. Yet these contingencies are far less damaging then the demeaning consequences of a helper's role that is largely patronizing or indifferent to the client's despair.

The critical search for alternatives and the need to rethink and reconceptualize one's state of being is exemplified in the following incident. Workers providing refuge and counsel to battered wives were troubled by the fact that so many of their clients returned to their husbands and the prospect of continued violence. Since the workers were deeply committed to the well-being of these wives and had the opportunity to influence their clients in the midst of their crises, a consultant suggested that at this decisive point the wives could be encouraged to consider the possibility of healthier options. Some of the workers protested that the women had only two alternatives: either remain with their abusive husbands or take their children and leave without support of any kind. Clearly, the two alternatives were products of the workers' premises. Being "realistic" and following a pragmatic either-or way of reasoning, their presuppositions precluded the possibility that their clients might conceive of other solutions or at least imagine another way of life.

After all, these women did not enter the marriage contract expecting to be violated and abused. They had certain ideals and hopes for their marriages. Were these expectations renounced? If so, did their resignation somehow encourage the kind of relationship with their mates that allowed these circumstances to emerge? Did their search for assistance indicate that they still might be clinging to a shred of hope for something other than this destructive lifestyle? Such questions are proposed as a means of unsettling stagnant premises and inviting more authentic responses to a tormented existence. Basically, it is the spirit of the strategy and not the tactic that provides the greatest influence. If the human services worker's commitments do not express powerful beliefs about the essential rights of the person to preserve his dignity, any of his interventions will be inconsequential.

Where the client's system is marked by patterns of disorganization severe enough to hinder concept learning, the worker's role, particularly in the early stages of helping, is clearly that of a teacher. Using his evaluation of the thematic, structural, and communicational patterns, the worker assumes responsibility for managing the change process in setting necessary limits, identifying priorities, providing guidance and information, and assuring topic continuity.

The literature on family treatment includes a number of strategies directly and indirectly addressed to changing the conceptual climate of the family to modify specific behaviors, relationships, and communications. Minuchin and Montalvo refer to specific techniques that "are warranted by obstacles to interpersonal problem solving such as faulty mechanisms regulating communication and the undifferentiated cognitive style."[2] These techniques include changing the composition of the family's subgroups, shifting the family's observations to enable the members to differentiate their global responses, encouraging transitions from observation to reflection about members' roles, and the use of the therapist's own affective responses to problematic behaviors. These approaches would effect rethinking and reconceptualization as an alternative to habitual and mindless behavior and encourage a shift from convergent to divergent modes of reasoning.

Minuchin also describes how the obscure forces controlling family interaction observed by the therapist can be made explicit and accessible to the coping techniques of the various family members. The family members are instructed to continue to deal with the conflict that troubles them. Although they are urged to use their typical styles, they are asked to do so within a different kind of emotional context. For example, if their usual style is largely competitive they are supposed to resolve the problem in a cooperative fashion.[3] This strategy succeeds in conceptualizing the difficulty and bringing it into the open as something real and tangible. It is then reconceptualized in contrary emotional terms, changing the former intentionality of behavior. If communicational behavior can be changed from self-enhancing motives (competitiveness) to self-extending motives (cooperativeness) by means of conceptual reorganization, the change should alter the way the members define themselves and perceive and relate to the others.

A few other family and systemic strategies also deserve consideration. Gerald Zuk places the family therapist in what he calls the "go-between" role. He acts as a broker who defines the issue causing serious conflict within the family. However, the therapist openly and deliberately sides with or against certain family members to change the valence of interaction, altering what had been fixed and unyielding patterns of communication.[4] The need to modify communication patterns to change self-reinforcing and mutually destructive networks of interaction is emphasized by Jackson and Weakland. The therapist makes these networks explicit and subject to manipulation by framing his own messages and reframing and reinterpreting the messages of the family members to disclose the purposive intentions that lie behind them.[5] As these intentions are explicated and linked with the conceptions of reality that they represent, a more positive understanding of behavior results, one that makes sense of what was seen as craziness and that reveals congruence instead of incongruence. The teaching role of the worker also is implied by Peggy Papp, but in relation to practice with groups of couples. She suggests the strategy of "family choreography" in which certain tasks are prescribed and group interactions are called on to sustain and amplify the redefining process.[6]

These systemic strategies depend on the worker's ability to appraise and make sense of the group's purposes and patterns of interaction. With this knowledge he is able to restructure relations and redirect conceptualizations that correspond with the values and ethos of the system. Such strategies foster concept learning both on literal and symbolic levels.

They also provide the leverage required to dislodge people from their habitual response patterns and to foster the need to learn and experiment with other more rewarding behaviors. As the individual tries to be more genuine in his responses to others, he also invites others to react in a similar fashion thereby changing the conceptions and premises that previously supported their game plan.

Resource and Service Systems

The possibility that the human services organization itself imposes serious obstacles to learning and change cannot be overlooked. In the North American context, these organizations are characterized by their specialized and partialized approach to personal and social problems. This approach represents a pragmatic orientation that assumes that these problems are best managed when they are allocated to certain categories that, by their nature, are artificial and inconsistent. Some categories embrace such specially defined social problems as mental illness and alcoholism. Others cover distinct age groups. Still others include the disabled and handicapped, the offenders, and the dependent. Since human needs and problems rarely conform to such tidy arrangements, it is quite possible that a particular system is unable to provide the range of services required to improve the quality of living and to enhance the learning and growth of some of its clientele. Who, for instance, would lay claim to the dependent family having marital problems that appear to stem from the father's heavy drinking that is the consequence of his helpless feelings about being unable to earn enough money to provide care for his elderly mother or services for his retarded child?[7]

A categorical model of service delivery may well be expeditious in relation to certain criteria—funding, administration, clarity of function, and the definition of personnel roles and specializations. It often has the advantage of assuring that special populations will receive the services they are entitled to. But in many cases, this model also assures that only certain facets of any one client's existence will receive attention, depending on where in the service structure he finds himself.

Within this categorical model it is likely that the human services worker will be constrained by the narrow functions and mandate of his agency as well as his own specialization if he finds the client has needs that do not quite fit the agency's functions. If the worker is in private practice he may find himself working outside of the mainstream of human services. If the client with extraneous problems is to get the help he needs, the worker must call on or refer him to the appropriate resources. Matching people with resources in an effective way is rarely a simple task. Complications develop over waiting lists, eligibility requirements, admissions procedures, and the client's own doubts and uncertainties.

Making it possible for the client to receive the service he needs requires something more than steering him in the proper direction. The process entails a measure of concept learning because the client needs to gather the knowledge and skills that are requisite to his moving into the relevant helping circumstances. The following are particular strategies aimed at facilitation and learning:

1. *Providing essential information.* The worker cannot assume that the client knows anything about the operations of the service delivery system. The client must be apprised of the available resources, what his choices are, and how he might go about making the appropriate choices. He needs to know in some detail what to expect, whom to see, the procedures to be followed, and the conditions that he will probably encounter. He should be informed of his rights and recourses as well as his obligations.

2. *Dealing with expectancies and dissonance.* Information in itself may not be sufficient for the client to move towards the appropriate resources. In some instances fear, misperceptions, or negative expectations could block his progress and they should be dealt with just as any other obstacles that impede problem solving.

3. *Advocacy.* Even if the client has the necessary information and is eager to seek out the resources, connection between the person and the service can be difficult to effect. Jurisdictional problems may arise about which agency should assume responsibility for the problem. For example, should a disturbed family with an abused child go to a family counseling service, a mental health clinic, or a child protection service? There may be disagreements about eligibility requirements. In any case, the worker should act on behalf of his client. This may involve representing the client, clarifying discrepancies, and even manipulating the system and its procedures to assure an effective relationship.

343

4. *Intermediation.* When the individual or his family are clients of a number of human services organizations, intermediation strategy is often required. A family may be receiving financial aid from one service, housing from another, and physical rehabilitation from a third. The worker's intent is to forestall fragmentation of service and person and to attempt to foster a holistic approach to the client's problems of living.

5. *Professional responsibility.* Actions and strategies only marginally related to the needs and problems of the specific client may fall in the purview of professional responsibility. The worker cannot help but become aware of the lacks, gaps, and inequities prevailing in the broad system of human services. Beyond his responsibility to his clients, he is also responsible as a professional and as an "expert" in social living for the welfare of his community. He is obligated to become a spokesman who makes these deficiencies known and to use his knowledge and authority to facilitate needed changes. This can be a prodigious undertaking requiring collection of convincing data and evidence, active involvement in critical decision-making processes, and the use of political tactics. In some instances, political action is most effective when the client constituencies of the service system are involved. This does not suggest that vulnerable clients should be exploited as part of a power play; rather, clients who are willing should be encouraged to contribute to planning for quality services.

Reference to ecological factors reaffirms the contention that personal and social change cannot be effected within a social void. The ecology of change is now recognized as a field of study in its own right with its own substantial and growing body of literature.[8]

COGNITIVE STRATEGIES

Cognitive strategies are directed toward changing personal or shared misconceptions of reality that obstruct healthy adaptation and problem solving. The individual may be hampered by the lack of proper knowledge or may unwittingly misunderstand himself, others, or conditions in his environment. It is possible that his reasoning is confused, resulting in personal meanings that tend to distort reality in unhelpful ways. Misconceptions also arise when the individual is uncertain or in conflict about his goals and expectations.

344

Conceptual Reorientation

When the individual's conceptions of self and world are marked by certain deficits, gaps, or inconsistencies, he is thwarted in his attempts to resolve his problems of living—particularly those problems that appear novel and unfamiliar. Inadequate knowledge or discontinuities in the way reality is represented thrusts the person into repetitively frustrating patterns of maladaptation. The modification or expansion of the client's conceptual understanding may be all that he requires to proceed toward his desired goals. In other instances, the resolution of this conceptual problem may be a necessary first step toward working out distortions in his reasoning or his intentions.

THE HELPER AS A MODEL   The human services worker is something more than a technician applying expedient tactics to effect change. Though he may use the basic techniques of his profession, his methods are inevitably personalized by his manner of relating and by the unique way that he expresses caring, interest, and curiosity. More than a "doer," the worker creates a presence that makes a difference. He stimulates learning and change not only by his planned interventions but also by the way he presents himself. As Strupp says, "The therapist comes to serve as a *new model of reality* by the time-proven method of setting an example. . . ."[9]

As an exemplar, the worker cannot expect his clients to express themselves clearly if he phrases his ideas ambiguously or resorts to baffling professional jargon. He cannot expect that his clients will be open and direct if he wears a mask of professional detachment and arrogance. He cannot expect his clients to acknowledge their frailties if he insists on disguising his own fallibilities, e.g., that he is capable of misunderstanding or frustrated when he cannot find the words that disclose what he believes and feels.

What the worker wishes his client would learn about human relationships and communication is best taught and transferred to the client by his own interpersonal conduct. As he demonstrates his willingness to listen and his ability to respond authentically, he offers his client a model of behavior that the client may be willing to try in his other relationships.

Many opportunities for vicarious learning present themselves in the moment-to-moment exchanges of the learning relationship. The client is especially open to new learning in the beginning phase as a consequence of his uncertainty about the question of expectations. He may be more keenly observant of the worker in his attempt to puzzle out the worker's role; in this case he would be more willing to follow the worker's lead. The client's discomfort could also induce him to resort to well-worn but inept evasive tactics. The worker's awareness of these gambits can open the way for the client to experience a more honest and trusting manner of relating. However, in all phases of the change event, the worker's presence (his presentation of self as a secure yet fallible human being) is a powerful influence on vicarious learning. His ability to disclose his humanness distinguishes the worker's role as a vital and caring teacher from that of the omniscient expert.

INFORMATION AND ADVICE   Except in educational and role development programs or in social action groups, the idea of giving information and direction to clients is sometimes viewed with some suspicion. Some say such actions may intensify the client's dependency on the worker or relieve the client of the responsibility that he should assume. These disclaimers may be valid only if that they are not overgeneralized to the point where they penalize those clients who can profit from informed direction. It is often evident that the client lacks the knowledge that would enable him to progress in his pursuits. To deny him this information for the sake of an abstract principle would probably increase his feelings of incompetence and reinforce his helplessness and dependency. The decision to provide guidance depends on some clarity about long- and short-range objectives. It is often useful to help the client out of some of his immediate dilemmas so that he can move on to tackle greater obstacles.

CONNECTING THINKING WITH EXPERIENCE   It cannot be assumed that clients who appear unable to acknowledge the existence of a problem obvious to others are blinded by a particular psychological motive. Although avoidance patterns may be operating, it is also possible that such blindness may be the consequence of a conceptual deficit that can take two forms: the client lacks the organizing concepts that would make it possible for him to recognize the difficulty, or he may be able to conceptualize the problem vaguely, but cannot understand how the concept is related to the problematic condition. The turmoil going on "out there" either is not perceived because of the lack of a proper cognitive framework, or if it is perceived, it does not fit the mind set of the person.

The field of marriage and family counseling offers a rather common example. People seek help after discovering that their mates have filed for divorce; it is a crisis because they saw no indication that divorce was a possibility. A client might protest: "Why is she doing this? We don't have any real problems! We seemed to be getting along OK!" A few queries might elicit such candid responses as, "Sure, we fought every once in awhile," or, "No, she hasn't wanted to have sex with me for a long time," or "Sure, I drink too much sometimes, but. . . ."

If these statements are not judged as signs of "denial" or "repression," the speaker might be seen as naive or possibly stupid. But such statements are often not classical psychological maneuvers, and looking at other aspects of the couple's life, these partners may be able to manage the less intimate parts of living quite well. Why then does the client fail to see the meaning of what he verbalizes? There are at least three possibilities for this conceptual discrepancy. (1) Whatever he feels about these conditions, in his own mind they are not classified as "problems" in the sense of something that needs to be resolved or changed. (2) In regard to the way he defines his existence, these troubles are understood as ordinary contingencies of living, i.e., they are "natural." (3) Even if he acknowledges that fighting, sexual problems, or heavy drinking may cause some discord, he is unable to generalize this awareness to other aspects of his marriage, i.e., the possibility that his spouse would become sufficiently distressed to want to end the marriage.

It would be foolish to suggest that this type of problem stems only from any one of these cognitive deficits. It may be evident in the way this client expresses his anguish that certain aspects of the self are in conflict and are distorting his perceptions. Yet, the conceptual void that he is enduring is the major obstacle that must be resolved before he can grapple with personal and interpersonal factors. The practitioner must resist the inclination to reach back into his stock of psychological explanations and select one that classifies this behavior. This tendency will only increase the frustration, particularly if the client feels that he is being charged with having motives that have no apparent bearing on his problem.

The worker's basic intent is to help the client discover the conceptual connections that would permit him to appreciate and make sense of the confusing conditions that surround him. The learning task involves a careful, step-by-step, developmental approach in which the client gains the ability to decipher the meanings and implications of his unfathomable problem. Variations in interventive approaches may be required, depending on the source of the deficit. The client may lack the proper level of conceptual maturity. Prior experience may be lacking and the problem may seem unprecedented. The client's essential beliefs may also preclude understanding. In a marital conflict, religious convictions could exclude the possibility of divorce; thus disturbing behavior would not be seen as a "problem" because, within the client's frame of reference, his actions could not possibly lead to separation.

It may be necessary to begin with an analysis of what the elemental term "problem" means to the client. "Problem" is a commonly used term, but one that is highly abstract. Unlike concepts such as chair or dog, it does not arouse a specific and communicable mental picture. It has no exact referent or meaning other than what the speaker assumes. The husband who is bewildered by his wife's threats to divorce him could therefore define his problem in a number of ways.

COUNSELOR: You really don't know why your wife is getting a divorce?
CLIENT: No . . . it's stupid! We don't have any real problems.
COUNSELOR: No real problems? What do you mean?
CLIENT: I mean a real problem. Why I've never so much as looked at another woman. I've always been absolutely faithful. So what is she doing? She must be nuts.
COUNSELOR: Yes. But you said something about drinking?
CLIENT (a bit puzzled): I have a drink now and then, but that don't mean anything. Now if she caught me in bed with another woman! Well, then she'd have something to be sore about. . . .

To this man, the idea of a problem has something to do with being unfaithful; obviously, his wife defines the term in very different ways. The difference is not a matter of contrariness or obstinacy but of conclusions and premises derived from past experience, ideals and image of self, and the individual's essential value system. The starting point in attempting to help the client achieve a more meaningful congruence between concept and reality is the client's own frame of reference. It is pointless to try to convince this client that he is wrong; such an admission would be tantamount to a disconfirmation of self, since that self is rooted in certainties about the nature of reality. If his symbolic reality is not theatened, he may be helped to contemplate other possible meanings or appreciate that others do define the same event in accord with their own particular frames of reference. Thus, the bewildered husband could react in the following way:

COUNSELOR: Yes, I can see that from your point of view going to bed with another woman would really be the worst, the rottenest thing you could do. But, like you said, your wife must be nuts. You mean all these years you've been married to a crazy lady?
CLIENT: Well, I didn't say that . . . but . . .
COUNSELOR: No, you said she's nuts. As far as you're concerned, there can't be any other explanation.
CLIENT: Well, I don't mean nuts exactly. I don't know, but why is she doing this?
COUNSELOR: Well, if she's not nuts then what is she?
CLIENT: Well, I guess, she's got her way of seeing things.
COUNSELOR (feigning surprise): Really? Like . . . what?
CLIENT (self-consciously): Well, she never liked my drinking . . . always bitching when I came home late—(catches himself and protests): But I really wasn't doing anything wrong and I . . .
COUNSELOR: I know . . . but was she bitching just to bitch or . . . well . . . how did she see it?
CLIENT: Well, she didn't like it.

The leverage for change is the client's own construction and meaning of reality. The worker is drawing this construction to its logical conclusions. The client's conceptions are essential to him, but they do not work. They do not enable him to understand or solve an overwhelmingly painful problem. Only when confronted with his own illogic can he begin to entertain other possible meanings and implications.

Another type of conceptual confusion arises when appropriate concepts are lacking or the person insists on using euphemistic terms that serve only to diffuse comprehension (e.g., being "irritated" instead of mad or angry). In the absence of definitive concepts, a person's attempts to resolve his problems of living inevitably become exercises in futility. If this lack represents a conflict between people, the result would be either an ongoing struggle or rejection and withdrawal. A husband and wife can be in painful disagreement about something but cannot explain what that "something" is. As a result, each takes turns lecturing the other, who does not listen or respond but turns his or her back on the speaker. These futile debates build to a point where the partners can barely restrain from striking each other.

JOHN (to counselor): She just doesn't listen! I try to tell her that she shouldn't let our three-year-old get away with things, but . . .
MARY (to counselor): Not listen? I'd like to be a little independent . . . get out to do the things that I would like, but he . . .
JOHN: And her parents! I've tried to tell her that I don't mind their coming around once in a while, but she keeps . . .
MARY: He just won't let me . . .

In many respects, this couple has devised a repetitive theme in their manner of relating, but since this theme is expressed largely in behavioral terms, neither John nor Mary are able to get a handle on it. In itself, understanding will not solve their dispute; however, until they are able to name the conflict that is at the core of their struggle, their relationship will continue to deteriorate. The worker's role would be to help them identify the concept that best represents the source of their discord. From one point of view *control*, and its attendant struggles, appears to be quite accurate. There is no doubt that this concept would arouse a number of powerful symbolic meanings; however, these divergent meanings are precisely what the worker would want to bring into the open, because basic feelings and beliefs underlie their charges and accusations and perpetuate the futile battle. The strategy that attempts to link conceptual understanding with outer reality requires that the worker assume the role of colleague and teacher. Assuming that the client is able to discriminate among the various elements of the problem, the worker guides the client's attempt either to piece these elements together into a conceptual whole or to see relationships that were unrecognized. Since conceptions are distinctly personal definitions of reality, it is important for this process to unfold within the client's frame of reference. Working within the medium of the family or the group can be most useful since it is the nature of the interpersonal relationship that clearly discloses the effects of conceptual deficits and voids.

ELICITING INHIBITED CONCEPTIONS   Often solutions to pressing problems are tightly circumscribed by the need to resort to conventional and proper forms of wisdom. The long process of socialization determines the "rightness," "propriety," or "goodness," of ideas, and the dependence on conventional wisdom is not merely a consequence of social habit, but also the fear of reprimand or ridicule. Additionally, an individual may be bound by the mind's logic—the closed system of thought represented by the verbal and analytic functions of the left hemisphere. Right hemispheric impressions are then cast aside by the precise logic of the left because they appear to be "weird" and indefensible. In either case a useful solution eludes the individual. Conformity to social pressures or to a pointless logic isolates the person from the potentials of his own inventiveness. Sidney Jourard, in writing of the importance of self-disclosure, said: "Growth is our experience of our concepts and percepts being detotalized and then retotalized into newly meaningful entities."[10]

The disclosure of the more knowing "other self" does not occur readily. Given the weight of social or personal inhibiting forces, the felt risk would be something to contend with. Moreover, the sense that a person is losing control of something when these exceptional notions are expressed is not at all rare. Once he admits to his more curious impressions of reality the situation becomes rather hazardous: he cannot predict what will happen next or what another's response will be, and having revealed these unusual ideas, he cannot recall or deny them. Hence, he would be quite conscious of his vulnerability and would consider self-disclosure with considerable hesitancy.

Whatever psychotherapy may be, it is assumed that it nurtures an intimate and accepting relationship that ought to invite self-disclosure and minimize its risks. Yet even within this secure and protected atmosphere this "other self" emerges haltingly, each statement uttered with misgivings. This apprehension is portrayed by "Ginny," a client who recorded her silent reflections of her therapy as part of her contract with her therapist:

I think during the session that I am bragging, trying to show myself off good. I am dropping little self-indulgent hints and facts, like me being pretty (a real static fact), like the acting group, like the good sentence I wrote (treading water in front of your face). I know these are a waste of time since they don't do me any good and are things that go through my head every day with or without you. Even when you say, "I don't understand," that is a kind of flattery to my worst old habits of being elusive in word and deed. And inside me I don't understand either. God knows I know the difference between the things I say and the things I feel. And my sayings are not satisfying most times. The few times in therapy when I react in a fashion not predestined by my mind, I feel alive in an eternal way. [11]

How can this self-disclosure be hastened to enable the client to come to terms with his secreted and creative wisdom? There is no more powerful influence than the worker's presence insofar as he is able and secure enough to demonstrate that revelation of private conceptions may be painful but not damaging. In more specific terms, "Ginny's" therapist has this to say in his own recorded reflections:

The therapist begins in a variety of ways to help the patient observe himself. The here-and-now focus of the therapist-patient relationship is thus a two pronged one: first, there is the lived experience as the patient and therapist interlock in a curious paradoxical embrace, at once artificial yet deeply authentic. Then the therapist, as tactfully as possible, shifts the frame so that he and the patient become observers of the very drama which they enact. . . . Enactment without reflection becomes simply another emotional experience, and emotional experiences occur all our lives without resultant change. On the other hand, reflection without emotion becomes a vacant intellectual exercise; we all know patients, iatrogenic mummies, so bound with insight and self-consciousness that spontaneous activity becomes impossible. [12]

The attempt to evoke symbolic impressions is not a discrete strategy to be pursued in its own right. The actuality of the human encounter becomes both the impetus and the frame for the revelation of symbolic meanings. Beyond the rational and literal meanings that form the surface of the interchange, the worker calls on the reflective self to observe self and other in interaction.

The problem of disclosure of private conceptions becomes even more complicated in practice with families and groups. These social units impose a variety of subtle and direct controls to avoid any one individual's departure from established themes and rules. Any member may find himself stifled by both his inner censor and the norms and restrictions of his group. It becomes necessary for the worker to deal with issues of structure and process at the same time. He helps the family or group loosen its structural norms to the extent that its members can essay a personal belief without retribution. The worker also takes account of the impact of any one individual's private conception or judgment in terms of the way it affects the integrity of the group.

COGNITIVE REVIEW   Victor Raimy's system of "cognitive review" complements the other strategies. Agreeing that "reality" is not an objective thing but dependent upon the circumstances of the individual, he notes: "If those ideas of the client or patient which are relevant to his psychological problems can be changed in the direction of greater accuracy where his reality is concerned, his maladjustments are likely to be eliminated."[13]

The purpose of engaging the client in cognitive review is to present the client with provocative "evidence" relative to the nature of his misconceptions. This approach is useful with those clients who need to reconceptualize their notions of reality but lack the tools of thought that would enable them to take the required step. At any rate, Raimy proposes four methods by which evidence may be presented: self-examination, explanation, self-demonstration, and vicariation.[14]

1. *Self-examination.* The client is encouraged to talk and think about himself and his problems to locate his misconceptions and to find the evidence that will modify or eliminate these distortions. The client may take another look at the way he has dealt with important issues. He may give closer scrutiny to the nature of his relationships to discover certain connections that he had previously ignored, or he could discover things about himself that he had not recognized before. One of the major drawbacks of this approach is the lack of required information or knowledge. If the client does not have a basis for comparison, he would not be able to alter his conceptions. The worker needs to discern this lack and provide what the client needs to know to avoid the client's going in circles.

2. *Explanation.* A number of approaches use explanation to provide the client with information that is more valid than that upon which his misconceptions are based. One approach is *interpretation* or *confrontation* that faces the client with information that the client has not recognized as relevant. *Reflection of feelings* is an approach that helps the client come to terms with the unrecognized significant messages contained in the emotions accompanying what he is saying. *Questioning* is useful for calling the client's attention to evidence that has apparently escaped him. *Suggestion* and *exhortation* are more direct means of pointing the client toward more functional ways of thinking and acting. Raimy advises that the practitioner's theoretical frame of reference is often used as a means of

educating the client in the "proper" ways to explain his problem, develop solutions, and so forth.

3. *Self-demonstration.* The client is placed in a situation where he can observe his own misconceptions and their effects. The situation may be real or contrived—the latter involving the use of imaginative thought by which the client creates an event in his mind and considers alternative ways of dealing with it. In either case, the client is urged to consider other possible conceptions and to attempt new solutions to old problems. The family and group context offers the medium for self-demonstration as does role sharing, role play, or psychodrama.

4. *Vicariation.* Involving imitation or modeling, vicariation is an observational approach that offers the client access to other conceptions of behavior and new modes of conduct. The worker is one significant model for the client to observe. Another source for a vicarious experience is the use of literature or drama that provides fictitious characters to serve as models. In a fixed role approach, the client and worker construct a sketch of a desirable personality type which the client may then enact. And finally, live models may be used. Here the client may observe others' behaviors which, to him, may be rather novel or even risky. Witnessing the results of their actions could then lead him either to modify his conceptions or his actions.

Conceptual reorientation or cognitive review represents a basic objective of concept learning since its aim is positive change in the fundamental concept structure that the client typically relies on in his attempts to resolve his problems of living. But misconceptions may also be indicative of more complex problems of thought and reasoning.

Changing Reasoning and Meaning

Confusion and demoralization reign when a person encounters an obstacle that will not yield to learned ways of understanding. But if he can discern its essential features, separate the significant factors from the unessential, and then go on to revise or add to his conceptual frame, it is possible that the problem will be unraveled and subject to some type of solution. There are situations, however, where conceptual reorientation by itself does not do the job. Although the individual may see the problem (or his attempts at solution) in new ways, his habitual or fixed modes of reasoning and interpreting may create a kind of mental paralysis that leaves the obstacle intact and unassailable.

In many respects, a person's inability to exercise understanding may be far more frustrating and self-defeating than the circumstances where the obstacle is unrecognized in the first place. If a problem cannot be identified, its existence can be denied; if denial is impossible, one can always plead ignorance or bestow the difficulty on another's shoulders for its solution. This sort of denial or retreat cannot be so easily claimed once the problem clearly shows itself.

The gap between knowing and acting sometimes characterizes an important segment of the planned change experience. If the initial exploratory phase is at all successful, the client will arrive at a preliminary explanation of the obstacle. Now that he is able to name and classify the difficulty, his next step is to develop methods of dealing with it. This works if his accustomed methods of thought are relevant to the obstacle in question. If they are not, he finds himself repeating the process again and again with increasing dismay.

The obstacle is the inability to reconceptualize or reorder thinking or interpretations in a way that yields new and effective solutions. Convergent thinking organizes incoming impressions by placing them in a more or less exclusive category. Thinking involves drawing together all that a person believes he knows about the event, thus creating a singular "fact." The derived fact is a product of thinking that moves from the general (all that is known) to the specific (the fact). Divergent thinking accepts the impression in its raw form and branches outward in more than one direction to create a number of associations or generalizations about it. Thinking begins with the specific (the impression) and moves toward the general (the many possibilities that the impression suggests). The individual's frame of reference, his schema, is expected to complement one or the other of the two styles of organization. Convergent thinking is associated with a rather narrow frame of reference, a simple and precise ascription of meaning. Divergent thinking calls for a variegated or fluid frame of reference that allows the person to contemplate a number of interpretations of his perceptions.

Considering the effect of these modes of thought on the process of concept formation, convergent thinking produces unipolar conceptions having rather literal and objective meanings. Divergent thought is somewhat more dialectical and generates subjective and symbolic meanings. Adequate adaptation to the varied demands of living requires the ability to shift from one mode to the other, depending on the nature of the problem.

A serious obstacle to learning and change arises when the individual habitually resorts to one style of thinking when the other is clearly more appropriate. When it comes to the human dilemmas, the ambiguous hurdles that accompany questions of personal choice and decision, interpersonal struggles, or social problems, it is evident that divergent thinking is the most creative and effective form. These dilemmas are shot through with inconsistencies, with symbolic implications, and other characteristics that preclude the use of simple conclusions or narrow categories. Convergent thinking tends to restrict solutions to human problems; divergent thought expands inventive possibilities.

Despite the obvious complexity of the human problem, many will still insist on depending on the convergent mode for solution. In some respects, this tendency is a product of the belief that good thinking is always logical and precise leading to specific and unipolar conclusions. Technological and pragmatic society gives high marks for the correct either-or solution; such solutions get the job done in a direct and uncomplicated fashion. Divergent thinking may be seen as disruptive since it hampers systematic planning by generating too many alternatives.

Convergent thinking becomes a likely refuge for personal reasons as well. When the problems encountered will not yield to accustomed solutions, a person is caught in an impasse. He must not only cope with the persistence of the problem, but also with his own inadequacies. If the bulk and intensity of the problem cannot be reduced, a simple way out of the impasse is to reduce its scope and meaning. If the attempt to wish the problem away does not work, a person might narrow it by redefinition or locate some spurious causes that serve to reduce his responsibility. Unfortunately, the chronic problem remains and productive solutions are subverted by this way of thinking.

The tendency to resort to convergent thinking when divergency is obviously required is illustrated in the following three examples:

1. Al presents himself as friendless, isolated, and generally unable to relate to others in a rewarding way. His worker encourages him to join a

singles group that is concerned with problems of loneliness. Al immediately protests that it would not help: "It's no use. I just can't trust anyone anymore. I've been hurt so many times that . . . well, I wouldn't believe that anyone cared no matter what they did."

2. Betty asserts that there is nothing more that she can do about her son's aggressive behavior. She admits that she is unable to control him, arguing that, "First I tried talking to that damn kid and that didn't work. Then I started beating on him. That didn't work either. That's all I know what to do . . . that's the way I was brought up. So I quit!"

3. A community worker approaches Carl to determine whether he would be interested in joining with other residents in his public housing development to discuss what can be done about rapidly deteriorating living conditions. Carl shrugs off the invitation saying, "Look, I know we are all getting the shaft. But we're kidding ourselves if we think we have any clout. Like they say, 'You can't fight city hall'."

These three statements reduce an apparently complex problem to a simple and self-justifying equation. At first glance, they appear to be reasonable explanations for the state of things. Could Al be expected to get anything from the group after what he has endured? Betty can't be judged too harshly because she has tried to do her best with what she has to work with. Carl has ample evidence that someone of his status in society would not be heard if he attempted to protest. Not only do these conceptions of the problem contain a semblance of "truth," but they also serve to foreclose further discussion. In this way, the speaker retains a measure of control over the interactional event. In the way the speaker creates the rules of the game, the listener appears to be left with either of two possible responses: he either can agree or sympathize with the plight of these people or he can disagree and find himself involved in a futile debate. In both cases, the speaker "wins" insofar as he is able to deal with his expectation that he might be challenged, condemned, or forced into an undesirable position. Moreover, his interpretation of reality remains intact, as does the integrity of the self. Obviously, nothing is solved.

If these conceptions are not accepted in their literal forms, and if these behaviors are not reduced to basic psychological defenses, it becomes possible to understand them as manifestations of a convergent mode of thinking. They can be appreciated as ineffective solutions to

357

problems of living, and the awareness of how this mode of thinking works can lead to possible avenues of helpful intervention.

Al, Betty, and Carl conceptualize their predicaments in unipolar terms thereby sidestepping the dialectical connotations of their explanations.

Al firmly states that "I just can't *trust* . . ." implying that trust falls into an either-or category. But experience tells us that trust is a relative concept, its essential meanings residing in its symbolic dimensions. If Al's logic is followed to its inevitable conclusions, he would have to say that he does *not* trust. Is "not trusting" total and absolute or conditional, depending on his circumstances? How does one "not trust"? And if "not trusting" is absolute, why then is he unhappy? Does he find himself being pulled by other inclinations?

Similarly, Betty protests that "nothing works," a statement that is an ingenuous summation of a rather complex human experience. A particular mechanical contrivance either works or does not work. But this either-or judgment does not apply to human events marked by such contingencies as values, perceptions, and relationships. Again, the logic breaks down. The fact that "nothing works" appears to justify her conclusion, "So I quit!" Can one walk away from a relationship as if it were a disabled automobile? Even if Betty attempts to remain detached from her son's actions she is still doing something, conveying some sort of message to him about her role, feelings, attitude toward him or other conditions that say something about the nature of their relationship.

Carl argues that people like himself have very little power to change their circumstances. Power is another concept that can be understood only in comparative and relational terms. Power implies a degree of control over something or someone. It is not a unipolar concept but a dialectic: thus it gives rise to questions similar to those related to the concept of "trust." If one is bereft of power, what takes its place and what are its implications?

Al, Betty, and Carl employ extremely symbolic terms as if they were concepts that point to a specific referent and express literal and straightforward meanings. These concepts are infused with highly personal meanings yet are extended to the listener with the tacit assumption that he will understand their meanings and not question them.

Pleading that "I have been *hurt* so many times" Al alludes to a qualitative state of being that is entirely subjective. The referent (what hurts) must be inferred by the listener since Al cannot point to the source of his pain. What is meant by "hurt" is not at all clear. Is Al referring to damaged self-esteem? The pain of rejection? An offended ego? A need to vindicate himself? Or are there other meanings in this abstraction?

Betty considers her son as a "damn kid." Although the listener may sympathize with her and appreciate how frustrated she must feel, the concept itself does not offer much information about the boy or what she feels about him. The listener might infer that Betty is angry, but this might not be the case. Symbolically, the pejorative term could stand for many feelings or attitudes that are either transient or long standing.

Carl acknowledges rather casually that "we are all getting the shaft." He employs a vernacular clearly symbolic in that its meanings depend on the kinds of imagery that the phrase evokes. Although the meaning of "getting the shaft" can be inferred, it is not clear exactly what the expression means to Carl. Does it mask anger or is it an indicator of his resignation? Or is it an excuse for inaction?

Although a single statement cannot fully reveal the speaker's world view, there is the possibility that it does express something about his general frame of reference. Al's convergent manner of defining his reality may well be supported by a perspective of hopelessness with the premise that nothing positive will be forthcoming and that nothing he can do will change anything. Betty's commentary suggests that her world image is constricted by the little that she has learned. What lies outside of the boundaries of what she already knows is of little consequence since it appears to her that one ought to stick with what one knows. She is not minimizing the seriousness of her son's behavior, but she is willing to resign, having exhausted her limited repertoire of discipline. Carl's perspective appears to be somewhat more decided and less fraught with anguish. To him, the control of his destiny lies in "their" hands—the indefinite "others" who determine the nature of his existence.

In all three instances, convergent thought supports a circular kind of reasoning that assures the status quo. This is what Watzlawick, Weakland, and Fisch call "first order change," a type of change that allows the system to remain invariant.[15] This kind of thinking creates a distressing version of reality. Given the individual's frame of reference and his essential premises about his I-world relations, this distress comes to be accepted as a natural contingency of his accustomed lifestyle.

Divergent Strategies

Clients locked into their troubles by convergent styles of thinking are not likely to be affected by rational or sensible approaches. If Al, Betty, and Carl typify this kind of thinking, it seems futile to confront them with the obvious errors in their conclusions since all of them could easily muster the evidence needed to justify their premises. The task is to make it possible for the client to essay a step outside of his literal and self-confining boundaries of thought and begin to grapple with the rudiments of divergent thinking. In many ways this intent corresponds with Watzlawick's conception of "second order change" or the movement into a radical level of change. [16]

This approach to change is dialogical in nature and in accord with the Socratic method of learning that seeks to uncover elemental premises and question basic certainties. It also bears some resemblance to the principles of Zen teaching and learning concerned with the process and symbols of human interaction. Writing about enlightenment, Kaplan points out: "What is being said doesn't matter so much—or rather, the words themselves are not a very good index of what is being communicated. . . . We must ask, what is the speaker up to, what is he getting at? It is not his words but the fact that he utters them, then and there and in just that way, that has latent meaning." [17]

The beginnings of the dialogical mode are guided by the well-worn precept: "Start where the client is." The attempt to erode the client's concretized versions of reality and to widen the space of his thinking about his difficulties commences with the acceptance of his reality. Acceptance does not necessarily connote agreement; it does, however, concede that the client "knows" his own truths and that he has convinced himself that he "knows he knows." By granting the client ownership of his interpretation of reality, he is also granted responsibility for its meanings and implications as far as his life situation is concerned.

Attempts to convince the client about what is or is not "true," "valid," or "real" about his circumstances places the burden of proof on the worker. The client is already certain about his beliefs; it is up to the worker to prove to him that he is wrong. This pointless struggle is avoided by respecting the client's ground rules for his existence, even though it is apparent that these rules are based on flimsy and inapt conceptions. Only when his rules and conceptions are amplified and extended to their logical outcomes will their absurdities and self-defending implications become apparent to the client. The intent is not to convince the client about the distortions in his thinking and solutions but to make it possible for him to convince himself. As he is convinced of the ineffectiveness of his constricted assumptions, his incentive to venture new ways of thinking increases.

The dialogical mode does not lend itself to being systematized; it is not possible to offer a scheme or formula that can be applied to certain cases. The efficacy of this approach depends in large part on the ingenuity and perceptivity of the worker. It is his ability to detect absurdities, to penetrate the fog of distortion, and to uncover self-fulfilling prophecies that fosters the dialogue of change. However, it is possible to identify four variant approaches to the problem of static and convergent thinking: (1) extracting meaning; (2) projecting meaning; (3) dialectic reversal; and (4) exchanging frames of reference.

EXTRACTING MEANING Starting with mutual agreement about the client's world view, he is led into the elaboration of his conceptions to the point where their meanings and implications become patently obvious to him. Within this dialogue, the "facts" as the client sees them are uncoiled with an "if-then" kind of logic. If these facts rest on faulty premises, as they are extended they will reveal the client's faulty solutions.

Al's predicament lends itself to this approach. He rejected the invitation to become part of a group because he had been hurt so many times that he could no longer trust anyone. After hearing Al's protests the dialogue could continue in this way:

WORKER: Yes, I see it. You're right—the group isn't for you. You'd be worried all the time about being hurt again. (Pause. Then fervently.) God! I'm sorry I suggested it! . . .
AL: Uh, that's O.K. . . .
WORKER: No, no it isn't. I can see why you don't trust anyone. If I really understood how much you were hurt I wouldn't have . . .
AL: Hey, wait! I didn't say I didn't trust you.
WORKER (astonished): Why should you trust me after what you've been through?

361

AL: Well . . . but you're different?

WORKER: Different? Me? Why am I different from any of the others?

AL: I dunno . . . I guess I feel safer with you.

WORKER: (surprised): But . . . Didn't you feel safe with some of the others? When you were hurt before? Why should I be any different?

AL: I guess you don't hurt people . . .

WORKER: Oh, you mean the others wanted to get you?

AL: No . . . wait . . . you're getting me confused! I didn't say they were out to get me . . . but like with Marj, the girl I was engaged to. We had everything all planned. Then all of a sudden she calls it off for no reason.

WORKER: If there was no reason, maybe she did want to hurt you?

AL: No . . . not Marj. This is dumb! I can't explain it. All I know is that I was really hurt. But I never really thought about why it happened.

WORKER: Maybe you and I could take a closer look at it to see what really went wrong. What do you think?

AL: I can see that maybe I better.

It is not only the worker's tactics but also his strong emotional response that illuminates the implications of Al's conceptions. The worker's intense reaction underscores the symbolic connotations of Al's rather literal statements. As the worker identifies with the extravagance of Al's convictions, Al finds it necessary to back off a bit and acknowledge that his "truths" are perhaps less absolute than he believed they were, especially since they do not lead to the proper conclusions. With the tacit admission that he is confused, perhaps he does not really understand what actually happened when he was so terribly hurt, and the path is now cleared of enough conceptual debris to permit a more helpful examination of Al's ambivalence and his role in his hurtful experiences. Al now seems ready to move from certainty to possibilities.

PROJECTING MEANING The conceptual impasse can be approached from the angle of projecting meaning. Directly or indirectly, the client is encouraged to demonstrate how his beliefs and premises work. In the direct approach, simulated situations are established in which the client can enact these premises. Role play is one such technique. The worker creates a verbal picture of a typical problematic event and asks the client to play out the way he might deal with it. As a variation, worker and client can switch roles, with the worker either mimicking the client's behavior or modeling what might be a more effective response to the situation. Whatever type of role play is used, the intent is to help the client observe

362

and confront the results of his maladaptive patterns, the active expressions of his rigidly conceived ideas about himself, his relations, and his world.

A more subtle and indirect form of projecting meaning involves careful questioning about the client's expectations of himself and what he thinks the results will be in a particular situation. An event is examined in terms of the client's projections about how he will deal with it and what will happen. The key to this approach is the use of *what* questions in place of the more common *why* questions. *Why* questions are posed with the presumption that causes of the problem can be defined or identified; if the cause can be found then a solution should follow. But people who organize reality in convergent terms already "know" the cause of their dilemma and tend to respond with neatly packaged and unassailable explanations. Questions about *why* things are as they are or *why* one does as he does will only generate a response that justifies what is believed in the first place.

The intent is to maneuver the client into circumstances where his certainty about cause or effect can be disabused. *What* questions serve this end since they put the individual into a simulated reality over which he has less control. In Carl's refusal to join with other neighbors to remedy certain community problems, his rejoinders to questions about *why* he thinks he is getting the shaft or *why* it won't do any good to confront the authorities can be readily imagined. With the use of *what* questions, the dialogue might work out in this way:

WORKER: From what you say, maybe you have been pushed around a lot in your time. And maybe you're right. It could be that what we are trying to do is pretty hopeless. But look, you've been around . . . you know what it's like. What I mean is . . . let's just suppose you were with your neighbors and are standing in front of the housing board . . .

CARL (firmly): They wouldn't listen!

WORKER: O.K., let's say they won't but you're still standing there with (lists other neighbors). You're there for a good reason. What do you do?

CARL: Nothing.

WORKER (puzzled): Nothing? I'm not sure what you mean. Look, here you are, standing with your neighbors trying to tell these bureaucrats that your development is going down the tubes. And they aren't listening . . .

CARL: Well, I guess I'd be a little sore, but . . .

WORKER: What do you do when you get sore?

CARL: Depends.

WORKER: What would happen if you got sore in the meeting?

CARL: Not sure . . . never thought that far ahead. (He is encouraged to go on.) Well, I'd have to say something, but it wouldn't do any good . . .

WORKER: What do you think you'd say?

CARL: I guess I'd ask them how they would like it living with rats in *their* kids' rooms, with garbage that is never picked up. (Carl goes on with other complaints.) But . . .

WORKER: But what about the fact that you're standing there with Ellerby, Jones. . . . how would they react?

CARL (enlightened): I know old Ellerby would back me up. Come to think of it . . . (laughs) he's like you. He's always over trying to get me to quit accepting things like they are . . .

Although this exchange shows only the beginnings of a breakthrough in Carl's way of thinking, it illustrates how rigid and convergent conceptions can be dissolved to some extent by creating imaginary but plausible conditions in which mindless patterns can be challenged. *What* questions are not in themselves threatening. Given the client's premises, they inquire about how his premises hold up in critical circumstances. When it becomes evident that his premises are not relevant, the client becomes vulnerable to the consideration of other divergent possibilities. "Clout" in this instance ceased to be an unattainable concept and at least in symbolic terms was transformed into something that could be shared with an ally.

DIALECTIC REVERSAL   The dialectic reversal approach also intends to create a climate in which the client's unipolar conception of reality is no longer tenable. A convergent orientation limits the individual's options and shields him from the anxiety that arises when he considers more ambivalent or dissonant conceptions. The worker's not debating with him or attempting to undermine his premises strips the client of his well-seasoned justifications of his plight. When the worker concedes that life must be just the way the client defines it, the client will often find himself in an existential void. To this point, the client's solipsistic conceptions offset the need to change his thinking about his problems and solutions. The critical issue is not whether the client is indeed weak or helpless. His ability to go on *proving* and *demonstrating* that he is weak or helpless supports a justifiable "disability." By granting that the client's reality may be valid, the worker shifts the weight of responsibility back onto the client's shoulders. If this succeeds in disturbing the stability of the self, the client might then reverse his field and consider the implications of the opposite side of his circumstances—the dialectics of his life. If he has laid claim to some sort of incapacitating infirmity he must now ponder what its opposite means to him.

Exaggeration or the well-placed caricature of the dialectical opposite can serve to place the client's unipolar conviction in doubt

FATHER: Seems like I can't do anything about what's going on in the family. It's not just the kids but my wife too. They all act as if I wasn't there.

WORKER: Yes, I guess it's really rough being invisible. (Pause.) But I bet it would feel good, if you *were* the real boss, the top honcho . . . all of them knowing that if they didn't follow you orders that you'd tell them off, reach out and grab 'em by the throat and . . .

FATHER (uncomfortably): No . . . no . . . that's being a tyrant . . . that's . . .

WORKER (surprised): Oh? I thought you wanted to run the show?

FATHER: Well, no . . . if I could just get them to listen to me.

WORKER: Say, I could call the family in and give them a lecture about how fathers should be listened to . . .

FATHER (smiling): Come on . . . you know that isn't what I mean. I'd have to be the one to be stronger, I guess, to take charge in some ways.

WORKER (honestly puzzled): But how can you do that? Like you said, "I just can't do anything."

FATHER: Well, that doesn't mean I can't do something!

WORKER: O.K. Let's take that problem you mentioned—about Tim's acting up at school. What kind of "something" can you do about that?

FATHER (after a thoughtful silence): Yes, that. I was hoping it would straighten out by itself, but I guess the first thing I ought to do is get down to his school and find out what's really going on.

Finding himself caught somewhere between the poles of the "helpless" and the "all-powerful" father, this client discovers that neither pole is tenable and that it is possible to think in ambivalent and middle-ground terms. He is just approaching the possibility that strength and weakness are not distinct opposites but coexist in the role of father. This is, of course, a divergent conception that will lead him to far more productive solutions than his convergent way of thinking allowed.

EXCHANGING FRAMES OF REFERENCE   In exchanging frames of reference the attempt is to appeal to the client's ability to relinquish a world view that restricts and stunts his options. Some people are either unable to act or

365

insist on repeating the same impotent attempts at solutions because of a schema that is vacant of the meanings that could free them to act with a greater sense of inventiveness and certainty. If it is assumed that Betty's protest, "That's all I know what to do, . . . that's the way I was brought up" is not a denial of personal responsibility, then it is possible that she is truly limited by her narrow frame of objective experience. What she is really saying is, "All I know is what I have been exposed to." If her difficulties in managing her relationship with her son were simply the consequences of the lack of experience and knowledge, she might profit from the provision of advice, guidance, or information. But often such difficulties are not the products of the lack of knowledge alone; they express the contents of a constricted and inflexible schema that compels the individual to repeat the same "solutions" until he is defeated in one way or another. As in most cases, the solution is the problem.

The attempt to help the client exchange or expand his frame of reference may be directed to the many levels of the perceptual process. It was proposed that whatever "knowing" is, it may be something that can transcend the rational intellect. In this instance, the worker shifts from practical and rational concerns to the awareness that might be unleashed by imagery, identification, or sentiency. Betty could be asked to review "the way I was brought up" not in narrative terms, but in a manner that reveals what she felt and imagined about the experience. Or, her identifications with one parent or the other might be explored. Any of these approaches may elicit hidden meanings that could add to her role as an effective mother. In more immediate terms, she could be encouraged to imagine another person in her role as mother. Since this mental picture is not constrained by actual circumstances, the client is freed to envision all sorts of possible solutions. Or, she might be asked to imagine a dialogue with her incorrigible son in which she can pursue any approach to the problem that might enter her mind. If the worker assumes that the powers of imagery and projection can override the intellectual boundaries of the mind, the possible ways he can help modify the client's schema are limited only by his own creativity and imagination.

Dialogical exchange is particularly relevant to the intent to question or challenge those premises that spring from a person's tendency to reduce his reality to concrete and simplistic levels. The four general strategies are by no means discrete and separable, but they do suggest the means of attacking reasoning that is convergently based.

Changing Purposive Conceptions

The preceding strategies of learning and change were directed toward the instrumental or practical functions of concept formation. The following approaches are concerned with the purposive or telic functions of the person's world view or the idea that people shape their conceptions of reality "for the sake of" something. This essential "something" is summed up by Ortega y Gasset: "Life is a struggle with things to maintain itself among them. Concepts are the strategic plan we form in answer to the attack."

The success of a person's attempts to cope with the contingencies of living depends on the extent to which he experiences himself as whole and congruent. This sense of harmony leads to behavior that is consistent and dependable. Conversely, ineffective coping can reflect the dissonance that arises when the individual's perceptions of his world, his valuation of self, and his incentives are in conflict. If dissonance cannot be resolved by authentic solutions, the individual contrives an illusory sense of integrity and tries to reduce his distress by a retreat to more fraudulent maneuvers. These maneuvers may be called maladaptive insofar as they generate additional problems and often disturb others. As far as the troubled person is concerned, they are indeed adaptive and purposeful since they enable him to survive, even though survival may be marginal.

These patterns are woven into the very character of the individual. They are the products of conceptions of reality that become organized into themes and rules of living. These themes and rules act as the premises that guide conduct in the manner in which a person presents himself, relates to others, and responds to his social and physical universe. They may be manifested in patterns of aimlessness, ambivalence, distortion, rigidity, or resignation.

Insofar as a person's conceptions are basic to the critical choices he makes about his approach to living, it appears that their purposes might best be understood within an existential perspective. The person confronted by a threat to his integrity can respond by ascribing the kind of meanings to himself and to the threat that would allow him to act in a manner that is more authentic and autonomous than it is inauthentic and submissive. Or he could elect the opposite course. These choices are illustrated by Bugental (Figure 5), who warns that this dichotomization of

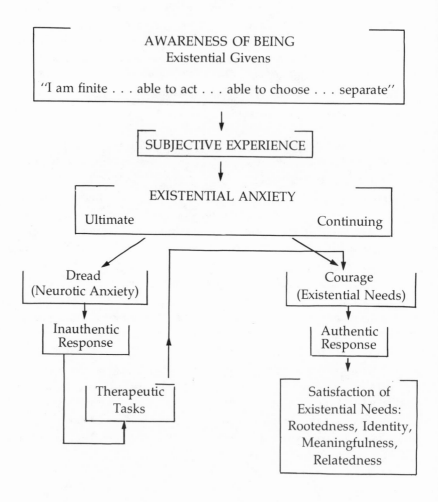

FIGURE 5. The Courage or Dread Confrontations

response oversimplifies the matter. [18] For in any given situation, human beings are capable of responding with both dread and courage, but one tends to dominate the other. [19]

Courage appears to express the existential givens that amount to one's autonomy; dread symbolizes the denial of these givens. Within this existential frame it is the subjective experience that either reaffirms or distorts these autonomous conceptions (by modes of thought and frames of reference). The consequence is anxiety; its form depends on the meanings that one creates.

The nature of this conceptual distortion and the inauthentic response that follows can be shown by an example. A mother and wife is able to discriminate among the many absurdities and troubles in the lifestyle of her family. She is a witness to her husband's controls and meaningless pursuits. She sees her children failing to achieve, unhappy, caught within the strains of the marriage. But she cannot act. In effect, she has resigned, drinks too much, and has become the "family problem." A selected fragment of an early interview shows her response to her worker and indicates what he might infer about her inner symbolic conceptions of her circumstances and her self.

Literal Statements	*Symbolic Meanings*
COUNSELOR: You're concerned about some serious problems in your family—yet, how do you see your part? What do you feel you can do?	Who are you, really? Can you be more than you believe you are?
CLIENT: Nothing. I'm just useless. Can't do anything but make others miserable.	I'm just not what they want me to be. If I were, they'd be happy, everything would be good, peaceful.
COUNSELOR: You really mean you have nothing to contribute, nothing you can do to change anything?	Are you just a helpless victim?
CLIENT: I don't know . . . I know what I believe . . . I mean, I think about some- things, but they . . . they . . . I don't know . . .	My ideas, values are different than theirs. I'm afraid to tell you. You might ridicule me too.
COUNSELOR: What would happen if you took a chance, tried? . . .	

CLIENT: It's no use . . . I can't . . . I just can't. | I *am* powerless. They control me.

COUNSELOR: And if you can't . . . if things don't change . . . then?

CLIENT: I know. It will only get worse . . . but . . . | I will get worse. I will be lost.

COUNSELOR: And if you really, *really* say what you think, what do you believe will happen? | Tell me the actual risk you face.

CLIENT: They will be even more miserable. | They will not like me. They will get angry. They will reject me. They will leave me. *I will be alone.*

Apparently experiencing conflict between her conception of herself and her ideals about the role of a woman, mother, and wife, this client adopts a pattern of resignation as a purposeful solution. This pattern and its underlying premises are scarcely authentic inasmuch as she has chosen to abdicate her ability to act and to deny her individuality. By this means she is able to ward off at least three powerful threats: (1) the need to acknowledge (first, to herself) her ambivalent feelings about herself, her husband, and her children; (2) the need to confront the risk that accompanies self-assertion and the intent to change the existing family balance; and (3) the fundamental dread of being abandoned.

The dilemma of this existential crisis must be considered before the approaches to change that pertain to this dimension of learning can be surveyed. Given the anguish that she is enduring, it could be assumed that any change in a positive direction would be seized. To the client, the idea of change may sound hopeful as a possible release from long-standing misery. But change also implies the need to abandon familiar and closely held solutions. To the client, her immediate solution not only "works" as an alternative to other types of dissonance, it also has become enmeshed in her identity as this identity is defined by self and others in relation. Thus, the thought of changing creates anguish of another order.

By whatever means the client is asked to change, an indispensable phase must be worked out well before any attempt to resolve problems of misconception and distortion. It involves the effort to gain the client's commitment. Basically, commitment denotes the client's willingness to choose to participate and accept responsibility for this choice and the willingness to endure the agony of having made a choice with little foreknowledge and less control over how the process will unfold. This attempt does not ask the client to accept something with blind faith; it requests her to make a critical determination about her existence and future, inasmuch as the immediate evidence predicts a dire outcome, should things remain as they are. This sort of commitment is not gained by placing an *either* (I will) or an *or* (I won't) set of choices before the client while the worker sits passively waiting for the client's decision. The need for a commitment does not grant the worker license to assign the client to a "motivated" or "unmotivated" category, depending on which direction the client elects. Rather, the client requires an amount of help to work out this commitment to whatever degree is possible for her: in many instances she would be able to enter into only a short-term contract that would need to be reworked again and again over the course of the change experience. Having made this commitment, the client also has taken the first critical step toward personal responsibility for her life circumstances. If this commitment is not forthcoming, the client is free to abdicate responsibility once again, to depart the experience that was not of her making in the first place.

Perhaps the term "principle" rather than strategy best covers the approach to this type of concept learning since what we are considering are general guidelines for practice. At any rate, learning comprises three interrelated tasks in this case: (1) redefinition and reconceptualization of the problem; (2) redefinition and reconceptualization of the dissonance experienced by the client; and (3) the consideration of the personal and interpersonal implications of new solutions to the client's difficulties. The three tasks are obviously not discrete and do not follow in a particular order.

The attempt to help the client redefine and rethink the problem and its personal and interpersonal consequences takes account of the distortions and misrepresentations that stand in the way of a reasonable solution. The first step in redefinition is a reframing of the nature of the problem in conceptual terms that more accurately represent its actuality. Often, this kind of reframing is qualitative, involving a significant change in conceptions about responsibility or the origins of the difficulty. For instance, the previous client was quite accurate when she indicated that the problem was her inability to act decisively. But she misrepresented the obstacle to action in the way that she implied that "I am powerless, they control me." If she were helped to reframe her beliefs in terms that portrayed what was really taking place she might then say, "I cannot do anything about my family's troubles because I *see myself* as powerless or subject to the controls of others," or "I have *chosen* to submit to others." This new conception shifts the locus of the problem from a nebulous force beyond my command to a conflict within myself that I can at least consider doing something about.

As this critical increment in understanding is achieved, many of the strategies subsumed under *conceptual reorientation* may assist in furthering the process of reconceptualization. The authenticity and decisiveness of the worker can serve as a new model of behavior that the client can observe and borrow from. Careful exploration of what actually transpires within this client's family may help her discover connections formerly unrecognized. Apparently, she sees no relation between her passive resignation and the ongoing turmoil in her family. Only when she appreciates that her chronic submissiveness and her retreat to alcohol are somehow intertwined with her family's distress can she consider some beginning attempts to change things.

The effort to elicit covert or forbidden sentiments is particularly indicated when the client's anguish is rooted in subverted premises and conceptions about her existence. This client justifies her sad lifestyle by repudiating, disguising, or stifling some critical conceptions. She will not allow herself to contemplate the idea of her differentness; if she attached any credibility to her individuality and femininity she would then need to become more assertive. Although she acknowledges her incompetence, she does so only to justify her passive state. Were she to admit to her real feelings of failure, she would also have to admit that she has violated her personal ideals and therefore confront her sense of futility. At the core of her sorrow, she cannot directly express her dread of abandonment and therefore can only conceive of herself as a hostage in a desolate relationship. Even the halting expression of these shrouded conceptions marks a shift toward the possibility of reexamining their meanings and implications. Only when the dread is named in some way and given reality can the client begin to contemplate what aspects of self she has at stake in perpetuating or changing her existing patterns. What is the cost of continuing to violate her self-conceptions and her aspirations? What does authentic action imply in terms of herself and her family? What does abandonment really mean to her?

The dialogical approach seems appropriate in these circumstances. The mutual pursuit of meaning can evolve into a challenge to the kind of convergent thinking that keeps her in dead center. This client employs a list of reductive conclusions that prove her helplessness; other clients might direct their assumptions outward by blaming others for their plight. In either case, dialogical questioning and the attempt to extract or project meaning strives to dislodge the client from her secure albeit tragic logic that discredits the worth, integrity, and power of the self.

As these purposes and their supporting premises are revealed, the client's inclinations to avoid responsible choice and action become less defensible. No longer able to resort to accustomed solutions, she now must contemplate other alternatives that may be more in line with her basic value commitments. This venture is by no means free of conflict as untested personal choices must be weighed against their unpredictable implications for significant others and for the client's own security in her system. It is a time when the worker must also be concerned with balance, as he attempts to work for continued reconceptualization while providing the support that clients require to risk probing this uncertain experience.

INDIRECT APPROACHES TO CONCEPT LEARNING

Concept learning like discrimination learning is not restricted to the planned interpersonal context of change. Although the dyadic relationship, the family, and the group provide powerful influences on learning and change, there are other resources that can be exploited. Again, the range of these resources is limited only by the creative spirit of the human services worker.

Diaries and Journals

Diary writing is of special benefit to concept learning directed to the way people organize and interpret their personal and experiential realities. The diary or journal provides a unique means of capturing and observing the meaningful thoughts and impressions that often go unheeded in the press of ordinary living.

The diary is unique in that it captures the essence of the heightened moment. . . . The diary shows constantly changing selves within one character; perceptions, perceptions only, of a swirling, rocky, unsteady external world; internally, images are drawn that are bigger, smaller, contradictory, complementary, expanding, contracting deeper into the mirror, on its surface, half-way in. But the gestalt, the completion, the totality can never be hoped for, can never be attained. Looking into a mirror facing a mirror, there is no entry into the region beyond the last face in the mirrors, yet it is there. Perhaps that is why diaries are usually not published or read till after the death of the diarist. It is a book without a true beginning or a true end. With the diary as with a true life, the only "real" denouement is death. . . .[20]

Seen in this way, the diary becomes a mirror of self that cannot be found in other realms of living. Its contents are not bound by the restrictions of grammar and syntax, nor does it require the coherence and rationality that are found in the normative conditions for proper human exchange. The writer also is not bound by any special audience and its expectations; his reflections may be directed toward himself, to his helper, to a mythical being, to posterity, or to no one at all. The diary may evolve into a "search for premises" that is circumscribed only by the writer's self-imposed limits.

Tristine Rainer points out that the diary can also be used in a deliberate fashion to complement the methods of change. She reports on a project where depressed people were asked to record their thoughts, particularly when they felt especially sad or depressed. This activity had the effect of helping these patients identify and correct the negative and unrealistic thought patterns that affected their low self-esteem.[21] Diaries and journals are a useful means for recording dreams and fantasies, giving credence to the levels of consciousness that support one's premises. Recorded personal reflections also help fill the space between meetings with the worker or the client's group and offer the opportunity to review what was discussed, reactions, and the issues needing further elaboration. Finally, the diary is another medium for eliciting tabooed conceptions, the thoughts and feelings that resist expression in the face-to-face encounter.

Homework and Directed Activity

Outside activities are a valuable means for expanding the client's conscious and focused attention to conditions of living that have gone unrecognized. Outside activities also have special benefits for concept learning, and their use derives from the assumption that cognition and behavior form a gestalt and are interdependent. There must be some degree of consonance between how an individual thinks and how he acts, otherwise strain and distress follows. It has been assumed that as an individual's construction of reality changes so will his conduct. Use of the reverse approach is an equally effective method of inducing change, particularly with those clients who experience some difficulty in articulating their thoughts and meanings. The selective assignment of specific tasks and behaviors followed by a detailed review of what actually transpired, how the outcome did or did not correspond with the client's expectations, and the implications that the experience has for the client's self-image can be most beneficial to the learning enterprise. This method is a behavioral version of the strategy that links conceptions with reality since it provides the worker and client with the experiential event in which this linkage can be forged.

A variation of this approach is the technique of *symptom prescription*, based on a theory of symptoms that explains them as expressions of human communication, and as spontaneous and inescapable problems over which the client believes he has no control. [22] The client conceives of himself as helpless insofar as his symptoms are concerned because they just "happen to me." The intent of symptom prescription is to create a paradox by instructing the client not to fight the symptom but to enact it. The client is placed in a bind. If he acts out the symptom it is no longer spontaneous, nor beyond his control; if he does not act it out, he is giving up a device that served an adaptive purpose. An example of this strategy involves a fat lady in her mid-thirties who had long complained about her unattractiveness and loneliness. She protested that she just could not stop herself from overeating and repeatedly proved the correctness of her premise to the therapists, physicians, and others from whom she sought help. She came to the attention of another worker who recognized the self-fulfilling prophecy in her symptom. His approach was to prescribe the symptom. Contrary to this client's expectations, he did not point out ways by which she might cut down on eating or interpret the psychological dynamics of her behavior. He gave her specific instructions to eat as much and as often as she could. He also embellished these instructions with vivid word pictures, adjectives that transformed ordinary eating habits into a gluttonous orgy. The woman soon reported that her desire to eat had abated tremendously; at the moment she found herself moving toward the refrigerator she was cognitively aware that this was no longer a spontaneous act and that she could stop and wanted to stop herself. Having dispensed with this obstacle, the worker and client could proceed to explore the more salient beliefs bearing on her adjustment to life. [23]

Victor Frankl offers another version of this method in what he calls *dereflection*, aimed at people whose hyperreflectiveness and overdetermination get in the way of the achievement of their goals. [24] The intent is to break into the self-defeating pattern brought on by preoccupation with the problem. Frankl cites the following case report:

> A young couple came in complaining of incompatibility. The wife had told the husband often that he was a lousy lover, and that she was going to start having affairs to satisfy herself. I asked them to spend at least one hour in bed together nude every evening for the next week. I said that it was okay to neck a little but under no circumstances were they to have intercourse. When they returned the following week they said they tried not to have sex but had intercourse three times. Acting irate, I demanded they try again next week to follow my instructions. Midweek, they called and said they were unable to comply and were having relations several times a day. They did not return. A year later I met the mother of the girl who relayed that the couple had not had a recurrence of the impotence problem. [25]

Jay Haley's technique involves giving directives or tasks to families in order to get people to behave differently. It intensifies the relationship with the therapist since the therapist becomes involved in the action, becomes an important person by issuing directives, and remains in the clients' minds between interviews. The technique also gathers information since the manner in which clients respond to these directives allows the therapist to learn things that would otherwise escape him. [26]

SUMMARY

Concept learning embraces strategies aimed at helping people revise those conceptions of self, relationships, and social environment that diminish quality of living and the capacity for capable problem solving. Personal and interpersonal change is always accomplished in some type of social system. If it is determined that the system is characterized by deprived or disorganized conditions, these deficits must be remedied before learning can proceed. Attention must also be given to the change organization itself to assess whether its established procedures in any way impede the learning experience.

Various strategies are directed toward resolving specific problems in the client's manner of understanding and responding to his world: cognitive reorientation, dialogue, divergent orientation, and the reexamination and reexperiencing of the existential implications of his world view. Concept learning is not, however, limited to the formal confines of the change event; the use of diaries and journals, homework, and other directed activities can also foster change. Once a person's conceptions are changed in a positive direction, more appropriate behavior will follow.

Chapter 12

Principle Learning and Problem Solving: The Gestalt of Learning and Change

An immediate and pragmatic measure of effective learning is the extent to which it leads to personally and/or socially rewarding solutions. A more durable measure takes account of the implications of learning for the total person. Learning that is something more than an expeditious tactic usually involves the person's values in important ways. Specifically, before a confident and consistent approach to problems of living can be pursued, the knowledge and skill gained in the process of concept learning would have to be balanced against the individual's essential beliefs and preferences. The integration of competent knowledge, value, and conduct is called *principle learning*. In addition, the personal meaning of learning is reflected in the extent to which a kind of ownership occurs. In this instance, ownership means that acquired abilities add to and enrich the individual's adaptive strengths thereby enhancing his aptitudes for dealing with other problems of living. This form of integration is called *problem solving*. The consideration of the two stages of learning represents the consummation of the planned change event and a return to a holistic view of social learning.

PRINCIPLE LEARNING

Robert Gagne limits the idea of principle learning to the field of education when he defines this typology as chains of concepts that make up what is called knowledge. [1] The objectives of formal education exceed the mastery of required concepts insofar as the learner is expected to

378

integrate these concepts into a set of rules or prescriptions that will serve as helpful guides to his behavior in special situations.

Education for practice in the human services field is a good illustration of this type of learning objective. The student will acquire a great deal of useful information about such select topics as personality and development, group leadership and interviewing skills, mental health, and interventive methods. His participation in class discussions and examinations may reveal a superior intellectual grasp of theoretical and practical content. However, the true test of his competency as a practitioner is demonstrated by his ability to integrate the acquired concepts into sets of guiding principles that allow him to deal with a variety of human problems in a confident, flexible, and responsive manner.

It is apparent that the cultivation of principles is not restricted to the field of formal education. Without well-set and well-tested principles the human experience would be random and without design or purpose. Principles guide serious and committed activities, whether they are enacted in close interpersonal relations, at work, or in the community. Crucial choices having important personal consequences often depend on the quality of humanistic, political, religious, or other ideologies that are central to one's principles. In human relations, individuals or groups tend to praise or condemn others depending on whether or not they judge them as persons of principle. Wars are fought, love affairs begun and ended, and pledges made because of the traditions, heritages and conventions that are basic to human principles.

It is also apparent that such guides to behavior rest on premises that are not readily discernible. In formal education, helpful principles derive from the ability to unite literal and factual concepts. In social learning and living, the emergence of personal principles depends not only on the integration of literal knowledge, but on the strength these principles draw from the less evident symbolic meanings and values that the individual ascribes to this knowledge. The principled person not only knows something but is committed to what he knows and to how this knowledge should be enacted. In definitional terms *a principle is a prototypical guide that is the product of the interplay* (or the dialectic) *among knowledge* (personal conceptions of reality), *personal values, and adaptive behavior.* Thus the aim of principle learning is to help people create a measure of harmony and reciprocity among what they know, what they value (their preferences and goals), and how they act. The more observable objective of this stage of learning is behavior that is confident and dependable largely because it is both a consequence and a validation of the person's wisdom and preference.

The term "prototypical" is included in the definition to differentiate actions based on principle from those determined either by dogma or by compulsion. Since principled behavior depends on reasoned judgment in relation to conscious values, it is more of a standard or general guide that offers the person a range of possible responses to the particular situation. For this reason, he is free to respond in a reasonable manner depending on how he evaluates his circumstances.

Some of the knotty predicaments of living originate in this inability to distinguish between principled reasoning and dogmatic imperative. In the latter case, the person behaves *as if* he is convinced that his actions were based on reasoned judgment when actually he is reacting reflexively. He asserts that he is rightfully expressing his value when actually he is echoing an adopted ideology. An example drawn from the late 1960s makes this point. A department of a southern university was torn by disagreement about the level of performance to be expected from certain groups of black students. These students were products of a segregated and second-rate educational system that had not prepared them for the rigors of advanced study. The faculty was split into opposing factions although both groups professed their commitment to the same humanistic and liberal values. Where they disagreed was in relation to educational standards of excellence. One group insisted that humanism and liberalism would best be served if these students were excused from the prevailing educational norms. They contended that since these students were "oppressed," "disadvantaged," and "victimized" by virtue of their minority status the department would be "racist" or "oppressive" if it expected these students to perform at a level comparable to that of other more privileged students. By their precepts, the only fair alternative was to allow these students to earn their degrees on the minority students' terms whether or not these terms corresponded with reasonable educational expectations.

The other group of teachers did not minimize the plight of these students; however, they seriously questioned whether the creation of artificial and inferior standards would serve fairness and justice. Would these students really benefit from receiving a spurious degree? How would it add to their confidence and self-esteem? Would this practice not be just another form of discrimination, one that officially sanctioned their inadequacies and set these students apart as special cases? Might it not be better to consider other alternatives of the kind that would promote greater equality?

The first faction exhorted rigid doctrines that, unlike principles, would not yield to thoughtful appraisal of the problem or to others' considered points of view. What appeared to be values were in fact creeds that pressed for uncompromising solutions. The teachers in the second faction were committed to values of equality in education and distributive justice, but these beliefs were tempered by well-tested knowledge. They were cognizant of the fact that equality as a value cannot be transformed into a commodity granted to someone as a handout and that distributive justice cannot be achieved by declaration or fiat. Moreover, they were aware that responsible action must represent a balance of knowledge and value if it is to avoid being seen as suspect and inept. Behavior that is essentially a product of one's value position (in this case, "everyone is equal and should be treated equally") comes to be seen as either naive or impulsive. On the other hand, behavior based on the intellect alone, thereby lacking the emotive qualities of one's beliefs, appears unconvincing and one-dimensional.

This example does not intend to suggest that a person's principles come into play only when his fundamental convictions and commitments are on the line. Principles assume a much more prosaic role in the course of day-to-day living; yet this role does not diminish the importance of principled behavior since it is in this ordinary sphere of living that the quality of being continues to be shaped.

Value Component of Principle Learning

Of the innumerable concepts that make up the vocabulary of human behavior, *value* ranks among the most abused. Too frequently it is used casually to denote a variety of personal dispositions that lack the power of a value. General preferences, attitudes, interests—even the short-lived and pragmatic choices made to achieve immediate goals—are called values. This looseness and ambiguity is understandable; the term has taken on such broad meanings that it lends itself to facile usage under a variety of human circumstances. Moreover, the concept has long eluded a universal definition despite the fact that the search for the meaning of and the criteria for human values has captured the interests of scholars for many centuries. Axiology is specifically committed to the study of the various types of human values and their nature and criteria.

A value is something more meaningful than an attitude, interest, or a simple preference or desire. The latter are time-limited, arising in response to a particular state or situation and are lacking in the special qualities of self-investment that are peculiar to value experiences. A value embodies the standards, preferences, and ideals that are integral to an individual's conception of self and serves as a determinant of his desired goals and the measure of his conduct in the attempt to achieve them. Milton Rokeach provides us with a useful definition and characterization. A value is *an enduring belief that a specific mode of conduct or end-state of existence is personally or socially preferable to an opposite or converse mode or end-state.*[2]

The first criterion of a value is *durability*. Interests, traits, and attitudes tend to change over time and circumstance; a value learned and acquired early in life endures and remains relatively constant. This is not to say that original values remain dominant for all time. With maturation and new learning people are exposed to and acquire newer values that may take their place with or stand in conflict with the old. Each person is not the proprietor of a random assortment of values; at any given time he possesses a hierarchy of values in which his essential beliefs and preferences are arranged in decreasing order of priority. It is safe to say that most people are committed to a similar range of values. This is why people are able to communicate approvingly with one another about such ideals as truth, beauty, honesty, love, goodness, and caring. They speak of these beliefs as if they have equal valence and as if they were invested in these beliefs in the same way. What differentiates one person from another and what is often the source of disappointment or disenchantment is the priority that is ascribed to a particular value in relation to all other values. Two people may form an instant friendship because as they exchange ideas they find that both value the right of people to make free choices about their lives. Sometime later one turns down the other's invitation to attend a pro-abortion rally claiming that his religious beliefs preclude support of such procedures. His friend is disillusioned, convinced that he really does not value free choice. But this may not be the case. He may indeed value free choice; however, his religious beliefs have greater meaning and are of higher priority in his personal value scheme.

A most troubling concern shared by many human service workers is the question about their impact on their clients' values. They wonder if they should be involved in changing other people's values and how circumspect they ought to be in revealing their own values. With regard to the second dilemma, it is immediately apparent that any serious interpersonal exchange is a value experience. A relationship will not evolve without at least a minimal awareness by the participants of each other's values. How people present themselves, their orientation to living, their vocabulary, interests, and countless other characteristics allow essential preferences and beliefs to come forward into the relationship. The obligation of the worker is not to create a value-free climate, but one in which his value stance is appropriately explicit. The criterion of durability makes the possibility of changing another's values highly improbable. People may adapt or change their attitudes and sentiments to accommodate what they believe is expected of them. But the individual's values, containing his essential premises and preferences, remain intact. Values are expressions of the primal self. Axiomatically, if values are altered in significant ways, the self also must undergo marked changes.

The idea of a hierarchy of values proposes the possibility of value change of another type. It is not the specific value that is tampered with; it is the priority that the individual ascribes to a value in relation to all of his other values. The client is helped to rethink his priorities and reconceptualize and realign that which he prizes; he is not asked to change his commitments. There are women who cling to mothering and caring for their children as their supreme value, but to the extreme where other self-enhancing and self-extending needs are virtually stifled. Such a woman feels overburdened and unrewarded, yet is driven to envelop herself in her mothering functions. If her secondary values were brought into cognitive awareness, would this constitute a rejection of her dominant value? As she struggles to find a measure of balance between the two virtues, it is likely that the value of mothering and caring may come to be even more rewarding as she discovers the fulfillment of other self-sustaining preferences.

The degree to which a value represents a powerful preference or belief is an "either-or" judgment: something is either "good" or "bad," either "right" or "wrong," either "desirable" or "undesirable." There are few halfway qualities in a value since it cannot tolerate compromise or middle ground. A value not only expresses a preference but also indicates its antithesis. (If I value honesty or caring for others, the strength of this value is not only in the degree to which I prize honesty or caring but also the extent to which I abhor dishonesty or indifference to others.)

A value therefore embodies serious cognitive, emotional, and behavioral elements. People believe in something or prefer something because they *know* it is right and proper to do so. Their conceptions of reality revolve around the core of these beliefs, which become the premises and justifications for the way they look at reality. Values are also capable of stirring intense feelings if they are threatened or blocked in any way. Sadness, helplessness, and hostility can be seen as consequences of depleted or frustrated ideals. The commitment to a particular value compels an individual to find the means of translating this belief into corresponding action. Principle learning is directed toward helping people arrive at a degree of correspondence among their beliefs, their passions, and the risks that sometimes accompany the intent to put them into suitable action.

Another criterion of a value is the extent to which it stands for a preferred mode of conduct and an end-state of being. The preferences related to modes of conduct are *instrumental values;* those associated with end-states of being are *terminal values.* Instrumental values affect immediate, day-to-day activities. They are the source of ongoing motivations, and they are guides to the manner in which people interact with others. Terminal values have a telic quality insofar as they represent cherished goals and ambitions projected into some future time. They are the hopes, expectations, and the ambitions people desire to fulfill. Optimally, both types of values complement each other: A person's current standards for himself should in some way correspond with where he sees himself heading; at the same time, his definition of prized goals should evoke those instrumental values that will enable him to achieve them.

When it comes to the matter of guiding principles and human motives, this kind of correspondence is sometimes painfully absent.

Some people create remarkable and laudable aspirations. Their goals are clearly sincere and deserving of all the effort and time they can muster. Yet despite the merit of their terminal values, they depend on images of themselves or their world or choose the kind of behaviors that will only confuse and frustrate their ambitions. Conversely, there are those who because of the strength of their instrumental values are able to manage their day-to-day activities quite well. Lacking worthwhile long-term goals, they discover that their well-ordered lives have become meaningless routines.

The ultimate test of the strength of a value is the extent to which it influences choice and action in a situation where something personally significant is at stake. Another university experience makes this point. Members of a faculty were pondering the disturbing fact that students were stealing books from the departmental library. In addition to the mounting costs of maintaining the library, these thefts created serious ethical questions. Some students who entered a helping profession with an express commitment to its humanistic ethics and principles chose to act in an unconscionable and unscrupulous fashion. Stealing was not only reprehensible, but it also deprived fellow students of access to these books. One instructor proposed that this pilferage might be tied to the pressure of term paper deadlines and examinations. Perhaps purchasing more of the required books and increasing their availability might stop or reduce the number of thefts. This was a practical solution if keeping books on the library's shelf was the only issue. Another instructor argued that this proposal missed the point. Would a good supply of textbooks resolve the questions of ethical and principled conduct? Was it fair to assume that these students were incorruptible just because there was no longer any test of their values? He observed that it was easy to proclaim righteous values as long as critical choice can be avoided. But these students clearly betrayed their commitments when caught between honest and dishonest alternatives for meeting a deadline. Having violated their expressed values in this common dilemma, how might they be expected to act when confronted with more serious choices in their practice with troubled people?

The strength of a value system is considerably more powerful than the kinds of pragmatic attitudes and preferences that can be manipulated to fit changing circumstances. In the course of living, a value is a certain and consistent force that assures basic standards of conduct and, without compromise, directs the choices and decisions that a person makes bearing on his life and the lives of others. Words such as *freedom, dignity, justice,* and *responsibility* are merely words if they do not represent dependable guides for conduct.

The brief reference to values is designed to underscore their significant role in principle learning. Value theory encompasses a vast body of literature.[3] D. Kinley Sturkie, for example, surveyed more than 120 references in his study of the implications of values for social work practice, but this number represented only a modest sample of literature on axiological theory.[4] His inquiry disclosed four broad and distinctive theories of human values, each deserving study in its own right. The concurrence of these theories in modern thought begins to explain why the value concept is so ambiguous. These theories include: (1) the *naturalistic* perspective on values, which claims that a true value is something that can be observed empirically and serves an instrumental purpose; (2) the *humanistic* perspective, which defines the individual, his rights, and his well-being as the ultimate value; (3) the *ontological* perspective, which sees the individual's values and his being as inseparable; and (4) the *theistic* perspective, which equates values with absolute precepts for desirable thought and behavior.

Criteria that distinguish the power of a value from other less substantial human inclinations also serve as touchstones of an individual's principles. The teacher who is sincerely guided by the principle of autonomy will use every appropriate opportunity to encourage his students to be active and decisive participants in the learning process. A husband who is committed to the principle of shared honesty and forthrightness will strive to maintain a climate in which openness will not incur penalty. The human services worker who is guided by the principle of self-determination will properly create the opportunities for his clients to define their own goals and decide on their choices. These commitments are not without the tempering effects of thoughtful judgments about the nature and needs of the immediate circumstances. Wisdom informs the person about the times when other principles—caring and concern for another, for example—must take precedence.

Israel Scheffler sees the acquisition of rules and principles as the highest form of learning because they derive from the supreme value of reason.[5] Reason is always a matter of abiding by general rules and principles in the judgment of particular issues; its opposite is inconsistency and expediency. In the cognitive realm, reason is justice to the nature of reality in the interests of truth. In the moral or value realm, reason is action on principle, action that does not bend with the wind or succumb to weakness. The individual who binds himself to a set of principles acts freely because his dignity derives from his power of choice. But commitment to his principles obligates him to obey them even when they rule against him since this is what fairness or consistency of conduct means. A rational man is one who is consistent in thought and action, abiding by impartial and generalized principles freely chosen as binding upon himself. The knower must earn the right to confidence in his belief by acquiring the capacity to make a reasonable case for the belief in question. His autonomy is evident in his ability to construct and evaluate fresh and alternative arguments, in the power to innovate, rather than to reproduce repetitively a stored and stale body of beliefs.

Characteristics of Principle Learning

Relatively little attention has been given to the idea of principle learning except in the field of moral philosophy and in a few educational theories. Two reasons may account for this lack of attention: (a) a principle is a rather lofty abstraction; its existence is not readily determined by empirical study and must be deduced, and (b) there are few discrete principles, those that are distinctly unattached to other approaches to living. The development of some consistent and temporarily unique rules of conduct might be observed in the behavior of a young child as he acquires certain characteristic patterns through instruction, observation, or vicariation. But the richness and complexity of an adult's prior experiences of living make it doubtful that his learning of new principles would be easy to discern. Each endeavor to revise former beliefs or to learn a new set of personal guides for action must contend with the authority of preexisting principles.

This tension between old and new learnings is evident in the case of the mature student engaged in educational preparation for practice in the human service fields. Typically, he enters the program with many seasoned and well-entrenched principles about human relations. Upon confronting some fresh and unfamiliar principles about interven-

387

tion into human problems, he is likely to experience an amount of conflict and misgivings—to the extent that these new ideas clash with his own unquestioned convictions. As a result of his life experiences, a particular learner might attach special importance to the value of self-determination. He is convinced that in virtually all instances people must be free to decide what is right for themselves if they are to evolve as self-realized beings. Moreover, he bases this belief on both practical and moral considerations. But he now finds himself getting his training in a setting that is concerned with social control (corrections, child abuse, or substance abuse, for example). He discovers that his personal rules of conduct and his wish to encourage self-determination would be counterproductive and contradict the objectives of the agency. Not only is he expected to impose strict controls on his clients' determinations, he must also grapple with the role of authority that he has been granted. How does he resolve this dilemma? He cannot readily forswear his ownership of the substantial precepts that are the elements of his integrity; at the same time, he cannot reject the new rules of professional conduct which, intellectually at least, are defensible and proper.

There are, of course, no easy solutions. It is one that must be lived through in its own special way by each individual as he attempts to resolve his personal value conflicts. Yet, out of this intensely personal struggle with seemingly irreconcilable principles, this worker may learn something of even greater moment. He may arrive at a deeper appreciation of his clients' plight as he attempts to encourage them to reevaluate the merit and consequences of *their* established principles in relation to the quality of their lives. Perhaps when he encounters his clients' tendencies to cling protectively to the worth of their past beliefs, he will be less prone to offend them with the label of "resistance" or intransigence.

The approach to principle learning does not lend itself to partition by specific strategies, because it is somewhat holistic in its orientation and is directed towards the self-directing potentials of the person. It is therefore more useful to consider the general climate and conditions of learnings. Previous strategies are not irrelevant to the development of principles, but having come this far, the task now is to enable the client to resolve his premises, conceptions, and values into his personal rules for growth and existence. This task depends far more on the worker's orientation and investment than it does on the use of specific interventions.

Climate and Conditions of Learning

Principle learning is a lifetime endeavor to make some sort of adequate adaptation to the protean nature of the world. Principles are enduring rules and guides for living; yet they cannot remain fixed and immutable in the face of rapid changes in major social values, technological advances, and shifting customs. As society becomes fragmented and its social laws become ambiguous, the individual must constantly reevaluate and revise his principles for purposes of self and social maintenance. For these reasons, principle learning as an exercise in value clarification and validation in the process of induced change takes on certain long-range implications. Although it is a necessary stage in the specific experience of effective problem solving, its consequences reach beyond the immediate experience. The practice of working out an integration of knowledge and value that leads to authentic behavior can offer the client something substantial to fall back on when later value problems are encountered.

The climate and conditions of principle learning can therefore be understood as a social model comprising people in a dialogical relationship attempting to resolve personally significant questions. The quality of this climate and the effectiveness of this model depend on the felt presence of honesty and openness. The client (whether an individual or a group) confronts a number of value dilemmas with some awareness that guaranteed or predictable solutions will not be forthcoming. The helper also realizes that his role cannot hinge on proven rules and procedures. His interventive guides are his own value commitments—his personal and professional principles on which he relies to assure that the dialogical experience will be as authentic as possible. The worker's principled conduct not only guides the sequence of learning, it also serves as an archetype that the client can observe and possibly borrow until his personal convictions are strengthened. The worker's principles are likely invested in a number of issues—self-determination, personal and social rights, and equality, for example.

The knowledge and values that guide the worker's approach to matters of power and authority deserve special attention because they have critical implications for the process, ethics, and outcome of learning and change. Power imbalance is an inescapable characteristic of the change relationship. Whether the worker is helping a voluntary client or one directed to him by an agency of social control, he acquires a position of authority and the responsibility for its effects on the change process. Whether this authority is granted or assumed, the worker comes to occupy a superordinate role in his relationship with his client; in its simplest equation, the worker is the provider and the client is the receiver.[6] According to the findings of Thibaut and Kelly, this role accrues three forms of power and control: contact control, fate control, and behavior control.[7] Contact control is the power to hold another in a relationship or to deprive him of that relationship. This power is evident in the extent to which the worker exerts his determinations about interpersonal conduct, how he and his client will work together, for how long, and how often. Fate control may be an overstatement of the worker's influence; nonetheless, the worker's decisions, his definition of the client's problem, and his procedures can have some short-run effects on the client's existence. For example, the client may have no other alternative than to rely on the worker for the things he needs for survival or for certain judgments that can affect his employment, family, or other critical aspects of his life. Behavior control connotes the power to influence another by varying one's own behavior. Direction, guidance, and request are the more overt forms of this control. More subtle forms of manipulation include giving or withholding approval, silence, facial expressions, and other more elusive reinforcements.

The professional role is further strengthened by a number of intrinsic status symbols, such as the office as a sanctum, the display of diplomas and certificates, the protective receptionist, and the dress, demeanor, and language of professionalism. Even the jeans and T-shirt worker who scorns more conventional attire indirectly informs his client that he has the power to choose what he wants to wear whenever he wants. The freedom that goes with this status may be uncomfortably evident to the client who has little choice.

Power imbalance tends to be maintained by the differential role definitions that are bound to arise from the transactions in the helping relationship. Even though the client may regard the relationship in positive and rewarding terms, he is aware that this association is unique and does not allow him the control of the kind that he has in his other more comfortable and familiar relationships. At this stage of learning he is also conscious of the fact that he has not yet overcome his problem and that he remains dependent on his worker and the relationship for continued support and help. Whether or not his feelings are justified, he may assume that his subordinate position leaves him little recourse other than a premature departure from the helping event that would be defeating.

The pivotal issue has less to do with the emergence of these and other attributes of power imbalance than it does with the principles that guide the human services worker's use of his power and authority. One derivative of his authority is his ability to foster a climate in which the client can observe and learn something about principles and behavior that express integrity, consistency, and fairness. The quality of interaction can help the client realize that authority and power need not be destructive and exploitive and that in his own role as parent, spouse, employee, or citizen, he, too, can exert his influence in a beneficial and humanitarian fashion.

Such a climate is scarcely possible if the worker even slightly abuses the trust placed in him for any sort of personal gain. Adopting the unqualified role of an expert or maintaining a cautious professional distance also adds little to the learning climate. Nor should he take a passive and tentative stance with the hope that the client will spontaneously grasp control of his own existence or at least will overlook the strains of power imbalance. Perhaps most harmful is the opposite extreme at which the worker places the client in a double bind by using his authority to disclaim his authority thereby attempting to persuade his client that they are, after all, equals. The discriminating client will perceive this type of equality as a hoax; if it can be granted it can also be retracted by the person in authority.

The principled worker will acknowledge and throw open for mutual consideration the existence of power imbalance (or any other value conflict) as a reality that both he and his client need to contend with as an inescapable condition of change. The forthright attempt to manage these tensions not only enhances the learning climate but also gives the client a learning experience that can be applied to other value dilemmas. Although the following examples are more indicative of activity in the opening phase of planned change, they serve to illustrate that the worker's authority can either become a hindrance or a positive means to a rewarding solution. Two hypothetical interviews between a parole officer and a parolee in a clearly authoritative situation involve the question of how the parole officer might be of help.

PAROLEE: Look I've heard it all before—all you guys want to help me. But you and I both know that you can send me back to the can anytime you want.
PAROLE OFFICER: But that's not why I'm here. I mean, I want to help you stay out and . . .
PAROLEE: Yeah, and if I get out of line just once . . . I've had it!
PAROLE OFFICER: Let's talk about what's really bothering you. Whether you know it or not, I am on your side . . .

If the parole officer is consciously open about the reality of his authority and their respective roles, the following dialogue might occur:

PAROLEE: Look, I've heard it all before—all you guys want to help me. But you and I both know that you can send me back to the can anytime you want.
PAROLE OFFICER: You are absolutely right. But think about this. You're the only one who can decide whether you go back in or stay out.
PAROLEE: What do you mean, *I'm* the only one?
PAROLE OFFICER: Whether we consider them fair or stupid, the fact is that you're stuck with a list of things you can't do as a condition of your parole. And I'm supposed to watch over what you do. Sure, there's a lot of things I can control . . . but one that I can't is whether or not you stick by the rules. It comes down to your choice. If you make the wrong choice it is *you* who is telling me to do what you know I have to do.
PAROLEE (bewildered): But what if I can't stop . . . I mean, sometimes . . .
PAROLE OFFICER: Let's talk about why "I can't stop." Maybe that's where I can help. That's why I'm here . . . to help with the "I can't stop" kind of problem.

The first interview represents a compromise of a shared truth and the dishonest avoidance of a painful fact. Such an unprincipled approach can only undermine any subsequent attempts to be helpful since trust would remain in doubt. Considering the kind of reality this client has to cope with, the flaccid model that the worker presents would be of small value. In the second example, the worker not only defines the conditions of the change experience but also augments the learning climate. He is willing to confront the uneasy tensions of their relationship, encourages his client to do the same, and acknowledges the real-life implications of the challenge they face. Thus, he obviates the need for deception and game playing and furthers the process of learning.

Reflection and Dialogue

The client who has reached this stage of learning has covered some important ground. He is more sensitive to his social reality; he is somewhat more conscious of his premises and commitments and is able to contemplate more authentic solutions to his problems of living. That he has come this far is, ironically, a source of further ambivalence and fear. Along the way, he has reluctantly given up certain misconceptions and fruitless solutions. He can admit that they were unrewarding (at least in retrospect); yet these approaches to living were familiar and, in whatever way they provide a measure of security, dependable. He may, in fact, look backwards to his former lifestyle with nostalgia. His new views may be preferable, yet they are still unproven and not yet organized into a set of valid principles. The worth of his intentions and how others will react to them are questions that have to be tested. This transitional period is a time of vulnerability and doubt; although a possible solution is in sight, uncertainty about the ability to achieve this end again arises.

This period of learning can be particularly out of joint when it is a family or group that is moving towards an active solution. Typically, channels of communication become impaired when former coalitions are no longer functional and expected patterns of interaction are weakened. A kind of self-consciousness also arises, precluding healthy interaction. Since new patterns of exchange have not been worked out, family or group members remain uncertain about how to reach out, state their differences, or assert their needs in a secure and predictable manner. The following illustrative statements of clients at this stage of learning only reveal the more outward quality of bewilderment that is experienced as the need to work out some effective principles for living is faced:

I've really felt good about myself in a new way. I know my daughter feels like she is doing the right thing in wanting to look after her old mother. Yet . . . how do I begin to tell her that I just have to be more independent without hurting her feelings or turning her away?

I think you've been pointing it out all along . . . but now we see it. My wife and I . . . the whole family . . . have to talk more and get things out in the open. It did no good to try to pretend we didn't have problems. But . . . I don't know . . . why can't you tell us how to do it?

It's strange how sure I was that being an engineer was what I wanted. Sure it was the right career as far as everyone else was concerned. But what's right for me? Sure, I've talked about doing some serious writing, but have I got what it takes? Do I deserve taking that kind of chance?

I'm not sure whether the rest of the group agrees with me, but I have to say it. We've been pussyfooting around for too long, not really facing what we really feel about each other. There's a lot of disagreement, but we sweep it under the rug. I wish there was some way to get it out in the open.

These clients are clearly able to perceive their circumstances more keenly than was previously possible. More important, they can conceptualize the obstacle and its ramifications and can therefore begin to think about alternative solutions. Their knowledge is evident and secure; the value issues and their implications for active and effective determinations remain unsettled. Such questions about rights and obligations, needs for independence and self-assertiveness, and issues of honesty and directness do not lend themselves to simple and straightforward resolution. How does the worker manage this hiatus and at the same time nurture the development of sound and compelling principles? His task is threefold: to provide the kind of *support* that will maintain balance and prevent disorganization; to *counteract* regressive tendencies; and to *persuade* forward movement.

Caught between knowing and action, the client may feel inadequate and helpless. He is aware that he has made some gains, but he might derogate their worth since they do not produce the proper solution. Assuming that the worker understands the nature of the client's emergency and is not enveloped by his hopelessness, his outlook is more optimistic. The worker prizes the learning and growth thus far accomplished and judges these gains as genuine and dependable. His regard for his client's potentials is not blighted by the anguish of the moment; although he is cognizant of the risks and dangers the client believes himself to be facing, he holds a longer view that takes account of the client's capabilities and possible goals. Moreover, if the worker and the client (individual, family, or group) have come this far together, there is the awareness that the relationship continues to be a source of sustenance and reinforcement.

Within the relationship, the worker fosters the kind of dialogue and reflection that will eventually free the client from his impasse. In being supportive, he avoids the sort of extravagance that could mislead the client by false reassurance and unqualified warmth. The worker is not unconditionally supportive; he is supporting something in the client's thoughts, beliefs, or actions that he perceives as meaningful. Support amounts to a reaffirmation of the images and ideas that the client himself has created—images of a role that is essential to his well-being, of his place in significant relationships, of his status in his community, and of his uncompromisable values. Active support is not always gentle and sympathetic; it may involve harsh and direct challenges to the client's tendency to disclaim his valid premises.

The attempt to counteract the inclination to retrogress centers on the intentional aspect of self and its impetus toward personal, shared, or transcendent goals. One strategy urges the client to recollect the costs, suffering, and self-defeat generated by the client's former coping patterns. But the worker's most powerful leverage comes from the client's own expressed commitments, values, and aspirations. Having already taken the critical step toward the clarification of his choices and objectives, the client can be challenged to consider what he truly has at stake in maintaining status quo or in moving toward his valued goals. This confrontation has the effect of enabling the client to achieve greater coherence between his terminal values and the instrumental means required to realize them.

The intent to persuade forward movement is accomplished when the client is helped to work out a degree of accord between what he knows and what he values. Through reflection and reconsideration of what has been learned and what is now valued the anguish accompanying responsible choice becomes crystallized. Both worker and client are acutely conscious that in gaining something meaningful, something else of value is being lost. In taking a principled stand based on reason and value, something is forfeited. A part of the client's history, no longer relevant for healthy adaptation, must be retired. Guarantees about future outcomes cannot be assured. Positive and approving responses of significant others cannot be promised.

Defining what they mean by their reference to the "whole person," Robert Carkhuff and Bernard Berenson indirectly yet effectively sum up the optimal consequences of principle learning: "The person who is in tune with and acts on the bases of his integrity is free to modify, incorporate, and learn from venturing into the unknown, with fear, but a knowledge that his inner being will not and cannot be destroyed. . . . The whole person realizes that life is empty without acting. The full person must discriminate among possible acts, make his choice, and ACT. The most significant learning comes from acting on those aspects of life the individual fears most. For the whole person there is only security in risks. In this way, and only in this way, can the individual gain or lose. In a life without risk, no one wins, no one loses, and *no one learns*."[8]

PROBLEM SOLVING

Since it encompasses the previous learning typologies, problem solving stands for a higher order of change that involves the distinctive and inclusive manner in which people confront and define their problems of living and go on to create and test alternative solutions to these problems. Problem solving may allude to the specific actions people take in response to isolated frustrations and obstructions; it is, as well, a characteristic approach to the ongoing demands of living. However maturity, autonomy, and personal and social well-being are defined, they are inseparably linked to personal capabilities for understanding, managing, and solving problems of living.

Benjamin Bloom and L. Broder found some critical differences between successful and unsuccessful problem solvers. The former can seize on some aspect of the problem quickly, utilize available information efficiently, and make workable assumptions even when complete knowledge is not at hand. The orderliness of their thinking allows successful problem solvers to simplify the intricacies of the problem and manage it more effectively. Unsuccessful problem solvers appear confused, constantly retrace their steps, and cannot sustain their thought processes. As a consequence, they project themselves into their problems and see themselves as powerless.[9] These findings reinforce the idea that it is not the actual solution that is of major importance but the manner in which the person goes about finding it. Thomas Banta explains: "Effective problem solving does not necessarily mean the achievement of correct solutions to conventional problems, but rather the development of behaviors which are useful in a world that presents problems demanding creative as well as conventional solutions."[10]

As a means of achieving a more gratifying and productive mode of living, the concept of problem solving rejects a static, pathological, or categorical view of people in distress. Although it refutes the notion that people are inescapably arrested or victimized by inner debilities or outer repressions, problem solving acknowledges the weight of emotions, inequity, deprivation, and other forces that obstruct healthy living. However, given the individual's capabilities and constraints, these conditions are not seen as intractable causes but as serious contingencies that must be redefined and mastered.

Problem-Solving Paradigms

Any thought about the formal structure of the problem-solving event should begin with John Dewey's theory. The problem-solving design that he proposed over fifty years ago, although refashioned in minor ways, persists as an authentic prototype of the actual experience of learning. Dewey reasoned that all thinking originates in problematic situations and that this thinking is one form in which the individual experiences his interactions with his environment. A problematic situation is one that cannot be resolved by the use of prior solutions. It is a fresh experience that can be settled only on its own terms.[11] Since prior solutions are unworkable, the person needs to proceed through five steps of reasoning to develop a new solution. These steps are (1) a difficulty is felt, (2) it is located and defined, (3) possible solutions are suggested, (4) consequences are considered, and (5) the solution is tested and accepted.[12]

Dewey advised that problem solving was not limited to the mental processes. In his attempt to resolve the dualism between knowing and doing, he regarded learning as an active experience involving "doing something" to things. Such experience has two parts. The first he called passive doing or an "undergoing" of something in which things may happen. But if this doing and undergoing is to become meaningful, it must involve thought and consideration about what the experience *meant*. A learning experience is of little value if the learner does not appreciate the consequences of his actions. We do not "learn by doing," . . . *"we learn by doing and realizing what came of what we did."*[13]

The implications of this model become clearer upon examination of how it has been embellished or modified by later theorists. Hugh Urban and Donald Ford believe that the basic five steps can be broken down to finer increments and add an evaluation and feedback loop. Their model is increased to include twelve steps of problem solving:

1. Initial recognition of a difficulty;
2. Identification and specification of a problem;
3. Analysis of the problem;
4. Summary and restatement of the problem;
5. Selection of objectives which are to be effected;
6. Depiction of criteria (values) by which solution will be judged;
7. Consideration of possible solutions;
8. Testing proposals against criteria;
9. Selection of a single final solution;
10. How it is to be done and who is to do it;
11. Implementation of solution; and
12. Subsequent evaluation[14]

Based on Dewey's logic, this model takes a rational approach to problem solving that resembles the process of formal decision making.

Ralph Garry and Howard Kingsley take a contrary position that views Dewey's formulation as much too rational. They argue that human affairs are somewhat less systematic than his model suggests. They propose that problem solving involves only four steps:

1. *The search phase:* Clarification of the nature of the problem narrows the range within which solutions can be found. The problem is reduced to simpler terms and to reformulation.

2. *The functional solution phase:* From data (observation, recall, imagination), inferences are made about a solution which depends on their functional effectiveness.

3. *The development of an actual solution:* A model of attack is applied until a solution is obtained.

4. *Validation:* The test of the outcome of the solution.[15]

In contrast with these two models (the first logical, the second processual), Karl Garrison and his colleagues offer a functional approach to problem solving. They also reduce the event to four stages: (1) an orientation function; (2) an information-gathering function; (3) a hypothesis-formation function; and (4) a hypothesis-testing function.[16] Garrison specifically, and the other theorists by inference, suggests that problem solving closely parallels the logic of the scientific method—or the use of a rational disciplined approach to the problems of living. Garry and

398

Kingsley soften this idea a bit, cautioning that as a human experience, problem solving must allow for the possibility of error, retrospection, and regression.

These contingencies were incorporated in a model of problem solving (Figure 6) that is pertinent to the actualities of the planned change event.[17] The steps of this model follow Dewey's formulation with the addition of a sixth step. This is the search for and survey of new information, a critical task of the change experience.

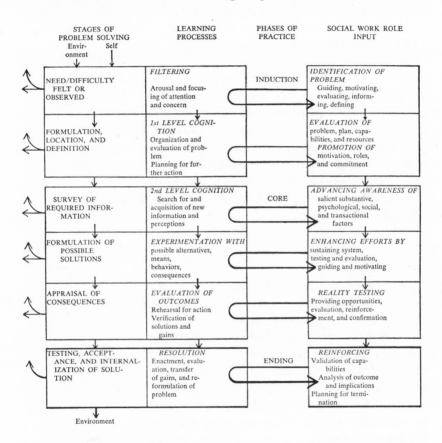

FIGURE 6. An Operational Model of Problem Solving and Related Input of the Social Worker's Role

To reflect the nature of the change experience, the model was divided into three phases (the induction, core, and ending), each accountable for specific functions of problem solving. The induction phase involves the definition of the problem and the roles and responsibilities essential to its solution. The core phase signifies the period in which respective roles are clarified and the participants are freed to invest themselves into the intensive work that is necessary for problem resolution. The ending phase concerns preparation for separation from the change experience and includes the enactment of the solution, its evaluation, and the consideration of ways in which the gained learnings can be transferred to other problem areas of the client's life.

The vertical arrows moving downward signify the logical sequence of problem-solving steps. The arrows looping back and upward indicate the possibility that at any stage error might occur, certain data may be lacking, or other reasons might require the individual to return to a prior stage. The horizontal arrows pointing outward signify the possibility of the individual departing the problem-solving experience at any stage of learning. Certain factors beyond the individual's control may act to abort the experience before it is consummated, or the person may discover along the way that the costs of learning and change are either too great or that the task itself exceeds his capabilities.

Paralleling each of these phases of problem solving are the educative and facilitating roles of the worker linked by a feedback loop indicating the transactional nature of the learning experience. The worker's interventions are not discrete, unilateral techniques; rather, they are responsive actions that are constantly open to modification as their effects and meanings are appraised. In generic terms, the worker's helping role involves management of the learning experience. His intent is to make it possible for the learning experience to unfold in a rewarding and effective manner that takes account of the client's motives, goals, values, energies, and capabilities. In specific terms, he contributes to the definition and evaluation of the problem, enhances motivation, provides guidance, information, focus, and directions, and deals with the feelings and values that bear on forward movement. The worker is also concerned with the extrarelational conditions that may impinge on the client's problem-solving efforts (e.g., system maintenance, the effects of change on significant others, and the resources and commodities required by the client for the successful completion of the problem-solving task).

Problem Solving and Social Learning

The process of problem solving can now be seen as the active expression of social learning as it was outlined in chapter seven. It is an endeavor that involves the interrelated variables of process, person, content, intent, and situation and is purposeful and adaptive when it serves as the means by which obstacles blocking movement toward a valued goal or objective are resolved. The obstacle may be something palpable and evident to all concerned; it can also be a personal construct existing only in the mind of the person who believes he is blocked. In either case, learning and problem solving are actuated when the obstacle resists solution by familiar or habitual practices and the individual is frustrated by the lack of proper alternatives. Rather than attempting new learning, the individual may fall back on certain maladaptive patterns. He can insist on repeating his habitual tactics despite consequences that show him that his actions are irrelevant to the problem. He can change his goals and therefore avoid having to confront the obstacle. He can abandon his objectives by minimizing their importance or altering his values. He can wait passively, hoping that the obstacle will dissolve or that someone else will give him the solution. But if his response is authentic he will try to use his rational, emotional, and perceptual faculties to find a new and more gratifying solution.

This authentic response is what has been termed learning and problem solving. The first stage of this effort involves at least an elemental awareness of or sensitivity to the presence of the obstacle or problem. It is at this point that contact is felt between person and predicament. Some authorities cited limit awareness to the level of sensation; others refer to the cognitive levels of "recognition," "clarification," or "reorientation." In operational terms, this stage calls for *discrimination learning* or the elaboration of abilities to distinguish between the important and unimportant elements in an individual's inner and outer environment. The learning task is the development of acuity of attentional skills, the deepening and expansion of consciousness, and the attainment of greater complementarity between the two.

The emergence of a keener awareness allows for movement to the second stage of learning where the gained impressions may be conceptualized (named, classified, ordered, interpreted) and placed in the service of problem resolution. This conceptual intent is expressed in such terms as identification and specification, definition, location, and formulation. In operational terms, this stage is called *concept learning*. Concepts come to be understood in relation to their literal meanings and their symbolic implications. Learning involves changes in the individual's styles of reasoning, thinking, and acting and in his frame of reference as these mental processes impede his search for new solutions to his problems.

The ability to reconceptualize the conditions of the dilemma opens the way to contemplate new alternatives and their implications. Moving beyond comprehension, the challenge is to make certain judgments involving value issues, priorities, appropriate behavior, consequences, and other issues bearing on the active solutions to the problem. Although other theorists make a point of outcome implications, Urban and Ford are most specific about the value and criteria factors critical to this stage of learning. Inasmuch as this stage is more directly concerned with the moral, ethical, and value questions crucial to a person's approach to his problems of living, it is designated as *principle learning*. The objective is the achievement of the degree of harmony and consistency among values, world view, and behavior that assures that no one of these qualities is compromised.

When an alternative is selected the person moves actively towards solution of the problem. Action does not cap off the experience of learning because the solution will probably generate other conditions that will call on the individual's coping abilities. First of all, the consequences of the solution should be tested against the individual's premises, conceptions, values, and expectations, taking account of Dewey's idea of "meaning" or the ongoing learning that arises from the realization of "what came of what I did." If the solution somehow affects significant others in the individual's social field, he needs to find ways of contending with the response that his action evoked, whether positive or negative, approving or disapproving. Ideally, prior attempts at an effective solution have reckoned with projections about the possible effects of the attempt, but under the best of circumstances, a person can go only so far in predicting how others will respond.

The problem-solving experience offers developmental and growth possibilities that exceed the purposes of the immediate solution. If this learning is seen as an expression of the self in action, the consequences of the successful endeavor should have positive implications for the person's self-concept, his further intentions and aspirations, and his world view. In other words, the gains accrued can be transferred to other important aspects of the client's existence—particularly if the helper is sensitive to these potentialities. Certainly the newly acquired skills may have practical applications to other problems; the client who has, for example, overcome his self-conscious passivity in his work relationships may find that his new-found and healthy assertiveness may add to the quality of his more intimate relationships. The thinking, acting, and feeling that contributed to the worth of the problem-solving experience can serve as prototypes for the way he tackles other problems of living. As he is able to transfer these modes to the new challenge he is likely to feel a greater sense of power and competency. The meaning of what has been accomplished should have a number of other enduring implications for the client and his place in his world. As a result of heightened self-image and the awareness that risks can be taken and problems can be confronted directly, the client may derive a deeper appreciation of himself as an autonomous and responsible being. This realization can serve as a source of courage in dealing with later contingencies of living.

Although the preceding generalizations accurately represent the stages and sequence of learning and problem solving, it is apparent that they cannot predict how any one experience will evolve. The process of learning is essentially idiosyncratic, dependent on such variables as personal maturity, cognitive style, imagery, and cultural and social influences.

Problem Solving and Creativity

Reports of experiences in which an individual attains a spontaneous insight about the nature of his predicament and its solution are not uncommon. There are many instances when a person is deeply immersed in a serious problem that appears to have no visible remedy. Concentrated thought only succeeds in driving the individual into deeper confusion, leading to a disgruntled rejection of the entire matter. After this person has given up and turned to other activities, the answer can suddenly appear with no forewarning. This phenomenon sometimes characterizes the climax of the planned change experience. The client troubled by a marital, financial, or other problem undergoes barren periods of mental and emotional toil. Then the client suddenly finds the answer, but in a way that appears to have little reference to his previous deliberations.

Do such spontaneous insights repudiate the explanatory value of the carefully detailed problem-solving scheme? Is it possible that apparently obdurate problems can be unraveled by sudden bursts of awareness that have nothing to do with developmental reasoning? Creative thinking is a product of this kind of reasoning, although it must be admitted that any or all of the sequential stages may involve other than the rational and conventional operations of the mind. Divergent thinking alone has the function of breaking through the ordinary boundaries of reasoning. The individual who grants some credibility to his divergent tendencies can find himself in somewhat unfrequented realms of reality. He encounters solutions that at first appear to be odd and inexplicable. Because the individual has not followed his familiar course of thinking and problem solving, his destination (the discovered solution) may take on a quality of strangeness.

Informative ideas about the nature and consequences of divergent thought can be found in some interesting theories by investigators of creative or spontaneous awareness. Earlier theories employed a phase principle not unlike Dewey's to explain creativity. Alexander Osborne, writing in 1953, listed seven sequential stages of creative evolution that parallel Dewey's model. His contribution was the concept of "incubation," the stage of problem solving where the letting up of active reasoning invites what appears to be a spontaneous generation of the solution. [18]

Jerome Bruner explains creative ability by distinguishing between analytic and intuitive thinking. Analytic thinking proceeds through explicit steps that can be reported by the thinker inasmuch as he is aware of the information he is dealing with and the operations he is using. Intuitive thought involves mental maneuvers that appear to be based on an implicit perception of the total problem. The thinker arrives at a solution with little if any awareness of the process that enabled him to reach it. Bruner speculates that intuitive thinking rests on a familiarity with a domain of knowledge that permits the thinker to leap about and take short cuts and that intuitive thinking is fostered by self-confidence, courage, and the willingness to make honest mistakes. [19]

Another perspective differentiates among the analytic, cause-effect, or if-then modes of thought and the emergence of seemingly inexplicable forms of consciousness. As reported by Ira Progoff, Carl Jung's doubts about the validity of causal explanations of human phenomena led him into areas of thought that questioned the dependability of causal explanations. He explored oriental philosophy, the ideas of David Hume, and the inquiries of physicists Nils Bohr and Wolfgang Pauli. Jung concurred with Hume's assumption that the idea of causality is no more than a habit of thinking, a convenient means for explaining observations. When a person simultaneously encounters two separate events, he immediately infers that they are causally connected in some way. This inference, based on past experiences and assumptions about how things are related, does not adequately represent reality. Jung proposed that the simultaneous occurrence of two separate events could best be explained by the principle of *synchronicity*.

This assumption involves a certain curious principle that I have termed synchronicity, a concept that formulates a point of view diametrically opposed to that of causality. Since the latter is merely a statistical truth and not an absolute, it is a sort of working hypothesis of how events evolve out of one another, whereas synchronicity takes the coincidence of events in space and time as meaning something more than mere chance, namely, a peculiar interdependence of objective events among themselves as well as the subjective (psychic) states of the observer or observers. [20]

Jung's ideas suggest that the insights and momentary glimpses of reality are not consequences of perceptions of logical relations. They are products of an inner process that immediately grasps the metaphorical meanings of the events, especially if the observer does not reject these meanings by resorting to the logic of causal connections. These events are the so-called strange coincidences that appear from time to time and which sometimes result in very important personal outcomes that could not have been anticipated. They could be dismissed as pure chance,

405

random occurrences bound to take place at one point or another. They could be ascribed to the usual products of periods of incubation except that no one is certain what takes place in whatever incubation happens to be. Even though the product of the experience might not be particularly momentous, the experience itself is significant enough not to be dismissed as a chance event.

As far as the concept of synchronicity is concerned, little is known about how it works—at least in Jungian terms. Jung was not able to develop his idea beyond some conjectures that there were many more potentials within human awareness than could be released by causal definitions of reality. Ira Progoff believes that creative people tend to be more open to synchronous events and their meanings. They can break away from a linear view of reality and are able to take advantage of the implications of unexpected events as they occur. Creativity arises when the individual can conceive of possibilities that others reject.

Arthur Koestler offers some explanations of the creative event. He defines *bisociation* or *bisociative thinking* as "the perceiving of a situation or idea . . . in two self-consistent and habitually incompatible frames of reference."[21] The situation or idea that is understood is not a product of thinking within one frame of reference or another but at the intersection of the two—thus the idea is *bi*sociated.

All forms of humor are examples of bisociative thinking since the source of laughter is the absurd impression that bursts forth when two incompatible ideas are placed in a contrapuntal relationship. Not infrequently, the sudden and spontaneous bloom of a new serious idea has an almost comic effect. There is a moment of elation, particularly when the person becomes aware of the incongruity in his associations of thought.

With regard to the bisociative act, Koestler states that there are two ways of escaping routine and mechanical manners of thinking and acting. One is to suspend rational thought by plunging into dream-like states. "The other way is also an escape—from boredom, stagnation, intellectual predicaments, and emotional frustrations—but an escape in an opposite direction; it is signalled by the spontaneous flash of insight which shows a familiar situation or event in a new light, and elicits a new response to it. The bisociative act connects previously unconnected matrices of experience; it makes us 'understand what it is to be awake, to be living on several planes at once.' "[22]

Bruner's ideas about intuition, Jung's synchronicity, and Koestler's bisociation begin to appear less distinctive or dissimilar when considered as variant expressions of the same phenomenon, specifically bimodal consciousness or the kinds of awareness that are products of left- and right-hemispheric thought.

Bruner posits that intuitive thinking rests on an already acquired domain of knowledge. It appears that the manipulation of this knowledge by the logical and analytic operations of the left hemisphere fail to produce the required insights or solutions. Can it be assumed that when the same knowledge is processed by the nonrational, holistic, relational, and concept-forming abilities of the right hemisphere that novel ideas will emerge? Right-hemispheric thought breaks the rational constraints of thinking and transmutes what was formerly known into new forms and arrangements. Since these operations are neither logical nor verbal, this could explain why the person cannot report how he arrived at his intuitive solution.

Jung's idea of synchronicity is similarly related to bimodal processes. It seems that the perception of causality derives largely from the logical and analytic styles of left-hemispheric thinking, which sorts phenomena into logical classes. By deduction, their causal connections are established. The ability to apprehend synchronous and noncausal relations depends on the extent to which one is able to reject conventional logic and rely on right-hemispheric thought. This thinking produces analogic impressions that cannot be framed in ordinary and communicable language.

Koestler's theory of bisociation confounds reasonable logic and analytic thinking. How does a person perceive two incompatible frames of reference at the same time? Left-hemispheric thinking would immediately subdivide the perception into two distinct units and examine them in linear terms. Hence, the bisociation of thought appears to be a right-hemispheric function that is comfortable in appreciating the metaphoric, ambiguous, and ungrounded nature of this kind of thinking.

Are these insights products of the processes of problem solving? The imaginative product may differ in many ways from conclusions arrived at

407

by thoughtful analysis, logic, and reasoning. Yet the processes are similar, despite the possibility that in creative thought there is much less order and sequence. At some point the individual needs to discriminate among all possibilities and scan his universe to gain a keener appreciation of the problem. A creative approach might attend to the wholes and relationships of the things in the person's perceptual field rather than to its discrete elements. This approach may also rely on the more extraordinary planes of consciousness that generate sentient images of the idea; the observer might "see" more of the things in his field than analytic thought would allow.

It is also probable that creative thinking produces conceptual images before discrimination takes place. But the images would be relatively meaningless if the person failed to discriminate among the conditions that would support his conceptual images. At any rate, there is a point in the process of creativity where conceptions must be formed. These concepts may be largely symbolic and metaphoric; nonetheless, they represent the organization of impressions that is a requisite to the development of useful solutions.

Principle learning in itself demands an amount of imaginative thought. At this stage in the act of problem solving, the individual is wrestling with rather abstract issues. The choice of alternatives requires the ability to engage in a kind of mental rehearsal. The individual must imagine and project where certain choices will lead and what their probable consequences might be. The need to bring his values and conceptions into an ethical and functional unity is largely a symbolic effort involving all sorts of personal images. Whether the solution obtains from systematic or creative thought and action, its worth can only be determined by active verification in a person's field of experience.

Although principle learning and problem solving are critical adaptive abilities inevitably owned by some individual, they can also be coping skills that are shared by members of a family or a working group. However wholesome family living may be defined in modern times, it seems obvious that its quality of life depends on the extent to which family members have achieved some measure of agreement about certain fundamental principles and are effective in resolving the host of problems that now challenge the family's survival and well-being. Agreement about basic principles (e.g., personal responsibility, interdependence, openness) may be equated with a common sharing of beliefs; it can also connote a commitment to a single overriding ideal that permits each family member to pursue his or her distinct convictions. In either case, the family must come to terms with a balance among knowledge, values, and action. Only as balance and accord is reached can the family move on to develop its unique approach to the resolution of the pragmatic and long-term existential problems of living.

These demands also apply to the formed group. However, where the generation of healthy principles and problem-solving techniques arises in a family's ongoing relationships and functions, the formed group must fulfill the need to create its own unique principles of operation and problem-solving methods as part of its developmental task. In short, the group must be helped to integrate a number of disparate values (representing the special preferences and beliefs of its individual members), grapple with many types of knowledge, and translate them into behaviors that will typify the group's ethos and intentions. Ideally, the resulting principles will come to characterize the group as an organism in its own right without violating the essential values of its members.

SUMMARY

The study of principle learning and problem solving reestablishes the idea of the holistic nature of social learning and change. Principle learning involves the attempt to reduce discrepancies between what the person knows, what he values, and how he acts. The effectiveness of this stage of learning depends more on its transactional climate than on deliberate change strategies. This climate is characterized by the human services worker's own principles and integrity. Within the helping experience, the worker's tasks include the provision of appropriate support, counteracting regressive tendencies, and encouraging continued progress forward.

Problem solving consolidates all of the stages and learning and change studied thus far. In accordance with confirmed theories of problem solving, discrimination learning corresponds with the elemental step at which the problem is first sensed or recognized. Concept learning concerns the stages at which the problem is formulated and given meaning. Principle learning is tied to the active consideration of pragmatic and existential alternatives. Problem solving, whether a rational and deliberate process or a seemingly spontaneous and imaginative enterprise, is a creative act insofar as it produces a solution to a baffling condition where before no solution existed.

Michael Mahoney and Diane Arnkoff sum up the central role of problem solving in the processes of behavior change. They state that "among the cognitive learning therapies . . . the problem-solving perspectives may ultimately yield the most encouraging results." Clients are not only taught specific coping skills, but also more general strategies of assessment and problem definition. This approach also allows substantial room for the uniqueness of the individual clients and adds a powerful humanistic component. Finally, since a problem-solving approach requires the active and responsible participation of the client in critical decisions and actions, it helps resolve some of the ethical issues of planned change. [23]

Chapter 13

Motivation: The Energy of Learning and Change

The study of motivation, as it involves issues of human needs, emotions, and aspirations, could have been appropriately introduced at the outset or in any of the previous sections of this book. Why people choose to pursue or refrain from pursuing a goal are questions that are not only critical to the actual planned changed experience but also to the philosophical and theoretical foundations of the human services. The decision to defer this study to this point was to assure that the concluding statements about learning and change give serious consideration to matters of incentive and self-determination as well as persons' rights to receive the help and services they require.

As it is ordinarily used, the concept of motivation presents few problems. Most listeners would have little trouble grasping the essential meanings of such statements as "He is a highly motivated person," or "I feel like I just lack the motivation to get the job done." The listener would assume that the speaker is referring to the presence or absence of some inner force or drive that affects his movement toward a particular goal. However, when the concept is employed for evaluative or judgmental purposes (as is often the case in planned change) to assess someone's willingness or readiness to change, it then becomes subject to misinterpretation and misuse. Some of the reasons for the ambiguity and the abuse of the concept are a result of semantic confusion; others arise from the interactive sphere of the planned change event.

Motivation, first of all, is not a precise concept, nor does it represent a specific referent. The presence, absence, or quality of another's motives must be inferred by the observer. Moreover, the motive may have literal or symbolic meanings in relation to whatever the observer selects as an indicator of motivation. As a literal concept it might refer to certain outward behaviors or attitudes or say something about another's apparent personality characteristics. Symbolically, a reference to another person's motives could convey the observer's own feelings or his images about that person's strengths, weaknesses, or worth. These reasons suggest that judgments of others' motivations are to some degree idiosyncratic and biased.

I have shown that concept formation (particularly in human relations) is something more than the simple abstraction and classification of observed or imagined phenomena. In addition to creating a "fact" the observer's definition of that "fact" is colored by the influence of his value system and personal frame of reference. If his valuation and interpretation of the event are imperative, it is likely that such qualities as "goodness" or "badness," "rightness" or "wrongness," or "effectiveness" or "ineffectiveness" will be attributed to it. If this is the case, the observer will tend to appraise the phenomenon in the kind of polar or diametric terms that exclude other possible options; simply, if something is seen as "bad," "wrong," or "ineffective" then it is appropriate to consider its opposite form as "good," "right," or "effective." The current hasty deinstitutionalization of mental patients because institutionalization is deemed harmful is one example of this questionable logic. The substitution of permissive, unstructured, standard-free educational programs for those that are judged as restrictive or overprogrammed is another. The concept of motivation is clearly subject to this type of polar thinking, especially when clients are classified as "unmotivated" because their attitudes and actions do not conform to the worker's conceptions of properly motivated behavior. In this either-or perspective, the "motivated" client will be welcomed as a "good" candidate for change; chances are the "unmotivated" client will be excluded or subjected to impersonal, controlling, or mechanical forms of treatment.

Unfortunately, some of the theories and the literature of behavior change tend to support this either-or perspective on motivation. Both by direction and implication, traditional theories and systems of change assume that demonstrated motivation is a precondition for successful change. By rule or intimation, the "good" client is seen as someone who actively seeks help, shows some insight about his anxiety or troubles, and most important, expresses a desire to change in some way. This dictum is expressed by Lewis Wolberg, who asserts that with nonvoluntary (un-motivated) people, "it is impossible to establish the kind of working relationship that permits the achievement of meaningful therapeutic goals."[1]

Confusion about the concept of motivation also stems from the cognitive errors that are bound to arise in human interaction. The flaws and blind spots in perception and cognition and the consequences of the imbalance that characterizes the worker-client relationship predict that misinterpretation of the inner state and intentions of the client is highly possible. In his review of pertinent research, Stanly Witkin notes that the interviewer in the helping situation maintains a considerable role advan-tage.[2] Since the interviewer usually decides what questions to ask and determines the flow of information exchange, a discrepancy results that inflates the perception of the interviewer's attributes while downgrading the client's own competence. The worker's theoretical and egocentric biases (and often cultural distance) also contribute to perceptions of deviancy, normality, and motivation for change that may diverge from the client's view of himself and his conditions and what he wishes to do about them. Witkin suggests that the identification of a greater incidence of emotional problems among low socioeconomic groups, the negative attitude of helpers toward treatment of the poor, and the negative relationship between socioeconomic class and outcome of service may be partially explained by these biases. Among others, these are the clients who do not eagerly seek help on their own, who appear confused and resist or question the services that are offered or pressed upon them, and who come to be classifed as "hard-to-reach," "nonvoluntary," or "un-motivated."

For the reasons noted, the concept of motivation deserves closer scrutiny and redefinition so as to achieve a more functional perspective on its role in the process of learning and change. Motivation will be defined in normative and transactional terms rather than in absolute or static terms. As a normative concept, it is understood as a *subjective* evaluation of one's will, energy, and desire to take some sort of action at a particular point in time and in relation to other sets of conditions—the person's antecedent state of being, the situation he is in, and social expectations, for example. This point of view assumes that motivation is not a singular prerequisite for change but a critical variable or dynamic of the change process requiring attention in its own right.

PRINCIPLES OF MOTIVATION

Emotion and *motive* are closely related, both terms coming from the same etymological root—*motus,* to move. It is apparent that they are also interdependent. The surge or press of a person's motives will usually be accompanied by a heightening of his emotions. Experiencing an impulse or incentive, he may also undergo intense feelings (pleasure, apprehension) related to the act. On the other hand, emotions can be powerful inducements to act or search out certain goals. The feeling of despair impels the pursuit of comfort or solace; passions seek fulfillment; affections want sharing. To understand another's motives it is necessary to appreciate his emotions, both those that excite the will to act and those aroused by the intention itself. Yet merely knowing how someone else feels will not always predict how he will act and observing his actions will not always disclose the emotions that prompted his behavior.

Ernest Hilgard's premises about the nature of human motives address the problems inherent in the attempt to discern another person's inclinations. Basically, the expressions of motives differ not only from culture to culture but also from person to person. A good many motives are learned out of specific experiences within the person's own cultural milieu. Yet, these learnings tend to be translated into personal motives that become a blend of cultural influences and individual attributes. For example, urban, middle-class American society advocates an assertive and direct attack on the obstacles that get in the way of valued goals. This doctrine is expressed in such terms as "overcoming," "making it," and "achievement." But within this larger system there are other populations who may indeed share the same intent. Rural dwellers, members of other classes, also may want to "overcome." But to the extent that their ambitions are typically pursued in somewhat less aggressive styles, these groups may be seen as aberrant by majority standards with the assumption that "they just don't care," or "they're content with their lot."

Similar motives may be expressed by unlike behavior. Where motives are judged by behavioral standards alone, grave misconceptions may be the consequence. This difficulty occurs in families where communication falters and the members are unaware of the others' intentions and expectations. It is quite possible that most of the family members do share common motives. However, each member leans towards his unique style of expression and, when recognition of shared intentions is lost, a struggle follows about the "oughts" of behavior.

Unlike motives may be expressed by similar behavior. The fact that a number of people can be observed acting in the same manner does not mean that they have any intentions in common. The first stages of group formation offer an interesting example of this variance. The leader observes the group acting almost in unison, as if all the members were striving towards a state of closeness and cohesion. Outwardly, they appear to agree about most issues and seem to have similar goals as far as the purposes of the group are concerned. The leader later discovers that this was not the case at all and that the apparent unity was short-lived. Although members' behaviors were similar it is quite possible that member A was motivated by a need for approval, member B by a need to control, and member C was moved by a need for security.

Any single act may express several motives. Hilgard argues that lists of motives can only be considered as a heuristic tool since the basic motives that dispose one toward certain actions must be inferred. Classification itself presents problems inasmuch as any given motivation may involve a number of others.[3]

Gordon Allport, in referring to the construction of theories of motivation, asserts that the theories should allow for many types and levels of human motives. He suggests the following criteria that place human motives in a transactional and phenomenological frame:

1. *Motivation theory should be concerned with the present state of the organism.* Individual motives are best understood in adaptational terms—that is, how the person perceives and interprets his circumstances in the here and now, how he intends to deal with them, and for what ends.

2. *The theory should ascribe dynamic force to the cognitive processes.* The idea that motivation has an intentional component implies that the person acts consciously. This quality of consciousness militates against the assumption that people are compelled to act because of blind,

irrational drives which, in turn, free them from responsibility for their behaviors. In short, conative behavior is conscious and purposeful rather than determined and involuntary.

3. *The theory should allow for the concrete uniqueness of motives.* Any one definition of motives cannot encompass all of the goals that men pursue. For this reason, allowance must be made for the idiosyncratic intentions of the person. This tells us that although we may be aware of the meaning of an individual's intentions and values relative to one of his goals, we cannot lose sight of the complex of many other motivations which also characterize this person.[4]

These principles encourage a cautious approach to the attempt to understand any one person's motives in any given situation. It is apparent that they argue against the use of the concept of motivation as a means for judging another person's energy, will, or intention relative to what he wishes to do about a problem. Not only must care be exercised in assuming what the person's motivations are in relation to the problem; how that person ranks and symbolizes the problem in comparison with the other motives and goals must also be considered. These principles militate against the absolute, fixed, or "either-or" notion of motivation and support the assumption that the term *"un*motivated" is gratuitous when applied to a client in the change experience.

THEORIES OF MOTIVATION

Based on assumptions about human free will and choice, theories of motivation fall into two schools of thought—the mechanistic and the organismic.[5] Mechanistic theories view the person as a machine propelled by various forces. The theories of E. T. Thorndike, C. L. Hull, B. F. Skinner, and othes, derived largely from the field of experimental psychology, are consonant with a mechanistic approach. Very briefly, these theories explain the neural consequences of drives and reinforcers and the movement of the organism toward a state of homeostasis. Motivation is aroused when the organism experiences discomfort caused by an unmet physiological need. The discomfort itself is an impelling force or drive that causes a search for fulfillment. When discomfort is sufficiently reduced, the drive is diminished and the organism returns to its former state. This theoretical position pictures man as reactive only to his physiological needs and ignores his ability to create and envision his own goals. According to Skinner, thoughts and feelings are not determiners of behavior but are either concomitants or consequences of behavior.

This point of view is disputed by Harry Harlow, who argues that physiological needs are less significant than many other sources of motivations—external influences, personal curiosity, and the need to manipulate one's environment.[6] In the case of learning, external influences such as the setting's climate and the expressed interest of others play an important role since they tend to sustain the learner's motivation over a prolonged period of time. The drive to reduce inner discomfort, in contrast, is short-lived and nonsustaining thus offering a minimal opportunity for learning. Even when the person seeks to reduce the discomfort of a pressing physiological need, upon fulfilling that need he does not immediately return to an inert homeostatic state but he may go on to explore his environment out of curiosity.

These active tendencies differentiate the organismic theories from the mechanistic.[7] Organismic approaches are concerned with humans in interaction with their environment and the manner in which they change and adapt to the environment. These approaches acknowledge the determining effects of cognition, emotion, and interaction but with some difference in emphasis. Some theorists, represented by Abraham Maslow and Henry Murray, underscore the importance of persons' psychological needs as motivational forces but give little attention to cognitive or relational factors. Others, represented by Lee Cronbach and Birch and Veroff, stress the role of cognition and the importance of the social field in which a person's motives are aroused.

Maslow's Hierarchy of Needs

Abraham Maslow's overall scheme is a hierarchic arrangement of needs in which the lower must be met before the individual can fulfill succeeding needs. Beginning with the basic needs, he establishes a hierarchy:

1. Physiological needs—hunger and thirst satisfaction, avoidance of pain and discomfort, for example.

2. Safety needs—a nonthreatening atmosphere including security, predictability, and stability.

3. Love and belongingness needs—the fulfillment provided by affiliation with others including affection and identification.

4. Esteem needs—the desire for advancement, competence, reputation, attention, appreciation, prestige, and self-respect.

5. The need for self-actualization.[8]

Maslow uses the elemental physiological needs as a base and moves up to more complex and interdependent needs. The last need, self-actualization, is the transcendent human motive representing the desire to realize an expansive and fulfilling sense of selfhood. In this realm of motivation, personal creativity emerges as a unique expression of the autonomous self. Maslow speaks of the *peak experience*, the extraordinary moment of self-realization.

Maslow's scheme corresponds in many respects to the motives of the intentional self. Physiological and safety needs and the latent love and belongingness needs are similar to the striving for self-enhancement; the more mature love and belongingness needs and the desire for esteem tend to conform with the press for self-extension; and self-actualization is another way of speaking of propriate striving. The difference is that Maslow's formulations do not take account of the role of perception in linking these inner motives with the actualities of the outer environment.

This hierarchy offers a simple way of understanding the reasons for clients' outward apathy toward the opportunity to do something about problems that others see as troublesome. For example, with the growth and expansion of the community mental health movement, mental health clinics have been established in rural comunities, ghettos, and working-class neighborhoods, usually for the first time. Moreover, the services of mental health professions are typically psychological therapies seeking to foster attainment of the higher needs (achievement, realization of personal potentials, richer interpersonal relationships, and abstract and somewhat transcendent goals). The motives of the residents are somewhat more concrete, and they may often reflect the basic needs of security, well-being, and physical survival. Thus, as counselor and client come together there is a disparity between what the worker offers and what the recipient actually needs.

Murray's Categories of Needs

Henry Murray's basic premises are quite similar to Maslow's; however, they differ in the way human motives are organized and in their scope. Murray does not employ a hierarchic approach other than in the way he differentiates primary from secondary needs.

Murray's primary needs are the viscerogenic requirements for physical sustenance and survival—food, water, and protection. The secondary needs are psychogenic and are the common human needs although they may differ in type and degree from person to person. Murray lists twenty-eight needs that can be categorized in accord with the seven functions they seem to represent.

The first category concerns the maintenance and control of the material and inanimate things that people value, including *acquisition*, to gain possession; *conservance*, to collect, repair, and clean; *order*, to arrange and organize; *retention*, to hold onto possessions; and *construction*, to organize or build.

The secondary category deals with needs for prestige and accomplishment and includes *superiority*, a complex involving the desire for power over others, things, and ideas and approval and status; *achievement*, the elementary ego need to overcome obstacles; *recognition*, the search for praise and commendations; and *exhibition*, the wish to attract attention to one's self.

The third category also reflects the desire for status but is more concerned with the avoidance of humiliation. Murray emphasizes the threats that may be encountered in the environment that Maslow only implies. These needs include *inviolacy*, the prevention of depreciation; *inavoidance*, the shunning of the experience of failure or shame; *defendance*, the defense or justification of one's actions; and *counteraction*, the need to attempt to overcome defeat.

The fourth category is primarily concerned with power needs. The intent is to exert power or to resist or cope with the power imposed by another: *dominance*, the wish to influence or control others; *deference*, to admire or follow a superior; *similance*, the need to imitate, identify with, or agree with another; *autonomy*, the need for independence; and *contrarience*, the desire to be unique or to take the other side.

The fifth category covers those needs that are related to the expression of socially unaccepted behavior. Murray acknowledges that all needs are not necessarily benign and that human motives can be malicious: *aggression*, the wish to assault, injure, or harm; *abasement*, the willingness to surrender and accept punishment; and *blame avoidance*, the need to obey so as to escape punishment.

The sixth category consists of affectional needs: *affiliation*, the search for friendship and human association and its opposite, *rejection*, the need to exclude others and remain aloof; *nurturance*, the drive to protect and care for others and its complement, *succorance*, the need to receive aid and protection.

The seventh category includes those motives that intend to express certain idiosyncratic features of the self. They include needs as basic as *play, cognizance*, the desire to express curiosity and exploration, and *exposition*, the wish to relate information and demonstrate knowledge.[9]

Murray's elaboration of needs verges on hair-splitting in the explication of human motives. His extensive inventory also runs the risk that often accompanies attempts to be overly exhaustive: something is bound to be omitted. The theorist operating on high levels of abstraction or dealing only with grand universes tends to side-step the possibility of accounting for possible omissions. What about the motive for intimacy? Is it merely implied in the category of affectional needs? Should the need to share or to be altruistic be included in this inventory?

Nonetheless, Murray's attempt does succeed in broadening the scope and diversity of human motives and in illuminating some of the nuances of human intent. His list includes the inevitable ambivalence that accompanies the more intense motives, and thus compensates for the problem involved in reducing behavior to discrete categories. Murray does indicate that a particular motive may take many forms: the need for status, for example, can be expressed by avoidance, by defensive behavior, or by counteraction. Human motives do not necessarily occur in an incremental or additive fashion and may be perverse.

Cronbach's Organization of Needs

Inasmuch as Lee Cronbach developed his scheme in the field of educational psychology, the following five needs are directly related to learning. Cronbach asserts that these needs must be present and satisfied if effective learning is to take place. The need for *competence and self-*

respect embodies the intention to know one's strengths and weaknesses and to set realistic goals. The need for *independence* also encompasses such motives as the desire for autonomous thought and action and the striving for creative expression.

Social and interactional factors are directly evident in the need for *approval by peers* and the need for *approval by authority*. These needs seem to conform to the socializing process that is part of learning and change. The motive to learn stems partly from the learner's perceptions of others' attitudes toward him, perceptions that serve as an impetus to go on with learning for its intrinsic value and to garner approval from colleagues and authorities.

Cronbach's reference to the *desire for affection* shows how significant learning evolves from serious interpersonal relationships. The basic principle is that an experience that is associated with other gratifications comes to be desired for itself. As an individual is involved in a cooperative, intimate, or otherwise satisfying relationship, the gains coming from the experience encourage him to seek other relationships that may yield similar satisfactions.

The possibility that the environment cannot or will not gratify this motive introduces the issue of contingency. Cronbach observes that from time to time changes in the social surroundings or in the demands placed on the person make it impossible for need satisfaction to occur by usual means. This condition frustrates the person's motives and calls for the kind of new learning that will fulfill these motives in different ways. If opportunities are available, these changes may spur new growth and a greater elaboration of learning potentials, competency, and eventual need fulfillment. Cronbach concludes that the motivational development of the individual is interlocked with the needs and the development of others around him. [10]

Cronbach's ideas serve as a bridge between theories of motivation that are largely based on personality and those that stress the transactional and cognitive components of conative strivings. Maslow stresses internal psychological drives. Murray also emphasizes the psychology of motivation, but suggests that there is also an interactional basis. Cronbach is far more explicit about the interactive social contingencies that encourage motivation to learn. Motivation is an essential dynamic to learning.

These schemes help to explain the motives that impel the voluntary client to seek assistance for his problems of living whether they are practical, personal, interpersonal, or social. His thoughts and feelings tell him that certain of his needs are unmet, and he generally anticipates the possibility of relief or fulfillment with a hopeful outlook. This is not to say that his understanding of his unmet need is necessarily accurate or that his motivation will endure or assure a successful outcome. Nonetheless, consciousness of the motive for need fulfillment enables the client to make contact with a helping person and serves as the necessary first step in the process of problem solving.

Understanding of the motivational problems of the so-called hard-to-reach client is not equally increased by these theories. Although they emphasize that lower or viscerogenic needs for food, shelter, and security must be satisfied, many human services workers know that the provision of these necessities does not automatically free the client to accept the kind of help that will enable him to achieve more rewarding relationships, self-sufficiency, or autonomy. In many instances, this individual not only remains a chronically dependent client but also appears motivated to resist the possibility of a more salutary and autonomous existence. If the human services organization is not fostering dependency or thwarting the client's growth and if the worker does not automatically assume that the client's resistance is a matter of obstinacy, irreversible conditioning, or an inner pathology, then it becomes evident that certain cognitive factors are distorting motivation for learning and growth. Something in the way that the client interprets the possibility of change or his role in the process stands in the way of more positive outcomes.

Birch and Veroff's Theory of Instrumental Activity

The theory of instrumental activity escapes the limits of psychological and unidirectional explanations of motivation by elaborating the cognitive and transactional features of human motives. David Birch and Joseph Veroff state that a pair of simultaneous events are set in motion when the motivation to act arises. One of these events includes the conditions within the individual's social environment that may influence the course of action he will take. The other involves the special characteristics of the person that modulate these environmental influences.

Therefore, the peculiarity of a person's motive is neither the consequence of a psychological drive nor the result of external environmental forces; rather it is the expression of the resonance between the two involving the functions of perception. As the link between self and social environment, perception is concerned with four intention-related factors: *availability, expectancy, incentive,* and *motive.*[11]

AVAILABILITY   Availability refers to the absence, presence, and quality of opportunities for the individual to carry out a particular instrumental act. Whether or not or what extent he is able to fulfill his motives depends on the relationship between the opportunities that exist in the person's field and his physical and perceptual characteristics.

Because it bears on the emergence of motivational tendencies, the concept of availability is especially relevant to the plight of clients who do not recognize the need to change but are urged to do so by others. These clients may be people who are asking for welfare aid, involuntary mental patients, those referred by a court for counseling help, parents of children having school problems, residents of inner city slums, parents charged with child abuse, substance abusers, delinquents, or others considered deviant.

Quite possibly, the environment of these clients could contain ample opportunities for positive change waiting to be seized by an eager consumer. But these clients are not eager because they perceive their circumstances in ways that isolate them from all the good that these opportunities might provide. Although they may be vaguely aware that something is wrong, they are not interpreting their conditions in the same manner as do others who are disturbed by what they observe. Therefore, despite the obvious presence of worthwhile services and promised benefits, these opportunities do not actually exist within these clients' phenomenological field. They do not see a meaningful connection between their needs and motives and the available services because their discriminatory skills are not turned in that direction and thus far have not conceptualized their state of being in problematic terms. Feeling pressured to do something about a problem that they do not understand, it is also possible that these clients' main motives might be to preserve a trace of dignity, to justify their notions of reality, to avoid additional penalties, or to somehow appease those who are imposing their authority. For the most part, these motives do little to encourage the use of available opportunities.

At the other extreme, opportunities in the client's environment may be so poor and indifferent as to nullify his emergent motivations. Some human services organizations devise their policies, procedures, and programs in a way that creates unnecessary obstacles separating clients from services that could be beneficial. The services may be "available," but they are obscured by a number of routines that are of greater benefit to the organization than to its constituents. For example, the unwilling client may be expected to pay a fee for a service that has no apparent value for him. He may be asked to give up his free time or leave his employment to appear for appointments that someone else sets for him. He may be expected to divulge personal information for reasons that he cannot comprehend. A procedure called "intake," "screening," or "admissions" often becomes a ritual designed to meet the organization's or the practitioner's requirements—to determine eligibility for service, to evaluate the client's motivation, or to allow the worker to diagnose the client and his problem.

Phyllis Silverman's study of clients who prematurely drop out of treatment suggests that these procedures should be reexamined. [12] The respondents were low-income blacks who were voluntary clients seeking help from a family services agency. All completed the initial intake process. It was learned that the clients were curious about their interviewer's credentials but never thought of questioning them, believing that such queries would be interpreted as a challenge. Many were concerned about practical matters of living, but they found themselves drawn into talking about "personal business." Some clients were willing to talk freely about their personal problems; although they felt somewhat relieved, they never did discover how this discussion was related to any kind of solution or plan. These people simply could not understand the process and did not find out what good all the talking would do; they accepted a second appointment but never returned.

Even when people do return and accept the client role, they become frustrated when the availability of opportunities is eclipsed by detrimental methods, attitudes, or policies. In a survey of Massachusetts' welfare recipients, one of the questions was, "Were there any other reasons why, when you needed help, you didn't ask for it?"[13] The following are some typical responses:

Because when you ask for help most of the time you don't get it, so you don't bother anymore.

Because if welfare does not tell you what services they will help you with, how can you ask?

Ridiculous amount of bureaucratic red tape you have to go through.

Because I can never locate my worker.

They stripped me of my dignity and made me feel it was out of their pockets.

Who needs the extra problem?

Understanding of one's motivation is inadequate if attention is not given to the matter of availability. People who do feel the incentive to find a remedy for their problem or discomfort tend to scan their environment for possible outlets or opportunities. When they encounter some of the obstacles noted, they are likely to endure them or take them in stride. But people who have not come to terms with their hardships and difficulties or who resist authoritative definitions of their problems will not readily perceive available opportunities since *availability* is not an objective fact but a subjective construct. If they happen to encounter baffling procedures, these conditions will only intensify their motives to withdraw from the experience.

EXPECTANCY   The concept of *expectancy* is defined by Birch and Veroff as the anticipation of outcomes that regulates activity aimed at particular goals. It is linked with past experiences and the pleasures that have accrued from similar events. The concept can be enlarged to include the broad range of cognitive impressions that have evolved over time, for example, the ideals and values of the self-image and the beliefs about what one ought to become in the future. The aspirations of the intentional self also bears on the kinds of goals and outcomes that might be anticipated. In addition, vicarious impressions of others' experiences will affect how a person thinks things will turn out.

The central role of expectancy in the process and outcome of behavior change has been extensively researched.[14] John Borghi's study designates expectancy as the key variable in the change process.[15] When people who terminated psychotherapy prematurely (Terminators) and those who continued (Remainers) were matched according to specific variables (e.g., demographic characteristics, diagnosis, results of psychological testing) expectation was the only significant variable. He concluded that Terminators can be identified by the unrealistic outcomes that are anticipated, where they place the source of the problem, or the kind of information sought, but not by personality characteristics.

Generally speaking, the voluntary client approaches the prospect of change with some positive expectations and hopes. His ability to define his problem allows him to envision what a rewarding solution might be like. Possibly, he has enjoyed prior success in dealing with some of his life's problems and is somewhat confident about his own role. The reluctant client does not share these positive expectations. Conforming with the definition of the Terminator, he is uncertain about the nature of his problem, doubtful about possible outcomes, and perplexed about what he should request or what he ought to be doing.

The value orientation and expectations of the helping person can also affect motivation. In their study of more than 3,000 mental health professionals, William Henry, John Sims, and Lee Spray found that the great majority are upwardly mobile. They had overcome, by their own efforts, the psychological barriers of their lower- or middle-class origins and had achieved the status of upper middle-class identification. They believed that aspiration and change were desirable values and that self-disclosure, introspection, and discussion were the best means of resolving personal problems.[16] Human services workers also hold other beliefs and perspectives that are translated into expectations of the client, his actions, and how change is best achieved. They are the bearers of their culture's, profession's, and organization's standards for normal behavior and proper adjustment. If the worker is an agent of an institution of social control, these standards and expectations will be even stronger. The professional worker typically subscribes to a theoretical orientation or a school or method of practice that prescribes how the problem in question should be defined and the steps that should be taken to change it.[17] The worker's own world image helps impose a formidable value climate with which a client must contend.

426

If the incoming client shares these values and expectations, the climate presents no serious difficulties. The probability of a successful outcome is actually enhanced by a mutual sharing of values.

The nonvoluntary client may see these values and expectations as foreign or at least as a lower priority than his other needs. This may well be the case when this client has a lower-class orientation or is identified with cultural, minority, ethnic, or racial groups whose approach to problem solving differs significantly from the middle- or upper middle-class worker. There is a large body of research that reveals that bias and the discrepancy of expectations have strong impacts on issues of the motivation and involvement of clients and the quality of services they receive. [18]

Arnold Goldstein refers to some specific discrepancies between the client's expectations and those of the helping professional. The lower- or working-class client usually defines help as something that he needs to cope with a concrete problem or an environmental crisis. If he does seek this help, it is often at the urging of others. He would like to get immediate relief by assuming a passive role and by being told what he is supposed to do. The professional sees this client as "unsuitable," expects minimal change, and brings the experience to a rapid close.

A number of psychiatric residents were divided into three groups to observe the same interview with a simulated patient. One group was informed that the patient was upper-class, the second that the patient was middle-class, and the third was told that he was lower-class. This information led to biased ratings that reflected the values of a status-oriented society: Despite the fact that the "patient" acted the same way and provided the same information in all three interviews, the residents who were told that the patient was lower-class offered a much poorer prognosis and lower judgments about this person's mental health.

Public school counselors were given information about a nine-year-old boy with behavior problems. Half of the counselors were told the boy was from an upper middle-class family; the other half were told that he was a lower-class child. The former group were far more likely to propose that the child needed help by meeting with the boy for counseling, scheduling a conference with his teacher, and making a home visit.

A study of the diagnostic tendencies of middle-class and lower-class therapists disclosed that the former more consistently rated patients' antisocial behavior in pathological terms than did the latter.

In a study of 425 alcoholic outpatients, upper-class patients were eight times more likely to be physician-referred than were lower-class patients. Most often, upper-class patients received psychotherapy while lower-class patients were treated with drug therapy.[19]

Beyond the expectations that the participants bring to the change event, the experience itself can create some additional problems. If the reluctant client does enter into some sort of dyadic or group relationship with a worker, what might he anticipate? Since this experience probably has no counterpart in the client's life, he would have no basis for determining what others want of him, what kind of role he ought to assume, or what to expect from others around him. If a relationship matures, he discovers that he is expected to discard his familiar protective social garments and reveal thoughts and feelings that he may have guarded to this point. Unsure about the purpose of these revelations and how the listeners will respond, he will need to struggle with feelings of vulnerability. Even if these fears are calmed to some extent, the client finds that he has to contribute something of himself to the relationship in the form of caring, regard, and trust. Inasmuch as ordinary living may be a demanding, energy-draining, and absorbing experience for the troubled client, the need to extend himself further may create an additional burden. The client may later discover that a relationship with a caring and committed person will offset many of the strains. Until this awareness ripens, he is understandably reluctant to invest any more of himself than he has to in this perplexing experience.

The effectiveness and development of the problem-solving enterprise stands or falls on the question of expectancy. Understanding a person's motivations is rather meaningless if close attention is not given to his elemental conceptions and expectations of the personal, interpersonal, and interactional attributes of the change event.

INCENTIVE AND MOTIVE Incentive and motive are interdependent variables of motivation and come into focus only after some of the basic expectancies are clarified and resolved. As these uncertainties are worked out, the client is free to give some thought to possible goals and what needs to done to achieve them.

Incentive refers to the feelings and attitudes that arise when an individual contemplates *what he will need to do* in order to reach a desired goal. Incentive concerns the *means* aspect of instrumental activity; its strength is measured by what a person believes he will actually accomplish should he desire to pursue a particular course of action.

Existing in some sort of balance with incentive, *motive* is primarily concerned with the *ends* themselves. In this sense, a person's "motives" refer to his thoughts, feelings, and perceptions about a particular goal—that is, whether he envisions it in desirable, undesirable, or ambivalent terms. If the goal seems desirable to him, he would be inclined or motivated in the direction of fulfillment; if it seems undesirable, other motives could arise relative to the intent to avoid that goal or to devise alternative goals.

Incentive and motive can be considered as a dialectic, as the tension between means and ends. There are four possible ways in which the two variables can stand in relation: they may be equally high; equally low; incentive may be high but motive low; or incentive may be low but motive high. If a person's incentives and motives are both consistently strong, he is committed to and deeply involved in the learning task. If incentive and motive are both weak, some antecedent problems have not yet been resolved.

The other two relationships represent the typical ambivalent nature of an individual's motivations about learning and change. Where incentives are strong but motive low, the person finds himself caught between the urge to change and the fear of what might happen if he does change. He has come to terms with the fact that his prior patterns of behaviors and the solutions he has attempted have been counterproductive; he wishes to learn new adaptive methods. Yet he is blocked by a fearful view of the consequences. This ambivalence may be expressed in such terms as "I'm really fed up with the way I have been living. I know I have to change. But if I do, I know that I'll just wind up alone!" "Sure, getting together with the other patients might change things around this ward. But I'm not sure how it will look on my chart. I want to get out of this place someday."

A person's motives may be strong and his ambitions compelling, but his incentive lags as he is confronted with what he will need to do if he wishes to achieve the goal. The client's visions of a cherished goal may be most poignant to him, but the realization that he would need to change his familiar adaptive styles may be most threatening. For example, the problem of mid-life transition is receiving increasing attention. At this crucial point of living, a time when a person may look back to reexamine his prior choices and the existential meanings of his life, the question of what to do with the time remaining arises. He may conclude that delivery from whatever dissatisfaction he now feels lies in a substantial change in his familiar lifestyle or in an entirely different career. These goals may stir much anticipation and excitement, but the person must take account of what he will have to do if the ends are to be realized. He considers the upheaval that he will have to endure and the backlash that will follow when others in his family or larger society find what will be expected of them in the process.

The client caught in either of these dilemmas will present the worker with difficult and challenging behaviors, behaviors that may evoke frustration, discouragement, and disappointment. Assuming that the client has come far enough in the problem-solving venture to resolve expectancy problems and to be able to conceptualize what needs changing, this ambivalence can be very disturbing. He may seriously contemplate departure and discover all sorts of excuses for so doing. He may demean his own intentions or capabilities and see himself as "unrealistic." He may become passive or dependent, hoping someone else will take over his problem. He may blame the worker or the group for the "wild goose chase" he has been on.

These clients are not "unmotivated," or "unsuited for change." The source of their conflict is a powerful wish to change either certain life patterns or goals, not unwillingness. It is because they do want something better and more rewarding that they find themselves in a dilemma.

This conflict is not solely the property of the nonvoluntary client; however, he would probably feel the pinch of ambivalence somewhat more acutely, because he may have less confidence and proof of success to fall back on. In any case, there comes a time in the process of change when whatever the bright vision was that the client cherished starts to come apart. The contingencies, demands, and the implications of change begin to loom as serious problems to be dealt with in their own right. Even the most eager client will turn a corner at some stage in the process and discover that his incentive does not match his motives, or vice versa. This is the nature of learning and change that stirs fundamental conflicts in values and principles as people confront the implications of their intent. The need of the person to reexamine and reconceptualize the existential

430

choices he will have to make about either action or goal is at issue, not the question of motivation.

Problems of motivation become more comprehensible and therefore open to resolution when the contingencies of availability, expectancy, incentive, and motive are given proper consideration. Arbitrary judgments about resistance, recalcitrance, or unreadiness dissolve when these contingencies are appreciated as adaptive needs; these judgments can then be supplanted by a helpful sensitivity to the cognitive and interactional obstacles that must be dealt with *before* the more apparent problem can be attacked. This perspective increases the possibility that people whose behavioral, cultural, or attitudinal dispositions do not conform to the helping person's standards will not be deprived of the assistance they require or subjected to inferior forms of service. As far as the human services worker is concerned, the ability to regard motivational inclinations from the client's angle of perception may offset or at least diminish the dismay and threat generated by the unaccommodating client—especially when this client's responses are interpreted as a hostile repudiation of the worker's expertise, his good intentions, or the organization's value.

An ex-social worker who defines herself as "burned out" describes the personal cost and the destruction of "idealism, spirit, and health" that results from trying to help such "ungrateful" clients: "Even the most idealistic among us eventually succumbs to such symptoms when defeat begins to equal, and sometimes surpass, success. After awhile, workers acquire a sixth sense for determining which cases are almost predestined to failure. We come to refer to such assignments as 'garbage cases.' One reading of the case record and a few personal contacts with the clients revealed to our trained eyes that nothing short of divine intervention would do any good."[20]

With no intention to minimize the challenge of working with people who are not asking for help, this point of view, emphasizing concerns with "defeat," "success," or "failure," indicates the demeaning struggle that is bound to escalate when the client's motivation is appraised in either-or, absolute, or otherwise disapproving terms.

THE NATURE AND CONDITIONS OF MOTIVATION

Motivation can be understood as the conscious desire to fulfill a particular need or set of needs. Such needs may concern the primary necessities of living (food, shelter, security) or the higher intentions involving self-enhancement, self-extension, or transcendent strivings. It is assumed that the intensity of a motive is measured by the value and meaning that is ascribed to it. If the individual's environment and/or his capabilities do not allow for the fulfillment of his needs then (a) the environment can be changed or augmented to provide the required resources, or (b) he will have to change inappropriate adaptive patterns by means of new learning and problem solving. The latter requirement compounds the problem of motivation; the individual may not only need to reconsider the value and meaning of his original motive and his desire to pursue it, he also must reckon with the demands and rewards of learning and change. In this regard, he must contemplate questions of the accessibility of assistance, the uncertainties of what he and significant others expect, and the value of the means and ends of change. The original motive for need-fulfillment must now be expanded to include the motivation for the kind of change required if these needs are to be fulfilled.

Drawing from prior assumptions about the nature of learning and change, it is apparent that other cognitive and affective conditions can strongly influence the person's self-determining motives. These conditions include:

1. *Lack of cognitive awareness or denial of the motive and problem.* This state may be reactive to the perceived risks and costs of change or the overwhelming complexity of the challenge.

2. *Inability to conceptualize need and motive.* The individual may sense or be emotionally aware of a pressing need but cannot translate his awareness into conceptual terms. It is also possible that the lack of fulfillment may be an accustomed part of the person's lifestyle; therefore it is not discerned as something requiring attention.

3. *The effects of the pressure of authority or other external forces.* The felt imposition of persuasive forces may shift the individual's priorities to self-protective motives involving the need to cope with or resist these influences.

4. *Perceived absence of alternative goals.* Despite the presence of acute

dissatisfaction with his present state, the individual does not envision other options fitting his versions of reality.

4. *Perceived absence of alternative roles.* The individual may be aware of the need to change but cannot project himself into other roles that promise to be more rewarding.

6. *Systemic factors.* Consciousness of personal needs and motives may be suppressed by negative expectations about the impact of self-determined action on the stability of the individual's immediate system.

7. *Stresses of living.* Energies that could be devoted to the fulfillment of growth-enhancing motives may be depleted by the unrelenting demands of daily living.

Chapter 14

Overview and Basic Principles

Whether we call the experience planned change, induced change, behavior change, psychotherapy, social action, family treatment, or any of the group approaches to change, some important parts of the experience will elude our understanding. The number of variables involved in the structure and process of the change event makes it impossible to produce a finely detailed blueprint of how the event ought to work or a concise report on how it did work. The mere fact that any of these forms of change comprises two or more people in transaction makes it certain that the experience will be somewhat kaleidoscopic, regardless of the planning and deliberation invested in it. Each participant presents a complex of selves in tension that strive to maintain equilibrium amidst change and constancy amidst movement. Each participant expresses many perceptions, motives, values, needs, and emotions. Each participant bears an unspoken autobiography of symbols and meanings that have substance to himself alone. Whatever the change experience happens to be at any given moment, we can only be sure that it will be qualitatively different the next.

Taking account of these human conditions, planned change is intelligible. This book has developed an anatomy of social learning and change that closely approximates the manner in which people ordinarily go about dealing with their problems of living. The processes that unfold in the planned change experience differ mainly in structure and purpose when compared with the processes that unfold in the business of ordinary living. We can look at the anatomy of change in the same way that we understand human anatomy. It comprises elements that are common to all people; yet, each person is differentiated from all others by the peculiarity of his special features. Social learning and problem solving can also be viewed as a matrix, a cognitive frame that can be applied to the experience of learning and change. The actual experience, however, will evolve in a manner that corresponds with the characteristics, style, and goals of its constituents.

The relevance of a problem-solving scheme for personal, interpersonal, and social change is finding greater advocacy in professional literature. [1] Although Hugh Urban and Donald Ford restrict their conclusions to the field of psychotherapy, their observations appear to be equally relevant to other modalities of change.

One of the conclusions with which the writers have emerged is the inherently sensible relationship that obtains between what has been called the "problem-solving approach" and the practice of psychotherapy. This approach is a way of conceptualizing what is involved in undertakings such as psychotherapy represents, and one that has evolved in contexts separate and distinct from psychotherapy theory and practice. The potential applicability of such developments to the business of psychotherapy and behavioral change, however, seems impressive indeed. We propose therefore, that one of the ways to encompass the heterogeneity that the "field" of psychotherapy represents is within the framework of the problem-solving approach.

. . .

. . . psychotherapists can be thought of as consultants to people about their problems, consultants who may elect to collaborate with those persons in the solution of their difficulties. And, one can consider the psychotherapeutic process in terms of the cooperation between one individual who has at hand information about his behavior "in the field" as it were, and another who is something of a behavior specialist, with each of them representing an area of particular knowledge. . . . The relevance of this manner of thinking to the practice of psychotherapy is not that it is characteristically accomplished in precisely this fashion. Rather, it is proposed that the situation with respect to psychotherapy is much as Dewey suggested for problem solving in general, *viz.* that there is a pattern of thinking inherent in the psychotherapist's approach to the resolution of behavioral difficulties, that every psychotherapist *implicitly* proceeds in such fashion to a greater or lesser extent, and that the process would become more efficient if it were (a) rendered explicit, (b) made specific, (c) laid out in an orderly and systematic progression, and (d) followed in a conscientious fashion. [2]

The expressed idea of the helping person as a consultant to people about their problems suggests that a cognitive approach to problem solving and social learning is germane to other professional helping roles as well. This approach applies to reeducation, rehabilitation, the many forms of mental health practice that have a family and community orientation, and work with all types of groups. Problem solving is the effective method by which people can solve their problems of living. A cognitive approach represents the medium by which problems are understood and defined and alternative solutions are devised and tested. An existential orientation takes account of personal and interpersonal considerations of choice and responsibility relative to the search for alternatives. The overall process is called social learning, a process involving the transactional and educative nature of change.

The assumptions and strategies described strive to maintain integrity, consistency, and effectiveness. Although these principles are directed toward human services practice in general, they intend to emphasize the crucial issues that are pertinent to practice with the outwardly reluctant and disadvantaged client.

1. *Accessibility of human services.* The question of accessibility has as much to do with the extent to which people are aware of and are able to gain easy entry to services as it does with the quantity of services placed in a given area. Even if a sufficient number of human service agencies or personnel existed, it would not necessarily mean that they would be accessible to potential consumers. Major barriers stand between needy people and the opportunity to resolve at least a few of their problems of living.

The splintering of human services into categories of problem or population means that each organization must define its particular boundaries to determine who shall be included or excluded. Boundary definitions are all too often framed in accord with the agency's needs, rather than as a response to the consumer's needs.[3] Rules for eligibility are also contrived from boundary definitions. Over time, these rules are multiplied and elaborated as more and more contingencies are encountered. Rules tend to persevere long after their utility has vanished. Having to cope with these obstacles, the person needing help is subjected to a complex problem-solving task well before he can begin to speak about his own problems.

There are other factors that may intervene to further distance the consumer from the needed service or to leave him trapped between the boundaries of a number of organizations. There is the confusing and obstructive nature of the screening and admission protocols, and the risk of depersonalization that often arises when a person attempts to penetrate a bureaucratic structure.

The committed and effective human services worker must be as aware, or even more so, of the coping deficiencies of his organization as he is aware of those of his clientele. He must be alert to the established conditions and procedures that appear to complicate the lives and the problems of his client. In principle, this worker cannot fall back on the "I just work here" syndrome. He must have some say in the creation and the revision of those policies and procedures that affect his practice and his clientele. The worker is on the line; he is the one who can provide an objective measure of the value or the penalties of the organizational rules. Accessibility, the productive link between person and effective service, depends on the worker's role at this level of change.

2. *Social forces affecting problem solving.* Problems of living inevitably are expressions of conditions within their own social field. People cannot proceed through the course of working out their problems without attention to (a) the conditions in their social field that support or contribute to the nature of the problem, and (b) the effect of the perceived solution on others in that field. A systemic or ecological orientation that takes account of the interlocking relations existing among persons and between the person and the other constituents of his social system will inform the worker about the critical forces involved.

In a more positive sense, the worker should look beyond the immediate circumstances of his clients to explore the possibilities for help and support that may be present in their personal network. The family, other natural or formed groups, the attributes of the client's culture, and other identifications may provide sources of assistance that had been untapped and unrecognized.

3. *It is the solution that is important, not the problem.* The tendency to focus on, diagnose, or classify the client's problem is a form of profes-

sional myopia. Problems of living are unavoidable when people are involved in living; the absence of problems reveals an empty and meaningless existence. It is not the problem that is the problem but the unsuitable and habitual solutions that people insist on applying to their problems of living that create their troubles. It could even be the absence of a solution in its own right. Problem solving connotes a search for new and more rewarding solutions to the demands of living.

4. *Starting where the client is.* The beginning point of practice is the client's unique version of his own reality. This version may not necessarily be approved or condoned, but it should be sincerely appreciated as his world view. This beginning has a number of advantages: (a) it grants the client at least a bit of the confirmation of self that he requires; (b) it forestalls pointless debate about whose reality is valid; (c) it does not place the client in a position where he must accommodate or become socialized to the worker's theoretical reality; and (d) it invites the client to explain and justify his conception, to reveal his underlying premises, and to discover for himself how these premises and conceptions are distorted or lacking in some way.

5. *The worker's management of the learning and change event.* The human services worker has the expertise to assume the responsibility for creating the climate and opportunity for people to find solutions to problems of living, a responsibility exercised with a strong measure of dignity, trust, privacy, and confidentiality. The worker may serve as a consultant, teacher, advocate, mediator, or enabler; yet however he defines his role, he becomes a manager. He anticipates obstacles, keeps the learning process on track, provides needed supports, and is prepared to meet and contend with the anguish, ambivalence, and fear that are often corollaries of change.

6. *The learning style of the client.* Since people are the final experts about the nature of their own existence, the problem-solving venture will be more meaningful, enduring, and effective if it is undertaken in close accord with their own style of learning. The worker should augment the client's approach to his problems; however, it is the client's values, priorities, cultural identifications, language and other important attributes that should guide the process rather than the worker's protocols or theoretical system for change.

438

7. *Values and action.* Primary aims of social learning and problem solving are enabling clients to bring their major values into open view and creating the space and opportunity for these values to be translated into reasonable and responsible behaviors. Moreover, the client should be helped to bring his instrumental values (choices and preferences bearing on effective daily living) and his terminal values (future goals or ends-in-sight) into more meaningful accord. If the worker can prize his clients' values and the alien territory of the client's value system, it is more likely that the client can begin to come to terms with his own principles for living.

8. *Risk taking.* Ordinarily, problem solving is understood as a deliberate and planful approach to the development of new solutions. Problem solving also depends on the less rational and the imaginal levels of thought when this level can permit the expression of personal symbols and meanings and the kind of intuitiveness of "knowing" that is not based on logical foundations. The extent to which the worker can tolerate and support these ambiguous and enigmatic thought processes enriches the quality of learning and urges the client toward a deeper consciousness of his true existence.

Risk taking also is an inevitable part of practice with families and groups. At some point the members come to realize that the familiar patterns and perceptions must be relinquished. The path ahead is most uncertain since old styles of relating are obsolete and new ways have yet to be determined and tried. Both clients and worker confront a void that, to reduce tension, the worker may be tempted to fill with his own solutions. The family or group, with the worker's assistance, must define its own route and design its own standards and expectations.

9. *Transferability of learning.* It is apparent that the immediate task of social learning and problem solving is the development of new solutions to a particular problem. These solutions will hold more enduring meanings for the client's self-concept and confidence if they can be extended to other problems of living. The intent is to help the client see the implications of his achievements as they bear on other realms of his existence.

10. *The question of motivation.* In work with the unwilling client, attention must be given to the personal conflicts that separate the client

from the attempt to find a solution before the apparent problem can be attacked. Rather than being judged as "resistant" or "unmotivated," the reasons for his need to distance himself from help and change must be understood. These reasons could include the need to preserve self-esteem; doubts about personal ideals and competency; value conflicts; misconceptions about the nature of change; inability to envision alternatives; and his expectancies about self, others, and possible outcomes.

11. *Clarity and openness.* Candor and an authentic presentation of self are essential to effective practice, particularly with the reluctant client. However he finds himself facing the human services worker, it usually is not by his choice or determination, and the experience is confusing and threatening or disturbing. The worker is likely to be seen in negative terms, if he is acknowledged at all. It is incumbent on the worker to take the lead in attempting to clear the atmosphere of misconceptions and distortions, but it should be in a bilateral fashion: the worker should explain his role, purpose, and function with clarity and in the client's terms; he also must elicit the client's perceptions and expectations of the event.

When the worker is occupying an authoritative role that may impose certain controls over the client, this reality must be clarified and the client must know the boundaries and limits with which he must contend. These issues must be addressed with sensitivity, timing, and tact, otherwise they may be interpreted as coercion or threat. The purposes of this sort of candor and openness may have less to do with what the client actually accepts of what is expressed than it does with creating an easier climate within which the client can begin to risk a degree of trust.

12. *Immediacy.* Practice with voluntary clients can usually progress at a relaxed pace without undue concerns about the use of time and continuance. Work with the involuntary client poses other demands. If he is troubled about something, he is looking for immediate relief or a solution. Quite possibly, the abstract notion of an extended period of talk is inconceivable to him. Each contact with this client should be treated as if it were the last—as if further contacts were in doubt. Each experience of working together should be a productive problem-solving exercise from which the client can come away with something concrete.

13. *The use of contracts.* The voluntary client's commitment represents a tacit contract involving his responsibility in the mutual agreement about the structure, process, and ends of the problem-solving venture. With the nonvoluntary client a specific contract should be made so that the obligations of all concerned are made explicit. The client can be encouraged to express his own goals and expectations, a first step in cognitive understanding and learning. Each contract must be relevant to the special characteristics of the individual event. It may be relatively simple and short-termed, an agreement only to meet at a specific time or to deal with a specific issue, e.g., what will be discussed next week. These agreements should be reworked periodically. The contract may also be more complex and extensive as, for example, the preparation for and the follow-up of discharge from a hospital.

14. *Advice, guidance, and direction.* It is proper and helpful for the worker to draw from his special expertise and knowledge to provide the client with the required information and direction. Obviously, this must be accomplished in a manner that does not detract from the client's ability to find his own useful solutions. A critical realm of knowledge that belongs to the worker is his acquaintance with the intricate workings of the human services and social welfare systems, their machinations, and procedures. This information should be imparted to the client to avoid a costly trial-and-error search for what he needs.

15. *The locus of practice.* Offices and agencies are routinely thought of as the optimal setting for the problem-solving enterprise. Quite often, this setting is more to the worker's or the organization's advantage if only because it allows for a more efficient use of time. But "getting the client to come to the office," also is used as a challenge to be won or as "proof" of the client's motivation. In the final analysis, these issues are irrelevant to the problem-solving task.

Arnold Goldstein states, "The most appropriate place for an interview should depend on the topic of discussion, but it should be a place directly relevant to the discussion." He questions why interviews are typically in the professional's office and proposes that they can be held quite helpfully in the client's home, in his place of employment, in bars, automobiles, and on park benches.[4]

16. *Security and stability*. The client approaching the change event with serious misgivings often bases his doubts on the few rewards that accrue to him in his usual life situation. He may be convinced that he has little if any control over the things that affect his destiny. He may be overwhelmed by the continuous crisis and disorder that characterize his circumstances. He may also suffer from certain material deprivations, from discrimination, or from the attitudes that cast him into the role of the deviant. Given that he has few dependable options to fall back on, the expectation that he must do something about his problems can further disrupt what meager securities or sense of control that he does cling to.

The worker may need to assume a number of roles that are protective and that serve to create a measure of stability, for example, acting on the client's behalf to assure that he receives the basic necessities of living. Such activities raise the specter of "dependency." It is a rather disreputable term in the lexicon of the profession and it has stopped many workers from providing sorely needed assistance out of the ill-grounded fear that the client will become helpless. This fear is baseless because the worker's interventions are aimed at enhancing the eventual growth of productive independence. The security that arises from the healthy reliance on another may be the means by which an individual can discover his own worth and power.

17. *Hope*. Social learning and problem solving deal with the literal and symbolic dimensions of human cognition. One of these symbols is *hope*, an expectancy of possible outcomes. Without hope and expectation of something better, the client tends to cling to what is and ignore what might be, irrespective of how vividly the worker paints the future. Perhaps the client is reluctant because he believes he has been cheated by hope. He has no sound basis for anticipating that the problem solving will be other than another disappointment.

Somehow, it is the worker who must breed a quality of hopeful anticipation into the experience—but in a careful and realistic fashion. His client, sensitized to futile promises, is acutely aware of sham and pretense. The worker can attempt to elicit the client's expectations as the first step toward uncovering his basic premises and world view. The worker has also the advantage of being able to see both more and less than his client can about the nature of the present and the future. In one way, he

442

can sense but cannot fully comprehend the anguish of his client's existence; in another, he is far enough removed to look beyond it and envision the possibilities that the client cannot. These possibilities cannot be conveyed by words alone; it is the worker's sense of vitality and inspiration that may come to generate a strain of hope.

18. *Autonomy*. Autonomous action and choice is a fundamental need of people and an obligation to pursue a style and course of existence that creates a semblance of personal meaning and social solidarity. Autonomy has nothing to do with the "Looking to be Me" syndrome of the current age, nor does it encourage a self-protective retreat from social interests and obligations.

Autonomy constitutes a consciousness of a person's ability to choose and act within the limitations of his existence, responsibly and considering the implications of his choices and actions for others. Autonomy also is the necessity for retaining a measure of control over the critical conditions that affect a person's being. For it is through choosing and acting in a self-determined fashion that the meaning of existence is discovered. In this way, a person counters the extraneous meanings that the external world attempts to impose on him. The well-being of the community depends on the extent to which its members can define themselves as autonomous; it is the obligation of the community to nurture and preserve the autonomy of its members.

It may seem foolish to apply this principle to people who feel hopeless even about something as basic as a decent life for themselves and their families. Clients living on the margins of society have little time and energy left to grapple with what may appear to them as questions of choice and dignity. Daily hazards fill the space of their lives and leave little room for reflection.

The more comfortable and affluent client, apparently free to reflect on his essential needs, may also be alienated from his values and ideals and may find himself to be a victim of another sort. It is quite possible that he has compromised his belief in the pursuit of consensually "good" but personally meaningless goals. He has also compromised his more authentic coping abilities. As Jerome Frank observes, it is not so much the symptom that brings people into the change situation but the sense of *demoralization* that ensues when one is unable to cope with the circumstances of living in accord with either his own expectations or those of others. [5]

The experience of learning and problem solving urges either client, the dispossessed or the over-socialized conformist, toward the realization of something more than the mastery of and solutions to his immediate problems of living. Such learning should offer these clients the opportunity to become aware of their critical ideals and images that are basic to their existence as authentic and vital social beings. The worker cannot provide a blueprint of living for his clients; this is the challenge and task that the client must confront. But over the course of problem solving, the worker can be mindful of this dimension of existence and grasp the opportunities that do stir the client's consciousness about the critical issues of living that involve autonomous and self-determined action.

Notes

CHAPTER ONE

1. Robert E. Ornstein, *The Mind Field* (New York: Grossman, 1976), 6–7.

2. B. F. Skinner, *Beyond Freedom and Dignity* (New York: Condon, 1972).

3. William Glasser has, in fact, developed a system of psychotherapy that is aimed at the human tendency to use explanations of the past to avoid responsibility for present actions. See *Reality Therapy: A New Approach to Psychiatry* (New York: Harper & Row, 1965).

4. Jean-Paul Sartre, *The Words* (New York: George Braziller, 1964).

5. This traditional approach is best represented by the work of Talcott Parsons. See, for example, *The Social System* (Glencoe, Ill.: Free Press, 1951), and Parsons and Edward Shils, *Toward a General Theory of Action* (Cambridge: Harvard University Press, 1951). An excellent discussion of some sociological and psychological attitudes about man and his existence can be found in Floyd Matson, *The Idea of Man* (New York: Delacorte Press, 1976), 181–210.

6. John Spiegel, *Transactions: The Interplay Between the Individual, Family, and Society.* Edited by John Papajohn. (New York: Science House, 1971), 1–84.

7. Ibid., 3–21.

8. Ibid., 42.

9. Ibid., 42–43.

10. Robert C. Ziller, "A Helical Theory of Personal Change," *Journal of Theory of Social Behavior* 1 (1973):33–73.

11. For a more comprehensive view of phenomenological thought, see Marvin Farber, *The Foundations of Phenomenology* (New York: Paine, Whitman, 1962), and Quentin Lauer, *Phenomenology: Its Genesis and Prospect* (New York: Harper & Row, 1958). A succinct discussion about the relationship of phenomenology and existentialism can be found in James R. Barclay, *Foundations of Counseling Strategy* (New York: John Wiley, 1971), 315–18.

12. F. A. Hayek, "The Primacy of the Abstract," in *Beyond Reductionism,* edited by Arthur Koestler and J. R. Smythies (Boston: Beacon Press, 1969), 309–33.

445

13. Anatol Rapoport, *Operational Philosophy: Integrating Knowledge and Action* (San Francisco: International Society for General Semantics, 1969), 54–56.

14. Philip Roth, *Reading Myself and Others* (New York: Farrar, Straus and Giroux, 1975), 96–97.

15. Anais Nin, *The Novel of the Future* (New York: Collier, 1968), 11.

16. An elaboration of Maurice Friedman's concept of the image of man can be found in his following books: *Problematic Rebel: An Image of Modern Man* (New York: Random House, 1963), and *To Deny Our Nothingness: Contemporary Images of Modern Man* (New York: Delta, 1968).

17. Maurice Friedman, *The Hidden Human Image* (New York: Delacorte Press, 1974), 19–27.

18. William McDougall, "The Hormic Psychology," in *Theories of Motivation in Personality and Social Psychology*, edited by Richard Teveen and Robert Birney (New York: Van Nostrand, 1964), 54–58.

19. Barclay, *Foundations*, 68–69.

20. Ernest Becker, *Angel in Armor* (New York: Free Press, 1969), 138.

21. Rapoport, *Operational*, 66–68.

22. Ibid., 70–72.

23. Ervin Laszlo, *The Systems View of the World* (New York: George Braziller, 1972), 58.

24. K. W. Wild, *Intuition* (Cambridge: The University Press, 1938), 184–85.

25. Within the field of psychotherapy there have been some recent attempts to integrate the two polar positions. See William D. Hitt, "Two Models of Man," *American Psychologist* 24 (1969):651–58; Judd Marmor, "Dynamic Psychotherapy and Behavior Therapy: Are They Irreconcilable?" in *Annual Review of Behavior Theory and Practice*, edited by Cyril M. Franks and G. T. Wilson (New York: Brunner/Mazel, 1973), 57–71; and Dennis Saleeby, "A Proposal to Merge Humanist and Behaviorist Perspectives," *Social Casework* 58 (1975):468–79.

26. H. J. Eysenck and H. R. Beech, "Counterconditioning and Related Methods," in *Handbook of Psychotherapy and Behavior Change*, edited by Allen Bergin and Sol Garfield (New York: John Wiley, 1971), 543–611.

27. Hugh Urban and Donald H. Ford, "Behavior Therapy," in *Treating Mental Illness*, edited by Alfred M. Freedman and Harold I. Kaplan (New York: Atheneum, 1972), 146–61.

28. Robert L. Stewart and Maurice Levine, "Individual Psychoanalysis and Psychoanalytic Therapy, in *Treating Mental Illness*, edited by Alfred M. Freedman and Harold I. Kaplan (New York: Atheneum, 1972), 69–120.

29. Ernest Becker, *The Revolution in Psychiatry* (New York: Free Press, 1964), 9–10. A more recent critique of the reasons for medicine's assumption of responsibility for treatment of the mind can be found in E. Fuller Torrey, *The Death of Psychiatry* (New York: Chilton, 1974).

30. Abraham Kaplan, *The New World of Philosophy* (New York: Vintage Books, 1961), 22–23.

31. John M. Lincourt and C. Olczak, "C. S. Peirce and H. S. Sullivan on the Human Self," *Psychiatry* 37 (1974):78–87.

32. William James, "The Self," in *The Self in Social Interaction*, vol. 1, edited by Chad Gordon and Kenneth Gergen (New York: John Wiley, 1968), 41–49.

33. John Dewey, *Human Nature and Conduct* (New York: Modern Library, 1930).

34. Lincourt and Olczak, "Peirce and Sullivan," 78–87.

35. Harry Stack Sullivan, *The Interpersonal Theory of Psychiatry* (New York: W. W. Norton, 1953), 165.

36. McDougall, "Hormic Psychology," 10–59.

37. Heinz Ansbacher and R. R. Ansbacher, eds., *The Individual Psychology of Alfred Adler* (New York: Harper & Row, 1956), 92.

38. Arthur W. Combs and Donald Snygg, *Individual Behavior: A Perceptual Approach to Behavior*, rev. ed. (New York: Harper, 1959).

39. Victor E. Frankl, "Reductionism and Nihilism," in *Beyond Reductionism*, edited by Arthur Koestler and J. R. Smythies (Boston: Beacon Press, 1969), 396–416.

40. Abraham H. Maslow, ed., *New Knowledge in Human Values* (New York: Harper, 1959), 126.

41. Albert Mehrabian, *An Analysis of Personality Theories* (Englewood Cliffs, N.J.: Prentice-Hall, 1968), 121–52.

42. Victor Raimy, *Misunderstandings of Self* (San Francisco: Jossey-Bass, 1975), 7–26.

43. Seymour Krim, "The Insanity Bit," in *The Inner World of Mental Illness*, edited by Bert Kaplan (New York: Harper & Row, 1964), 62–79.

44. Howard Goldstein and Linda L. Goldstein, "The Concept of Deviancy Revisited," *Canada's Mental Health* 23 (1975):10–14.

45. Dewey, *Human Nature*, 103.

CHAPTER TWO

1. Walter L. Wallace, *The Logic of Science in Sociology* (New York: Aldine-Atherton, 1971), 89–100.

2. Joseph F. Rychlak, *The Psychology of Rigorous Humanism* (New York: Wiley Interscience, 1977), 508.

3. See, for example, the provocative essay, "In the Beginning: God and Science," *Time*, Feb. 5, 1979, 149–50.

4. Rychlak, *Psychology*, 168.

5. Henri Bergson, *Creative Evolution* (New York: Modern Library, 1944), 360.

6. A definition of social systems relative to its application to practice with social problems can be found in Howard Goldstein, *Social Work Practice: A Unitary Approach* (Columbia: University of South Carolina Press, 1973), 105–19. Comprehensive theoretical orientations to systems include Ludwig von Bertalanffy, *General Systems Theory* (New York: George Braziller, 1968), and Walter Buckley, *Sociology and Modern Systems Theory* (Englewood Cliffs, N.J.: Prentice-Hall, 1967).

7. Howard Goldstein, "Some Critical Observations on the Relevance of Social Systems Theory for Social Work Practice," *Canadian Journal of Social Work Education* 1 (1975):13–23.

8. Maurice Friedman, *Problematic Rebel: Melville, Dostoievsky, Kafka, Camus,* 2nd ed. (Chicago: University of Chicago Press/Phoenix Books, 1970), 470–72.

9. Michael Wertheimer, "Humanistic Psychology and the Humane but Tough-Minded Psychologist," *American Psychologist* 33 (1978):739–45.

10. For a critical discussion on the limitations of theory relative to practice, see Robert R. Carkhuff and Bernard G. Berenson, *Beyond Counseling and Therapy* (New York: Holt, Rinehart & Winston, 1967), 61–130.

11. Anatol Rapoport, *Operational Philosophy: Integrating Knowledge and Action* (San Francisco: International Society for General Semantics, 1969), 22.

CHAPTER THREE

1. Paul Tibbetts, ed., *Perception: Selected Readings in Science and Phenomenology* (Chicago: Quadrangle Books, 1969), 60.

2. *Time*, Sept. 20, 1976, 60.

3. Neil Gilbert and Harry Specht, "Advocacy and Professional Ethics," *Social Work* 21 (1976):288–93.

4. Chad Gordon and Kenneth Gergen, eds., *The Self in Social Interaction*, vol. 1 (New York: John Wiley, 1968), 2–7.

5. Gordon W. Allport, *Becoming* (New Haven: Yale University Press, 1955), 35–56.

6. Ibid.

7. Ibid.

8. Ibid.

9. Robert E. Ornstein, *The Psychology of Consciousness* (New York: Viking Press, 1972), 210–13.

10. Erving Goffman, *Asylums: Essays on the Social Situation of Mental Patients and Other Inmates* (New York: Doubleday, 1961).

11. Tom Wicker, *Facing the Lions* (New York: Viking Press, 1973), 152.

12. It would be legitimate to refer to the person as a system providing all factors contributing to a systemic state are taken into account. In addition to the psychological and social, these would include neurological, chemical, glandular, cellular, and other physiological and anatomic subsystems.

13. Walter Buckley, *Sociology and Modern Systems Theory* (Englewood Cliffs, N.J.: Prentice-Hall, 1967).

14. An informative perspective on the historical self is expressed in Chad Gordon, "Self Conceptions: Configurations of Content," in *The Self in Social Interaction*, vol. 1, edited by Chad Gordon and Kenneth Gergen (New York: John Wiley, 1968), 115–36. For research findings on how people reconstruct conceptions of an historical self, see Mark Snyder and Seymour Uranowitz, "Reconstructing the Past: Some Cognitive Consequences of Person Perception," *Journal of Personality and Social Psychology* 36 (1978):941–50.

15. F. Scott Fitzgerald and Zelda Fitzgerald, "Show Mr. and Mrs. F to No.—," in *The Crack Up* (New York: New Directions, 1945), 41–55.

16. Kurt Lewin's development of the theory of the social field can be found in his following works: *A Dynamic Theory of Personality* (New York: McGraw-Hill, 1935); 'Field Theory and Learning," in *41st Yearbook of National Society for the Study of Education* (Bloomington, Ill.: Public School Press, 1942); and *Principles of Topological Psychology* (New York: McGraw-Hill, 1936).

17. Erich Fromm, *The Art of Loving* (New York: Harper & Row, 1956), 20.

18. Katherine Mansfield, *The Journal of Katherine Mansfield*, edited by J. Middleton Murry (New York: A. A. Knopf, 1928), 174–75.

19. The process of "conscientization" is central to the following books by Paulo Freire: *Pedagogy of the Oppressed* (New York: Herder and Herder, 1968); and *Education for Critical Consciousness* (New York: Seabury Press, 1973). See also Rosa P. Resnick, "Conscientization: An Indigenous Approach to International Social Work," *International Social Work Journal* 19 (1976):21–29.

20. Gordon, "Self Conceptions," 115–36.

21. Karl Marx, "On Alienated Labor," in *Marx's Concept of Man*, edited by Erich Fromm (New York: Frederick Ungar, 1961), 95–106.

22. Karen Horney, *Neurosis and Human Growth: The Struggle Toward Self Realization* (New York: W. W. Norton, 1950), 155–67.

23. R. D. Laing, *The Divided Self* (New York: Pantheon Books, 1960), 40–56.

24. Robert Pirsig, *Zen and the Art of Motorcycle Maintenance: An Inquiry into Values* (New York: Morrow, 1974), p. 374.

25. Maurice Friedman, *The Hidden Human Image* (New York: Delacorte Press, 1974), 18.

26. See: Mary C. Jones, et al., eds., *The Course of Human Development: Selected Papers from the Longitudinal Studies*, Institute of Human Development, University of California, Berkeley (Waltham, Mass.: Xerox College Publishers, 1971); Henry S. Maas and J. A. Kuypers, *From Thirty to Seventy* (San Francisco: Jossey-Bass, 1974); Gail Sheehy, *Passages* (New York: E. P. Dutton, 1976); G. E. Vaillant, "Natural History of Male Psychological Health," *Archives of General Psychiatry* 31 (1974):15–22; and, Daniel J. Levinson, *The Seasons of a Man's Life* (New York: A. A. Knopf, 1978).

27. James F. T. Bugental, *The Search for Authenticity: An Existential-Analytic Approach to Psychotherapy* (New York: Holt, Rinehart & Winston, 1965), 287–88. For other existential approaches see also Rollo May, E. Angel, and Henri Ellenberger, eds., *Existence: A New Dimension in Psychiatry and Psychology* (New York: Basic Books, 1958); Eugene Minkowski, *Lived Time: Phenomenological and Psychopathological Studies* (Evanston, Ill.: Northwestern University Press, 1970); Medard Boss, *Psychoanalysis and Daseinsanalysis* (New York: Basic Books, 1963); H. F. Thomas, "The Existential Attitude in Working with Individuals and Groups," in *The Challenges of Humanistic Psychology*, edited by James F. T. Bugental (New York: McGraw-Hill, 1967); and, Donald F. Krill, *Existential Social Work* (New York: Free Press, 1978).

CHAPTER FOUR

1. Carolyn W. Sherif and Muzafer Sherif, *Attitude, Ego-Involvement and Change* (New York: John Wiley, 1967), 458–67.

2. Floyd H. Allport, *Theories of Perception and the Concept of Structure* (New York: John Wiley, 1955).

3. For a discussion on recent advances in the study of the physiology of perception, see Sir Russell Brain, "Some Reflections on Brain and Mind," in *Perception*, edited by Paul Tibbetts (Chicago: Quadrangle Books, 1969), 19–48.

4. See: Allport, *Theories of Perception;* Jerome S. Bruner, "On Perceptual Readiness," *Psychological Review* 64 (1957):123–152; Mark Cook, *Interpersonal Perception* (Middlesex, Eng.; Penguin, 1971); Robert L. Fantz, "The Origin of Form Perception," *Scientific American*, May, 1961, 66–72; and Herschel W. Leibowitz, ed., *Visual Perception* (New York: Macmillan, 1965).

5. See: D. French, "Relationship of Anthropology to Studies in Perception and Cognition," in *Psychology: A Study of a Science*, vol. 6, edited by Sigmund Koch (New York: McGraw-Hill, 1963), 388–428; M. H. Segall, Donald T. Campbell, and Melville J. Herskovits, *The Influence of Culture on Visual Perception* (Indianapolis: Bobbs-Merrill, 1966); and Claude Lévi-Strauss, *The Savage Mind* (Chicago: University of Chicago Press, 1967).

6. See: Maurice Merleau-Ponty, *The Structure of Behavior* (Boston: Beacon Press, 1963); T. W. Wann, ed., *Behaviorism and Phenomenology* (Chicago: University of Chicago Press, 1964); and William H. Werkmeister, "On Describing a World," *Philosophy and Phenomenological Research* 11 (1951):303–25.

7. Allport, *Theories of Perception*.

8. Gustav Ichheiser, *Appearances and Realities: Misunderstandings in Human Relations* (San Francisco: Jossey-Bass, 1970).

9. D. L. Rosenhan, "On Being Sane in Insane Places," *Science*, Jan. 19, 1973, 250–58.

10. John Spiegel, *Transactions; the Interplay Between the Individual, Family and Society*, edited by John Papajohn. (New York: Science House, 1971), 20.

11. Ralph Garry and Howard Kingsley, *The Nature and Conditions of Learning* (Englewood Cliffs, N.J.: Prentice-Hall, 1970), 370–99.

12. Julian Jaynes, *The Origins of Consciousness in the Breakdown of the Bicameral Mind* (Boston: Houghton Mifflin, 1976), 64.

13. For a more extensive discussion of the concept "threshold," see Conrad G. Mueller, *Sensory Psychology* (Englewood Cliffs, N.J.: Prentice-Hall, 1965), 5–6.

14. Jerome S. Bruner, *Toward a Theory of Instruction* (New York: W. W. Norton, 1966), 9–12.

15. Carl G. Jung, *Collected Works* (New York: Pantheon Books, 1953).

16. Ernest L. Rossi, *Dreams and the Growth of Personality* (New York: Pergamon Press, 1972), 152.

17. Jaynes, *The Origins*, 46.

18. Gordon R. Taylor, *The Natural History of the Mind* (New York: E. P. Dutton, 1979), 179–84.

19. Virginia Woolf, *A Room of One's Own* (New York: Harcourt, Brace & World, 1929), 100–101.

20. Alan Watts, *Nature, Man and Woman* (New York: Vintage Books, 1970), 181.

21. Albert Bandura, *Social Learning Theory* (New York: General Learning Press, 1971).

22. Rossi, *Dreams*, 188–89.

23. Charles B. Truax and Kevin M. Mitchell, "Research on Certain Therapist Interpersonal Skills in Relation to Process and Outcome," in *Handbook of Psychotherapy and Behavior Change*, edited by Allen Bergin and Sol Garfield (New York: John Wiley, 1971), 299–344.

24. Irving Howe, *World of Our Fathers* (New York: Harcourt Brace Jovanovich, 1976), 322–23.

25. For a more specific discussion of Jung's concept of "psyche," see Jung, *Collected Works;* Henri F. Ellenberger, *The Discovery of the Unconscious* (New York: Basic Books, 1970), 703–19; and Edward C. Whitmont, "Carl Jung," in *Interpreting Personality*, edited by Alfred M. Freeman and Harold I. Kaplan (New York: Atheneum, 1972), 131–43.

26. A comparison of Lockean and Kantian models and an analysis of their impact on modern psychology can be found in Joseph F. Rychlak, *The Psychology of Rigorous Humanism* (New York: Wiley Interscience, 1977), 86–95.

27. Abraham Kaplan, *The New World of Philosophy* (New York: Vintage Books, 1961), 305.

28. C. M. Owens, "Zen Buddhism," in *Transpersonal Psychologies*, edited by Charles T. Tart (New York: Harper & Row, 1975), 155–202.

29. Watts, *Nature*, 76–77. For further study of the meanings and implications of Zen, see Philip Kapleau, ed., *Three Pillars of Zen: Teaching, Practice and Enlightenment* (New

York: Harper & Row, 1967); D. T. Suzuki, *Zen Buddhism* (New York: Grove Press, 1960); and two other books by Watts, *The Way of Zen* (New York: Pantheon Books, 1957), and *Psychotherapy East and West* (New York: Ballantine, 1961).

30. Robert E. Ornstein, *The Psychology of Consciousness* (New York: Viking Press, 1972), 196–204.

31. Michael S. Gazzaniga, "The Split Brain in Man," in *Nature of Human Consciousness,* edited by Robert E. Ornstein (San Francisco: Freeman, 1973), 87–100. A related article in same text is Joseph E. Bogen, "The Other Side of the Brain: An Appositional Mind," 101–25.

32. Arthur J. Deikman, "Bimodal Consciousness," in Ornstein, *Nature of Human Consciousness,* 67–86.

33. Ibid.

CHAPTER FIVE

1. J. P. Guilford, *The Nature of Human Intelligence* (New York: McGraw-Hill, 1967), 253–54.

2. Ibid., 359–60.

3. Kurt Lewin, *Principles of Topological Psychology* (New York: McGraw-Hill, 1936).

4. James R. Barclay, *Foundations of Counseling Strategy* (New York: John Wiley, 1971), 43–44.

5. Salvador Minuchin et al., *Families of the Slums* (New York: Basic Books, 1967), 4–5.

6. Basil Bernstein, "Language and Social Class," *British Journal of Sociology* 11 (1960):271–76. For additional discussion of this issue, see Martin Deutsch, "The Role of Social Class in Language Development and Cognition," *American Journal of Orthopsychiatry* 35 (1965):78–88.

7. For some examples of the rich literature on deviance theory, see Howard S. Becker, ed., *The Other Side* (New York: Free Press, 1964); Albert K. Cohen, *Deviance and Control* (Englewood Cliffs, N.J.: Prentice-Hall, 1966); Howard Goldstein and Linda Goldstein, "The Concept of Deviancy Revisited," *Canada's Mental Health* 23 (1975):10–14; and Alexander Liazos, "The Poverty of the Sociology of Deviance: Nuts, Sluts and Preverts," *Social Problems* 20 (1972):103–20.

8. Geoffrey Pearson, *The Deviant Imagination: Psychiatry, Social Work, and Social Change* (London: Macmillan, 1975), 127–28.

9. Erwin W. Straus, "The Expression of Thinking," in *Perception,* edited by Paul Tibbetts (Chicago: Quadrangle Books, 1969), 261–78.

10. Similar definitions of thought and cognition can be found in D. E. Berlyne, *Structure and Direction of Thinking* (New York: John Wiley, 1965); John Dewey, *How We Think* (Boston: D. C. Heath, 1910); and Peter C. Wason and P. N. Johnson-Laird, eds., *Thinking and Reasoning* (New York: Peter Smith, 1968).

11. Gordon R. Taylor, *The Natural History of the Mind* (New York: E. P. Dutton, 1979), 266–68.

12. Guilford, *Human Intelligence,* 148.

13. Israel Scheffler, "Philosophical Models of Teaching," in *Problems and Issues in Contemporary Education,* edited by editors of *The Teaching Record* and *The Harvard Educational Review* (Chicago: Scott Foresman, 1966), 90–100.

14. Guilford, *Human Intelligence.*

15. E. P. Torrance, "Causes for Concern," in *Creativity,* edited by Philip E. Vernon (Baltimore: Penguin, 1970), 355–70.

16. Anthony Davis, "Psychodynamic and Sociocultural Factors Related to the Intolerance of Ambiguity," in *The Study of Lives*, edited by Robert W. White (New York: Atherton, Press, 1969), 161–77.

17. As reported in Floyd Matson, *The Idea of Man* (New York: Delacorte Press, 1976), xv.

18. Silvano Arieti, *Creativity: The Magic Synthesis* (New York: Basic Books, 1976), 12.

19. Joseph F. Rychlak, *The Psychology of Rigorous Humanism* (New York: Wiley Interscience, 1977), 294.

20. Benjamin De Mott, "Hot-Air Meeting," *Harpers*, July 1975, 71.

21. Jean-Paul Sartre, *Existentialism*, translated by B. Frechtman (New York: Philosophical Library, 1947), 44.

22. Albert Mehrabian, *An Analysis of Personality Theories* (Englewood Cliffs, N.J.: Prentice-Hall, 1968).

23. See Gordon W. Allport's essay "Perception, Proception, and Public Health," in his book *Personality and the Social Encounter* (Boston: Beacon Press, 1960), 295–310. In his discussion of the evolvement of perception he uses the term "proception" as another way of explaining what is referred to here as "schema." Other Gestaltist approaches can be found in Arthur W. Combs and Donald Snygg, *Individual Behavior: A Perceptual Approach to Behavior*, rev. ed. (New York: Harper, 1959); Ernest R. Hilgard, "The Place of Gestalt Psychology and Field Theories in Contemporary Learning Theory," in *Theories of Learning and Instruction*, Chapter 3, The 63rd Yearbook of the National Society of Education, Part I (Chicago: University of Chicago Press, 1964); and George A. Kelly, *A Theory of Personality* (New York: W. W. Norton, 1963).

CHAPTER SIX

1. Salvatore Maddi, *Personality Theories* (Homewood, Ill.: Dorsey Press, 1976).

2. This issue of duality or the question of the subjective and objective nature of things has generated philosophical debate over the centuries between two opposing schools of thought. The Idealist point of view (expressed by Berkeley in the 18th century) states that physical objects cannot be conceived as existing independently of someone's perception. When we talk about physical things we are referring to sensory experiences that cannot be justified or defended. The Realists, on the other hand, insist that physical objects exist independently of experience and possess intrinsic qualities.

3. Arthur Koestler, *Janus: A Summing Up* (New York: Random House, 1978), 19.

4. Ibid., 303.

5. Henri Bergson, *Creative Evolution* (New York: Modern Library, 1944), 36.

6. Leon Festinger, *A Theory of Cognitive Dissonance* (Evanston, Ill.: Row, Peterson, 1957).

7. The paradox of competition and conformity is described by Charles Reich in his controversial book, *The Greening of America* (London: Allen Lane, Penguin, 1971). Referring to the contradictory pulls of society, Reich's concept of Consciousness I represents the pioneer spirit, the merits of industriousness, righteousness, competitiveness, and acquisitiveness. These values lead to war, suffering, rejection, loneliness, and injustice. Consciousness II supports the idea of the corporate man, advocates conformity to established values, efficiency, control, and bureaucracy. These values result in the liberal-democratic ethic of welfare-ism, which outwardly opposes suffering but covertly supports the system that makes suffering inevitable.

8. Walter Kaufmann, *Without Guilt and Justice* (New York: Delta, 1973).

9. Paul Watzlawick et al., *Pragmatics of Human Communication* (New York: W. W. Norton, 1967). See also Ernest G. Beier, *The Silent Language of Psychotherapy* (Chicago: Aldine, 1966).

10. Elizabeth Carter and Monica Orfanidis, "Family Therapy with One Person and the Therapist's Own Family," in *Family Therapy: Theory and Practice,* edited by Philip J. Guerin (New York: Gardner Press, 1976), 193–219.

11. Quotation taken from Salvatore Maddi's article, "The Existential Neurosis," *Journal of Abnormal Psychology* 72 (1967):311–25.

12. Vernon W. Grant, *Great Abnormals* (New York: Hawthorne, 1968), 52–53.

13. Lara Jefferson, "I am Crazy Wild This Minute. How Can I Learn to Think Straight?" In *The Inner World of Mental Illness,* edited by Bert Kaplan (New York: Harper & Row, 1964), 3–42.

14. Bernard Malamud, *The Tenants* (New York: Farrar, Straus and Giroux, 1971), 182–84.

15. David Riesman et al., *The Lonely Crowd* (New Haven: Yale University Press, 1950).

16. David Riesman, "On Autonomy," in *The Self in Social Interaction,* edited by Chad Gordon and Kenneth Gergen (New York: John Wiley, 1968), 445–61.

17. George Konrad, *The Case Worker* (New York: Harcourt Brace Jovanovich, 1974), 12–13.

18. Ibid., 13–14.

19. William C. Rhodes, *Behavioral Threat and Community Response* (New York: Behavioral Publications, 1972), 47–61.

20. Max Siporin, "Deviant Behavior Theory," *Social Work* 10 (1965):59–67.

21. Contrasting with this tendency to arrange people into neat and sterile categories are some books that document people's words about the actual nature of their lives. The dreams, ambitions, and ideas about survival of the poor, specifically, may not fit into the conventional mold. Yet, pride and dignity are no less a part of their reality. A recent book of this type is Robert Coles and Jane H. Coles, *Women of Crisis: Lives of Struggle and Hope* (New York: Delacorte Press, 1978), in which a migrant, a mountain woman, a Mexican-American, an Eskimo, and a White House maid disclose their inner thoughts and experiences. See also: James Agee and Walker Evans, *Let Us Now Praise Famous Men* (Boston: Houghton Mifflin, 1939), an account of the daily lives of sharecroppers; and Oscar Lewis, *Five Families* (New York: Basic Books, 1959), and *The Children of Sanchez* (New York: Random House, 1961), both studies of poor Mexican families.

22. William S. Sahakian, *Psychopathology Today* (Itasca, Ill.: F. E. Peacock, 1970), 473–74.

23. *The Cleveland Plain Dealer,* Oct. 25, 1978.

24. Steven P. Segal and Uri Aviram, *The Mentally Ill in Community-Based Sheltered Care* (New York: John Wiley, 1978).

25. Sheldon J. Korchin, *Modern Clinical Psychology* (New York: Basic Books, 1976), 104.

26. Robert E. Ornstein, *The Mind Field* (New York: Grossman, 1976), 39–54.

27. Ibid., 49.

28. Paul Watzlawick et al., *Change: Principles of Problem Formulation and Problem Resolution* (New York: W. W. Norton, 1974), 48.

29. Ibid., 56.

30. Ibid., 48.

31. See Roy Bailey and Mike Brake, eds., *Radical Social Work* (London: Arnold, 1975);

Jeffrey Galper, *Radical Social Work: Theory and Practice* (New York: MSS Modular Publications, 1970); N. Goroff, "Social Welfare as Coercive Social Control," *Sociology and Social Welfare* 2 (1974):19–26; and Willard Richan and Allan Mendelsohn, *Social Work: The Unloved Profession* (New York: New Viewpoints, 1973).

32. Seymour Halleck, *The Politics of Therapy* (New York: Science House, 1971), 243.

33. Perry London, *Behavior Control* (New York: Harper & Row, 1969), 48–51.

34. Michael A. Weinstein, *The Tragic Sense of Political Life* (Columbia: University of South Carolina Press, 1977), 123–26.

35. Some relevant books dealing with these issues include: Nicholas N. Kittrie, *The Right to Be Different* (Baltimore: Johns Hopkins Press, 1971); London, *Behavior Control*; and Thomas S. Szasz, *Law, Liberty and Psychiatry* (New York: Macmillan, 1963).

CHAPTER SEVEN

1. Perry London, *Behavior Control* (New York: Harper & Row, 1969), 50–51.

2. Hans H. Strupp, *Psychotherapy: Clinical, Research and Theoretical Issues* (New York: Jason Aronson, 1973), 94.

3. Jerome D. Frank, *Psychotherapy and the Human Predicament* (New York: Schocken Books, 1978), 14–16.

4. William Bennett, Jr., and Merle C. Hokenstad, Jr., "Full Time People Workers and Conceptions of the Professional," *Sociological Review Monograph No. 20, Professionalism and Social Change*, University of Keele, Dec. 1973, 21–45.

5. A similar approach to these dimensions of learning and adaptation can be found in Robert C. Carson, *Interaction Concepts of Personality* (Chicago: Aldine, 1969), 85–86.

6. As quoted in John F. Travers, *Learning, Analysis and Application* (New York: McKay, 1965).

7. In Travers, *Learning.*

8. Ralph Garry and Howard Kingsley, *The Nature and Condition of Learning* (Englewood Cliffs, N. J.: Prentice-Hall, 1970), 3–4.

9. Jean Piaget and Barbel Inhelder, *The Psychology of the Child* (New York: Basic Books, 1969), 158.

10. Orville G. Brim, Jr., "Socialization Through the Life Cycle," in *The Self in Social Interaction*, vol. 1, edited by Chad Gordon and Kenneth Gergen (New York: John Wiley, 1968), 227–40.

11. Variations can be found in James F. Y. Bugental, *The Search for Authenticity: An Existential Approach to Psychotherapy* (New York: Holt, Rinehart & Winston, 1965); Victor E. Frankl, *Man's Search for Meaning* (New York: Simon and Schuster, 1962); Donald F. Krill, *Existential Social Work* (New York: Free Press, 1978); and Jean-Paul Sartre, *Existentialism*, translated by B. Frechtman (New York: Philosophical Library, 1947).

12. A major work formulating a theory of crisis situations is Gerald Caplan, *Principles of Preventive Psychiatry* (New York: Basic Books, 1964). See also: Allen R. Darbonne, "Crisis: A Review of Theory, Practice and Research," *International Journal of Psychiatry* 6 (1968):371–79 and J. R. Taplin, "Crisis Theory: Critique and Reformulation," *Community Mental Health* 7 (1971): 13–23.

13. Gerald Caplan, *An Approach to Community Mental Health* (New York: Grune & Stratton, 1961), 18.

14. Verta Taylor, "Good News About Disaster." *Psychology Today*, Oct., 1977, 93.

15. Robert Anderson, *I Never Sang for My Father* (New York: Random House, 1968), 113.

16. Martin Buber, *I and Thou* (New York: Charles Scribner's, 1958), 28–29.

17. *Time*, Dec. 5, 1977, p. 19.

18. Though it is the perceiver who grants meaning and significance to the event, he must contend with its intrinsic qualities or what is seen as the more or less universal meaning ascribed to the event by the majority group or culture. Chronic unemployment, for example, would have intrinsic significance in relation to the work ethic.

19. The concept of intelligence is open to many questions and more than one definition. Ideas about the nature of intelligence in this work are drawn from the theory of J. P. Guilford. In his article, "Intelligence Has Three Facets," (*Science* 160 1968: 615–20), he states that whatever we call intelligence is not unitary and it does not stay fixed for life. Given intellectual abilities do not have equal valence; any one individual may display greater or lesser competence in coping with one type of obstacle than with another. These intellectual abilities include memory and recall, evaluation and judgment, comprehending classes, relations, and transformations, and dealing with material on figural, semantic, symbolic, and behavioral levels.

20. Ernest Becker, *Escape from Evil* (New York: Free Press, 1975), 149.

CHAPTER EIGHT

1. The idea that learning comprises a series of specific stages and functions is borrowed from educational theorists who have derived their assumptions about complex human learning from systematic observations of people in actual learning situations rather than from a controlled and experimental environment. The theorists to whom I am most indebted are Robert Gagne, author of *Conditions of Learning* (New York: Holt, Rinehart & Winston, 1965), and Ralph Garry and Howard Kingsley, authors of *The Nature and Conditions of Learning* (Englewood Cliffs, N.J.: Prentice-Hall, 1970).

2. Sonia F. Osler, "Cognitive Studies in Disadvantaged Children," in *Cognitive Studies*, vol. 1, edited by Jerome Hellmuth (New York: Brunner/Mazel, 1970), 258–74.

3. Herbert Zimilies, "Conceptual Thinking in Young Children as a Function of Age and Social Class," in Hellmuth, *Cognitive Studies*, 230–57.

4. Salvador Minuchin et al., *Families of the Slums* (New York: Basic Books, 1967), 193–94.

5. Ibid., 194.

6. H. Myklebust and M. Brutten, "A Study of the Visual Perception of Deaf Children," *Acta Oto-Laryngol* (Stockholm, Suppl. No. 105, 1953).

7. Jane W. Kessler, "Contributions of the Mentally Retarded Toward a Theory of Cognitive Development," in Hellmuth, *Cognitive Studies*, 11–209.

8. Louis Gottschalk and Robert Davidson, "Sensitivity Groups, Encounter Groups, Training Groups, Marathon Groups and the Laboratory Movement," in *Sensitivity Through Encounter and Marathon: Modern Group Book IV*, edited by Harold H. Kaplan and Benjamin Sadock (New York: E. P. Dutton, 1972), 59–94.

9. See: Erving Goffman, *Asylums: Essays on the Social Situation of Mental Patients and Other Inmates* (New York: Doubleday, 1961); E. M. Gruenberg, "The Social Breakdown Syndrome—Some Origins," *American Journal of Psychiatry* 123 (1967):1481–89; Maxwell Jones, *Therapeutic Community* (New York: Basic Books, 1953), and *Social Psychiatry in the Community, in Hospitals and in Prisons* (Springfield, Ill.: Thomas, 1962); Fritz Redl, *Group Living in a Childrens Institution* (New York: Association Press, 1951); and John K. Wing and G. W. Brown, *Institutionalism and Schizophrenia: A Comparative Study of Three Mental Hospitals, 1960–68* (Cambridge: The University Press, 1970).

Notes for Chapter Nine

10. Ernest L. Rossi, *Dreams and the Growth of Personality* (New York: Pergamon Press, 1972), 14.

11. Albert Ellis, "Rational-Emotive Therapy," in *Operational Theories of Personality*, edited by Arthur Burton (New York: Brunner/Mazel, 1974), 318–44.

12. Annie Dillard, *Pilgrim at Tinkers Creek* (New York: Harper Magazine Publishing 1974).

13. Robert E. Ornstein, *The Mind Field* (New York: Grossman, 1976), 96.

CHAPTER NINE

1. Eric Partridge, *Origins: A Short Etymological Dictionary of Modern English* (New York: Macmillan, 1958).

2. Robert M. Gagne, *Conditions of Learning* (New York: Holt, Rinehart & Winston, 1965), 126–39.

3. Ralph Garry and Howard Kingsley, *The Nature and Conditions of Learning* (Englewood Cliffs, N.J.: Prentice-Hall, 1970), 428–56.

4. John Dewey, *How We Think* (Boston: D. C. Heath, 1910), 56.

5. Jerome Bruner, *Toward a Theory of Instruction* (New York: W. W. Norton, 1966), 40–41.

6. Arnold Goldstein et al., *Psychotherapy and the Psychology of Behavior Change* (New York: John Wiley, 1966), 213.

7. Joseph F. Rychlak, *The Psychology of Rigorous Humanism* (New York: Wiley Interscience, 1977), 55.

8. Ibid., 55–57.

9. Paul Watzlawick, *The Language of Change* (New York: Basic Books, 1978), 14–17.

10. Ibid., 23–24.

11. Ibid., 140–41.

12. Silvano Arieti, "The Role of Cognition in the Development of Inner Reality," in *Cognitive Studies*, vol. 1, edited by Jerome Hellmuth (New York: Brunner/Mazel, 1970), 91–110.

13. Jean Piaget and Barbel Inhelder, *The Psychology of the Child* (New York: Basic Books, 1969).

14. See: Benjamin Bloom, *Stability and Change in Human Characteristics* (New York: John Wiley, 1964); W. Dennis, "Causes of Retardation Among Institutional Children," *Journal of Genetic Psychology* 96 (1960):47–59; and Maya Pines, *Revolution in Learning: The Years from Birth to Six* (New York: Harper & Row, 1967).

15. Extract from a personal letter.

16. These presuppositions are also called "locus of control." See Herbert M. Lefcourt, *Locus of Control* (Hillsdale, N.J.: L. Erlbaum Associates, 1976), for amplification of the concept.

17. Hanna Levenson, "Multidimensional Locus of Control in Psychiatric Patients," *Journal of Consulting and Clinical Psychology* 41 (1973):397–404.

18. Julian B. Rotter, "Generalized Expectancies for Internal vs. External Control of Reinforcement," *Psychological Monographs* 80, 1, no. 609 (1966).

19. Rychlak, *Psychology*, 91.

20. B. Claude Mathis et al., *Psychological Foundations for Education* (New York: Academic Press, 1970), 195–96.

21. Joseph R. Newton and Audrey B. Bohnengel, "Psychoeducational Meetings with

Spouses of ESRD Patients," *Dialysis and Transplantation: Journal of Renal Technology* 7 (1978):32–37.

CHAPTER TEN

1. Paul Watzlawick, *The Language of Change* (New York: Basic Books, 1978), 141.

2. More extensive discussion of the concept of metacommunication can be found in Paul Watzlawick et al., *Pragmatics of Human Communication* (New York: W. W. Norton, 1967), 39.

3. Henri Bergson, *An Introduction to Metaphysics* (New York: Putnam, 1912).

4. Watzlawick, *Language*, 140.

5. In addition to literature cited, the following references on the role of communication in change deserve attention: Richard Bandler and John Grinder, *The Structure of Magic I: A Book about Language and Therapy* (Palo Alto: Science & Behavior Books, 1975), and *The Structure of Magic II: A Book about Communication and Change* (Palo Alto: Science & Behavior Books, 1976); Ernest G. Beier, *The Silent Language of Psychotherapy* (Chicago: Aldine, 1966); Peter Farb, *Word Play: What Happens When People Talk* (New York: A. A. Knopf, 1974); and Jurgen Ruesch, "General Theory of Communication," in *American Handbook of Psychiatry*, vol. 2, edited by Silvano Arieti (New York: Basic Books, 1959).

6. See: Arnold P. Goldstein, *Therapist-Patient Expectancies* (New York: Pergamon, 1962); Russell A. Jones, *Self-Fulfilling Prophecies* (Hillsdale, N.J.: L. Erlbaum Associates, 1977); Edward Murray and Leonard Jacobson, "The Nature of Learning in Traditional and Behavioral Psychotherapy," in *Handbook of Psychotherapy and Behavior Change*, edited by Allen Bergin and Sol Garfield (New York: John Wiley, 1971), 709–47; and Julian B. Rotter, *Social Learning and Clinical Psychology* (Englewood Cliffs, N.J.: Prentice-Hall, 1954).

7. Rotter, *Social Learning*, 102.

8. The ambiguity of the change relationship is deliberately exploited by the psychoanalytic method. It is intensified by the absence of face-to-face contact, the analyst's protracted silence, and the use of the couch to promote free association and the development of transference.

9. Michael Weinstein, *The Tragic Sense of Political Life* (Columbia: University of South Carolina Press, 1977), 114–15.

10. Walter Kaufmann, *Existentialism: Dostoevsky to Sartre* (New York: New American Library, 1975), 11.

11. Don D. Jackson and John H. Weakland, "Conjoint Family Therapy: Some Considerations on Theory, Technique and Results," in *Changing Families*, edited by Jay Haley (New York: Grune & Stratton, 1971), 13–35.

12. Murray Bowen, "The Use of Family Theory in Clinical Practice," in Haley, *Changing Families*, 159–92.

13. Ross Speck and Carolyn N. Attneave, *Family Networks: Retribalizing and Healing* (New York: Pantheon Books, 1973).

14. Thomas F. Fogarty, "Systems Concepts and the Dimensions of Self," in *Family Therapy: Theory and Practice*, edited by Philip Guerin (New York: Gardner Press, 1976), 144–53.

15. Jules Riskin and Elaine Faunce, "Family Interaction Scales," in *The Interactional View*, edited by Paul Watzlawick and John Weakland (New York: W. W. Norton, 1977), 101–27.

16. For further discussion of the double-bind concept, see Gregory Bateson et al.,

"Toward a Theory of Schizophrenia," *Behavioral Science* 1 (1956):251–64; Jackson and Weakland, "Conjoint Family Therapy"; Watzlawick, *Pragmatics;* and Paul Watzlawick, "A Review of the Double Bind Theory," *Family Process* 2 (1963):132–53.

17. The concept of an institutional theme is, of course, only one of many approaches to the understanding of institutional life. See: Peter M. Blau and W. Richard Scott, *Formal Organizations: A Comparative Approach* (San Francisco: Chandler, 1962); Peter F. Drucker, "Managing the Public Service Institution," *Public Interest* 33 (1973):43–60; Amitai Etzioni, *Modern Organizations* (Englewood Cliffs, N.J.: Prentice-Hall, 1964); Thomas Holland, "Organizational Structure and Institutional Care," *Journal of Health and Social Behavior* 14 (1973):241–51; and James D. Thompson, *Organizations in Action* (New York: McGraw-Hill, 1967).

18. See: *O'Connor* v. *Donaldson*, 95 Supreme Court 2846 (1975); "The First Landmark: Mental Patients' Rights, *Civil Liberties* 289 (Sept. 1972); and R. K. Schwitzgebel, "The Right to Effective Treatment," *California Law Review* 63 (1974):936–56.

CHAPTER ELEVEN

1. Abraham. H. Maslow, *Toward a Psychology of Being* (Princeton, N.J.: Van Nostrand, 1962).

2. Salvador Minuchin and Braulio Montalvo, "Techniques for Working with Disorganized and Low Socioeconomic Families," in *Changing Families*, edited by Jay Haley (New York: Grune & Stratton, 1971), 202–211.

3. Salvador Minuchin, "Conflict Resolution Family Therapy," in Haley, *Changing Families*, 146–58.

4. Gerald H. Zuk, "Family Therapy," in Haley, *Changing Families*, 212–26.

5. Don D. Jackson and John H. Weakland, "Conjoint Family Therapy: Some Considerations on Theory, Technique and Results," in Haley, *Changing Families*, 13–35.

6. Peggy Papp, "Brief Therapy with Couples in Groups," in *Family Therapy: Theory and Practice*, edited by Philip Guerin (New York: Gardner, 1976), 350–63.

7. For further analysis of this categorical dilemma, see Howard Goldstein, "Generalist Social Work Practice," in the forthcoming work, *Handbook of Social Work Programs and Methods*, edited by Neil Gilbert and Harry Specht (Englewood Cliffs, N.J.: Prentice-Hall).

8. See: Carel B. Germain, ed., *Social Work Practice: People and Environments* (New York: Columbia University Press, 1979), and Carel B. Germain and Alex Gitterman, *The Life Model of Social Work Practice* (New York: Columbia University Press, 1979).

9. Hans H. Strupp, *Psychotherapy: Clinical, Research and Theoretical Issues* (New York: Jason Aronson, 1973), 39.

10. Sidney M. Jourard, *Disclosing Man to Himself* (New York: Van Nostrand, 1968), 165.

11. Irvin Yalom and Ginny Elkins, *Every Day Gets a Little Closer* (New York: Basic Books, 1974), 14.

12. Ibid., 218.

13. Victor Raimy, *Misunderstandings of Self* (San Francisco: Jossey-Bass, 1975), 7.

14. Ibid., 42–60.

15. Paul Watzlawick et al., *Change: Principles of Problem Formulation and Problem Resolution* (New York: W. W. Norton, 1974), 10.

16. Ibid., 10–11.

17. Abraham Kaplan, *The New World of Philosophy* (New York: Vintage Books, 1961), 308–309,

18. James F. T. Bugental, *The Search for Authenticity: An Existential-Analytic Approach to Psychotherapy* (New York: Holt, Rinehart & Winston, 1965), 287–88.

19. Ibid., 290.

20. Linda L. Lehmann, *Household Accounts* (forthcoming).

21. Tristine Rainer, *The New Diary* (Los Angeles: Tarcher, 1978), 287–88. See also Susan C. Nichols, "The Personal Journal: A Mental Health Proposal," (Ph.D. diss., 1973).

22. Watzlawick et al., *Change*, 114.

23. Appreciation is extended to Richard Kushner, M.S.W., of the Center for Human Services, Cleveland, Ohio, for this report of his work.

24. Victor E. Frankl, *The Unheard Cry for Meaning* (New York: Simon and Schuster, 1978), 150–51.

25. Ibid., 154–55.

26. Jay Haley, *Problem-Solving Therapy* (San Francisco: Jossey-Bass, 1977), 49–50.

CHAPTER TWELVE

1. Robert M. Gagne, *Conditions of Learning* (New York: Holt, Rinehart & Winston, 1965), 142–56.

2. Milton Rokeach, *The Nature of Human Values* (New York: Free Press, 1973), 5.

3. For additional study of values, see Franz Adler, "The Value Concept in Sociology," *American Journal of Sociology* 62 (1956):272–73; Charlotte Buhler, *Values in Psychotherapy* (Glencoe; Free Press, 1962); John Dewey, "The Meaning of Value," *Journal of Philosophy* 22 (Jan.–Dec. 1925); Charles Frankel, "Social Values and Professional Values," *Journal of Education for Social Work* 5 (1969):29–35; Abraham H. Maslow, ed., *New Knowledge in Human Values* (New York: Harper, 1959); Charles Morris, *Varieties of Human Values* (Chicago: University of Chicago Press, 1956); Walter D. Nunokawa, ed., *Human Values and Abnormal Behavior* (Chicago: Scott Foresman, 1965); Raymond Plant, *Social and Moral Theory in Casework* (London: Routledge and Kegan Paul, 1970); and William H. Werkmeister, *Man and His Values* (Lincoln: University of Nebraska Press, 1967).

4. D. Kinley Sturkie III, "Value Systems and Social Work: The Implications of Axiological Theory for Social Work" (Master's thesis, University of South Carolina, 1973).

5. Israel Scheffler, "Philosophical Models of Teaching," in *Problems and Issues in Contemporary Education*, edited by the editors of *The Teaching Record* and *The Harvard Educational Review* (Chicago: Scott Foresman, 1966), 90–100.

6. Peter M. Blau in *Exchange and Power in Social Life* (New York: John Wiley, 1964) refers to the "power-dependence" relationship that arises from the transactions between persons when one has the competence, the commodities, or the services that the other needs. The person needing assistance finds himself in an unequal relationship where there is little he can do to reciprocate and to restore the state of equality that characterizes most other social relationships. If he does not depart or deny his needs, he would therefore have to grant the helper or provider with a degree of authority or power.

7. John W. Thibaut and Harold H. Kelly, *The Social Psychology of Groups* (New York: John Wiley, 1959).

8. Robert R. Carkhuff and Bernard G. Berenson, *Beyond Counseling and Therapy* (New York: Holt, Rinehart & Winston, 1967), 198.

9. Benjamin Bloom and L. Broder, "Problem-Solving Processes of College Students," *Supplementary Educational Monographs*, no. 73 (Chicago: University of Chicago Press, 1950), 1–31.

10. Thomas J. Banta, "Tests for the Evaluation of Early Childhood Education: The

Cincinnati Autonomy Test Battery (CATB)," in *Cognitive Studies*, vol. 1, edited by Jerome Hellmuth (New York: Brunner/Mazel, 1970), 424–90.

11. John Dewey, *Experience and Nature* (New York: Grove Press, 1929).

12. James R. Barclay, *Foundations of Counseling Strategy* (New York: John Wiley, 1971), 366.

13. Ibid., 367.

14. Hugh Urban and Donald H. Ford, "Some Historical and Conceptual Perspectives on Psychotherapy and Behavior Change," in *Handbook of Psychotherapy and Behavior Change*, edited by Allen Bergin and Sol Garfield (New York: John Wiley, 1971), 3–35.

15. Ralph Garry and Howard Kingsley, *The Nature and Conditions of Learning* (Englewood Cliffs, N.J.: Prentice-Hall, 1970), 463–73.

16. Karl Garrison et al., *Educational Psychology*, 2nd ed. (New York: Appleton-Century-Crofts, 1964).

17. Howard Goldstein, *Social Work Practice: A Unitary Approach* (Columbia: University of South Carolina Press, 1973), 174.

18. Alexander F. Osborne, *Applied Imagination* (New York: Scribners, 1953).

19. Jerome S. Bruner, *The Process of Education* (New York: Vintage Books, 1960), 57–65.

20. Ira Progoff, *Jung, Synchronicity and Human Destiny* (New York: Dell, 1973), 22–23. Jung's definition of synchronicity originally appeared in his foreword for *I Ching*, translated by R. Wilhelm and C. Baynes, Bollingen Series XIX (Princeton: Princeton University Press, 1950, 1969).

21. Arthur Koestler, *The Act of Creation* (New York: Dell, 1964), 35.

22. Ibid., 45.

23. Michael J. Mahoney and Diane Arnkoff, "Cognitive and Self-Control Therapies," in *Handbook of Psychotherapy and Behavior Change*, 2nd ed., edited by Sol L. Garfield and Allen E. Bergin (New York: John Wiley, 1978), 689–722.

CHAPTER THIRTEEN

1. Lewis R. Wolberg, *The Technique of Psychotherapy* (New York: Grune & Stratton, 1954), 275.

2. Stanley Witkin, "Cognitive Processes and the Intuitive Practitioner: Implications for Practice," Paper read at the Sixth National Association of Social Workers Symposium, November 17, 1979, at San Antonio. Mimeographed.

3. Ernest R. Hilgard, "Human Motives and the Concept of Self," *American Psychologist* 4 (1949):374–82.

4. Gordon W. Allport, *Pattern and Growth in Personality* (New York: Holt, Rinehart & Winston, 1961), 19.

5. Edward L. Deci, *Intrinsic Motivation* (New York: Plenum, 1975), 5–13.

6. Harry Harlow, "Motivation as a Factor in the Acquisition of New Responses," in *Current Theory and Research in Motivation*, edited by J. Brown (Lincoln: University of Nebraska Press, 1953).

7. Deci, *Intrinsic Motivation*, 13–14.

8. Abraham H. Maslow, *Motivation and Personality* (New York: Harper, 1954).

9. Henry A. Murray, *Explorations in Personality* (New York: Oxford University Press, 1938).

10. Lee J. Cronbach, *Educational Psychology*, 2nd ed. (New York: Harcourt Brace, 1963).

11. David Birch and Joseph Veroff, *Motivation: A Study of Action* (Monterey: Brooks/ Cole, 1966).

12. Phyllis R. Silverman, "A Reexamination of the Intake Procedure," *Social Casework* 51 (1970):625–34.

13. William J. Sahlein, *A Neighborhood Solution to the Social Services Dilemma* (Toronto: Heath, 1973), 108–9.

14. See: Edward S. Bordin, "The Implications of Client Expectations for the Counseling Process," *Journal of Consulting Psychology* 2 (1955):17–21; James V. Clark, "Task Group Therapy: Goals and the Client System," in *Interpersonal Dynamics*, 3rd ed., edited by Warren Bennis et al. (Homewood, Ill.: Dorsey Press, 1973), 574–91; Arnold P. Goldstein, *Therapist-Patient Expectancies* (New York: Pergamon, 1962); Russell A. Jones, *Self-Fulfilling Prophecies* (Hillsdale, N.J.: L. Erlbaum Associates, 1977); T. J. Powell, "Negative Expectations of Treatment: Some Ideas about the Source and Management of Two Types," *Clinical Social Work Journal* 1 (1973):177–86; and Wallace Wilkins, "Expectancy of Therapeutic Gain; An Empirical and Conceptual Critique," *Journal of Consulting and Clinical Psychology* 40 (1973):69–77.

15. John H. Borghi, "Premature Termination of Psychotherapy and Patient-Therapist Expectations," *American Journal of Psychotherapy* 22 (1968):460–73.

16. William Henry, John H. Sims, and S. Lee Spray, *The Fifth Profession* (San Francisco: Jossey-Bass, 1971).

17. In his book, *Psychotherapy: Clinical, Research and Theoretical Issues* (New York: Jason Aronson, 1973), 523–36, Hans Strupp observes that therapists are quite clear about patients who are "suitable" for psychotherapy. In a study of therapists' attitudes, there was high agreement about such desirable characteristics as "capacity for insight," "motivation for therapy," and "agreement about the degree of improvement expected."

18. Pioneer studies of the relationship between social class and treatment include: August B. Hollingshead and Frederick C. Redlich, *Social Class and Mental Illness* (New York: John Wiley, 1958), and Richard Jessor, "Social Values and Psychotherapy," *Journal of Consulting Psychology* 20 (1956):246–66. More recent studies include: Eugene Baum et al., "Psychotherapy, Dropouts, and Lower Class Patients," *American Journal of Orthopsychiatry* 36 (1966):629–35; Wilmatene Blake, "The Influence of Race on Diagnosis," *Smith College Studies in Social Work* 43 (1973):184–92; Milton Bloombaum and Joe Yamamoto, "Cultural Stereotyping Among Psychotherapists," *Journal of Consulting and Clinical Psychology* 32 (1968):99–104; Robert R. Carkhuff and Richard Pierce, "Differential Effects of Therapist Race and Social Class upon Patient Depth of Self-Exploration in the Initial Interview," *Journal of Consulting Psychology* 31 (1967):632–34; Charles W. Cobb, "Community Mental Health Services and the Lower Socioeconomic Classes," *American Journal of Orthopsychiatry* 42 (1972):404–14; Shirley Cooper, "A Look at the Effects of Racism on Clinical Work," *Social Casework* 54 (1973):76–84; Stephen D. Lee and Maurice K. Temerlin, "Social Class, Diagnosis and Prognosis for Psychotherapy," *Psychotherapy: Theory, Research and Practice* 7 (1970):181–85; Barbara Lerner and Donald Fiske, "Client Attributes and the Eye of the Beholder," *Journal of Consulting and Clinical Psychology* 40 (1973):272–77; and Raymond P. Lorion, "Research on Psychotherapy and Behavior Change with the Disadvantaged," in *Handbook of Psychotherapy and Behavior Change*, 2nd ed., edited by Sol L. Garfield and Allen E. Bergin (New York: John Wiley, 1978), 903–38.

19. Arnold P. Goldstein, *Structured Learning Therapy: Psychotherapy for the Poor* (New York: Academic Press, 1973).

20. J. Corley, "Burned Out," *Cleveland Magazine*, July 1979, 101.

Notes for Chapter Fourteen

CHAPTER FOURTEEN

1. See: Jay Haley, *Problem-Solving Therapy* (San Francisco: Jossey-Bass, 1977); J. R. Strong, "A Marital Conflict Resolution Model: Redefining Conflict to Achieve Intimacy," *Journal of Marital and Family Counseling* 1 (1975):269–76; Irving Tallman, "The Family as a Small Problem-Solving Group," *Journal of Marriage and the Family* (Feb. 1970), 94–104; and S. Valle and R. Marinelli, "Training in Human Relations Skills as a Preferred Mode of Treatment for Married Couples," *Journal of Marriage and Family Counseling* 1 (1975):359–65.

2. Hugh Urban and Donald H. Ford, "Some Historical and Conceptual Perspectives on Psychotherapy and Behavior Change," in *Handbook of Psychotherapy and Behavior Change,* edited by Allen Bergin and Sol Garfield (New York: John Wiley, 1971), 3–35.

3. Carol Meyer, "Direct Services in Old and New Contexts," in *Shaping the New Social Work,* edited by Alfred Kahn (New York: Columbia University Press, 1973), 25–64.

4. Arnold P. Goldstein et al., *Psychotherapy and the Psychology of Behavior Change* (New York: John Wiley, 1966), 227.

5. Jerome D. Frank, *Psychotherapy and the Human Predicament* (New York: Schocken Books, 1978), 1–12.

Bibliography

Adler, Franz. "The Value Concept in Sociology." *American Journal of Sociology* 62 (1956):272–73.

Agee, James, and Walker Evans. *Let Us Now Praise Famous Men*. Boston: Houghton Mifflin, 1939.

Alexander, Franz. "The Dynamics of Psychotherapy in the Light of Learning Theory." *American Journal of Psychiatry* 120 (1963):440–48.

Alinsky, Saul. "Of Means and Ends in Strategies of Community Organization." In *Strategies of Community Organization*, edited by Fred Cox, John Erlich, Jack Rothman, and John Tropman, pp. 199–208, Itasca, Ill.: F. E. Peacock, 1970.

———. "Citizen Participation and Community Organization in Planning and Urban Renewal." In *Strategies of Community Organization*, edited by Fred Cox, John Erlich, Jack Rothman, and John Tropman, pp. 216–25. Itasca, Ill.: F. E. Peacock, 1970.

Allen, Vernon A. *Psychological Factors in Poverty*. Chicago: Markham, 1970.

Allport, Floyd H. *Theories of Perception and the Concept of Structure*. New York: John Wiley, 1955.

Allport, Gordon W. *Becoming*. New Haven: Yale University Press, 1955.

———. *Personality and Social Encounter*. Boston: Beacon Press, 1960.

———. *Pattern and Growth in Personality*. New York: Holt, Rinehart & Winston, 1961.

———. "The Functional Autonomy of Motives." In *Theories of Motivation in Personality and Social Psychology*, edited by Richard Teveen and Robert Birney, pp. 60–79. New York: Van Nostrand, 1964.

———. "Is the Concept of Self Necessary?" In *The Self in Social Interaction*, vol. 1, edited by Chad Gordon and Kenneth Gergen, pp. 25–32. New York: John Wiley, 1968.

Anderson, Harold H., ed. *Creativity and Its Cultivation*. New York: Harper, 1959.

463

Bibliography

Anderson, Robert. *I Never Sang for My Father*. New York: Random House, 1968.
Andreski, Stanislav. *Social Sciences as Sorcery*. New York: St. Martin's Press, 1972.
Ansbacher, Heinz, and R. R. Ansbacher, eds. *The Individual Psychology of Alfred Adler*. New York: Harper & Row, 1956.
Arieti, Silvano. "The Role of Cognitive in the Development of Inner Reality." In *Cognitive Studies*, vol. 1, edited by Jerome Hellmuth, pp. 91–110. New York: Brunner/Mazel, 1970.
————. *Creativity: The Magic Synthesis*. New York: Basic Books, 1976.
Arnold, Magda, ed. *Feelings and Emotions: The Loyola Symposium*. New York: Academic Press, 1970.
Astin, Alexander. "The Functional Autonomy of Psychotherapy." *American Psychologist* 16 (1961):75–78.
Auld, F., Jr., and Alice White. "Sequential Dependencies in Psychotherapy." *Journal of Abnormal and Social Psychology* 58 (1959):100–104.
Ayllon, Teodoro, E. Haughton, and H. B. Hughes. "Interpretation of Symptoms: Fact or Fiction?" *Behavioral Research and Therapy* 3 (1965):1–8.
Ayres, Alice. "Neighborhood Services: People Caring for People." *Social Casework* 54 (1973):195–215.
Bailey, Roy, and Mike Brake, eds. *Radical Social Work*. London: Arnold, 1975.
Bandler, Richard, and John Grinder. *The Structure of Magic I: A Book about Language and Therapy*. Palo Alto: Science & Behavior Books, 1975.
————. *The Structure of Magic II: A Book about Communication and Change*. Palo Alto: Science & Behavior Books, 1976.
Bandura, Albert. "Psychotherapy as a Learning Process." *Psychological Bulletin* 58 (1961):143–59.
————, ed. *Psychological Modeling*. New York: Aldine-Atherton, 1970.
————. *Social Learning Theory*. New York: General Learning Press, 1971.
————, D. Ross, and S. A. Ross. "A Comparative Test of the Status, Envy, Social Power, and Secondary Reinforcement Theories of Identificatory Learning." *Journal of Abnormal and Social Psychology* 67 (1964):527–34.
Banta, Thomas J. "Tests for the Evaluation of Early Childhood Education: The Cincinnati Autonomy Test Battery (CATB)." In *Cognitive Studies*, vol. 1, edited by Jerome Hellmuth, pp. 424–90. New York: Brunner/Mazel, 1970.
Barclay, James R. *Foundations of Counseling Strategy*. New York: John Wiley, 1971.
Barnlund, Dean C. *Interpersonal Communication: Survey and Studies*. Boston: Houghton Mifflin, 1968.
Bateson, Gregory. *Mind and Nature: A Necessary Unity*. New York: E. P. Dutton, 1979.
————, Don Jackson and John Weakland. "Toward a Theory of Schizophrenia." *Behavioral Science* 1 (1956):251–64.
Bauer, Raymond A. "Social Psychology and the Study of Policy Formation." *American Psychologist* 21 (1966):933–42.

Baum, Eugene, Stanton Felzer, Thomas D'Zmura and Elaine Shumaker. "Psychotherapy, Dropouts, and Lower Class Patients." *American Journal of Orthopsychiatry* 36 (1966):629–35.

Beck, Aaron T. *Cognitive Therapy and the Emotional Disorders*. New York: International Universities Press, 1976.

——— et al. *Cognitive Therapy of Depression*. New York: Guilford Press, 1979.

Becker, Ernest. *The Revolution in Psychiatry*. New York: Free Press, 1964.

———. *Angel in Armor*. New York: Free Press, 1969.

———. *Escape from Evil*. New York: Free Press, 1975.

Becker, Howard S., ed. *The Other Side*. New York: Free Press, 1964.

Beier, Ernst G. *The Silent Language of Psychotherapy*. Chicago: Aldine, 1966.

Bem, Daryl J. "Self-Perception: An Alternative Interpretation of Cognitive Dissonance Phenomena." *Psychological Review* 74 (1967):183–200.

Bennett, William Jr., and Merle C. Hokenstad, Jr. "Full Time People Workers and Conceptions of the Professional." In *Sociological Review Monograph #20, Professionalism and Social Change*, pp. 21–45. Keele, Eng.: University of Keele, December 1973.

Bennis, Warren, David Berlew, Edgar Schein, and Fred Steele, eds. *Interpersonal Dynamics*. 3rd ed. Homewood, Ill.: Dorsey Press, 1973.

Benz, Loretta N. "Citizen Participation Reconsidered." *Social Work* 20 (1975):115–19.

Bergin, Allen E., and Sol L. Garfield, eds. *Handbook of Psychotherapy and Behavior Change*. New York: John Wiley, 1971.

Bergson, Henri. *An Introduction to Metaphysics*. New York: Putnam, 1912.

———. *Creative Evolution*. New York: Modern Library, 1944.

Berlo, David K. *The Process of Communication*. New York: Holt, Rinehart & Winston, 1960.

Berlyne, D. E. *Structure and Direction of Thinking*. New York: John Wiley, 1965.

Bermant, Gordon, Herbert Kelman, and Donald Warwick. *The Ethics of Social Intervention*. Washington: Hemisphere, 1978.

Berne, Eric. *Transactional Analysis in Psychotherapy*. New York: Grove Press, 1964.

———. *Principles of Group Treatment*. New York: Oxford University Press, 1966.

Bernstein, Basil. "Some Psychological Determinants of Perception." *British Journal of Sociology* 9 (1958):159–74.

———. "Language and Social Class." *British Journal of Sociology* 11 (1960):271–76.

Bertalanffy, Ludwig von. *General Systems Theory*. New York: George Braziller, 1968.

Beutler, Larry. "Value and Attitude Change in Psychotherapy: A Case for Dyadic Assessment." *Psychotherapy: Theory, Research and Practice* 9 (1972):362–67.

Birch, David, and Joseph Veroff. *Motivation: A Study of Action*. Monterey: Brooks/Cole, 1966.

Bibliography

Blake, Wilmatene. "The Influence of Race on Diagnosis." *Smith College Studies in Social Work* 43 (1973):184–92.

Blau, Peter M., and W. Richard Scott. *Formal Organizations: A Comparative Approach.* San Francisco: Chandler, 1962.

Bloom, Benjamin. *Stability and Change in Human Characteristics.* New York: John Wiley, 1964.

―――― and L. Broder. "Problem-Solving Processes of College Students." *Supplementary Educational Monographs.* No. 73. Chicago: University of Chicago Press, 1950.

――――, M. D. Englehart, E. J. Furst, W. H. Hill and D. R. Kratwohl. *Taxonomy of Educational Objectives, Handbook 1: Cognitive Domain.* New York: McKay, 1956.

Bloombaum, Milton, and Joe Yamamoto. "Cultural Stereotyping Among Psychotherapists." *Journal of Consulting and Clinical Psychology* 32 (1968):99–104.

Bloomberg, Morton, ed. *Creativity.* New Haven: Yale University Press, 1973.

Bogen, Joseph E. "The Other Side of the Brain: An Appositional Mind." In *The Nature of Human Consciousness,* edited by Robert E. Ornstein, pp. 101–25. San Francisco: Freeman, 1973.

Bordin, Edward S. "Curiosity, Compassion and Doubt: The Dilemma of the Psychologist." *American Psychologist* 21 (1966):116–21.

Borghi, John H. "Premature Termination of Psychotherapy and Patient-Therapist Expectations." *American Journal of Psychotherapy* 22 (1968):460–73.

Boss, Medard. *Psychoanalysis and Daseinsanalysis.* New York: Basic Books, 1963.

Bowen, Murray. "The Use of Family Theory in Clinical Practice." In *Changing Families,* edited by Jay Haley, pp. 159–92. New York: Grune & Stratton, 1971.

Bowles, Dorcas. "Making Casework Relevant to Black People." *Child Welfare* 48 (1969):468–75.

Brain, Sir Russell. "Some Reflections on Brain and Mind." In *Perception: Selected Readings in Science and Phenomenology,* edited by Paul Tibbetts, pp. 19–48. Chicago: Quadrangle Books, 1969.

Briggs, Dennie. "De-Clienting Social Work." *Social Work Today* 3 (1973):3–6.

Brim, Orville G., Jr. "Socialization Through the Life Cycle." In *The Self in Social Interaction,* vol. 1, edited by Chad Gordon and Kenneth Gergen, pp. 227–40. New York: John Wiley, 1968.

Bronowski, Jacob. "The Logic of the Mind." *American Scientist* 54 (1966):1–14.

Brown, J. J., ed. *Current Theory and Research on Motivation.* Lincoln: University of Nebraska Press, 1953.

Bruner, Jerome S. "On Perceptual Readiness." *Psychological Review* 64 (1957):123–52.

――――. *The Process of Education.* New York: Vintage Books, 1960.

――――. "The Course of Cognitive Growth." *American Psychologist* 19 (1964):1–15.

――――. *Toward a Theory of Instruction.* New York: W. W. Norton, 1966.

Buber, Martin. *I and Thou.* New York: Charles Scribner's, 1958.

466

Buckley, Walter. *Sociology and Modern Systems Theory.* Englewood Cliffs, N.J.: Prentice-Hall, 1967.

Bugental, James F. T. *The Search for Authenticity: An Existential-Analytic Approach to Psychotherapy.* New York: Holt, Rinehart & Winston, 1965.

————, ed. *Challenges of Humanistic Psychology.* New York: McGraw-Hill, 1967.

Buhler, Charlotte. *Values in Psychotherapy.* Glencoe: Free Press, 1962.

Bullough, Bonnie. "Poverty, Ethnic Identity and Preventive Health Care." *Journal of Health and Social Behavior* 13 (1972):347–59.

Burton, Arthur, ed. *Operational Theories of Personality.* New York: Brunner/Mazel, 1974.

Buss, Allan R. *A Dialectical Psychology.* New York: Irvington Pub., 1979.

Campbell, Donald T. "Methodological Suggestions from a Comparative Psychology of Knowledge Processes." *Inquiry* 2 (1959):152–82.

Camus, Albert. *The Stranger.* New York: A. A. Knopf, 1946.

Caplan, Gerald. *An Approach to Community Mental Health.* New York: Grune & Stratton, 1961.

————. *Principles of Preventive Psychiatry.* New York: Basic Books, 1964.

Carkhuff, Robert R., and Bernard G. Berenson. *Beyond Counseling and Therapy.* New York: Holt, Rinehart & Winston, 1967.

———— and Richard Pierce. "Differential Effects of Therapist Race and Social Class upon Patient Depth of Self-Exploration in the Initial Interview." *Journal of Consulting Psychology* 31 (1967):632–34.

Carrier, J., and I. Kendall. "Social Policy and Social Change: Explanations of the Development of Social Policy." *Journal of Social Policy* 2 (1973):209–24.

Carson, Robert C. *Interaction Concepts of Personality.* Chicago: Aldine, 1969.

Carter, Elizabeth, and Monica Orfanidis. "Family Therapy with One Person and the Therapist's Own Family." In *Family Therapy: Theory and Practice,* edited by Philip J. Guerin, pp. 193–219. New York: Gardner Press, 1976.

Cassirer, Ernst. *Essay on Man.* New Haven: Yale University Press, 1944.

Clark, James V. "Task Group Therapy: Goals and the Client System." In *Interpersonal Dynamics,* 3rd ed., edited by Warren Bennis, David Berlew, Edgar Stein and Fred Steele, pp. 574–91. Homewood, Ill.: Dorsey Press, 1973.

Cobb, Charles W. "Community Mental Health Services and the Lower Socioeconomic Classes: A Summary of Research Literature on Outpatient Treatment." *American Journal of Orthopsychiatry* 42 (1972):404–14.

Cohen, Albert K. *Deviance and Control.* Englewood Cliffs, N.J.: Prentice-Hall, 1966.

Cohen, Arthur R. *Attitude Change and Social Influence.* New York: Basic Books, 1964.

Coles, Robert, and Jane H. Coles. *Women of Crisis: Lives of Struggle and Hope.* New York: Delacorte Press, 1978.

Combs, Arthur W., and Donald Snygg. *Individual Behavior: A Perceptual Approach to Behavior.* Rev. ed. New York: Harper, 1959.

467

Bibliography

Cook, Mark. *Interpersonal Perception.* Middlesex, Eng.: Penguin, 1971.
Cooper, Shirley. "A Look at the Effect of Racism on Clinical Work." *Social Casework* 54 (1973):76–84.
Coopersmith, Stanley. *The Antecedents of Self-Esteem.* San Francisco: Freeman, 1967.
Cox, Fred, John Erlich, Jack Rothman, and John Tropman, eds. *Strategies of Community Organization.* Itasca, Ill.: F. E. Peacock, 1970.
Cronbach, Lee J. *Educational Psychology.* 2nd ed. New York: Harcourt Brace, 1963.
Crowne, Douglas, and D. Marcowe. *The Approval Motive.* New York: John Wiley, 1964.
Darbonne, Allen R. "Crisis: A Review of Theory, Practice and Research." *International Journal of Psychiatry* 6 (1968):371–79.
Datan, Nancy, and Leon Ginsberg, eds. *Life Span Developmental Psychology.* New York: Academic Press, 1975.
Davis, Anthony. "Psychodynamic and Sociocultural Factors Related to Intolerance of Ambiguity." In *The Study of Lives,* edited by Robert W. White, pp. 161–77. New York: Atherton Press, 1969.
De Bono, Edward. *Lateral Thinking.* New York: Harper & Row, 1970.
Deikman, Arthur J. "Bimodal Consciousness." In *The Nature of Human Consciousness,* edited by Robert E. Ornstein, pp. 67–86. San Francisco: Freeman, 1973.
De Levita, D. J. *The Concept of Identiy.* New York: Basic Books, 1965.
De Mott, Benjamin. "Hot-Air Meeting." *Harpers,* July 1975, p. 71.
Dennis, W. "Causes of Retardation Among Institutional Children." *Journal of Genetic Psychology* 96 (1960):47–59.
Deutsch, Martin. "The Role of Social Class in Language Development and Cognition." *American Journal of Orthopsychiatry* 35 (1965):78–88.
Development and Participation: Operational Implications for Social Welfare. Proceedings of the XVIIth International Conference on Social Welfare. New York: Columbia University Press, 1975.
Dewey, John. *How We Think.* Boston: D. C. Heath, 1910.
———. "The Meaning of Value." *Journal of Philosophy* 22, Jan.–Dec. 1925.
———. *Experience and Nature.* New York: Grove Press, 1929.
———. *Human Nature and Conduct.* New York: Modern Library, 1930.
———. *Experience and Education.* New York: Macmillan, 1938.
Dillard, Annie. *Pilgrim at Tinkers Creek.* New York: Harper Magazine Publishing, 1974.
Dollard, John, and Neal E. Miller. *Personality and Psychotherapy.* New York: McGraw-Hill, 1950.
Douglas, Jack D., ed. *Deviance and Respectability: The Social Construction of Moral Meanings.* New York: Basic Books, 1970.
Dreikers, Rudolph. "The Adlerian Approach to Psychodynamics." In *Contempo-*

rary Psychotherapies, edited by Morris I. Stein, pp. 60–79. New York: Free Press, 1961.

Drucker, Peter F. "Managing the Public Service Institution." *Public Interest* 33 (1973):43–60.

Dubey, Sumati, and Morris Grant. "Powerlessness Among Disadvantaged Blacks." *Social Casework* 51 (1970):285–90.

Dukes, William F. "Psychological Studies of Values." *Psychological Bulletin* 52 (1955):24–50.

Duncan, Carl P. *Thinking: Current Experimental Studies.* Philadelphia: Lippincott, 1967.

Duncker, Karl. "On Problem Solving." *Psychological Monographs.* No. 5, 58 (1945):1–14.

Edelstein, Rosalind. "Early Intervention in the Poverty Cycle." *Social Casework* 53 (1972):418–24.

Ellenberger, Henri F. *The Discovery of the Unconscious.* New York: Basic Books, 1970.

Ellis, Albert. *Reason and Emotion in Psychotherapy.* New York: Lyle Stuart, 1962.

———. "Goals of Psychotherapy. In *The Goals of Psychotherapy,* edited by A. R. Mahrer. New York: Appleton-Century-Crofts, 1967.

———. "Rational-Emotive Theory." In *Operational Theories of Personality,* edited by Arthur Burton, pp. 308–44. New York: Brunner/Mazel, 1974.

Epstein, Norman, and Anne Shainline. "Paraprofessional Parent-Aides and Disadvantaged Families." *Social Casework* 55 (1974):230–36.

Erikson, Kai T. "Notes on the Sociology of Deviance." In *The Other Side,* edited by Howard Becker, pp. 9–22. New York: Free Press, 1964.

Etzioni, Amitai. *Modern Organizations.* Englewood Cliffs, N.J.: Prentice-Hall, 1964.

Ewing, A. C. *The Fundamental Questions of Philosophy.* New York: Collier Books, 1962.

Eysenck, H. J. "The Effects of Psychotherapy." *International Journal of Psychiatry* 1 (1965):99–142.

——— and H. R. Beech. "Counterconditioning and Related Methods." In *Handbook of Psychotherapy and Behavior Change,* edited by Allen Bergin and Sol Garfield, pp. 543–611. New York: John Wiley, 1971.

Fagan, Joen, and Irma Sheperd, eds. *Gestalt Therapy Now.* Palo Alto: Science and Behavior Books, 1970.

Fantz, Robert L. "The Origin of Form Perception." *Scientific American,* May 1961, pp. 66–72.

Farb, Peter. *Word Play: What Happens When People Talk.* New York: A. A. Knopf, 1974.

Farber, Marvin. *The Foundations of Phenomenology.* New York: Paine, Whitman, 1962.

Bibliography

Farrell, Ronald A., and Victoria L. Swigert. *Social Deviance*. Philadelphia: Lippincott, 1975.

Farrelly, Frank, and Jeffrey Brandsma. *Provocative Therapy*. San Francisco: Shields, 1974.

Ferm, Vergilius, ed. *A History of Philosophical Systems*. Paterson: Littlefield, Adams, 1965.

Festinger, Leon. *A Theory of Cognitive Dissonance*. Evanston, Ill.: Row, Peterson, 1957.

Filstead, William J., ed. *An Introduction to Deviance: Readings in the Process of Making Deviants*. Chicago: Markham, 1972.

First Landmark: Mental Patients Rights. Civil Liberties 289, Sept. 1972.

Fishbein, Martin, ed. *Readings in Attitude Theory and Measurement*, New York: John Wiley, 1967.

Fiske, Donald, and D. Cartwright. "Are Psychotherapeutic Changes Predictable?" *Journal of Abnormal and Social Psychology* 69 (1964):418–26.

Fitzgerald, F. Scott. *Crack Up*. New York: New Directions, 1945.

Fogarty, Thomas F. "Systems Concepts and the Dimensions of Self." In *Family Therapy: Theory and Practice*, edited by Philip Guerin, pp. 144–53. New York: Gardner Press, 1976.

Frank, Jerome D. *Persuasion and Healing: A Comparative Study of Psychotherapy*. Baltimore: Johns Hopkins Press, 1961.

———. *Psychotherapy and the Human Predicament*. New York: Schocken Books, 1978.

Frankel, Charles. "Social Values and Professional Values." *Journal of Education for Social Work* 5 (1969):29–35.

Frankl, Charles. "Positivism." In *A History of Philosophical Systems*, edited by Vergilius Ferm. Paterson: Littlefield, Adams, 1965.

Frankl, Victor E. *Man's Search for Meaning*. New York: Simon and Schuster, 1962.

———. *Psychotherapy and Existentialism: Selected Papers on Logotherapy*. New York: Washington Square Press, 1967.

———. "Reductionism and Nihilism." In *Beyond Reductionism*, edited by Arthur Koestler and J. R. Smythies, pp. 396–416. Boston: Beacon Press, 1969.

———. *The Unheard Cry for Meaning*. New York: Simon and Schuster, 1978.

Franks, Cyril M., and G. T. Wilson, eds. *Annual Review of Behavior Theory and Practice*. New York: Brunner/Mazel, 1973.

Freedman, Alfred M., and Harold I. Kaplan, eds. *Interpreting Personality*. New York: Atheneum, 1972.

———, eds. *Treating Mental Illness*. New York: Atheneum, 1972.

Freire, Paulo. *Pedagogy of the Oppressed*. New York: Herder and Herder, 1968.

———. "The Adult Literacy Process as Cultural Action for Freedom." *Harvard Educational Review* 40 (1970):215.

———. *Education for Critical Consciousness*. New York: Seabury Press, 1973.

French, D. "Relationship of Anthropology to Studies in Perception and Cognition." In *Psychology: A Study of a Science*, vol. 6, edited by Sigmund Koch, pp. 388–428. New York: McGraw-Hill, 1963.

Freud, Sigmund. *Collected Papers.* London: Hogarth Press, 1925.

Friedman, Maurice. *Problematic Rebel: An Image of Modern Man.* New York: Random House, 1963.

———. *To Deny Our Nothingness: Contemporary Images of Modern Man.* New York: Delta, 1968.

———. *Problematic Rebel: Melville, Dostoievsky, Kafka, Camus.* 2nd ed. Chicago: University of Chicago Press/Phoenix Books, 1970.

———. *The Hidden Human Image.* New York: Delacorte Press, 1974.

From, Franz. *Perception of Other People.* New York: Columbia University Press, 1971.

Fromm, Erich. *The Art of Loving.* New York: Harper & Row, 1956.

———. "Value, Psychology and Human Existence." In *New Knowledge in Human Values*, edited by Abraham A. Maslow, pp. 151–64. New York: Harper, 1959.

———, ed. *Marx's Concept of Man.* New York: Frederick Ungar, 1961.

Gagne, Robert M. *Conditions of Learning.* New York: Holt, Rinehart & Winston, 1945.

Galper, Jeffrey. *Radical Social Work: Theory and Practice.* New York: MSS Modular Publications, 1970.

Garrison, Karl, A. Kingston, and A. McDonald. *Education Psychology.* 2nd ed. New York: Appleton-Century-Crofts, 1964.

Garry, Ralph, and Howard Kingsley. *The Nature and Conditions of Learning.* Englewood Cliffs, N.J.: Prentice-Hall, 1970.

Gazzaniga, Michael S. "The Split Brain in Man." In *Nature of Human Consciousness*, edited by Robert E. Ornstein, pp. 87–100. San Francisco: Freeman, 1973.

Gerard, Harold, Stephan Blevans, and Thomas Malcolm. "Self Evaluation and the Evaluation of Choice Alternatives." *Journal of Personality* 32 (1964):395–410.

Gergen, Kenneth. "Personal Consistency and the Presentation of Self." In *The Self in Social Interaction*, edited by Chad Gordon and Kenneth Gergen, pp. 299–308. New York: John Wiley, 1968.

Germain, Carel B., ed. *Social Work Practice: People and Environments.* New York: Columbia University Press, 1979.

———, and Alex Gitterman. *The Life Model of Social Work Practice.* New York: Columbia University Press (forthcoming).

Getzels, J. W., and P. W. Jackson. "The Meaning of 'Giftedness': An Examination of an Explanatory Concept." *Phi Delta Kappan* 40 (1958):75–77.

Giglioli, Pier P., ed. *Language and Social Context.* Baltimore: Penguin, 1972.

Gilbert, Neil, and Harry Specht. "Advocacy and Professional Ethics." *Social Work* 21 (1976):288–93.

———, eds. *Handbook of Social Work Programs and Methods.* Englewood Cliffs, N.J.: Prentice-Hall (forthcoming).

Bibliography

Gitterman, Alex, and Alice Schaeffer. "The White Professional and the Black Client." *Social Casework* 53 (1972):280–91.

Glasser, William. *Reality Therapy*. New York: Harper & Row, 1965.

Goffman, Erving. *Asylums: Essays on the Social Situation of Mental Patients and Other Inmates*. New York: Doubleday, 1961.

———. *Behavior in Public Places*. New York: Free Press, 1963.

———. *Stigma: Notes on the Management of Spoiled Identity*. Englewood Cliffs, N.J.: Prentice-Hall, 1963.

Goldstein, Arnold P. *Therapist-Patient Expectancies*. New York: Pergamon, 1962.

———. *Structured Learning Therapy: Psychotherapy for the Poor*. New York: Academic Press, 1973.

———, Kenneth Heller, and Lee Sechrest. *Psychotherapy and the Psychology of Behavior Change*. New York: John Wiley, 1966.

——— and Norman R. Simonson. "Social Psychological Approaches to Psychotherapy Research." In *Handbook of Psychotherapy and Behavior Change*, edited by Allen Bergin and Sol Garfield, pp. 154–95. New York: John Wiley, 1971.

Goldstein, Howard. *Social Work Practice: A Unitary Approach*. Columbia: University of South Carolina Press, 1973.

———. "Some Critical Observations on the Relevance of Social Systems Theory for Social Work Practice." *Canadian Journal of Social Work Education* 1 (1975):13–23.

———. "A Unitary Approach: Its Rationale and Structure and Implications for Education and Practice." In *The Proceedings of the Dundee Conference*. Dundee, Scotland: University of Dundee, 1975.

———. "Theory Development and the Unitary Approach to Social Work Practice." In *Integrating Social Work Methods*, edited by Harry Specht and Ann Vickery, pp. 60–72. London: George Allen & Unwin, 1977.

———. "Generalist Social Work Practice." In *Handbook of Social Work Programs and Methods*, edited by Neil Gilbert and Harry Specht. Englewood Cliffs, N.J.: Prentice-Hall (forthcoming).

——— and Linda L. Goldstein. "The Concept of Deviancy Revisited." *Canada's Mental Health* 23 (1975):10–14.

Gordon, Chad. "Self Conceptions: Configurations of Content." In *The Self in Social Interaction*, Vol. 1, edited by Chad Gordon and Kenneth Gergen, pp. 115–36. New York: John Wiley, 1968.

——— and Kenneth Gergen, eds. *The Self in Social Interaction*. New York: John Wiley, 1968.

Goroff, N. "Social Welfare as Coercive Social Control." *Journal of Sociology and Social Welfare* 2 (1974):19–26.

Goslin, David, and D. E. Glass. *Handbook of Socialization Theory and Research*. Chicago: Rand-McNally, 1966.

Gottschalk, Louis, and Robert Davidson. "Sensitivity Groups, Encounter

Groups, Training Groups, Marathon Groups and the Laboratory Movement." In *Sensitivity Through Encounter and Marathon; Modern Group Book IV*, edited by Harold H. Kaplan and Benjamin Sadock, pp. 59–94. New York: E. P. Dutton, 1972.

Gould, Robert E. "Dr. Strangeclass: Or How I Stopped Worrying about Theory and Began Treating the Blue Collar Worker." *American Journal or Orthopsychiatry* 37 (1967):78–86.

Grant, Vernon W. *Great Abnormals*. New York: Hawthorne, 1968.

Gruenberg, E. M. "The Social Breakdown Syndrome—Some Origins." *American Journal of Psychiatry* 123 (1967):1481–89.

Guerin, Philip J., ed. *Family Therapy: Theory and Practice*. New York: Gardner Press, 1976.

Guilford, J. P. *The Nature of Human Intelligence*. New York: McGraw-Hill, 1967.

———. "Intelligence has Three Facets." *Science* 160 (1968):615–20.

Gurwitsch, Aron. "The Phenomenology of Perception: Perceptual Implications." In *Perception*, edited by Paul Tibbetts, pp. 248–60. Chicago: Quadrangle Books, 1969.

Guthrie, Victor, and Jane Gasdick. "Rehabilitation through Improvement in Social Skills." *Social Casework* 54 (1973):42–44.

Haley, Jay, ed. *Changing Families*. New York: Grune & Stratton, 1971.

———. *Problem-Solving Therapy*. San Francisco: Jossey-Bass, 1977.

Hall, Edward T. *The Silent Language*. Garden City, N.Y.: Doubleday, 1959.

Halleck, Seymour. *The Politics of Therapy*. New York: Science House, 1971.

Harlow, Harry. "Motivation as a Factor in the Acquisition of New Responses." In *Current Theory and Research in Motivation*, edited by J. Brown. Lincoln: University of Nebraska Press, 1953.

———. "Recent Research on Human Problem Solving." *Psychological Bulletin* 56 (1959):397–429.

Harris, Dale B. *The Concept of Development: An Issue in the Study of Human Behavior*. Minneapolis: University of Minnesota Press, 1957.

Hart, William, and Louise Bassett. "Delivery of Services to Lower Socioeconomic Groups by Suburban Community Mental Health Centers." *American Journal of Psychiatry* 2 (1972):191–96.

Hayek, F. A. "The Primacy of the Abstract." In *Beyond Reductionism*, edited by Arthur Koestler and J. R. Smythies, pp. 309–33. Boston: Beacon Press, 1969.

Heller, Kenneth, J. Davis, and R. Myers. "The Effects of Interviewer Style in a Standardized Interview." *Journal of Consulting Psychology* 30 (1966):501–508.

Hellmuth, Jerome, ed. *Cognitive Studies*, vol. 1. New York: Brunner/Mazel, 1970.

Henry, William, John H. Sims, and S. Lee Spray. *The Fifth Profession*. San Francisco: Jossey-Bass, 1971.

Hilgard, Ernest R. "Human Motives and the Concept of Self." *American Psychologist* 4 (1949):374–82.

———. *Introduction to Psychology*. 3rd ed. New York: Harcourt Brace, 1962.

Bibliography

————. "The Place of Gestalt Psychology and Field Theories in Contemporary Learning Theory." In *Theories of Learning and Instruction,* Chapter 3, The 63rd Yearbook of the National Society of Education, Part I. Chicago: University of Chicago Press, 1964.

———— and Gordon H. Bower. *Theories of Learning.* New York: Appleton-Century-Crofts, 1966.

Hitt, William D. "Two Models of Man." *American Psychologist* 24 (1969):651–58.

Holland, Thomas. Organizational Structure and Institutional Care." *Journal of Health and Social Behavior* 14 (1973):241–51.

Hollender, M. H. "Selection of Patients for Definitive Forms of Psychotherapy." *Archives of General Psychiatry* 19 (1964):361–69.

Hollingshead, August B., and Frederick C. Redlich. *Social Class and Mental Illness.* New York: John Wiley, 1958.

Hopkins, Thomas. "The Role of the Agency in Supporting Black Manhood." *Social Work* 18 (1973):53–58.

Horney, Karen. *Neurosis and Human Growth: The Struggle Toward Self Realization.* New York: W. W. Norton, 1950.

Hovland, C. I., and Irving L. Janis. *Personality and Persuasibility.* New Haven: Yale University Press, 1959.

Howe, Irving. *World of Our Fathers.* New York: Harcourt Brace Jovanovich, 1976.

Hudgins, Bryce B. "Effects of Group Experience on Individual Problem Solving." *Journal of Educational Psychology* 51 (1960):37–42.

Hughes, Everett. *The Sociological Eye.* Vol. 2. New York: Aldine-Atherton, 1971.

Hull, C. L. *Principles of Behavior.* New York: Appleton-Century-Crofts, 1943.

Ichheiser, Gustav. *Appearances and Realities: Misunderstandings in Human Relations.* San Francisco: Jossey-Bass, 1970.

Jackson, Don D., and John H. Weakland. "Conjoint Family Therapy; Some Considerations on Theory, Technique and Results." In *Changing Families,* edited by Jay Haley, pp. 13–35. New York: Grune & Stratton, 1971.

Jacobs, Daniel, Edward Charles, Theodore Jacobs, Henry Weinstein, and David Mann. "Preparation for the Treatment of the Disadvantaged Patient." *American Journal of Orthopsychiatry* 42 (1972):666–74.

James, William. "The Self." In *The Self in Social Interaction,* Vol. 1, edited by Chad Gordon and Kenneth Gergen, pp. 41–49. New York: John Wiley, 1968.

Jaques, Elliot, ed. *Levels of Abstraction in Logic and Human Action.* London: Heinemann, 1978.

Jaynes, Julian. *The Origins of Consciousness in the Breakdown of the Bicameral Mind.* Boston: Houghton Mifflin, 1976.

Jefferson, Lara. "I am Crazy Wild This Minute. How Can I Learn to Think Straight?" In *The Inner World of Mental Illness,* edited by Bert Kaplan, pp. 3–42. New York: Harper & Row, 1964.

Jessor, Richard. "Social Values and Psychotherapy." *Journal of Consulting Psychology* 20 (1956):246–66.

—— and Seymour Feschbach. *Cognition, Personality and Clinical Psychology.* San Francisco: Jossey-Bass, 1967.

Jones, Edward E., and Harold B. Girard. *Foundations of Social Psychology.* New York: John Wiley, 1967.

Jones, Maxwell. *Therapeutic Community.* New York: Basic Books, 1953.

——. *Social Psychiatry in the Community, in Hospitals and in Prisons.* Springfield, Ill.: Thomas, 1962.

Jones, Mary C., N. Bayley, J. W. MacFarlane, and M. Honzik, eds. *The Course of Human Development: Selected Papers from the Longitudinal Studies.* Institute of Human Development, University of California, Berkeley. Waltham, Mass.: Xerox College Publishers, 1971.

Jones, Russell A. *Self-Fulfilling Prophecies.* Hillsdale, N.J.: L. Erlbaum Associates, 1977.

Jourard, Sidney M. *Disclosing Man to Himself.* New York: Van Nostrand, 1968.

Jung, Carl G. *Collected Works.* New York: Pantheon, 1953.

Kaam, Adrian van. *Existential Foundations of Psychology.* Pittsburgh: Duquesne University Press, 1966.

Kahn, Alfred J., ed. *Shaping the New Social Work.* New York: Columbia Univesrity Press, 1973.

Kanfer, Frederich H. "Comments on Learning in Psychotherapy." *Psychological Reports* 9 (1961):681–99.

——. "Issues and Ethics in Behavior Manipulation." *Psychological Reports* 16 (1965):187–96.

—— and A. R. Marston. "Determinants of Self-Reinforcement in Human Learning." *Journal of Experimental Psychology* 66 (1963):245–54.

Kaplan, Abraham. *The New World of Philosophy.* New York: Vintage Books, 1961.

Kaplan, Bert, ed. *The Inner World of Mental Illness.* New York: Harper & Row, 1964.

Kaplan, Harold I., and Benjamin J. Sadock, eds. *Sensitivity Through Encounter and Marathon: Modern Group Book IV.* New York: E. P. Dutton, 1972.

Kaplan, Howard B. "Social Class and Self Derogation: A Conditional Relationship." *Sociometry* 34 (1971):41–64.

Kapleau, Philip, ed. *Three Pillars of Zen: Teaching, Practice and Enlightenment.* New York: Harper & Row, 1967.

Kaufmann, Walter. *Existentialism: Dostoevsky to Sartre.* New York: New American Library, 1975.

——. *Without Guilt and Justice.* New York: Delta, 1973.

Keith-Lucas, Alan. "Philosophies of Public Social Service." *Public Welfare* 31 (1973):21–24.

Kelly, George A. *The Psychology of Personal Constructs.* Vols. 1 and 2. New York: W. W. Norton, 1955.

——. *A Theory of Personality.* New York: W. W. Norton, 1963.

Kessler, Jane W. "Contributions of the Mentally Retarded Toward a Theory of

Cognitive Development." In *Cognitive Studies*, Vol. 1, edited by Jerome Hellmuth, pp. 111–209. New York: Brunner-Mazel, 1970.

Kitsuse, John I. "Societal Reactions to Deviant Behavior; Problems of Theory and Method." *Social Problems* 9 (1962):247–56.

Kittrie, Nicholas N. *The Right to Be Different*. Baltimore: Johns Hopkins Press, 1971.

Klausmeier, Herbert J., and William L. Goodwin. *Learning and Human Abilities*. New York: Harper & Row, 1966.

Klausner, Samuel Z., ed. *The Quest for Self-Control*. New York: Free Press, 1965.

Knowles, Malcolm. *The Modern Practice of Adult Education: Androgogy Versus Pedagogy*. New York: Association Press, 1970.

Koch, Sigmund, ed. *Psychology: A Study of a Science*, Vols. 5 and 6. New York: McGraw-Hill, 1963.

Koestler, Arthur. *The Act of Creation*. New York: Dell, 1964.

———. *Janus: A Summing Up*. New York: Random House, 1978.

——— and J. R. Smythies, eds. *Beyond Reductionism*. Boston: Beacon Press, 1969.

Kogan, M. "Social Policy and Public Organizational Values." *Journal of Social Policy* 3 (1974):97–111.

Konrad, George. *The Case Worker*. New York: Harcourt Brace Jovanovich, 1974.

Korchin, Sheldon J. *Modern Clinical Psychology*. New York: Basic Books, 1976.

Kramer, Ralph. *Participation of the Poor*. Englewood Cliffs, N.J.: Prentice-Hall, 1969.

Kratwohl, Donald F., and Benjamin S. Bloom, and B. B. Masia. *Taxonomy of Educational Objectives, Handbook II: Affective Domain*. New York: McKay, 1964.

Krill, Donald F. *Existential Social Work*. New York: Free Press, 1978.

Krim, Seymour. "The Insanity Bit." In *The Inner World of Mental Illness*, edited by Bert Kaplan, pp. 62–79. New York: Harper & Row, 1964.

Kroeber, Theodore C. "The Coping Functions of the Ego Mechanisms." In *The Study of Lives*, edited by Robert R. White, pp. 179–98. New York: Atherton, 1969.

Laing, R. D. *The Divided Self*. New York: Pantheon Books, 1960.

———. *The Politics of Experience*. New York: Pantheon Books, 1967.

———. *Self and Others*. New York: Pantheon Books, 1969.

Lampman, R. J. "What Does It Do for the Poor? A New Test for National Policy." *Public Interest* 34 (1974):66–82.

Lance, Evelyn. "Intensive Work with the Deprived Family." *Social Casework* 50 (1969):454–60.

Laszlo, Ervin. *The Systems View of the World*. New York: George Braziller, 1972.

Lauer, Quentin. *Phenomenology: Its Genesis and Prospect*. New York: Harper & Row, 1958.

Lazarus, Richard S. *Psychological Stress and the Coping Process*. New York: McGraw-Hill, 1966.

———, J. R. Averill, and E. M. Opton. "Toward a Cognitive Theory of Emotion."

In *Feelings and Emotions: The Loyola Symposium*, edited by Magda Arnold. New York: Academic Press, 1970.

Lee, Stephen D., and Maurice K. Temerlin. "Social Class, Diagnosis and Prognosis for Psychotherapy." *Psychotherapy: Theory, Research and Practice* 7 (1970):181–85.

Leeper, Robert S. "The Motivational and Perceptual Properties of Emotions as Indicating Their Fundamental Character and Role." In *Feelings and Emotions: The Loyola Symposium*, edited by Magda Arnold. New York: Academic Press, 1970.

Lefcourt, Herbert M. *Locus of Control.* Hillsdale, N.J.: L. Erlbaum Associates, 1976.

Lehmann, Linda L. *Household Accounts* (forthcoming).

Leibowitz, Herschel W., ed. *Visual Perception.* New York: Macmillan, 1965.

Lepley, Ray, ed. *Language of Value.* New York: Columbia University Press, 1957.

Lerner, Barbara, and Donald Fiske. "Client Attributes and the Eye of the Beholder." *Journal of Consulting and Clinical Psychology* 40 (1973):272–77.

Levenson, Hanna. "Distinctions Within the Concept of Internal-External Control" *Proceedings of the 80th Annual Convention, American Psychological Association* 7 (1972):259–60.

———. "Multidimensional Locus of Control in Psychiatric Patients." *Journal of Consulting and Clinical Psychology* 41 (1973):397–404.

Levinson, Daniel J. *The Seasons of a Man's Life.* New York: A. A. Knopf, 1978.

Lévi-Strauss, Claude. *The Savage Mind.* Chicago: University of Chicago Press, 1967.

Levy, Charles S. "Values and Planned Change." *Social Casework* 53 (1972):488–93.

———. "The Value Base of Social Work." *Journal of Education for Social Work* 9 (1973):34–42.

Lewin, Kurt. *A Dynamic Theory of Personality.* New York: McGraw-Hill, 1935.

———. *Principles of Topological Psychology.* New York: McGraw-Hill, 1936.

———. "Field Theory and Learning." In *41st Yearbook of National Society for the Study of Education.* Bloomington, Ill.: Public School Press, 1942.

Lewis, Oscar. *Five Families.* New York: Basic Books, 1959.

———. *The Children of Sanchez.* New York: Random House, 1961.

Liazos, Alexander. "The Poverty of the Sociology of Deviance: Nuts, Sluts and Preverts." *Social Problems* 20 (1972):103–20.

Lichtenberg, Philip. "Introduction of a Radical Theory and Practice in Social Work Education: Personality Theory." *Journal of Education for Social Work* 12 (1976):10–16.

Lincourt, John M., and C. Olczak. "C. S. Peirce and H. S. Sullivan on the Human Self." *Psychiatry* 37 (1974):78–87.

Lorion, Raymond P. "Research on Psychotherapy and Behavior Change with the Disadvantaged." In *Handbook of Psychotherapy and Behavior Change,* 2nd ed., edited by Sol L. Garfield and Allen E. Bergin, 903–38. New York: John Wiley, 1978.

London, Perry. *Modes and Morals of Psychotherapy*. New York: Holt, Rinehart & Winston, 1964.

———. *Behavior Control*. New York: Harper & Row, 1969.

Luria, A. R. *The Working Brain*. New York: Basic Books, 1973.

Lyon, Harold C., Jr. *Learning to Feel—Feeling to Learn: Humanistic Education for the Whole Man*. Columbus: Charles E. Merrill, 1971.

Maas, Henry S., and Kuypers, J. A. *From Thirty to Seventy*. San Francisco: Jossey-Bass, 1974.

McDougall, William. *Character and the Conduct of Life*. London: Methuen, 1921.

———. *Outline of Psychology*. New York: Scribners, 1923.

———. *Outline of Abnormal Psychology*. New York: Scribners, 1926.

———. "The Hormic Psychology." In *Theories of Motivation in Personality and Social Psychology*, edited by Richard Teveen and Robert Birney, pp. 10–59. New York: Van Nostrand, 1964.

McLaughlin, Barry. *Learning and Social Behavior*. New York: Free Press, 1971.

McLeish, John, Wayne Matheson, and James Park. *The Psychology of the Learning Group*. London: Hutchinson, 1973.

Maddi, Salvatore. "The Existential Neurosis." *Journal of Abnormal Psychology* 72 (1967):311–25.

———. *Personality Theories*. Homewood, Ill.: Dorsey Press, 1976.

Mahoney, Michael J., and Diane Arnkoff. "Cognitive and Self-Control Therapies." In *Handbook of Psychotherapy and Behavior Change*. 2nd ed., edited by Sol L. Garfield and Allen E. Bergin, 689–722. New York: John Wiley, 1978.

Malamud, Bernard. *The Tenants*. Toronto: Simon and Schuster, 1972.

Maltzman, Irving M. "Awareness, Cognitive Psychology vs. Behaviorism." *Journal of Experimental Research in Personality* 1 (1966):161–65.

Manis, Jerome, and Bernard Meltzer, eds. *Symbolic Interaction*. Boston: Allyn & Bacon, 1967.

Mansfield, Katherine. *The Journal of Katherine Mansfield*. Edited by J. Middleton Murry. New York: A. A. Knopf, 1928.

Marmor, Judd. "Dynamic Psychotherapy and Behavior Therapy: Are They Irreconcilable?" In *Annual Review of Behavior Theory and Practice*, edited by Cyril M. Franks and G. T. Wilson, pp. 57–71. New York: Brunner/Mazel, 1973.

Marquart, Dorothy. "Group Problem Solving." *Journal of Abnormal Psychology* 41 (1965):103–13.

Marx, Karl. "On Alienated Labor." In *Marx's Concept of Man*, edited by Erich Fromm, pp. 95–106. New York: Frederick Ungar, 1961.

Maslow, Abraham H. *Motivation and Personality*. New York: Harper, 1954.

———, ed. *New Knowledge in Human Values*. New York: Harper, 1959.

———. *Toward a Psychology of Being*. Princeton, N.J.: Van Nostrand, 1962.

Mathis, B. Claude, John Cotton, and Lee Sechrest. *Psychological Foundations for Education*. New York: Academic Press, 1970.

Matson, Floyd. *The Idea of Man*. New York: Delacorte Press, 1976.

Matza, David. *Becoming Deviant*. Englewood Cliffs, N.J.: Prentice-Hall, 1969.

May, Rollo, E. Angel, and Henri Ellenberger, eds. *Existence: A New Dimension in Psychiatry and Psychology*. New York: Basic Books, 1958.

Mayer, John, and Noel Timms. "Clash in Perspective Between Worker and Client." *Social Casework* 50 (1969):32–40.

Mazer, Milton. "Characteristics of Multi-Problem Households: A Study in Psycho-social Epidemiology." *American Journal of Orthopsychiatry* 42 (1974): 792–802.

Mead, George H. *Mind, Self and Society*. Chicago: University of Chicago Press, 1934.

Mehrabian, Albert. *An Analysis of Personality Theories*, Englewood Cliffs, N.J.: Prentice-Hall, 1968.

———. *Nonverbal Communication*. Belmont, Calif.: Wadsworth, 1971.

Melton, Arthur W. *Categories of Human Learning*. New York: Academic Press, 1964.

Merleau-Ponty, Maurice. *The Structure of Behavior*. Boston: Beacon Press, 1963.

———. *The Primacy of Perception and Other Essays*. Evanston, Ill.: Northwestern University Press, 1964.

Meyer, Carol. "Direct Services in Old and New Contexts." In *Shaping the New Social Work*, edited by Alfred Kahn, pp. 25–64. New York: Columbia University Press, 1973.

Milio, N. "Values, Social Class and Community Health Services." *Nursing Research* 16 (1967):26–31.

Miller, Henry. "Value Dilemmas in Social Casework." *Social Work* 13 (1968):27–33.

Miller, Walter B. "Implications of Urban Lower-Class Culture for Social Work." *Social Service Review* 33 (1959):219–36.

Minkowski, Eugene. *Lived Time: Phenomenological and Psychopathological Studies*. Evanston, Ill.: Northwestern University Press, 1970.

Minuchin, Salvador. *Families and Family Therapy: A Structural Approach*. Cambridge: Harvard University Press, 1974.

———. "Conflict-Resolution Family Therapy." In *Changing Families*, edited by Jay Haley, pp. 146–58. New York: Grune & Stratton, 1971.

———, Braulio Montalvo, Bernard Guerney, Bernice Rosman and Florence Schumer. *Families of the Slums*. New York: Basic Books, 1967.

———, and Braulio Montalvo. "Techniques for Working with Disorganized and Low Socioeconomic Families." In *Changing Families*, edited by Jay Haley, pp. 202–11. New York: Grune & Stratton, 1971.

Mogulof, Melvin. "Involving Low Income Neighborhoods in Anti-Delinquency Programs." *Social Work* 10 (1965):51–59.

Bibliography

Morris, Charles. *Varieties of Human Values*. Chicago: University of Chicago Press, 1956.

Mossman, Beal M., and Robert Ziller. "Self Esteem and the Consistency of Social Behavior." *Journal of Abnormal Psychology* 73 (1968):363–67.

Moustakas, Clark E. *The Self: Explorations in Personal Growth*. New York: Harper & Row, 1956.

Mueller, Conrad G. *Sensory Psychology*. Englewood Cliffs, N.J.: Prentice-Hall, 1965.

Murray, Edward, and Leonard Jacobson. "The Nature of Learning in Traditional and Behavioral Psychotherapy. In *Handbook of Psychotherapy and Behavior Change*, edited by Allen Bergin and Sol Garfield, pp. 709–47. New York: John Wiley, 1971.

Murray, Henry A. *Explorations in Personality*. New York: Oxford University Press, 1938.

Myklebust, H., and M. Brutten. "A Study of the Visual Perception of Deaf Children." *Acta Oto-Laryngol*. Stockholm, Suppl. No. 105, 1953.

Newcomb, Theodore, Ralph Turner, and Philip Converse. *Social Psychology: The Study of Human Interaction*. New York: Holt, Rinehart & Winston, 1965.

Newton, Joseph R., and Audrey B. Bohnengel. "Psychoeducational Meetings with Spouses of ESRD Patients." *Dialysis and Transplantation: Journal of Renal Technology* 7 (1978):632–37.

Nichols, Susan C. "The Personal Journal: A Mental Health Proposal." Ph.D. diss. San Francisco: California School of Professional Psychology, 1973.

Nin, Anaïs. *The Novel of the Future*. New York: Collier, 1968.

Nunokawa, Walter D., ed. *Human Values and Abnormal Behavior*. Chicago: Scott Foresman, 1965.

Oakes, William F. "Reinforcement of Bales' Categories in Group Discussion." *Psychological Reports* 11 (1962):427–35.

Ornstein, Robert E. *The Psychology of Consciousness*. New York: Viking Press, 1972.

———, ed. *The Nature of Human Consciousness*. San Francisco: Freeman, 1973.

———. *The Mind Field*. New York: Grossman, 1976.

Osborne, Alexander F. *Applied Imagination*. New York: Scribners, 1953.

Osler, Sonia F. "Cognitive Studies in Disadvantaged Children." In *Cognitive Studies*, Vol. 1, edited by Jerome Hellmuth, pp. 258–74. New York: Brunner/Mazel, 1970.

Owens, C. M. "Zen Buddhism." In *Transpersonal Psychologies*, edited by Charles T. Tart, pp. 155–202. New York: Harper & Row, 1975.

Packwood, William T., and Clyde A. Parker. "A Method for Rating Counselor Social Reinforcement and Persuasion." *Journal of Counseling Psychology* 20 (1973):38–43.

Papp, Peggy. "Brief Therapy with Couples in Groups." In *Family Therapy: Theory and Practice*, edited by Philip Guerin, pp. 350–63. New York: Gardner, 1976.

Parsons, Talcott. *The Social System*. Glencoe, Ill.: Free Press, 1951.
──── and Edward Shils. *Toward a General Theory of Action*. Cambridge: Harvard University Press, 1951.
Patterson, C. H. "The Place of Values in Counseling and Therapy." In *Human Values and Abnormal Behavior*, edited by Walter Nunokawa, pp. 94–101. Chicago: Scott Foresman, 1965.
Pearson, Geoffrey. *The Deviant Imagination: Psychiatry, Social Work and Social Change*. London: Macmillan, 1975.
Peck, Harris, Seymour Kaplan, and Melvin Roman. "Prevention, Treatment and Social Action: A Strategy of Intervention in a Disadvantaged Urban Area." *American Journal of Orthopsychiatry* 36 (1966):57–69.
Peirce, Charles S. *The Collected Papers of Charles Sanders Peirce*, Vols. 1–6, edited by Charles Hartshorne and Paul Weiss, Vols. 7 and 8, edited by A. Burks. Cambridge: Harvard University Press, 1965.
Percy, Walker. "Toward a Triadic Theory of Meaning." *Psychiatry* 35(1972):1–19.
Perls, Fritz. *Gestalt Therapy Verbatim*. Lafayette, Calif.: Real People Press, 1969.
────, Ralph F. Hefferline, and Paul Goodman. *Gestalt Therapy*. New York: Julian Press, 1951.
Petro, Olive, and Betty French. "The Black Client's View of Himself." *Social Casework* 53 (1972):466–74.
Piaget, Jean, and Barbel Inhelder. *The Psychology of the Child*. New York: Basic Books, 1969.
Pines, Maya. *Revolution in Learning: The Years from Birth to Six*. New York: Harper & Row, 1967.
Pirsig, Robert. *Zen and the Art of Motorcycle Maintenance: An Inquiry into Values*. New York: Morrow, 1974.
Plant, Raymond. *Social and Moral Theory in Casework*. London: Routledge and Kegan Paul, 1970.
Popper, Karl R. *Conjectures and Refutations: The Growth of Scientific Knowledge*. New York: Basic Books, 1962.
────, "On the Source of Knowledge and Ignorance." *Encounter* 19 (1962):42–57.
Postman, Leo. "Perception and Learning." In *Psychology: A Study of a Science*, Vol. 6, edited by Sigmund Koch, pp. 30–113. New York: McGraw-Hill, 1963.
Powell, T. J. "Negative Expectations of Treatment: Some Ideas about the Source and Management of Two Types." *Clinical Social Work Journal* 1 (1973):177–86.
Pratt, L. "The Relationship of Socioeconomic Status to Health." *American Journal of Public Health* 61 (1971):281–91.
Progoff, Ira. *Jung, Synchronicity and Human Destiny*. New York: Dell, 1973.
Rabkin, Richard. *Strategic Psychotherapy*. New York: Basic Books, 1977.
Raimy, Victor. *Misunderstandings of Self*. San Francisco: Jossey-Bass, 1975.
Rainer, Tristine. *The New Diary*. Los Angeles: Tarcher, 1978.
Rainwater, Lee. "Neutralizing the Disinherited: Some Psychological Aspects of

Understanding the Poor." In *Psychological Factors in Poverty*, edited by Vernon A. Allen, pp. 9–28. Chicago: Markham, 1970.

Rapoport, Anatol. *Operational Philosophy: Integrating Knowledge and Action*. San Francisco: International Society for General Semantics, 1969.

Redl, Fritz. *Group Living in a Children's Institution*. New York: Association Press, 1951.

Reich, Charles. *The Greening of America*. London: Allen Lane, Penguin, 1971.

Reinhardt, Adina, and Robert Gray. "Anomia, Socioeconomic Status and Mental Disturbance." *Community Mental Health Journal* 8 (1972):109–19.

Renner, John, and Vivian Renner. "Shall We Be Therapists or Educators?" *Canada's Mental Health* 21 (1973):3–10.

Resnick, Rosa P. "Conscientization: An Indigenous Approach to International Social Work." *International Social Work Journal* 19(1976):21–29.

Rhodes, William C. *Behavioral Threat and Community Response*. New York: Behavioral Publications, 1972.

Richan, Willard, and Allan Mendelsohn. *Social Work: The Unloved Profession*. New York: New Viewpoints, 1973.

Riesman, David. "On Autonomy." In *The Self in Social Interaction*, Vol. 1, edited by Chad Gordon and Kenneth Gergen, pp. 445–61. New York: John Wiley, 1968.

———, Nathan Glazer, and Reuel Denny. *The Lonely Crowd*. New Haven: Yale University Press, 1950.

Riessman, Frank. "Role Playing and the Lower Socioeconomic Group." *Group Psychotherapy* 17(1964):36–48.

Riskin, Jules, and Elaine Faunce. "Family Interaction Scales." In *The Interactional View*, edited by Paul Watzlawick and John Weakland, pp. 101–27. New York: W. W. Norton, 1977.

Rogers, Carl R. *Client Centered Therapy*. Boston: Houghton Mifflin, 1951.

———. "The Necessary and Sufficient Conditions of Therapeutic Personality Change." *Journal of Consulting Psychology* 21(1957):95–103.

———. "Interpersonal Relationships: Year 2000." *Journal of Applied Behavioral Science* 4(1968):265–80.

Rokeach, Milton. *The Nature of Human Values*. New York: Free Press, 1973.

Rosen, A. "The Treatment Relationship: A Conceptualization." *Journal of Consulting and Clinical Psychology* 38(1972):329–37.

Rosengren, William R., and M. Lefton. *Organizations and Clients*. Columbus; Charles E. Merrill, 1970.

Rosenhan, D. L. "On Being Sane in Insane Places." *Science*, Jan. 19, 1973, 250–58.

Rosenthal, David. "Changes in Some Moral Values Following Psychotherapy." *Journal of Consulting Psychology* 19(1955):431–36.

Rossi, Ernest L. *Dreams and the Growth of Personality*. New York: Pergamon Press, 1972.

Roth, Philip. *Reading Myself and Others*. New York: Farrar, Straus and Giroux, 1975.

Rotter, Julian B. *Social Learning and Clinical Psychology*. Englewood Cliffs, N.J.: Prentice-Hall, 1954.

———. "Generalized Expectancies for Internal vs. External Control of Reinforcement." *Psychological Monographs* 80, 1, no. 609 (1966).

Ruesch, Jurgen. "General Theory of Communication." In *American Handbook of Psychiatry*, Vol. 2, edited by Silvano Arieti. New York: Basic Books, 1959.

Russell, Roger W. "Biochemical Substrates of Behavior." In *Frontiers in Physiological Psychology*, edited by Roger W. Russell, pp. 185–246. New York: Academic Press, 1966.

Rychlak, Joseph F. *The Psychology of Rigorous Humanism*. New York: Wiley Interscience, 1977.

Sahakian, William S. *Psychopathology Today*. Itasca, Ill.: F. E. Peacock, 1970.

Sahlein, William J. *A Neighborhood Solution to the Social Services Dilemma*. Toronto: Heath, 1973.

Saleeby, Dennis. "A Proposal to Merge Humanist and Behaviorist Perspectives." *Social Casework* 56(1975):468–79.

Sarbin, Theodore R., and James C. Mancuso. "Failure of a Moral Enterprise: Attitudes of Public Toward Mental Illness." *Journal of Counseling and Clinical Psychology* 35(1970):159–73.

Sartre, Jean-Paul. *Existentialism*. Translated by B. Frechtman. New York: Philosophical Library, 1947.

———. *The Words*. New York: George Braziller, 1964.

Sawrey, J., and C. Telford. *Educational Psychology*. 2nd ed. Boston: Allyn & Bacon, 1964.

Schachter, Stanley, and J. E. Singer. "Cognitive, Social and Physiological Determinants of Emotional States." *Psychological Review* 69(1962):379–99.

Scheerer, M. "Problem Solving." *Scientific American* 208(1963):118–28.

Scheff, Thomas J. *Being Mentally Ill*. Chicago: Aldine, 1966.

Scheflen, Albert E. *A Psychotherapy of Schizophrenia: Direct Analysis*. Springfield, Ill.: Thomas, 1961.

Scheffler, Israel. "Philosophical Models of Teaching." In *Problems and Issues in Contemporary Education*, edited by the editors of *The Teaching Record* and *The Harvard Educational Review*, pp. 90–100. Chicago: Scott Foresman, 1966.

Schorr, Alvin L. "Who Promised Us a Rose Garden?" *Social Work* 20(1975):200–205.

Schramm, Wilbur L. *The Process and Effects of Mass Communication*. Urbana, Ill.: University of Illinois Press, 1954.

Schur, Edwin. *Labeling Deviant Behavior: Its Sociological Implications*. New York: Harper & Row, 1971.

Bibliography

———. *The Awareness Trap: Self Absorption Instead of Social Change.* New York: McGraw-Hill, 1976.

Schwitzgebel, R. K. "The Right to Effective Treatment." *California Law Review* 63(1974):936–56.

Sears, Robert R. "Identification as a Form of Development." In *The Concept of Development: An Issue in the Study of Human Behavior,* edited by Dale B. Harris. Minneapolis: University of Minnesota Press, 1957.

Secord, Paul F., and Carl W. Backman. *Social Psychology.* New York: McGraw-Hill, 1964.

Segal, Steven P., and Uri Aviram. *The Mentally Ill in Community-Based Sheltered Care.* New York: John Wiley, 1978.

Segall, M. H., Donald T. Campbell, and Melville J. Herskovits. *The Influence of Culture on Visual Perception.* Indianapolis: Bobbs-Merrill, 1966.

Selye, Hans. *The Stress of Life.* Rev. ed. New York: McGraw-Hill, 1976.

Sexton, Anne. *To Bedlam and Part Way Back.* Boston: Houghton Mifflin, 1960.

Sheehy, Gail. *Passages.* New York: E. P. Dutton, 1976.

Sherif, Carolyn W., and Muzafer Sherif. *Attitude, Ego-Involvement and Change.* New York: John Wiley, 1967.

Shoben, Edward J. "Psychotherapy as a Problem in Learning Theory." *Psychological Bulletin* 46(1949):366–92.

Silverman, Phyllis R. "A Reexamination of the Intake Procedure." *Social Casework* 51(1970):625–34.

Sinsheimer, Robert S. "The Existential Casework Relationship." *Social Casework* 50(1969):67–73.

Siporin, Max. "Deviant Behavior Theory." *Social Work* 10(1965):59–67.

Skinner, B. F. *Science and Human Behavior.* New York: Macmillan, 1953.

———. *Beyond Freedom and Dignity.* New York: Condon, 1972.

Solis, Faustina. "Socioeconomic and Cultural Conditions of Migrant Workers." *Social Casework* 52(1971):308–15.

Smith, Henry C. *Sensitivity to People.* New York: McGraw-Hill, 1966.

Snyder, Mark, and Seymour Uranowitz. "Reconstructing the Past: Some Cognitive Consequences of Person Perception." *Journal of Personality and Social Psychology* 36(1978):941–50.

Specht, Harry, and Ann Vickery, eds. *Integrating Social Work Methods.* London: George Allen & Unwin, 1977.

Speck, Ross, and Carolyn N. Attneave. *Family Networks: Retribalizing and Healing.* New York: Pantheon Books, 1973.

Spicker, Stuart F. *The Philosophy of the Body: Rejections of Cartesian Dualism.* Chicago: Quadrangle Books, 1970.

Spiegel, John. *Transactions: The Interplay Between the Individual, Family, and Society.* Edited by John Papajohn. New York: Science House, 1971.

Staats, Arthur W., ed. *Human Learning.* New York: Holt, Rinehart & Winston, 1964.

————, and Carolyn Staats. *Complex Human Behavior.* New York: Holt, Rinehart & Winston, 1963.

Stapledon, William D. *A Modern Theory of Ethics: A Study of the Relation of Ethics and Psychology.* London: Methuen, 1929.

Stewart, Robert L., and Maurice Levine. "Individual Psychoanalysis and Psychoanalytic Psychotherapy." In *Treating Mental Illness,* edited by Alfred M. Freedman and Harold I. Kaplan, pp. 69–120. New York: Atheneum, 1972.

Straus, Erwin W. "The Expression of Thinking." In *Perception,* edited by Paul Tibbetts, pp. 261–78. Chicago: Quadrangle Books, 1969.

Strong, J. R. "A Marital Conflict Resolution Model: Redefining Conflict to Achieve Intimacy." *Journal of Marriage and Family Counseling* 1 (1975):269–76.

Strupp, Hans H. *Psychotherapy: Clinical, Research and Theoretical Issues.* New York: Jason Aronson, 1973.

Sullivan, Harry S. *The Interpersonal Theory of Psychiatry.* New York: W. W. Norton, 1953.

————. *The Psychiatric Interview.* New York: W. W. Norton, 1954.

————. *The Fusion of Psychiatry and Social Science.* New York: W. W. Norton, 1964.

Suzuki, D. T. *Zen Buddhism.* New York: Grove Press, 1960.

————. *Essays in Zen Buddhism.* New York: Paragon Book Gallery, 1971.

Swartz, Robert J. *Perceiving, Sensing and Knowing.* New York: Anchor Books, 1965.

Szasz, Thomas S. *Law, Liberty and Psychiatry.* New York: Macmillan, 1963.

————. *The Manufacture of Madness.* New York: Harper & Row, 1970.

Tallman, Irving. "The Family as a Small Problem-Solving Group." *Journal of Marriage and the Family,* Feb. 1970, pp. 94–104.

————. *Passion, Action and Politics.* San Francisco: Freeman, 1976.

Taplin, J. R. "Crisis Theory: Critique and Reformulation." *Community Mental Health* 7(1971):13–23.

Tart, Charles T., ed. *Transpersonal Psychologies.* New York: Harper & Row, 1975.

Taylor, Gordon R. *The Natural History of the Mind.* New York: E. P. Dutton, 1979.

Taylor, Verta. "Good News About Disaster." *Psychology Today,* Oct. 1977, p. 93.

Teveen, Richard C., and Robert C. Birney, eds. *Theories of Motivation in Personality and Social Psychology.* New York: Van Nostrand, 1964.

Thevenaz, Pierre. *What Is Phenomenology?* Chicago: Quadrangle Books, 1962.

Thibaut, John W., and Harold H. Kelley. *The Social Psychology of Groups.* New York: John Wiley, 1959.

Thomas, H. F. "The Existential Attitude in Working with Individuals and Groups." In *Challenges of Humanistic Psychology,* edited by James F. T. Bugental, pp. 227–32. New York: McGraw-Hill, 1967.

Thompson, James D. *Organizations in Action.* New York: McGraw-Hill, 1967.

Thorndike, Edward L. *Animal Intelligence.* New York: Macmillan, 1911.

485

Tibbetts, Paul, ed. *Perception: Selected Readings in Science and Phenomenology.* Chicago: Quadrangle Books, 1969.

Toch, Hans. *The Social Psychology of Social Movements.* Indianapolis: Bobbs-Merrill, 1965.

Torrance, E. P. "Causes for Concern." In *Creativity,* edited by Philip E. Vernon, pp. 355–70. Baltimore: Penguin, 1970.

Torrey, E. Fuller. *The Death of Psychiatry.* New York: Chilton, 1974.

Travers, John F. *Learning, Analysis and Application.* New York: McKay, 1965.

Truax, Charles B., and Robert R. Carkhuff. *Toward Effective Counseling and Psychotherapy.* Chicago: Aldine, 1967.

———, and Kevin M. Mitchell. "Research on Certain Therapist Interpersonal Skills in Relation to Process and Outcome." In *Handbook of Psychotherapy and Behavior Change,* edited by Allen Bergin and Sol Garfield, pp. 299–344. New York: John Wiley, 1971.

Urban, Hugh, and Donald H. Ford. "Some Historical and Conceptual Perspectives on Psychotherapy and Behavior Change." In *Handbook of Psychotherapy and Behavior Change,* edited by Allen Bergin and Sol Garfield, pp. 3–35. New York: John Wiley, 1971.

———. "Behavior Therapy." In *Treating Mental Illness,* edited by Alfred M. Freedman and Harold I. Kaplan, pp. 146–61. New York: Atheneum, 1972.

Vaillant, G. E. "Natural History of Male Psychological Health." *Archives of General Psychiatry* 31(1974):15–22.

Valle, S., and R. Marinelli. "Training in Human Relations Skills as a Preferred Mode for Treatment of Married Couples." *Journal of Marriage and Family Counseling* 1(1975):359–65.

Vattano, Anthony J. "Power to the People: Self-Help Groups." *Social Work* 17(1972):7–15.

Vernon, Philip E., ed. *Creativity.* Baltimore: Penguin, 1970.

Wachspress, M. "Goals and Functions of the Community Mental Health Center." *American Journal of Psychiatry* 129(1972):101–4.

Wallace, Walter L. *The Logic of Science in Sociology.* New York: Aldine-Atherton, 1971.

Wann, T. W., ed. *Behaviorism and Phenomenology.* Chicago: University of Chicago Press, 1964.

Wason, Peter C., and P. N. Johnson-Laird, eds. *Thinking and Reasoning.* New York: Peter Smith, 1968.

Watts, Alan. *The Way of Zen.* New York: Pantheon Books, 1957.

———. *Psychotherapy East and West.* New York: Ballantine, 1961.

———. *Nature, Man and Woman.* New York: Vintage Books, 1970.

Watzlawick, Paul. "A Review of the Double Bind Theory." *Family Process* 2(1963):132–53.

———. *The Language of Change.* New York: Basic Books, 1978.

————, Janet Beavin, and Don Jackson. *Pragmatics of Human Communication.* New York: W. W. Norton, 1967.

————, and John Weakland, eds. *The Interactional View.* New York: W. W. Norton, 1977.

————, and Richard Fisch. *Change: Principles of Problem Formulation and Problem Resolution.* New York: W. W. Norton, 1974.

Weinstein, Michael A. *The Tragic Sense of Political Life.* Columbia: University of South Carolina Press, 1977.

Werkmeister, William H. "On Describing a World." *Philosophy and Phenomenological Research* 11 (1951):303–25.

————. *Man and His Values.* Lincoln: University of Nebraska Press, 1967.

Werner, Harold D. *A Rational Approach to Social Casework.* New York: Association Press, 1965.

Wertheimer, Michael. "Humanistic Psychology and the Humane but Tough-Minded Psychologist." *American Psychologist* 33 (1978):739–45.

White, Robert W., ed. *The Study of Lives.* New York: Atherton, 1969.

Whitmont, Edward C. "Carl Jung." In *Interpreting Personality,* edited by Alfred M. Freedman and Harold I. Kaplan, pp. 131–43. New York: Atheneum, 1972.

Wicker, Tom. *Facing the Lions.* New York: Viking Press, 1973.

Wild, K. W. *Intuition.* Cambridge: The University Press, 1938.

Wilding, Paul, and Vic George. "Social Values and Social Policy." *International Social Policy* 4(1975):373–90.

Wilkins, Wallace. "Expectancy of Therapeutic Gain: An Empirical and Conceptual Critique." *Journal of Consulting and Clinical Psychology* 40(1973):69–77.

Wing, John K., and G. W. Brown. *Institutionalism and Schizophrenia: A Comparative Study of Three Mental Hospitals, 1960–1968.* Cambridge: The University Press, 1970.

Wolberg, Lewis R. *The Technique of Psychotherapy.* New York: Grune & Stratton, 1954.

Woolf, Virginia. *A Room of One's Own.* New York: Harcourt, Brace & World, 1929.

Wyatt, Frederick. "The Reconstruction of the Individual and of the Collective Past." In *The Study of Lives,* edited by Robert W. White, pp. 305–20. New York: Atherton, 1969.

Wylie, Ruth. *The Self Concept.* Lincoln: University of Nebraska Press, 1961.

Yalom, Irvin, and Ginny Elkin. *Every Day Gets a Little Closer.* New York: Basic Books, 1974.

Ziller, Robert C. "A Helical Theory of Personal Change." *Journal of Theory of Social Behavior* 1(1973):33–73.

Zimilies, Herbert. "Conceptual Thinking in Young Children as a Function of Age and Social Class." In *Cognitive Studies,* Vol. 1, edited by Jerome Hellmuth, pp. 230–57. New York: Brunner/Mazel, 1970.

Zuk, Gerald H. "Family Therapy." In *Changing Families,* edited by Jay Haley, pp. 212–26. New York: Grune & Stratton, 1971.

Index of Names

Index of Names

Index of Names

Index of Subjects